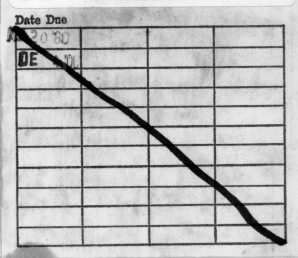

LEADING CASES
ON THE
CONSTITUTION

By Paul C. Bartholomew

About the Author

1. Present Position: Professor of Political Science, University of Notre Dame. Sometime Visiting Professor at Northwestern University, Michigan State University, St. Mary's College, Loyola University (Chicago), the University of Tennessee, the University of Chicago, and the National University of Ireland, Dublin. Consultant: Department of the Navy, U. S. House of Representatives, State of Indiana, and the City of Chicago.

2. <u>Publications</u>: *A Manual of American Government* (Burgess, 1936 and 1939); *A Manual of Political Science Research* (Notre Dame, 1940); *Public Administration* (Littlefield, Adams, 1958); co-author, *For Americans Only* (Nesterman, 1944); *American Government Under the Constitution* (Brown, 1947, 1949 and 1956). Has written a number of articles and reviews for various journals in the field including "Constitutional Law," 1956 and subsequent editions, *Encyclopedia Americana*, as well as "Checks and Balances" and "Constitution", 1968 Edition. His annual analysis of the work of the Supreme Court appears in the December issue of the *Western Political Quarterly*.

About the Book

1. Cases are arranged alphabetically but with indexes by plaintiff, by defendant, by popular name, and by subject matter. Dates of decisions and official citations are supplied in the first index.
2. Each case carries citations to the official reports and applicable citations to the Supreme Court Reporter and the Lawyers' Edition.
3. Concise presentation is made of each case under the headings of facts, question, decision, and reason for the decision.
4. Correlative cases are listed after each case to suggest additional sources on the same phase of constitutional interpretation.
5. The arrangement provides immediate, convenient information on the gist of the most frequently cited cases.

Summaries of
Leading Cases
on the
Constitution

by

Paul C. Bartholomew
Professor of Political Science
University of Notre Dame

Sixth Edition

1968

LITTLEFIELD, ADAMS & CO.
Totowa, New Jersey

Pri⬛⬛⬛⬛⬛⬛⬛⬛⬛ca

PREFACE

The purpose of this little volume is to make readily available in convenient form the gist of the major decisions of the United States Supreme Court since its establishment. No previous book has done just that. For the student, for the teacher, for the casual reader who wishes to know the basic points of a case, the matter is contained herein. For the person who wishes to go beyond that, a listing of leading correlative cases has been appended to each case covered.

Possibly the greatest use this volume will have will be by those who, in reading or studying, come upon references to cases and wish to know something of the nature of the cases or to refresh their memories on them. There is no attempt here at commentary or at the presentation of the political and economic background or "climate" in which decisions have been handed down. Those matters have been done well by others, and repetition would be at variance with the basic purpose of the book.

The selection of cases to be included has offered great difficulty. In the final determination every effort was made to take into consideration various interests and factors—historical, legal, political, economic—that would influence a reader in his quest for cases. I hope that some success has resulted from this effort. Two indexes are provided, one, alphabetical by plaintiff, by defendant, and by popular name, the other, by subject matter of the cases. The cases covered run through the October, 1966 Term which ended June 12, 1967 and the October, 1967 Term through February 1968.

I want to make special acknowledgment of very real assistance to my wife, Agnes, to Francis Carey, to Dr. Redmond Allman of Boston College, to Professor Bernard J. Feeney of the Law School of DePaul University, to Professor Joseph F. Menez of Loyola University, Chicago, and to Professor Rocco J. Tresolini of Lehigh University. Also, I am indebted to Mr. Bennett H. Fishler, Jr., Counsellor at Law of Ridgewood, New Jersey, who read the entire manuscript and offered many valuable suggestions.

Paul C. Bartholomew.

TO TOM AND BOB

CONTENTS

ALPHABETICAL INDEX OF CASES

By Plaintiff, By Defendant And By Popular Name

Cases below are arranged alphabetically by plaintiff, by defendant, and by popular name. See *Index* for alphabetical listing of cases by subject matter.

CONTENTS

CONTENTS

CONTENTS

INTRODUCTION

The Federal Judiciary *

THE CONSTITUTION OF THE UNITED STATES

ARTICLE III

Section 1. The judicial Power of the United States, shall be vested in one supreme Court, and in such inferior Courts as the Congress may from time to time ordain and establish. The Judges, both of the supreme and inferior Courts, shall hold their Offices during good Behavior, and shall, at stated Times, receive for their Services, a Compensation which shall not be diminished during their Continuance in Office.

Section 2. 1. The judicial Power shall extend to all Cases, in Law and Equity, arising under this Constitution, the Laws of the United States, and Treaties made, or which shall be made, under their Authority;—to all Cases affecting Ambassadors, other public Ministers and Consuls;—to all Cases of admiralty and maritime Jurisdiction; to Controversies to which the United States shall be a Party;—to Controversies between two or more States;—between a State and Citizens of another State;—between Citizens of different states;—between Citizens of the same State claiming Lands under Grants of different States, and between a State, or the Citizens thereof, and foreign States, Citizens or Subjects.

2. In all Cases affecting Ambassadors, other public Ministers and Consuls, and those in which a State shall be Party, the supreme Court shall have original Jurisdiction. In all the other Cases before mentioned, the supreme Court shall have appellate Jurisdiction, both as to Law and Fact, with such Exceptions, and under such Regulations as the Congress shall make.

---

* This is a reprint of a revised portion of Chapter Seven, Paul C. Bartholomew, *American Government under the Constitution* (Dubuque, Iowa: Brown Publishing Co. 1956.)

3. The trial of all Crimes, except in Cases of Impeachment, shall be by Jury, and such Trial shall be held in the State where the said Crimes shall have been committed; but when not committed within any State, the Trial shall be at such Place or Places as the Congress may by Law have directed.

America's Contribution—Article Three is the most original of all the parts of the Constitution. Here the Constitution sets up independent courts to judge the legality of acts of Congress and the President. Thus, because of judicial review, we have America's greatest contribution to the science of government. The "judicial power" referred to is the power to hear and determine cases in accordance with law and legal methods—a government of laws and not of men. The lack of a judiciary was one of the prime defects of the Articles of Confederation.

Federal Court Organization—The only court definitely provided for by the Constitution is the Supreme Court, although Congress is empowered to constitute lesser courts. Even as regards the Supreme Court, the Constitution is very sparing of details, no provision being included as to the number of judges or their qualifications as judges. The Constitution specifies[1] that all federal judges shall be named by the President with the consent of the Senate. All federal judges hold office for life and may be removed only by the impeachment process. The salary of a Supreme Court justice is $39,500 that of the Chief Justice $40,000. The Supreme Court apparently regards itself as having power to determine the validity of appointments made to it, as evidenced by the action of the Court in assuming jurisdiction in a case involving Justice Hugo L. Black.[2]

The Supreme Court—In the Judiciary Act of 1789 Congress set the number of justices on the Supreme Court at six. This number was changed in 1801, the Federalists amending the law to provide that any vacancy appearing on the Court should not be filled, so as to reduce the total number of justices to five. The purpose of the Federalist Congress in doing this was to prevent the Jeffersonian Republicans from getting control of the Court as soon as they might otherwise. In 1802 the Republicans simply repealed this law and returned the number to six. At this time the law provided that

[1] Article II, Section 2, Clause 2.
[2] Ex parte Albert Levitt, 302 U. S. 633 (1937)

the Supreme Court justices should "ride the circuit." In fact, a Circuit Court of that day was composed of one Supreme Court justice (originally it had been two Supreme Court justices) and the federal judge of the District Court within whose limits the case was being heard. There were no circuit judges as such. Therefore, every time a new Circuit Court was established, it was necessary to increase the size of the Supreme Court. Thus, in 1807 the number of Supreme Court justices was increased to seven, in 1837 to nine, and in 1863 to ten, as, with the opening of the West, new Circuit Courts were established. In 1866, as a result of the fight between President Johnson and the Congress, a law was enacted providing that no vacancies on the Court should be filled until it had been reduced to seven justices. This was to prevent Johnson from making any appointments to the Court. In 1869, with Johnson out of the way, Congress repealed this law and set the number at nine, where it has remained until the present time. Incidentally, Supreme Court justices no longer "ride the circuit," the Courts of Appeals of today being made up of regularly-appointed judges. Members of the Supreme Court are, however, assigned to the Courts of Appeals, one to a circuit. They do not sit and hear cases on the circuits, although they could if they had the time and the inclination. In fact, there being ten circuits, plus the District of Columbia circuit, and only nine justices, two Supreme Court justices are named to two circuits.

On the Supreme Court today, six justices constitute a quorum and a majority (at least four in case of the minimum quorum of six) must concur on a decision. Otherwise, either the decision of the lower court is upheld, or a rehearing is ordered. Sessions are held in the Court's beautiful building across the Plaza from the Capitol. The Court is in session from October to June each year, subject to recesses, normally about every two weeks to study cases and write opinions. It receives and *disposes* of over 2000 cases or applications each year. Decisions may be handed down on any day and no sessions are held on Fridays or Saturdays. The Court now holds sessions from 10 A.M. to 12:30 P.M. and from 1:00 P.M. to 2:30 P.M. Special sessions of the Court may be called by the Chief Justice, as in the case of the German saboteurs[3] in 1942, and the Rosenbergs

[3] Ex parte Quirin, 317 U. S. 1 (1942)

[4] Rosenberg et ux. v. United States, 346 U. S. 273 (1953). The Court also held a special session in 1958 on the school integration question. Aaron v. Cooper, 357 U. S. 566.

in 1953[4]. The 1942 special session was the first such session since 1920. Following oral arguments in a case, the justices study the briefs, and discuss the matter. They then vote at a Saturday conference in one of the conference rooms in the rear of the Court building. On votes, taken orally, the members vote in order of seniority of service, the youngest justice first and with the Chief Justice always voting last. If no agreement can be reached, a reargument will be ordered. If agreement is reached, the Chief Justice, if he is a member of the majority, will assign the task of writing the opinion to one of the members of the majority. Otherwise the senior associate justice of the majority will assign the opinion. One or more members of the majority may voluntarily write concurring opinions, indicating that the justice or justices in question agree with the decision set forth in the opinion, but for different reasons. For instance, the decision in a case may uphold federal rent control and the opinion may justify this on the basis of the war power, while a concurring opinion may hold that such control is valid under interstate commerce. If the decision is not unanimous, any member of the minority may file a dissenting opinion in which he publicizes his stand. These opinions are published each year under the title of *United States Reports*. An average of about 100-125 cases are decided each year by full published opinions. In the early days of the Court, the opinions were published under the name of the court reporter for that term of the Court. These, in order, were Dallas, (1790-1800), Cranch (1801-1815), Wheaton (1816-1827), Peters, (1828-1842), Howard (1843-1860), Black (1861-1862), Wallace (1863-1874), and Otto (1875-1882). Since that time the "U.S." citation has prevailed.

Inferior Courts, The District Courts—In the field of "inferior courts" below the Supreme Court are the eleven Courts of Appeals and eighty-six District Courts, not including the territories. These are "constitutional" courts and the limitations in the Constitution on such matters as appointment of judges, security of tenure, and compensation reduction, apply just as they do to the justices of the Supreme Court. On the other hand the territorial courts and the special federal courts —Court of Claims, Customs Court, Court of Customs and Patent Appeals, the Tax Court, the United States Court of Military Appeals, and the Emergency Court of Appeals—are Congressional or "legislative" courts, not established under

under legislative powers of Congress. The Constitutional limitations regarding judges do not apply to such courts. The Court of Claims has recently been declared by Congress to be a "constitutional court."

The lowest category of regular federal court is the **District Court.** There is at least one such court in each state, the number varying upwards from that to four each in Texas and New York, according to the amount of litigation in the state. There are also District Courts in the District of Columbia, Puerto Rico, Guam, the Virgin Islands, and the Canal Zone. District Courts, obviously, have only original jurisdiction where civil and criminal trials both with and without jury are conducted. Only one judge will be assigned to a District Court with two exceptions: (1) Where there is a great amount of litigation coming before the particular court, two or more judges are permanently assigned to that court, but they sit separately and hear cases in "divisions" simultaneously. For example, the District Court in New York City has twenty-four judges, those in Chicago and Brooklyn, ten and eight respectively and in Cleveland, six.[5] (2) Under present law, whenever an application is made for an injunction to restrain the enforcement of an allegedly unconstitutional federal or state law, a court of three judges must pass on such application in the District Court.[6] This panel will be made up of other District or Circuit judges. Appeals from these three-judge hearings then go directly to the Supreme Court.[7] District Court judges receive $30,000 a year. District Courts currently receive about 58,000 civil cases and 38,000 criminal cases annually.

The Courts of Appeals—Above the District Courts are the federal courts of intermediate grade, the Courts of Appeals. The entire territory of the United States has been divided into eleven areas, and in each of these areas there is one Court of Appeals. Sometimes these courts hold all sessions at one city, as does the Seventh Circuit with its seat at Chicago. Other courts move about and hold sessions at different cities, as does the court in the Fourth Circuit. The number of judges appointed to these courts varies from three to nine depending on the amount of work in a circuit, but in all cases judges sit together on a case; these are collegial, appellate courts. Two

---

[5] Title 28, United States Code Annotated, Sec. 133.
[6] Title 28, U. S. C. A., Secs. 47 and 380.
[7] Title 28, U. S. C. A., Sec. 345.

judges constitute a quorum. The judge with the longest service is the Chief Judge. As the name indicates, the Courts of Appeals have only appellate jurisdiction. Their chief function is to serve as a sort of "buffer state" between the District Courts and the Supreme Court. The original purpose in establishing the Courts of Appeals was to relieve the Supreme Court of a part of its business, and, under present laws, the Court is in most cases the court of last resort unless the Supreme Court sees fit to review the case. Circuit Court judges receive an annual salary of $33,000. The eleven Courts of Appeals receive about three thousand cases every year. In addition to appeals from the lower Federal courts, the Courts of Appeals receive many cases to review actions of various Federal administrative agencies for errors of law.

The Supreme Court, incidentally, has held that the imposition of a general income tax on the salary of a federal judge does not violate the restrictions as to diminution of salary.[8]

The Legislative Courts—The "legislative courts" referred to, as established by Congress under power granted by other than the judicial section of the Constitution, are of four types. The Court of Claims, formerly under this category, has recently been declared by Congress to be a Constitutional court established under Article III. The Court of Claims is a federal adaptation of the continental system of administrative courts. "The King can do no wrong," so no government can be sued against its wishes. However, Congress has provided for suits under certain circumstances, those provisions under present law being rather broad. Such suits may be brought in the District Courts in many cases under recent legislation, but the Court of Claims is a special court established for just such suits. Five judges are named by the President with the consent of the Senate for life. The court holds its sessions in Washington.

The Customs Court was set up to determine the validity of customs valuations when the judgment of officials is disputed by owners. Nine judges named by the President with the consent of the Senate for life make up the Court, which has its seat in New York City, although some sessions are held elsewhere. Appeals from decisions of this court are taken to the Court of Customs and Patent Appeals, as are appeals from decisions of the Patent Office. Final appeal may then be taken to the Supreme Court. The Court of Customs and Patent Appeals consists of five judges named by the President with the consent of the Senate for life. This Court holds most

[8] O'Malley v. Woodrough, 307 U. S. 277 (1938)

of its sessions in Washington, although sessions are at times held elsewhere. Both of these courts have recently been declared by Congress to be constitutional courts established under Article III of the Constitution.

In 1942 Congress provided for another Court, called the United States Emergency Court of Appeals. This court heard certain appeals which arose in price and rent control cases and litigants could apply to the Supreme Court for review of its decisions. The United States Emergency Court of Appeals was and the District Courts were assigned to these courts to hear these price and rent cases whenever they arose.

The Tax Court, also established in 1942, consists of sixteen judges named by the President with the consent of the Senate. It hears appeals from decisions of federal revenue collection agencies.

The United States Court of Military Appeals, established in 1950, consists of three civilian judges named by the President and the Senate. It reviews court martials.

The Federal Judicial Conferences and Councils—Some unity has been brought into the regular federal judiciary by the establishment, in 1922, of the federal Judicial Conference. This conference, composed of the senior judge of each of the ten Courts of Appeals in the states, and the Chief Justice of the District of Columbia Court of Appeals, meets in Washington each September with the Chief Justice of the Supreme Court presiding. The function of the conference is to survey the situation among the courts, to make recommendations to the courts, and to assign and transfer judges among the districts and circuits. In addition there are judicial councils and conferences in each of the eleven circuits. The judicial councils consist of the judges of the Courts of Appeals and have power to take such steps, including particularly the assignment of judges, as may be necessary to dispose properly of the volume of cases in each district. The judicial conferences in the several circuits consist of all the district and circuit judges in the particular circuit and sometimes also invited members of the bar meeting together once a year to discuss common problems.

The Administrative Office of U. S. Courts—In 1939 Congress went a step further and set up the Administrative Office of United States Courts. This office is headed by a director and assistant director named by the Supreme Court for indefinite terms. It has two general functions handled by two divisions

—business administration, taking care of supplies, budgeting, auditing and disbursements, housing of courts, clerical services and other material needs of the courts; and procedural studies and statistics, a research unit. In general, this office is subordinate to the annual federal judicial conferences and councils.

District Attorney, Marshal, Commissioner—In each District there is a district attorney named by the President, with the consent of the Senate for a four-year term. He is the federal equivalent of the prosecuting attorney in state systems, presenting cases to the grand jury, and conducting the trials on behalf of the government in cases of indictment. Each District Court also has attached to it a marshal, a sort of federal sheriff, named by the President with the consent of the Senate for a term of four years. He and his deputies conduct arrests, serve summons and legal processes issuing from the court, and protect the judge, among other duties. Finally, each District Court judge names one or more United States Commissioners for a term of four years, but removable at any time by the judge. The functions of the Commissioner include such matters as administering oaths, issuing subpoenas and warrants, and conducting preliminary hearings of accused persons.

Federal Court Jurisdiction—The federal courts, like other federal units, operate under the doctrine of delegated powers. Therefore, the types of cases outlined in the constitution constitute the entire jurisdiction of the federal courts. These cases are capable of classification under two heads: (1) those that may be brought in the federal courts because of the parties involved, and (2) those that may be so brought because of the subject matter involved.

Parties—Under the first of these categories—parties—there is, first, the matter of all cases affecting ambassadors, ministers, and consuls. By international law, diplomats are immune from prosecution or suit in the country to which they are accredited, regardless of the seriousness of the civil or criminal matter. Therefore, this particular provision acts only to prevent the states from attempting to assume jurisdiction in such cases. Consuls, however, are not immune from suit except in so far as such immunity may be set up by treaties existing between their home country and the country to which they are sent.

Secondly, among cases that may be brought in the federal courts are those to which the United States is a party, but, of course, the United States cannot be sued for damages without its consent.

Thirdly, are the cases to which a state is a party. As regards this latter category, suits by an individual against a state for damages cannot be brought in the federal courts, under the terms of the Eleventh Amendment. Most cases coming in the federal courts under this provision of Article Three are those between states, such as Missouri v. Illinois,[9] Kansas v. Colorado,[10] Kentucky v. Indiana,[11] and Virginia v. West Virginia,[12] involving water contamination, water diversion, an agreement to construct a bridge, and debt payment, respectively.

Fourthly, are cases involving diversity of citizenship, that is, cases involving suit brought by a citizen of one of our states, Indiana, for example, against a citizen of another state, say California, or suits involving citizens of a foreign country and those of a state. However, in order to come into the federal courts, such cases must involve over $10,000. This does not include suits between citizens of the District of Columbia or of the territories and citizens of the states since the District and the territories are not states. A corporation is presumed to be a citizen, under this clause, of the state in which it was incorporated.

Finally, the Constitution provides for cases between citizens of the same state claiming lands under grants of different states. With the passing of the frontier, such cases are rare indeed. Such provision was necessary because of the uncertainty of state boundaries in some instances, and because two or more states claimed certain lands. Thus, there might be conflicting claims by individuals under state land grants, and a federal court seemed the best place to get an unprejudiced decision.

Subject Matter—The second category of cases that may be brought in the federal courts are those that may be brought there because of the subject matter of the cases involved. The first of these is cases of admiralty and maritime law.

---

[9] 200 U. S. 496 (1906)
[10] 185 U. S. 125 (1902)
[11] 281 U. S. 163 (1930)
[12] 246 U. S. 565 (1918)

For all practical purposes the two can be regarded as synonymous, but, strictly speaking, admiralty refers to the location of the act (an American ship on the high seas or the navigable waters of the United States) while maritime refers to the character of the act, such as marine insurance and contracts for transportation by water or service on shipboard.

Probably most important of all the types of cases that may be brought before the federal courts are those arising under the Constitution, laws, and treaties of the United States. These cases involve what is known as a "federal question." Whenever a case arises which involves some interpretation of or a right that is claimed under the federal Constitution, laws, or treaties of the United States, and if it is a matter that must be settled for the proper determination of the case, then the federal courts may properly take jurisdiction.

These, then, are the cases, under the Constitution and the doctrine of delegated powers, over which the federal courts may take jurisdiction. Only *cases,* or actual controversies, may come in the federal courts, therefore the Supreme Court has held that no *advisory opinions* may be handed down by the Supreme Court.[13] In about eleven states the state Supreme Court may, on request of the governor, or the legislature, give its "curbstone opinion" as to the constitutionality of either existing or proposed legislation. In such an instance, there is no actual controversy or case, and the decision of the Court is not binding on either the court itself, in the event of future actual litigation, or on those who request the opinion. On the other hand, all of the federal courts can hand down *declaratory judgments,* where there is an actual controversy, and the court is asked to declare what are the rights and duties of the parties involved. Requests for such a determination come from private parties, and the decisions are binding. In more than half of the states this procedure is also available in the state courts.

Law and Equity—The federal courts are given jurisdiction in cases, as noted, "in law and equity." The distinction is one primarily of procedure or remedy. Common law arose before statutory law, and involved the judicial enforcement of custom. Thus, the first law in our system was a matter of the government putting its enforcement power behind what at least a part of the people had already determined. As common

[13] Muskrat v. United States, 219 U. S. 346 (1911)

law developed there evolved certain forms of procedure, and all suits that were brought were fitted into one of these stereotyped forms, such as, damages, trespass, replevin, trover, or assumpsit. With increasing frequency, however, cases arose that involved matters that simply would not fit into one of the stereotyped forms if justice was to be done. For example, damages might be entirely inadequate as a form of relief because possibly the defendant might be unable to pay any judgment for money damages, or because of the nature of the contract it might be very difficult if not impossible to estimate the damages, or, again, a contract might appear valid on its face but fraud might be involved. A proceeding in law would not go beyond the face of the agreement, while equity would go behind the "window dressing" and investigate the circumstances surrounding the making of the contract. When cases of this sort arose in early England, the matters were referred to the King, who in turn, referred them to the Chancellor as the "keeper of the king's conscience." Appeals of this sort became so numerous that a special court, called the Chancery Court, for obvious reasons, was established. Here a real effort was made to give a degree of justice not possible under the available procedures at law. As time went on, procedure here, too, became stereotyped, so that today, there is no "going into a trance" on the part of the judge, followed by his coming up with the right answer, but simply a determination that the case in question requires a certain procedure—injunction, specific performance, bill of discovery, or some other form. For example, in a case where an individual or a group threatens irreparable damage to property, a court in equity might issue an injunction, a court order, which would prohibit the action on the part of those who would cause the damage. The temporary, or preliminary, or interlocutory, restraining order would be issued on request. Later there would be a hearing to determine whether the order should be made permanent or dissolved. Thus, equity is sometimes referred to as "preventive justice," preventing the occurrence of the injury. In some states, separate courts, after the original English pattern, called Courts of Chancery, apply equity, but in the federal system and in most of the states the regular courts have jurisdiction in both law and equity procedure. Therefore, equity simply provides for a remedy or procedure that gives a person a degree of justice that otherwise would not be possible. Equity applies only to civil cases, a jury is not used, and the final determination is sometimes known as a decree.

Political Questions—The federal courts, being judicial bodies, do not take jurisdiction over cases involving political questions, which are matters of policy. The most obvious of such questions are matters of the foreign relations of the United States, the need for calling out the militia, the acquisition of territory, the question of recognition of a foreign government, or a determination as to the republican form of a state's government.[14] When the Supreme Court determines that a political question is involved, the decision of the political units of the government—Congress or the President—will be taken as final and binding on the courts. This is, of course, a self-imposed limitation on the part of the courts.

Judicial Review—In the clause of the Constitution extending federal judicial power to all cases under the Constitution,[15] there is the "major premise" of the Constitutional basis of the power of the Supreme Court to declare acts of the President or Congress unconstitutional. The Court is given final jurisdiction over the determination of questions involving an interpretation of the Constitution. That Constitution is declared (Article VI) to be the supreme law of the land, and no law can be contrary to it. Therefore, when the Supreme Court exercises its granted jurisdiction and takes a case that involves an interpretation of the Constitution, and the Court finds that a lesser law—federal or state—is contrary to the Court's interpretation of the Constitution, the lesser law is declared void for that reason. That is all that is meant by declaring an act unconstitutional. It cannot be emphasized too strongly or too often that the Supreme Court is a judicial body, not a political or policy-determining body, not a "third house" of Congress. Its job is judicial. It is not the function of the Court to decide whether a certain action is good or bad for us, whether we need it or not. Its proper function is to decide whether an action that has been taken is or is not permitted or authorized under the Constitution. As Justice Roberts pointed out on one occasion,[16] the job of the Supreme Court is to place the Constitution on the table, and to place alongside it the

---

[14] Luther v. Borden, 7 How. 1 (1849)

[15] Article III, Section 2, Clause 1.

[16] United States v. Butler, 297 U. S. 1 (1936)

law or act in question. If the two agree, all is well. If they disagree, if the Constitution says "no" and the law says "yes," the law is simply declared no law. Again, in spite of the obvious oversimplification in this statement, that is all that is meant by declaring an act unconstitutional. From the point of view of policy, the matter may be very desirable, but the Court, in its interpretation of the Constitution, is only to determine judicially whether the matter is good or bad. Under the doctrine of *stare decisis* whenever the Court decides a case, that decision will serve as a precedent and will be followed in future cases of the same sort. The Court, however, can and does overrule prior decisions, so the doctrine of *stare decisis* is not ironclad.

It is a common misapprehension that the Supreme Court declares acts unconstitutional with considerable regularity. However, such is not the case. Through its entire history the Supreme Court has held only seventy-nine acts of Congress unconstitutional in whole or in part, ranging from Marbury v. Madison in 1803 and the Dred Scott case in 1857 to Afroyim v. Rusk, in 1967.

How Cases May Be Brought in the Federal Courts: Original Jurisdiction—Cases may be brought in the federal courts through original jurisdiction, removal, or appeal. Original jurisdiction is first-hand jurisdiction, the first time a case is heard by any court. In the federal system, the Supreme Court has original jurisdiction in two types of cases—those involving diplomats and consuls accredited to the United States, and those to which a state is a party. Other federal cases go by original jurisdiction to the District Courts, plus the fact that cases involving consuls may also be brought by original jurisdiction in District Courts. The Courts of Appeals, as the name implies, have only appellate, or second-hand jurisdiction, reviewing cases that have already had a hearing. Since the original jurisdiction of the Supreme Court is specifically set down in the Constitution, Congress cannot either increase or decrease this jurisdiction.[18] The Supreme Court's appellate jurisdiction may be changed as Congress sees fit within the limits of federal case jurisdiction. In fact, on at least one occasion, Congress has taken appellate jurisdiction from the

[17] Marbury v. Madison, 1 Cranch 137 (1803); Dred Scott v. Sandford, 19 Howard 393 (1857); Afroyim v. Rusk, 387 U.S. 253 (1967).   500 (1964).

[18] Marbury v. Madison, 1 Cr. 137 (1803)

Supreme Court so as to forestall a decision.[19] This provision giving Congress control over the Court's appellate jurisdiction has given Congress considerable influence over the exercise of federal court jurisdiction. Not only does Congress have power to regulate the Supreme Court's appellate jurisdiction, but Congress also has control over the jurisdiction of the lower federal courts.

Removal—In addition to original jurisdiction, cases may be brought in the federal courts by *removal*, which is the transfer of a case from a state system to the federal system. To be eligible for removal, a case must be a matter of concurrent jurisdiction, that is, a case over which both federal and state courts have jurisdiction. Specifically, such cases are those of diversity of citizenship if they involve over ten thousand dollars, and cases under the Constitution, federal laws (with some exceptions), and treaties. As noted, the removal must take place before a final verdict has been rendered by any court. After a verdict, appeal is the only recourse. The reason for permitting removal is to place the defendant on the same plane of equality with the plaintiff. The plaintiff first determines in which court the case is to be filed. Then the defendant may ask to have the case removed to the other court system, if it is a matter of concurrent jurisdiction.

Appeal—A third way by which cases may be brought in the federal courts is by appeal. Appeals through the federal system are determined by laws of Congress, just as the state legislatures determine the laws of appeals for their particular courts. There is no common law right of appeal. It is a matter of statute or indulgence. Any case that can be brought in a District Court can be taken by mandatory appeal to a Court of Appeals. For most cases that is the end of the legal line; the decision of the Court of Appeals stands. Appeals to the Supreme Court can be classified as either mandatory or optional; the former includes cases that the Supreme Court must take, the latter, cases that the Supreme Court may or may not take as the justices decide. Mandatory appeals normally cannot be carried beyond the Court of Appeals in the federal system, nor from the highest appellate court in a state to the United States Supreme Court, unless there is a federal question involved. Specifically, a case may be appealed in this manner from the Court of Appeals to the Supreme Court only when

[19] Ex parte McCardle, 7 Wall. 506 (1869)

the statute of a state has been determined to be repugnant to the Constitution, laws, or treaties of the United States. Mandatory appeals may be taken from the highest court of a state having final jurisdiction only when a federal law has been declared invalid, or a state law has been declared not repugnant to the Constitution, laws, or treaties of the United States.

Optional appeal may be taken by either of two methods, certification or writ of certiorari. An appeal may be taken by *certification* only from the Court of Appeals. Any question in any case may go to the Supreme Court in this manner. In this procedure the judges of the Court of Appeals request the Supreme Court to answer certain questions involved in the case. The Supreme Court may then either answer the questions certified to it for answer, or it may direct that the entire case be sent to the Supreme Court.

The second method of optional appeal is by *writ of certiorari*, which is simply an order issued by the high court compelling the Court of Appeals to transmit a case to it for review and decision. The Supreme Court may do this upon the request of any of the parties to the suit in any case. A writ of certiorari may be used also to force a state court to transmit a case to the United States Supreme Court. This may be done whenever the validity of a federal law or treaty, the repugnance of a state law to the Constitution, laws, or treaties of the United States, or a right, privilege, title, or immunity under the Constitution, laws, treaties, or authority of the United States—in other words, a "federal question"— has been determined finally by a state court.

LEADING CASES
ON THE
CONSTITUTION

STATE AUTHORITY OVER FEDERAL OFFICERS

Ableman v. Booth, 21 Howard 506; 16 L. Ed. 169 (1859)

Booth was held in the custody of Ableman, a United States marshal, pending his trial in a district court of the United States on the charge of having aided the escape of a fugitive slave from the custody of a deputy marshal in Milwaukee. The Supreme Court of Wisconsin issued a writ of habeas corpus.

OPINION BY MR. CHIEF JUSTICE TANEY

(No evidence from the report that the decision was not unanimous.)

Question—Can a state court grant a writ of habeas corpus to a prisoner arrested under the authority of the United States and in Federal custody?

Decision—No.

Reason—No state judge or court, after being judicially informed that the party is imprisoned under the authority of the United States, has the right to interfere with him, or to require him to be brought before them. And if the authority of the state, in the form of judicial process or otherwise, should attempt to control the marshal or other authorized officer or agent of the United States in any respect, in the custody of his prisoner, it would be his duty to resist it, and to call to his aid any force that might be necessary to maintain the authority of federal law against illegal interference. No judicial process, whatever form it may assume, can have any lawful authority outside the limits of the jurisdiction of the court or judge by whom it is issued; and an attempt to enforce it beyond these boundaries is nothing less than lawless violence.

Corollary cases

Watkins Case, 3 Peters 202
Tennessee v. Davis, 100 U. S. 257

Tarble's Case, 13 Wallace 397
In re Neagle, 135 U. S. 1

ESPIONAGE AND FREE SPEECH

Abrams v. United States, 250 U. S. 616; 40 S. Ct. 17; 63 L. Ed. 1173 (1919)

In this case, Abrams and four other Russians were indicted for conspiring to violate the Espionage Act. They published two leaflets that denounced the efforts of capitalist nations to interfere with the Russian Revolution, criticized the President and the "plutocratic gang in Washington" for sending American troops to Russia, and urged workers producing munitions in the United States not to betray their Russian comrades.

OPINION BY MR. JUSTICE CLARKE
(Vote: 7-2)

Question—Does the Espionage Act violate the First Amendment?

Decision—No.

Reason—The court reasoned that the plain purpose of their propaganda was to excite, at the supreme crisis of the war, disaffection, sedition, riots, and, as they hoped, revolution, in this country, for the purpose of embarrassing, and if possible defeating, the military plans of the government in Europe.

Corollary cases

Schenck v. United States, 249 U. S. 47

Frohwerk v. United States, 249 U. S. 204

Lancaster v. Collins, 115 U. S. 222

Evans v. United States, 153 U. S. 608

Claassen v. United States, 142 U. S. 140

Debs v. United States, 249 U. S. 211

Stromberg v. California, 283 U. S. 359

Herndon v. Lowry, 301 U. S. 242

Schaefer v. United States, 251 U. S. 466

Gorin v. United States, 312 U. S. 19

DUE PROCESS AND CRIMINAL PROSECUTION

Adamson v. California, 332 U. S. 46; 67 S. Ct. 1672; 91 L. Ed. 1903 (1947)

Adamson, a citizen of the United States, was convicted, without recommendation for mercy, by a jury in the Superior Court of the State of California of murder in the first degree. Sentence of death was affirmed by the Supreme Court of the state.

The provisions of California law which were challenged permit the failure of a defendant to explain or deny evidence to be commented upon by the court and by counsel, and to be considered by the court and by the jury. These were challenged as invalid under the Fourteenth and Fifth Amendments.

OPINION BY MR. JUSTICE REED
(Vote: 5-4)

Question—Do the provisions of the California state constitution and its penal law abridge the guarantee against self-incrimination and of due process?

Decision—No.

Reason—The clause of the Fifth Amendment is not made effective by the Fourteenth Amendment as a protection against state action. The clause in the Bill of Rights is for the protection of the individual from the federal government, and its provisions are not applicable to the states. As a matter of fact, the Fourteenth Amendment forbids a state from abridging privileges of citizens of the United States, leaving the state free, so to speak, to abridge, within the limits of due process, the privileges and immunities of state citizenship.

A right to a fair trial is undoubtedly guaranteed by the Fourteenth Amendment. However, the due process clause does not include all the rights of the federal Bill of Rights under its protection. The purpose of due process is not to protect the accused against a proper conviction, but against an unfair conviction. The Court held that the state may control such a situation as this, where the defendant remains silent, with its own ideas of efficient administration of criminal justice.

Corollary cases

Barron v. Baltimore, 7 Peters 243

Twining v. New Jersey, 211 U. S. 78

Palko v. Connecticut, 302 U. S. 319

Wolf v. Colorado, 338 U. S. 25

Powell v. Alabama, 287 U. S. 45

Chambers v. State of Florida, 309 U. S. 227

Haley v. State of Ohio, 332 U. S. 596

United States v. Baldi, 344 U. S. 561

MINIMUM WAGE LAWS AND DUE PROCESS

Adkins v. Children's Hospital, 261 U. S. 525; 43 S. Ct. 394; 67 L. Ed. 785 (1923)

The Minimum Wage Act of 1918 provided for the creation in the District of Columbia of a Minimum Wage Board. The Board was authorized to investigate and ascertain the wages of women and minors and to set up standard minimum wages, which employers were forbidden to lower. The Children's Hospital employed several women at less than the minimum wage fixed by the Board. Through the action of the Minimum Wage Board, these women lost their jobs. They were satisfied with their pay and working conditions. A suit was brought by the women seeking to enjoin the enforcement of the minimum wage law and to permit the taking of whatever jobs they desired.

OPINION BY MR. JUSTICE SUTHERLAND
(Vote: 5-3)

Question—Is the Minimum Wage Act a violation of the due process clause of the Fifth Amendment?

Decision—Yes.

Reason—The right to contract about one's affairs is part of the liberty of the individual protected by the Fifth Amendment. There is no such thing as absolute freedom of contract, but freedom is the rule and restraint is the exception. The statute in question is simply a price-fixing law forbidding two parties to contract in respect to the price for which one shall render service to the other.

The price fixed by the board has no relation to the capacity and earning power of the employee, the number of hours worked, the character of the place or the circumstances or surroundings involved, but is based solely on the presumption of what is necessary to provide a living for a woman and preserve her health and morals.

The law considers the necessities of one party only. It ignores the necessities of the employer by not considering whether the employee is capable of earning the sum. If the police power of a state may justify the fixing of a minimum wage, it may later be invoked to justify a maximum wage, which is power widened to a dangerous degree. To uphold individual freedom is not to strike down the common good, but to further it by the prevention of arbitrary restraint upon the liberty of its members. (This case was overruled by West Coast Hotel Co. v. Parrish.)

Corollary cases

Lochner v. New York, 198 U. S. 45
Holden v. Hardy, 169 U. S. 366
Bunting v. Oregon, 243 U. S. 426
Morehead v. New York ex rel. Tipaldo, 298 U. S. 587

Stettler v. O'Hara, 243 U. S. 629
Muller v. Oregon, 208 U. S. 412
McLean v. Arkansas, 211 U. S. 539
West Coast Hotel Co., v. Parrish, 300 U. S. 379

DUE PROCESS AND SUBVERSIVE ACTIVITY

Adler v. Board of Education of the City of New York, 342 U. S. 485; 72 S. Ct. 380; 96 L. Ed. 517 (1952)

The Feinberg Law of New York State provides that any person who is a member of an organization advocating the unlawful overthrow of the government of the United States shall not be eligible for employment in the public schools of the state. The Board of Regents, after full notice and hearing, is to make a list of such subversive organizations, according to the law. The law retains the right to a full hearing for anyone fired or denied employment with representation by counsel and the right to judicial review.

OPINION BY MR. JUSTICE MINTON
(Vote: 6-3)

Question—Do these legal provisions violate the due process clause of the Fourteenth Amendment?

Decision—No.

Reason—The state has the right to inquire of its employees relative to their fitness and suitability for public service. If persons do not wish to work for the school system on the reasonable terms set down by the proper authorities, they are at liberty to retain their beliefs and associations and go elsewhere. "A teacher works in a sensitive area in a school-room. . . . One's associations, past and present, as well as one's conduct, may properly be considered in determining fitness and loyalty. From time immemorial, one's reputation has been determined in part by the company he keeps. . . . Disqualification follows therefore as a reasonable presumption from such membership and support. Nor is there a problem of procedural due process. The presumption is not conclusive but arises only in a hearing where the person against whom it may arise has full opportunity to rebut it."

Corollary cases

Garner v. Los Angeles Board, 341 U. S. 716
Gerende v. Board of Supervisors of Baltimore City, 341 U. S. 56
Joint Anti-Fascist Refugee Committee v. McGrath, 341 U. S. 123
United Public Workers v. Mitchell,

330 U. S. 75
American Communications Ass'n. v. Douds, 339 U. S. 382
Gitlow v. New York, 268 U. S. 652
Cole v. Young, 351 U. S. 536
Konigsberg v. State Bar of California, 366 U. S. 36
Keyishian v. Board of Regents, 385 U.S. 589

STATE LEGISLATION AND INTERSTATE COMMERCE

Aero Mayflower Transit Co. v. Board of Railroad Commissioners of Montana, 332 U. S. 495; 68 S. Ct. 167; 92 L. Ed. 99 (1947)

The state of Montana levied two similar taxes on trucking firms for the use of the highways in Montana. The tax money was placed in the general tax fund. The appellant was a Kentucky corporation and was exclusively in the business of interstate commerce. The appellant complied with the tax law from 1935 to 1937 and then ceased to pay. Montana sought to stop the company from operating in Montana and this was upheld in the state Supreme Court.

OPINION BY MR. JUSTICE RUTLEDGE
(No evidence from the report that the decision was not unanimous.)

Question—Can a state pass two identical taxes affecting the same party?

Decision—Yes.

Reason—The Court reasoned that in this case the taxes did not discriminate against interstate commerce. Each tax applied alike to local and interstate operations. Both taxes applied exclusively to operations wholly within the state or the proceeds of such operations, although those operations were interstate in character. The Court held it was of no consequence that the state had seen fit to lay two taxes, substantially identical, for the state does not exceed its constitutional powers by imposing more than one form of tax. As to the state's use of the tax money collected, the Court held that it was immaterial whether it had been placed with the general tax fund, as long as it had been identified as a tax for the privilege of the use of the Montana highways.

Corollary cases

Clark v. Poor, 274 U. S. 554

Interstate Transit v. Lindsey, 283 U. S. 183

McCarroll v. Dixie Greyhound Lines, 309 U. S. 176

Morf v. Bingaman, 298 U. S. 407

Memphis Gas Co. v. Stone, 335 U. S. 89

Clark v. Gray, 306 U. S. 583

Dixie Ohio Express Co. v. State Revenue Commission, 306 U. S. 72

Lloyd A. Fry Roofing Co. v. Wood, 344 U. S. 157

City of Chicago v. Willett Co., 344 U. S. 574

Bode v. Barrett, 344 U. S. 583

FEDERAL COURT JURISDICTION

Aetna Life Insurance Co. of Hartford v. Haworth, 300 U. S. 227; 57 S. Ct. 461; 81 L. Ed. 617 (1937)

Haworth in 1911, 1921, 1928, and 1929 bought a total of five life insurance policies from the Aetna Life Insurance Co. in amounts aggregating $40,000. They were to be ordinary life policies with the provision that if the insured became totally and permanently disabled they would then become paid-up policies and he would not have to pay further premiums. Further, he was to be entitled to the stipulated disability benefits. In 1930 and 1931 the insured ceased to pay the insurance premiums of the last four policies that he bought but continued to pay the premiums on the first one. He claimed that he was totally and permanently disabled. In 1934 he ceased to pay the premiums on the first policy and claimed the disability clause. By this time Haworth had taken loans on his policies and the last four had no value, while the first one was worth only $45. If, however, the plaintiff was to be judged totally and permanently disabled, as he claimed, the five policies would be regarded as being in full force, and the company would be obliged to pay accrued benefits. The complaint of the plaintiff was dismissed from the District Court on the grounds that it had no jurisdiction.

OPINION BY MR. CHIEF JUSTICE HUGHES

(No evidence from the report that the decision was not unanimous.)

Question—Does the District Court have jurisdiction in the suit under the Federal Declaratory Judgment Act?

Decision—Yes.

Reason—The Constitution limits the exercise of judicial power to either cases or controversies. Controversies are distinguished from cases in that they are less comprehensive than cases and they include suits of a civil nature. The facts before the Court were not of a hypothetical situation. It was a concrete case. When there is such a concrete case admitting of an immediate and definite determination of the legal rights of parties in an adversary proceeding upon the facts alleged, the judicial function may be properly exercised and the District Court must hear the case. Therefore, a suit for a declaratory judgment is a controversy under the Constitution.

Corollary cases

Chisholm v. Georgia, 2 Dallas 419

Muskrat v. United States, 219 U. S. 346

Osborn v. Bank of United States, 9 Wheaton 738

De La Rama S. S. Co., The, v. United States, 344 U. S. 386

State of New Jersey v. State of New York, 345 U. S. 369

SEARCH AND SEIZURE

Agnello v. United States, 269 U. S. 20; 46 S. Ct. 4; 70 L. Ed. 145 (1925)

Two government revenue agents went to the home of one, Alba, to purchase narcotics. They were given samples and arranged to come again. The second visit they brought more agents and the police. This time Alba sent an accomplice to Agnello's home, and then the two of them returned to Alba's, with Agnello carrying the narcotics. After transacting the sale of the drugs, all three participants were arrested for conspiracy to violate the Harrison Act. The police then searched Agnello's home, where they discovered some drugs. At first this was excluded from the trial since the police searched Agnello's home without a warrant. However, when Agnello denied knowledge of the conspiracy to sell narcotics, the court allowed the evidence of the search to be presented.

OPINION BY MR. JUSTICE BUTLER

(No evidence from the report that the decision was not unanimous.)

Question—Did the search of the house of Agnello and seizure of the narcotics without a search warrant violate the

Fourth Amendment, and did admission of the evidence of such search and seizure violate the Fifth Amendment?

Decision—Yes.

Reason—Persons arrested while committing a crime and at the place where the arrest is made may lawfully be searched to find and seize things connected with the crime. After arrest for conspiracy to violate the Harrison Act, search without warrant of a house of one of the alleged conspirators, several blocks distant from the house where the arrest was made, was held violative of the Fourth Amendment and not justifiable. Belief, however well founded, that an article sought is concealed in a house, furnishes no justification for search without warrant, and this notwithstanding facts unquestionably showing probable cause. Properly invoked, the Fifth Amendment protects every person from incrimination by the use of evidence obtained through search or seizure made in violation of the Fourth Amendment. Here the seizure was not incidental to the arrest.

Corollary cases

Carroll v. United States, 267 U. S. 132

Weeks v. United States, 232 U. S. 383

Silverthorne Lumber Co. v. United States, 251 U. S. 391

Boyd v. United States, 116 U. S. 616

Adams v. New York, 192 U. S. 585

Isaacs v. United States, 159 U. S. 487

Olmstead v. United States, 277 U. S. 438

Frank v. Maryland, 359 U. S. 360

Henry v. United States, 361 U. S. 98

DUE PROCESS AND STATE LAW

Allgeyer v. Louisiana, 165 U. S. 578; 17 S. Ct. 427; 41 L. Ed. 832 (1897)

A Louisiana statute forbade one, under penalty of $1,000 for each offense, to effect insurance on property in the state with companies who had not complied with the laws of the state. E. Allgeyer & Co. made a contract in New York with a New York insurance company not doing business in Louisiana, for an open policy of marine insurance for $200,000 upon future shipments of cotton. By the terms of the policy, Allgeyer was to notify the company from time to time of shipments applicable to the policy, which he did, and remitted the premium from New Orleans. A state court held them liable for the penalty.

OPINION BY MR. JUSTICE PECKHAM

(No evidence from the report that the decision was not unanimous.)

Question—Is this an interference in the "liberty" of the individual under the Fourteenth Amendment?

Decision—Yes.

Reason—The "liberty" contained in the Fourteenth Amendment is not simply physical freedom of his person, but freedom of all the faculties of the individual. Likewise, he is free to use these faculties in all lawful ways, to live and work where he will, and, as in this case, is free to make contracts which may be necessary or proper.

The Court did not intend to say that in no such case could the state exercise its police power. How far it might extend such power, the Court said, would be determined as cases arose. The contract in this case was valid, made outside the state, to be performed outside the state, and was not invalidated by the fact that the subject was temporarily within the state. The sending of the notice did not violate the statute, it being merely an act necessary to the valid contract. The doctrine of this case regarding substantive due process is no longer controlling.

Corollary cases

Butchers' Union Slaughter-house Co. v. Crescent City Live Stock Landing Co., 111 U. S. 746

Powell v. Pennsylvania, 127 U. S. 678

Nebbia v. New York, 291 U. S. 502

West Coast Hotel Co. v. Parrish, 300 U. S. 379

Osborn v. Ozlin, 310 U. S. 53

Olsen v. Nebraska, 313 U. S. 236

Phelps Dodge Corp. v. N.L.R.B., 313 U. S. 177

LIBERTY AND NON-COMMUNIST OATHS

American Communications Association v. Douds, 339 U. S. 382; 70 S. Ct. 674; 94 L. Ed 925 (1950)

Section 9 (h) of the Taft-Hartley Act, the Labor-Management Relations Act of 1947, provides that no investigation shall be made by the National Labor Relations Board of any question unless all officers of a labor organization concerned in the dispute sign an affidavit that they are not Communists and that they are not advocates of overthrowing the United States Government by force or by illegal means.

OPINION BY MR. CHIEF JUSTICE VINSON
(Vote: 5-1)

Question—Is Section 9 (h) of the Taft-Hartley Act contrary to the First Amendment of the Constitution?

Decision—No.

Reason—The freedoms of speech, press or assembly, established in the First Amendment, are dependent on the power of constitutional government to survive. If it is to survive it must have power to protect itself against unlawful conduct. Thus freedom of speech does not comprehend the right to speak on any subject at any time. Also, this is not merely a matter of speech. The government's interest "is in protecting the free flow of commerce from what Congress considers to be substantial evils of conduct that are not the products of speech at all. Section 9 (h) . . . regulates harmful persons who may be identified by their political affiliations and beliefs. . . . Section 9 (h) is designed to protect the public not against what Communists and others identified therein advocate or believe but against what Congress has concluded they have done and are likely to do again." There was no violation of the ex post facto prohibition because here the law was intended to prevent future action rather than to punish past action.

Corollary cases

Dennis v. United States, 339 U. S. 162

Whitney v. California, 274 U. S. 357

Hague v. C.I.O., 307 U. S. 496

Bridges v. California, 314 U. S. 252

Thomas v. Collins, 323 U. S. 516

Terminiello v. Chicago, 337 U. S. 1

TERRITORIAL COURTS

American Insurance Co. v. Canter, 1 Peters 511; 7 L. Ed 242 (1828)

The plaintiffs sued for restitution of 356 bales of cotton, part of a ship's cargo they had insured. The ship was bound from New Orleans to France but sank off the coast of Florida, near Key West. The cargo was partly recovered and was carried into Key West, where it was sold to satisfy the salvors under order of an inferior court established by act of the Florida Territorial legislature.

OPINION BY MR. CHIEF JUSTICE MARSHALL
(No evidence from the report that the decision was not unanimous.)

Question—Was this tribunal of the territory of Florida able to have jurisdiction in this case?

Decision—Yes.

Reason—Florida was not yet a state, and Congress in legislating for it exercised the combined powers of the national government and of a state government. It had been held that this court did not have the jurisdiction to hear this case, since the Constitution says, "all cases of admiralty and maritime jurisdiction must be vested in one Supreme Court and in such inferior courts that Congress may establish." Thus the territorial court established in Florida could not hear cases of this type. However, the courts established by the territorial legislature in Florida under authority of act of Congress were not constitutional courts.

"They are legislative courts, created in virtue of the general right of sovereignty which exists in the government, or in virtue of that clause which enables Congress to make all needful rules and regulations, respecting the territory belonging to the United States. The jurisdiction with which they are invested, is not a part of that judicial power which is defined in the Third Article of the Constitution, but is conferred by Congress, in the execution of those general powers which that body possesses over the territories of the United States. Although admiralty jurisdiction can be exercised in the states, in those courts only which are established in pursuance of the Third Article of the Constitution; the same limitation does not extend to the territories. In legislating for them, Congress exercises the combined powers of the general, and of a state government."

Corollary cases

Sere v. Pitot, 6 Cranch 332
Late Corporation of the Church of Jesus Christ v. United States, 136 U. S. 1

DeLima v. Bidwell, 182 U. S. 1
Balzac v. Porto Rico, 258 U. S. 298

EQUAL PROTECTION

Asbury Hospital v. Case County, N. D., 326 U. S. 207; 66 S. Ct. 61; 90 L. Ed. 6 (1945)

A North Dakota law stated that all land used or usable for agriculture, that was owned by corporations both domestic and foreign, must be disposed of within ten years except for such as was reasonably necessary in the conduct of their business. If not sold within this period, the county was to take it over and sell it to the highest bidder and give the proceeds, less expenses, to the former owner. The appellant obtained the land in satisfaction of a mortgage indebtedness and had been unable to sell it for an amount equal to the original mortgage. It was claimed that the statute violated the privileges and immunities clause, the contract clause, the due process clause, and the equal protection clause of the Fourteenth Amendment, and prayed for a judgment that the statute was unconstitutional and void as applied to appellant.

OPINION BY MR. CHIEF JUSTICE STONE
(Vote: 7-1)

Question—Does the North Dakota statute deny equal protection of the laws?

Decision—No.

Reason—The state of North Dakota had granted no charter or incorporation rights to the appellant, nor issued any permit to do business or own property in the state, so the appellant had no contract rights against the state. The Fourteenth Amendment does not deny a state the right to forbid a foreign corporation from doing business or acquiring property within its borders. Neither does the due process clause guarantee that a foreign corporation when lawfully excluded shall recapture its cost. It is sufficient that the corporation be given a fair opportunity of sale.

The Court held that a corporation is neither a "citizen of a state" nor a "citizen of the United States" within the privileges and immunities clause of the Constitution or the Fourteenth Amendment. The Fourteenth Amendment does not deny to a state power to exclude a foreign corporation from doing business or acquiring or holding property within it. A state's power to exclude a foreign corporation, or to limit the nature of the business it may conduct within the state, does not end as soon as the corporation has lawfully entered the state and there acquired immovable property.

Equal protection was not denied because corporations whose business is dealing in farm lands were exempt from the statute. The legislature is free to make classifications, if the differences between them are pertinent.

Corollary cases

Horn Silver Mining Co. v. New York, 143 U. S. 305

Hammond Packing Co., v. Arkansas, 212 U. S. 342

Metropolitan Insurance Casualty Co. v. Brownell, 294 U. S. 580

Terrace v. Thompson, 263 U. S. 197

Oyama v. California, 332 U. S. 633

Union Brokerage Co. v. Jensen, 322 U. S. 202

Western Union Telegraph Co. v. Kansas, 216 U. S. 1

Barrows v. Jackson, 346 U. S. 249

District of Columbia v. John R. Thompson, Co., 346 U. S. 100

THE CONSTITUTION AND ELECTRIC POWER

Ashwander v. Tennessee Valley Authority, 297 U. S. 288; 56 S. Ct. 466; 80 L. Ed. 688 (1936)

The T.V.A., an agency of the federal government, entered into a contract with the Alabama Power Company, providing for the purchase by the T.V.A., among other items, of certain transmission lines and real property. Also included in the contract were the interchange of hydroelectric energy and the sale by the T.V.A. to the power company of the surplus power from the Wilson Dam. The plaintiffs, who held preferred stock in the power company, were unable to get results in protesting the contract to the power company. Therefore they sought a decree restraining these activities as repugnant to the Constitution. The District Court issued a decree annulling the contract and the Circuit Court of Appeals reversed.

OPINION BY MR. CHIEF JUSTICE HUGHES
(Vote: 8-1)

Question—Is the contract of the T. V. A. with the Alabama Power Co. beyond the constitutional power of the Federal Government?

Decision—No.

Reason—The Court first considered the constitutional authority for the construction of the Wilson Dam, which was supported on the grounds that it was constructed under the exercise of war and commerce powers, that is, for the purpose of national defense and the improvement of navigation.

Secondly, the Court considered the constitutional authority to dispose of electric energy generated at the Wilson Dam. Here it was held that the authority to dispose of property constitutionally acquired by the United States is expressly granted to Congress by Section 3 of Article 4 of the Constitution. This section provides: "The Congress shall have Power to dispose of and make all needful Rules and Regulations respecting the Territory or other property belonging to the United States; and nothing in this Constitution shall be so construed as to prejudice any claims of the United States, or of any particular State."

Corollary cases

Dodge v. Woolsey, 18 Howard 331

Pollock v. Farmers' Loan & Trust Co., 157 U. S. 429

McCulloch v. Maryland, 4 Wheaton 316

Linder v. United States, 268 U. S. 5

Green Bay & M. Canal Co. v. Patten Paper Co., 172 U. S. 58

United States v. Chandler-Dunbar Water Power Co., 229 U. S. 53

United States v. Sweet, 245 U. S. 563

Pan American Petroleum & Transport Co. v. United States, 273 U. S. 456

Kaukauna Water-Power Co. v. Green Bay & M. Canal Co., 142 U. S. 254

Tennessee Electric Power Co. v. T.V.A., 306 U. S. 118

INVOLUNTARY SERVITUDE

Bailey v. Alabama, 219 U. S. 219; 31 S. Ct. 145; 55 L. Ed. 191 (1911)

Bailey received $15 under a written contract to work for a certain employer in Alabama. Bailey, for reasons undisclosed, refused to do the work or repay the money received and fulfill the terms of the written contract. There was an Alabama statute that made the refusal to carry out the labor conditions of a contract prima facie evidence of attempt to defraud.

OPINION BY MR. JUSTICE HUGHES
(Vote: 7-2)

Question—Is the Alabama statute constitutional?

Decision—No.

Reason—The Thirteenth Amendment prohibits involuntary servitude except for a crime, and empowers Congress to enforce this provision. In pursuance of this an act was passed by Congress, stating in effect that all laws requiring the enforcement of voluntary or involuntary labor of any persons in liquidation of a debt or obligation, or otherwise, should be declared null and void. Therefore, the Court concluded that to make evidence of refusal to work prima facie evidence of the crime of fraud is in conflict with the Thirteenth Amendment and the federal laws. This is compulsory service, this is peonage.

Corollary cases

Kelly v. Jackson, 6 Peters 632

Fong Yue Ting v. United States, 149 U. S. 698

Robertson v, Baldwin, 165 U. S. 275

Butler v. Perry, 240 U. S. 328

Taylor v. Georgia, 315 U. S. 25

Pollock v. Williams, 322 U. S. 4

United States v. Reynolds, 235 U. S. 133

Tot v. United States, 319 U. S. 463

Selective Draft Law Cases, 245 U. S. 366

USE OF FEDERAL TAX POWER TO REGULATE CHILD LABOR

Bailey v. Drexel Furniture Co., 259 U. S. 20; 42 S. Ct. 449; 66 L. Ed. 817 (1922)

The Child Labor Tax Law of 1919 passed by Congress required that those employing children under the age of fourteen must pay a tax amounting to 10 per cent of their net profits. In this case the Drexel Furniture Co. hired a boy under the age of fourteen and was assessed the tax by Bailey, Collector of Internal Revenue. The Company paid the tax under protest. Seeking a refund, they contended that the Child Labor Tax Law violated the states' powers under the Tenth Amendment. The defendants contended the law was passed under the federal government's power of taxation.

OPINION BY MR. CHIEF JUSTICE TAFT
(Vote: 8-1)

Question—Did Congress exercise constitutional power in passing the Child Labor Tax Law?

Decision—No.

Reason—The Court was of the opinion that the tax required in the Child Labor Tax Law was passed by Congress for the purpose of enforcing police power legislation. Although the Child Labor Law did not declare the employment of children illegal, the same purpose was accomplished by imposing the tax. The Court did not deny the power of Congress to tax. However, the tax in this law seemed to accomplish the purpose of a penalty for not obeying the employment standards set down by Congress. The employment standard within a state is clearly a state power. Therefore, the Court ruled that the power to tax by Congress must be reasonably adapted to the collecting of a tax and not solely to the achievement of some other purpose plainly within the power of the states.

Corollary cases

Hammer v. Dagenhart, 247 U. S. 251

McCray v. United States, 195 U. S. 27

Flint v. Stone Tracy Co., 220 U.S. 107

United States v. Doremus, 249 U. S. 86

United States v. Darby, 312 U. S. 100

United States v. Kahriger, 345 U. S. 22

Marchetti v. United States, 390 U. S. 38 (1968)

Grosso v. United States, 389 U. S. 62 (1968)

THE COURTS AND LEGISLATIVE REDISTRICTING

Baker v. Carr, 369 U. S. 186; 82 S. Ct. 691; 6 L. Ed. (2d) 663 (1962)

This was a civil action alleging that the apportionment of the Tennessee General Assembly by means of a 1901 statute debased the votes of the plaintiffs and denied them equal protection of the law under the Fourteenth Amendment. The Constitution of Tennessee mandates a decennial reapportionment but all proposals for such since 1901 have failed to pass the General Assembly. In this period the relative standings of Tennessee counties in terms of qualified voters have changed significantly. The appellants asserted that the voters in certain counties have been placed in a position of constitutionally unjustified inequality *vis-a-vis* voters in irrationally favored counties. The appellants claimed injunctive and declaratory judgment relief. The plaintiffs alleged that any change in the apportionment that would be brought about by legislative action would be difficult or impossible.

OPINION BY MR. JUSTICE BRENNAN
(Vote: 6-2)

Questions — 1. Do federal courts have jurisdiction of cases involving state legislative reapportionment?
2. Does the case state a justiciable cause of action?

Decisions — 1. Yes.
2. Yes.

Reason — This is a cause of action that arises under the Constitution according to Article III, Section 2 since the complaint alleges an apportionment that deprives the appellants of the equal protection of the laws in violation of the Fourteenth Amendment. Further, the claim is not "so attenuated and unsubstantial as to be absolutely devoid of merit." Moreover, "the appellants do have standing to maintain this suit. Our decisions plainly support this conclusion." Voters who allege facts showing disadvantage to themselves as individuals have standing to sue. Finally, the matter presented is justiciable. The mere fact that a suit seeks protection of a political right does not mean that it presents a nonjusticiable political question. The nonjusticiability of a political question is primarily a function of the separation of powers, the relationship between the judiciary and the coordinate branches of the Federal Government, and not the federal judiciary's relationship to the states.

The case was remanded to the District Court for trial and further proceedings consistent with this opinion.

Corollary cases

See also cases under Colegrove v. Green, 328 U. S. 549 and Fergus v. Marks, 321 Ill. 510 and Scholle v. Hare, 369 U. S. 429 W.M.C.A., Inc. v. Simon, 370 U. S. 190. Wesberry v. Sanders, 376 U. S. 1 (1964) Reynolds v. Sims, 377 U. S. 533 (1964)

STATE LAW AND INTERSTATE COMMERCE

Baldwin v. G. A. F. Seelig, Inc., 249 U. S. 511; 55 S. Ct. 497; 79 L. Ed. 1032 (1935)

G. A. F. Seelig, Inc. was engaged as a milk dealer· in the city of New York. It bought its milk, including cream, in Fair Haven, Vt. from the Seelig Creamery Corporation, which in turn bought from the producers on the neighboring farms. Upon arrival in New York, about 90 per cent was sold to customers in the original cans. About 10 per cent was bottled in New York and sold to customers in bottles.

The New York Milk Control Act set up a system of minimum prices to be paid by dealers to producers. A protective provision prohibited the sale of milk brought in from outside the state unless the price paid to the producers was one that would be lawful within the state.

Seelig bought its milk from the creamery in Vermont at prices lower than the minimum in New York. The Commissioner of Farms and Markets refused to license the transaction unless Seelig conformed to the New York regulations.

OPINION BY MR. JUSTICE CARDOZO
(No evidence from the report that the decision was not unanimous.)

Question—Is the New York law an unreasonable interference with interstate commerce?

Decision—Yes.

Reason—(1) New York has no power to project its legislation into Vermont. Such a power sets up a barrier in trade as effective as a customs duty. The imposition of imposts or duties upon commerce is placed without exception by the Constitution beyond the power of the states. The case in question is not one in which the state may regulate for the prevention of disease or to protect its inhabitants against fraudulent deception.

(2) The "original package" is not inflexible and final as regards interstate commerce. It is a convenient concept, and sufficient, except in exceptional cases. However, neither the police power nor the power to tax may be used with the aim or effect of setting up economic barriers against competition with the products of another state.

Corollary cases

International Textbook Co. v. Pigg, 217 U. S. 91

Asbell v. Kansas, 209 U. S. 251

Plumley v. Massachusetts, 155 U. S. 461

Brown v. Maryland, 12 Wheaton 419

Hood and Sons v. Du Mond, 336 U. S. 525

Gibbons v. Ogden, 9 Wheaton 1

THE CONSTITUTION AND THE TERRITORIES

Balzac v. People of Porto Rico, 258 U. S. 298; 42 S. Ct. 343; 66 L. Ed. 627 (1922)

Balzac was tried and convicted in Porto Rico in two criminal libel suits. In each case the defendant demanded a jury but this was denied. The Code of Criminal Procedure of Porto Rico granted a jury trial in cases of felony, but not in misdemeanors. The defendant was committed and sentenced to jail.

OPINION BY MR. CHIEF JUSTICE TAFT

(No evidence from the report that the decision was not unanimous.)

Question—Was the defendant under the protection of the Sixth Amendment?

Decision—No.

Reason—The Court reasoned that the only act of Congress indicating a purpose to make Porto Rico a part of the United States was the Organic Act of Porto Rico of March 2, 1917, known as the Jones Act. The act is entitled "An act to provide a civil government for Porto Rico and for other purposes." It does not indicate by its title that it has a purpose to incorporate the island into the Union. While this is not conclusive, it strongly tends to show that Congress did not have such an intention. The section called a "Bill of Rights" includes substantially every one of the guaranties of the federal constitution, except those relating to indictment by a grand jury in the case of infamous crimes and the right of trial by jury in civil and criminal cases. The Court reasoned on this evidence that if it was the purpose of Congress to incorporate Porto Rico, then the Islanders would have been entitled to the entire Bill of Rights. As for the classification of Porto Ricans as citizens of the United States, the Court reasoned that it enabled them to move into the continental United States and, becoming residents of any State there, to enjoy every right of any other citizen of the United States, civil, social and political. The citizen of the United States living in Porto Rico cannot there enjoy a right of trial by jury under the federal constitution any more than the Porto Rican. It is locality that is determinative of the application of the Constitution, in such matters as judicial procedure, and not the status of the people who live in the area. Therefore the Court found no evidence in the Organic Act showing intention of Congress to incorporate Porto Rico into the United States.

Corollary cases

Rasmussen v. United States, 197 U. S. 516

Dorr v. United States, 195 U. S. 138

De Lima v. Bidwell, 182 U. S. 1

Downes v. Bidwell, 182 U. S. 244

Hawaii v. Mankichi, 190 U. S. 197

THE STATES AND CONSTITUTIONAL LIMITATIONS
Barron v. Baltimore, 7 Peters 243; 8 L. Ed. 672 (1833)

The City of Baltimore in paving its streets diverted several streams from their natural course, with the result that they made deposits of sand and gravel near Barron's Wharf, which rendered the water shallow and prevented the approach of vessels. The wharf was rendered practically useless. Barron alleged that this action upon the part of the city was a violation of the clause in the Fifth Amendment that forbids taking private property for public use without just compensation. His contention was that this amendment, being a guarantee of individual liberty, ought to restrain the states, as well as the national government.

OPINION BY MR. CHIEF JUSTICE MARSHALL

(No evidence from the report that the decision was not unanimous.)

Question—Does the Fifth Amendment restrain the states as well as the national government?

Decision—No.

Reason—The Constitution was established by the people of the United States for their own government, not for the government of the individual states. The powers they conferred on that government were to be exercised by that government. Likewise, the limitations on that power, if expressed in general terms, are necessarily applicable only to that government.

The Fifth Amendment contains certain restrictions obviously restraining the exercise of power by the federal government. Since the Constitution is a document framed for the government of all, it does not pertain to the states unless directly mentioned.

Corollary cases

Gitlow v. New York, 268 U. S. 652

Palko v. Connecticut, 302 U. S. 319

Wolf v. Colorado, 338 U. S. 25

THE SENATE'S INVESTIGATORY POWER

Barry v. United States ex rel. Cunningham, 279 U. S. 597; 49 S. Ct. 452; 73 L. Ed. 867 (1929)

Acting upon the constitutional provision that "each House shall be the judge of the elections, returns, and qualifications of its own members" the Senate in 1926 refused to seat William S. Vare of Pennsylvania because of charges of fraud in his election. In the course of the investigation, Cunningham, an associate of Vare, refused to give the Senate committee an explanation of the source of $50,000 he had expended. He was arrested for contempt, and challenged the validity on the ground that the information was "private" and he did not have to reveal it.

OPINION BY MR. JUSTICE SUTHERLAND

(No evidence from the report that the decision was not unanimous.)

Question—Is the Senate able to compel a witness to appear and give testimony when the Senate is exercising a judicial function?

Decision—Yes.

Reason—The Constitution has conferred judicial powers upon the Senate, as well as legislative powers. That power carries with it the authority to take whatever steps are necessary to secure the proper information, in this case concerning elections. The Senate may do this by appointing a committee, or the Senate itself may deal with the matter.

Vare claimed that he was not a "member" of the Senate as yet, and so could not be investigated. However, such strictness does not apply here. Nor did the Senate's refusal to seat Vare deprive a state of its equal suffrage in the Senate any more than would the vote of the Senate vacating the seat of another member.

The Senate, in its capacity as a judicial tribunal may at times issue a warrant of arrest to compel attendance for the purpose of giving testimony. This applies to legislative as well as judicial functions.

Corollary cases

Reed v. County Commissioners, 277 U. S. 376

In re Chapman, 166 U. S. 661
Marshall v. Gordon, 243 U. S. 521

McGrain v. Daugherty, 273 U. S. 135	Jurney v. MacCracken, 294 U. S. 125
Kilbourn v. Thompson, 103 U. S. 168	Sinclair v. United States, 279 U. S. 263
Anderson v. Dunn, 6 Wheaton 204	United States v. Rumely 345 U. S. 41

DUE PROCESS AND COUNSEL

Betts v. Brady, 316 U. S. 455, 62 S. Ct. 1252, 86 L. Ed. 1595 (1942)

The defendant was indicted for robbery in a Maryland court and informed of his arraignment. Due to lack of funds he was unable to employ counsel, and requested that counsel be appointed for him. The request was denied, the judge informing him that it was not the practice in that county to appoint counsel for indigent defendants, save in prosecutions for murder and rape.

OPINION BY MR. JUSTICE ROBERTS
(Vote: 6-3)

Question—Does the Fourteenth Amendment imply that the state should furnish counsel for one indicted in a criminal offense?

Decision—No.

Reason—The Court concluded, after an extensive examination of constitutional, statutory, and other material, that in the great majority of the states, it has been considered the judgment of the people, their representatives, and their courts that appointment of counsel is not a fundamental right, essential to a fair trial. The matter has generally been deemed one of legislative policy. In the light of this evidence the Court was unable to say that the concept of due process incorporated in the Fourteenth Amendment obligates the state, whatever may be their own views, to furnish counsel in every such case. The circumstances in this case seemed not to demand counsel.

This decision has been overruled by Gideon v. Wainwright, 372 U. S. 335 (1963).

Corollary cases

McKnight v. James, 155 U. S. 685	Powell v. Alabama, 287 U. S. 45
Craig v. Hecht, 263 U. S. 255	Avery v. Alabama, 308 U. S. 444
United States v. Dawson, 15 Howard 467	Smith v. O'Grady, 312 U. S. 329
	Palko v. Connecticut, 302 U. S. 319

Hurtado v. California, 110 U. S. 516

Maxwell v. Dow, 176 U. S. 581

LaVallee v. Durocher, 377 U. S. 998 (1964)

Bute v. Illinois, 333 U. S. 640

Johnson v. Zerbst, 304 U. S. 458

Palmer v. Ashe, 342 U. S. 134

Miranda v. Arizona, 384 U. S. 436

Escobedo v. Illinois, 378 U. S. 478

Johnson v. New Jersey, 384 U. S. 719

DISCRIMINATION IN COMMERCE

Bob-Lo Excursion Company v. Michigan, 333 U. S. 28; 92 L. Ed. 455; 68 S. Ct. 358 (1948)

The Bob-Lo Excursion Company is engaged chiefly in round-trip transportation of passengers from Detroit to Bois Blanc Island, Canada, which lies some fifteen miles upstream from the mouth of the Detroit River. The island is known as "Bob-Lo," and has been styled Detroit's Coney Island.

The appellant holds almost all of Bois Blanc in fee, operating it as a place of amusement. It also operates two steamships for transporting the island's patrons back and forth. No freight, mail, or express is carried; the only passengers are the patrons bent on pleasure. The appellant has refused two classes—the disorderly and the colored. Miss Ray, colored, and forty white fellow members of a class conducted at Commerce High School planned an excursion. Miss Ray was rejected because she was colored. The courts of Michigan held the company guilty of violating the Michigan civil rights act.

OPINION BY MR. JUSTICE RUTLEDGE
(Vote: 7-2)

Question—Does the statute of the state of Michigan apply to this vessel, which is engaged in foreign commerce?

Decision—Yes.

Reason—The Bob-Lo Excursion Company must definitely be considered as engaged in foreign commerce. However, it would be very difficult to find a business touching foreign soil that would be more local in color. The island is economically and socially an adjunct of the city of Detroit. There are no established means of access from the Canadian shore to the island. The only means of transportation are the vessels of the appellant, carrying exclusively their own patrons. These facts insulate the island from all the commercial traffic characteristic of foreign commerce. The island is a local Detroit business, although carried on in Canadian waters, and for the present is of greater concern to Detroit and the state of Michigan than to the Dominion or Ontario.

That being the case, the state of Michigan is clearly justified in applying her civil rights act. The other cases cited do not apply to such a localization of the commerce involved. Nor is there any national interest or policy that could be found adverse to the application of the Michigan statute against discrimination. The Court held that the Michigan civil rights act will not impose an undue burden on the excursion company in its business in foreign commerce.

Corollary cases

Lord v. Steamship Co., 102 U. S. 541

Hall v. DeCuir, 95 U. S. 485

Morgan v. Virginia, 328 U. S. 373

South Covington and O. Street Ry. Co. v. Kentucky, 252 U. S. 399

DUE PROCESS AND SEGREGATION

Bolling v. Sharpe, 347 U. S. 497; 74 S. Ct. 693; 98 L. Ed. 884 (1954)

Here petitioners were Negro minors who sought to obtain admission to public schools of the District of Columbia attended by white children. The Negroes had been refused such admission, and the District Court had dismissed their complaint.

OPINION BY MR. CHIEF JUSTICE WARREN

(Vote: 9-0)

Question—Does segregation deprive children of due process of law under the Fifth Amendment?

Decision—Yes.

Reason—"We have this day held that the Equal Protection Clause of the Fourteenth Amendment prohibits the states from maintaining racially segregated public schools. The legal problem in the District of Columbia is somewhat different, however. The Fifth Amendment, which is applicable in the District of Columbia, does not contain an equal protection clause as does the Fourteenth Amendment which applies only to the states. But the concepts of equal protection and due process, both stemming from our American ideal of fairness, are not mutually exclusive. The 'equal protection of the laws' is a more explicit safeguard of prohibited unfairness than 'due process of law,' and, therefore, we do not imply that the two are always interchangeable phrases. But, as this Court has recognized, discrimination may be so unjustifiable as to be violative of due process."

"Although the Court has not assumed to define 'liberty' with any great precision, that term is not confined to mere freedom from bodily restraint. Liberty under law extends to the full range of conduct which the individual is free to pursue, and it cannot be restricted except for a proper governmental objective. Segregation in public education is not reasonably related to any proper governmental objective, and thus it imposes on Negro children of the District of Columbia a burden that constitutes an arbitrary deprivation of their liberty in violation of the Due Process Clause.

"In view of our decision that the Constitution prohibits the states from maintaining racially segregated public schools, it would be unthinkable that the same Constitution would impose a lesser duty on the Federal Government. We hold that racial segregation in the public schools of the District of Columbia is a denial of the due process of law guaranteed by the Fifth Amendment to the Constitution."

Corollary cases

See Brown vs. Board of Education of Topeka.

DUE PROCESS AND POLICE POWER

Bourjois v. Chapman, 301 U. S. 183; 57 S. Ct. 691; 81 L. Ed. 1027 (1937)

Bourjois, Inc., a New York corporation, brought suit asking that a Maine statute be restrained. The statute required that all cosmetics be registered and a certificate be secured from the department of health and welfare.

OPINION BY MR. JUSTICE BRANDEIS

(No evidence from the report that the decision was not unanimous.)

Question—Is the Maine statute a violation of the due process clause of the Constitution?

Decision—No.

Reason—None of the sixteen distinct charges of invalidity was well grounded. Among these contentions was the charge that the power conferred on the board to grant or deny a certificate was unlimited, and that neither the statute nor the board provided a hearing for the appellant. Delegation of power to exercise judgment as to injurious cosmetics does not require that the exercise of such power be preceded by the adoption of regulations.

The power to regulate or prohibit the sale of cosmetics containing poisonous, injurious, or harmful ingredients is not a violation of any provision of the federal Constitution. The requirement of due process is sufficiently guarded by an appeal to the superior court of the county.

Corollary cases

Shafer v. Farmers' Grain Co., 268 U. S. 189

Real Silk Hosiery Mills, Inc. v. Portland, 268 U. S. 325

Lemke v. Farmers' Grain Co., 258 U. S. 50

Hood and Sons v. Du Mond, 336 U. S. 525

Garner v. State of Louisiana, 368 U. S. 157

WAR POWERS AND RENT CONTROL

Bowles v. Willingham, 321 U. S. 503; 64 S. Ct. 641; 88 L. Ed. 892 (1944)

Section 2 (b) of the Emergency Price Control Act stated in part, "whenever in the judgment of the Administrator (Chester Bowles) such action is necessary or proper in order to effectuate the purposes of this Act, he shall issue a declaration setting forth the necessity for, and with recommendations with reference to, the stabilization or reduction of rents for any defense-area housing accommodations within a particular defense rental area." On April 28, 1942, the Administrator designated 28 areas in the United States, including Macon, Georgia, as defense rental areas. He recommended certain criteria for maximum rents and left certain housing accommodations to be adjusted by the rent director. Mrs. Willingham's apartments in Macon were judged by the rent director to have too-high rents. He sent Mrs. Willingham a notice informing her that he was going to issue an order directing her to reduce the rents on her apartments. Mrs. Willingham sued in a Georgia court to restrain the rent director's order on grounds that the statutes on which the order rested were unconstitutional. The state court issued a temporary injunction restraining the rent director, whereupon the O.P.A. administrator brought suit in the federal district court restraining Mrs. Willingham from further prosecutions and from violation of the Act, and restraining Sheriff Hicks of Macon from carrying out the instructions of the state court. The district court dismissed Mr. Bowles' suit on the grounds that the orders in question and provision of the Act on which they rested were unconstitutional.

OPINION BY MR. JUSTICE DOUGLAS
(Vote: 8-1)

Question—Are the provisions of the Emergency Price Control Act unconstitutional?

Decision—No.

Reason—"It has never been thought that price-fixing, otherwise valid, was improper because it was on a class rather than an individual basis. Indeed, the decision in Munn v. Illinois, 94 U. S. 113, 24 L. Ed. 77, the pioneer case in this Court, involved a legislative schedule of maximum prices for a defined class of warehouses and was sustained on that basis. We need not determine what constitutional limits there are to price-fixing legislation. Congress was dealing here with conditions created by activities resulting from a great war effort. Yakus v. United States, *supra*. A nation which can demand the lives of its men and women in the waging of that war is under no constitutional necessity of providing a system of price control on the domestic front which will assure each landlord a 'fair return' on his property.

"We fully recognize, as did the Court in Home Bldg. & Loan Association v. Blaisdell, ... that 'even the war power does not remove constitutional limitations safeguarding essential liberties.' But where Congress has provided for judicial review after the regulations or orders have been made effective it has done all that due process under the war emergency requires."

Finally, as to whether the Act violates the Fifth Amendment, the court held that Congress need not make provision for a hearing to landlords before the order or regulation fixing rents becomes effective. Congress provided for judicial review of the Administrator's action. Although the review came after the order was promulgated, the court held, as in Yakus v.

United States, that that review satisfied due process of
law.

Corollary cases

Toucey v. New York Life Ins. Co.,
314 U. S. 118

Lockerty v. Phillips, 319 U. S. 182

McKay v. Kalyton, 204 U. S. 458

Opp Cotton Mills, Inc., v. Administrator, 312 U. S. 126

Yakus v. United States, 321 U. S.
414

Munn v. Illinois, 94 U. S. 113

Tennessee v. Davis, 100 U. S. 257

Block v. Hirsh, 256 U. S. 135

Hamilton v. Kentucky Distilleries
Co., 251 U. S. 155

Woods v. Miller Co., 333 U. S. 138

Lichter v. United States, 334 U. S.
742

Gilbert v. Minnesota, 254 U. S. 325

FREE SPEECH AND PRESS

Bridges v. California (Times-Mirror Co., v. Superior Court of California) 314 U. S. 252; 62 S. Ct. 190; 86 L. Ed. 892 (1941)

"While a motion for a new trial was pending in a
case involving a dispute between an A.F.L. and a C.I.O.
union of which Bridges was an officer, he either caused to
be published or acquiesced in the publication of a telegram which he had sent to the Secretary of Labor. The
telegram referred to the judge's decision as 'outrageous,'
said that attempted enforcement of it would tie up the
port of Los Angeles and involve the entire Pacific Coast,
and concluded with the announcement that the C.I.O.,
union did 'not intend to allow state courts to override the
majority vote of members in choosing its officers and
representatives and to override the National Labor Relations Board.'"

Involved also were newspaper editorials that commented on pending action before the same court. "The
editorial thus distinguished was entitled 'Probation for
Gorillas?' After vigorously denouncing two members of a
labor union who had previously been found guilty of
assaulting nonunion truck drivers, it closes with the
observation: 'Judge A. A. Scott will make a serious
mistake if he grants probation to Matthew Shannon and
Kennan Holmes. This community needs the example of
their assignment to the jute mill'"

Both Bridges and the newspaper were cited for contempt and convicted.

OPINION BY MR. JUSTICE BLACK
(Vote: 5-4)

Question—Do the convictions violate rights of free speech and due process as guaranteed by the First Amendment made applicable to the States by the Fourteenth Amendment?

Decision—Yes.

Reason—The telegram that Bridges sent to the Secretary of Labor criticizing the decision of the court was merely a statement of the facts which the Secretary of Labor was entitled to receive regarding an action that might result in a strike. "Again, we find exaggeration in the conclusion that the utterance even 'tended' to interfere with justice. If there was electricity in the atmosphere, it was generated by the facts; the charge added by the Bridges telegram can be dismissed as negligible."

The influence of the editorials was likewise minimized by the Court.

"This editorial, given the most intimidating construction it will bear, did no more than threaten future adverse criticism which was reasonably to be expected anyway in the event of a lenient disposition of the pending case. To regard it, therefore, as in itself of substantial influence upon the course of justice would be to impute to judges a lack of firmness, wisdom, or honor, which we cannot accept as a major premise."

Corollary cases

Cantwell v. Connecticut, 310 U. S. 296

Gitlow v. New York, 268 U. S. 652

Toledo Newspaper Co. v. United States, 247 U. S. 402

Pennekamp v. Florida, 328 U. S. 331

Schenck v. United States, 249 U. S. 47

Abrams v. United States, 250 U. S. 616

EQUAL PROTECTION AND SEGREGATION

Brown v. Board of Education of Topeka, 347 U. S. 483; 74 S. Ct. 686; 98 L. Ed. 873 (1954).

A series of cases went to the Supreme Court from the states of Kansas, South Carolina, Virginia, and Delaware. Since all of the cases involved the same basic problem—Negro minors, through their legal representatives, seeking the aid of the courts in obtaining admission to the public schools of their respective communities on a nonsegregated basis—all were determined by one decision of the

Court. The Kansas case is taken as the nominal leading case. In the various states, the Negro children were of elementary or high school age or both. Segregation requirements were on a statutory and state constitutional basis except in Kansas where only statutory provisions were involved.

OPINION BY MR. CHIEF JUSTICE WARREN

(Vote: 9-0)

Question—Does segregation of children in public schools solely on the basis of race, even though the physical facilities and other "tangible" factors may be equal, deprive the children of the minority group of equal educational opportunities?

Decision—Yes.

Reason—Intangible factors involved in the separation of students of similar age and qualifications solely because of their race need very serious consideration. Such segregation of white and colored children in public schools has a detrimental effect upon the colored children, an impact that is greater when it has the sanction of law. It "generates a feeling of inferiority as to their status in the community that may affect their hearts and minds in a way unlikely ever to be undone. . . . We conclude that in the field of public education the doctrine of 'separate but equal' has no place. Separate educational facilities are inherently unequal. Therefore, we hold that the plaintiffs and others similarly situated for whom the actions have been brought are, by reason of the segregation complained of, deprived of the equal protection of the laws guaranteed by the Fourteenth Amendment."

The foregoing Bolling and Brown cases were the first of the Segregation Cases. Late in the 1954-1955 Term of the Court, the appropriate decrees for the implementation of Brown v. Board of Education and Bolling v. Sharpe were issued by the Court. Briefly, these called for the lower federal courts to supervise and enforce desegregation within a reasonable time. (349 U. S. 294; 75 S. Ct. 753; 99 L. Ed. 1083, 1955).

Corollary cases

Plessy vs. Ferguson, 163 U. S. 537

McCabe vs. Atchison, Topeka and Santa Fe Ry. Co., 235 U. S. 151

of Richmond County, 175 U. S. 528

Gong Lum vs. Rice, 275 U. S. 78

State of Missouri ex rel. Gaines vs. Canada, 305 U. S. 337

Sipuel vs. Board of Regents, 332 U. S. 631

Berea College vs. Kentucky, 211 U. S. 45

Henderson vs. U. S., 339 U. S. 816

Shelley vs. Kraemer, 334 U. S. 1

Mitchell vs. U. S., 313 U. S. 80

Morgan vs. Virginia, 328 U. S. 373

Cumming vs. Board of Education

Sweatt vs. Painter, 339 U. S. 629

McLaurin vs. Oklahoma State Regents, 339 U. S. 637

Buchanan vs. Warley, 245 U. S. 60

Cooper v. Aaron, 358 U. S. 1

Garner v. State of Louisiana, 368 U. S. 157

Shuttlesworth v. Birmingham Board of Education, 358 U. S. 101

THE "ORIGINAL PACKAGE" IN FOREIGN COMMERCE

Brown v. Maryland, 12 Wheaton 419; 6 L. Ed. 678 (1827)

There was a law in Maryland requiring all importers of foreign goods to have a license issued by the state. The indictment in this case charged Brown with having imported and sold some foreign goods without having a license to do so.

OPINION BY MR. CHIEF JUSTICE MARSHALL
(Vote: 6-1)

Question—Can the legislature of a state constitutionally require the importer of foreign goods to take out a license from the state, before he shall be permitted to sell the goods imported?

Decision—No.

Reason—The powers remaining with the states as a result of the Constitution may be so exercised as to come in conflict with those vested in Congress. When this happens, that which is not supreme must yield to that which is supreme. It results necessarily from this principle that the taxing power of the states must have some limits. Here the Court held that the Maryland statute authorizing a tax on imports interfered with the federal government's control of commerce with foreign countries. Although not denying the right of a state to tax property within the state, the court felt in this case the taxing of imports would obviously derange the measures of Congress to regulate commerce, and affect materially the purpose for which that power was given. "It is sufficient for the present to say, generally, that when the importer has so acted upon the thing imported, that it has become incorporated and mixed up with the mass of property in the country, it has, perhaps, lost its distinctive character as an import, and has become subject to the taxing power of the state; but while remaining the property of the importer, in his warehouse, in the original form or package in which it was imported, a tax upon it is too plainly a duty on imports to escape the prohibition in the Constitution."

Corollary cases

McCulloch v. Maryland, 4 Wheaton 316

Anglo-Chilean Nitrate Sales Corp. v. Alabama, 288 U. S. 218

Hooven and Allison Co. v. Evatt, 324 U. S. 652

Baldwin v. Seelig, 294 U. S. 511

Leisy v. Hardin, 135 U. S. 100

Woodruff v. Parham, 8 Wallace 123

Youngstown Sheet and Tube Co. v. Bowers, 358 U. S. 534

SUBSTANTIVE DUE PROCESS

Buck v. Bell, 274 U. S. 200, 47 S. Ct. 584, 71 L. Ed. 1000 (1927)

The superintendent of the State Colony for Epileptics and Feeble Minded in the State of Virginia ordered an operation upon Carrie Buck, the plaintiff in error, for the purpose of making her sterile. She contended that the Virginia statute authorizing the operation was void under the Fourteenth Amendment as denying to her due process of law and the equal protection of the laws. The evidence in this case showed that Carrie Buck's mother was feeble-minded, that Carrie Buck was feeble-minded, and that she had a child that was feeble-minded. All of them were committed to the State Colony. Under the procedure of the law, the rights of the patient were most carefully considered, and every step, as in this case, was taken in scrupulous compliance with the statute and after months of observation.

OPINION BY MR. JUSTICE HOLMES
(Vote: 8-1)

Question—Can this law under any circumstances be justified?

Decision—Yes.

Reason—The Court reasoned that more than once the public welfare may call upon the best citizens for their lives. The Court said that it would be strange if it could not call upon those who already sap the strength of the state for these lesser sacrifices, in order to prevent our being swamped with incompetence. "But, it is said, however it might be if this reasoning were applied generally, it fails when it is confined to the small number who are in the institutions named and is not applied to the multitudes outside. It is the usual last resort of constitutional arguments to point out shortcomings of this sort." The Court answered that "the law does all that is needed when it does all that it can, indicates a policy, applies it to all within the lines, and seeks to bring within the lines all similarly situated so far and so fast as its means allow." So far as the operations enable those who otherwise must be kept confined to be returned to the world, and thus open the asylum to others, the equality aimed at will be more nearly reached. (The philosophy of this case has been severely criticized.)

Corollary cases

Jacobson v. Massachusetts, 197 U. S. 11

Laurel Hill Cemetery v. City and County of San Francisco, 216 U. S. 358

Minnesota ex rel. Pearson v. Probate Court of Ramsey County, 309 U. S. 270

Skinner v. State of Oklahoma, 316 U. S. 535

EMPLOYER-EMPLOYEE LEGISLATION

Bunting v. State of Oregon, 243 U. S. 426; 37 S. Ct. 435; 61 L. Ed. 830 (1917)

A statute of Oregon required that any person employed in a mill, factory, or manufacturing establishment should not work more than ten hours a day, except for necessary repairs, or in an emergency. However, an additional three hours could be spent, but with payment of time and one-half for the overtime period. Bunting employed a man named Hammersly for thirteen hours one day, with no payment for overtime.

OPINION BY MR. JUSTICE McKENNA
(Vote: 5-3)

Question—Does this statute violate the Fourteenth Amendment?

Decision—No.

Reason—The Court held that this was a valid extension of state police power. The state found that it was injurious to men to work longer than ten hours in the types of establishments mentioned. This was not a wage law (which would have been in violation of the state constitution), since no attempt was made to fix standard wages, which were left to the contracting parties. The provision for overtime was simply for the purpose of giving an additional reason for not working overtime. This was adequate reasoning for the legislative judgment in this case.

"But we need not cast about for reasons for the legislative judgment. We are not required to be sure of the precise reasons for its exercise, or be convinced of the wisdom of its exercise. It is enough for our decision if the legislation under review was passed in the exercise of an admitted power of government."

Corollary cases

Coppage v. Kansas, 236 U. S. 1

Rast v. Van Deman & L. Co., 240 U. S. 342

West Coast Hotel Co. v. Parrish, 300 U. S. 379

Morehead v. New York ex rel. Tipaldo, 298 U. S. 587

Adkins v. Children's Hospital, 261 U. S. 525

Muller v. Oregon, 208 U. S. 412

United States v. Darby, 312 U. S. 100

Alstate Construction Co., v. Durkin, 345 U. S. 13

Thomas v. Hempt Bros., 345 U. S. 19

CENSORSHIP OF MOVIES

Burstyn v. Wilson, 343 U. S. 495; 72 S. Ct. 777; 96 L. Ed. 1098 (1952)

A highly controversial film, "The Miracle," produced in Italy and starring Anna Magnani, had at first been licensed for showing in New York and had been exhibited in the city for approximately eight weeks. Public reaction resulted in the license being withdrawn on the grounds that the movie was "sacrilegious." The distributor of the motion picture brought action in the state courts and ultimately in the Supreme Court of the United States to attempt to force Wilson, New York State Commissioner of Education, to grant the license.

<u>OPINION BY MR. JUSTICE CLARK</u>
(Vote: 9-0)

Question — Is the New York statute which permits state authorities to ban films on the ground that they are "sacrilegious" contrary to the First and Fourteenth Amendments?

Decision — Yes.

Reason — Motion pictures are a significant medium for the communication of ideas. The importance of movies as an organ of public opinion is not lessened by the fact that they are designed to entertain as well as to inform. Also, their production, distribution, and exhibition for profit do not affect the application of the liberty guaranteed by the First Amendment any more than in the case of books, newspapers, and magazines. Expression by means of motion pictures is included within the free speech and free press guaranty of the First and Fourteenth Amendments. A state cannot ban a film on the basis of a censor's view that it is "sacrilegious." Such a standard is too vague. From the standpoint of freedom of speech and press, the state has no legitimate interest in protecting any or all religions from views distasteful to them which is sufficient to justify prior restraint upon the expression of those views.

Corollary cases

Kingsley International Pictures Corp. v. Regents, 360 U. S. 684

Times Film Corp. v. City of Chicago, 365 U. S. 43

Freedman v. Maryland, 380 U. S. 51

Near v. Minnesota, 283 U. S. 697

Mutual Film Corp. v. Industrial Commission of Ohio, 236 U. S. 230

DUE PROCESS AND COUNSEL

Bute v. Illinois, 333 U. S. 640, 68 S. Ct. 763, 92 L. Ed. 986 (1948)

> Bute was charged with the crime of "taking indecent liberties with children" and was sentenced to 20 years imprisonment. The court record was silent on the subject of counsel for Bute's defense.

OPINION BY MR. JUSTICE BURTON
(Vote: 5-4)

Question—Was there a violation of the due process clause of the Fourteenth Amendment, since the court record does not show that the court inquired as to the petitioner's desire to have counsel assigned to him to assist him in his defense, or that such counsel was offered or assigned to him?

Decision—No.

Reason—The Court reasoned, after exhaustive consideration of the subject, that the Fourteenth Amendment does not, through its due process clause or otherwise, have the effect of requiring the several states to conform the procedure of their state criminal trials to the precise procedure of the federal courts as prescribed by the federal Constitution or Bill of Rights. There is nothing in the Fourteenth Amendment specifically stating that the long-recognized and then existing power of the states over the procedure of their own courts in criminal cases was to be prohibited or even limited. The states are free to determine their own practice as to the assistance of counsel, subject to the general limitation that such practice shall not deprive the accused of life, liberty, or property without due process of law. " . . . . This Court repeatedly has held that failure to appoint counsel to assist a defendant or to give a fair opportunity to the defendant's counsel to assist him in his defense where charged with a capital crime is a violation of due process of law under the Fourteenth Amendment . . . .

"In a noncapital state felony case, this Court has recognized the constitutional right of the accused to the assistance of counsel for his defense when there are special circumstances showing that, otherwise, the defendant would not enjoy that fair notice and adequate hearing which constitute the foundation of due process of law in the trial of any criminal charge. . . ." These were not capital charges and there were no special circumstances involved.

This decision has been overruled by Gideon v. Wainwright, 372 U. S. 355 (1963).

Corollary cases

Powell v. Alabama, 287 U. S. 45

Hebert v. Louisiana, 272 U. S. 312

Palko v. Connecticut, 302 U. S. 319

Snyder v. Massachusetts, 291 U. S. 97

Carter v. Illinois, 329 U. S. 173

Rice v. Olson, 324 U. S. 786

Betts v. Brady, 316 U. S. 455

DeMeerleer v. Michigan, 329 U. S. 663

Johnson v. Zerbst, 304 U. S. 458

House v. Mayo, 324 U. S. 42

Palmer v. Ashe, 342 U. S. 134

EX POST FACTO LEGISLATION

Calder v. Bull, 3 Dallas 386; 1 L. Ed. 648 (1798)

A dispute arose between Calder and his wife on one side and Bull and his wife on the other side concerning a right to property left by N. Morrison, a physician, in his will of March, 1793. The said will was rejected by the Probate Court of Hartford, and the decision was given in favor of Calder and his wife. As a result of a law enacted in 1795 by the state legislature, a new hearing of the case (which was not allowed according to the old law) took place, and the will involved in this case was approved, thus transferring the right of the property from Calder to Bull.

OPINION BY MR. JUSTICE CHASE

(No evidence from the report that the decision was not unanimous.)

Question—Was this statute of Connecticut an ex post facto law?

Decision—No.

Reason—Mr. Justice Chase defined ex post facto laws as contained in the prohibition of the Constitution as:

1. Every law that makes criminal an action done before the passing of the law and which was innocent when done, and punishes such an action.

2. Every law that aggravates a crime, or makes it greater than it was, when committed.

3. Every law that changes punishment, and inflicts a greater punishment, than the law annexed to the crime when committed.

4. Every law that alters the legal rules of evidence, and receives less or different testimony than the law required at the time of the commission of the offense, in order to convict the offender.

Thus a distinction must be made between retrospective laws and ex post facto laws. Likewise, ex post facto laws do not affect contracts, but only criminal or penal statutes.

Corollary cases

Thompson v. Utah, 170 U. S. 343

Malloy v. South Carolina, 237 U. S. 180

Thompson v. Missouri, 171 U. S. 380

Cummings v. Missouri, 4 Wallace 277

Ross v. Oregon, 227 U. S. 150

McDonald v. Massachusetts, 180 U. S. 311

DUE PROCESS AND FREEDOM OF RELIGION

Cantwell v. Connecticut, 310 U. S. 296; 60 S. Ct. 900; 84 L. Ed. 1213 (1940)

Newton Cantwell and others, members of the Jehovah's Witnesses, went from house to house in New Haven, Conn., selling books. They were equipped with a record player that described the books. They asked each householder for permission to play the record before doing so.

They were convicted under a statute that said that no person could solicit money for alleged religious purposes from someone not of their sect unless they have first secured a permit from the Secretary of the Public Welfare Council. The Secretary passed on all permits that were given.

OPINION BY MR. JUSTICE ROBERTS

(No evidence from the report that the decision was not unanimous.)

Question—Does this statute deprive the appellants of their liberty and freedom of religion in violation of the First Amendment as guaranteed by the Fourteenth Amendment?

Decision—Yes.

Reason—The act required an application to the Secretary of the Public Welfare Council of the state. He was empowered to determine whether the cause was a religious one, and the issuance of a certificate depended upon his affirmative action. If he found that the cause was not one of religion, it then became a crime to solicit for the cause. He did not issue the certificate as a matter of course. He must first appraise the facts, exercise judgment, and formulate an opinion. He was authorized to withhold certification if he believed the cause not to be religious. Such a censorship of religion as the means of determining its right to survive is a denial of liberty protected by the First Amendment as applied to the states by the Fourteenth Amendment.

Corollary cases

Cox v. New Hampshire, 312 U. S. 569

Chaplinsky v. New Hampshire, 315 U. S. 568

Murdock v. Pennsylvania, 319 U. S. 105

Martin v. Struthers, 319 U. S. 141

Follett v. Town of McCormick, 321 U. S. 573

Marsh v. Alabama, 326 U. S. 501

Tucker v. Texas, 326 U. S. 517

Prince v. Massachusetts, 321 U. S. 158

Kedroff v. St. Nicholas Cathedral of Russian Orthodox Church in North America, 344 U. S. 94

Fowler v. State of Rhode Island, 345 U. S. 67

Poulos v. State of New Hampshire, 345 U. S. 395

Kunz v. New York, 340 U. S. 290

CONGRESS AND INTERSTATE COMMERCE

Carter v. Carter Coal Co., 298 U. S. 238; 56 S. Ct. 855; 80 L. Ed. 1160 (1936)

This was a suit testing the validity of the Bituminous

Coal Conservation Act of 1935, commonly known as the Guffey Act. The purposes of the act, as declared by the title were "to stabilize the bituminous coal-mining industry and promote its interstate commerce; to provide for co-operative marketing of bituminous coal; to levy a tax on such coal and provide for a drawback under certain conditions; to declare the production, distribution, and use of such coal to be affected with a national public interest; to conserve the national resources of such coal; to provide for the general welfare, and for other purposes." Stockholders who brought suit had formally demanded of the board of directors that the company should not join the code (Bituminous Coal Conservation Act of 1935). The board of directors decided that, while they believed the act to be unconstitutional and economically unsound, they would join because of the penalty in the form of a 15 per cent tax on gross sales, which would seriously injure the company and might result in bankruptcy.

OPINION BY MR. JUSTICE SUTHERLAND
(Vote: 5-4)

Question—Can the labor provisions of the act be upheld as an exercise of the power to regulate interstate commerce?

Decision—No.

Reason—Commerce is "intercourse for the purposes of trade." Plainly the mining of coal does not constitute such intercourse, since the employment of men, fixing their wages, their hours of labor, and working conditions are purely local affairs. Everything that moves in interstate commerce has a local beginning; whatever may be done with the products does not change the local character.

The decision in the Schechter case was that federal power was asserted with respect to commodities that had come to rest after their interstate transportation. Here the case deals with commodities before interstate commerce begins. Federal regulatory power ends when interstate commercial intercourse ends, and conversely, does not begin until interstate commercial intercourse begins.

Corollary cases

United States v. E. C. Knight Co., 156 U. S. 1

Sunshine Anthracite Coal Co., v. Adkins, 310 U. S. 381

Kidd v. Pearson, 128 U. S. 1
Gibbons v. Ogden, 9 Wheaton 1
Coe v. Errol, 116 U. S. 517
Oliver Iron Mining Co. v. Lord, 262 U. S. 172

Schechter Poultry Corp. v. United States, 295 U. S. 495
N.L.R.B. v. Jones and Laughlin Steel Corp., 301 U. S. 1

TREATIES AND LAWS

Chae Chan Ping v. United States, (Chinese Exclusion Case), 130 U. S. 581; 32 L. Ed. 1068; 9 S. Ct. 623 (1889)

The appellant was a subject of the emperor of China, and a laborer by occupation, who resided in San Francisco from 1875 until June 2, 1887. When he left for China, he had in his possession a certificate entitling him to return to the United States. He returned on Oct. 8, 1888, presented his certificate to the proper custom-house officers, and demanded permission to land. The collector of the port refused, since the certificates had been annulled by an act of Congress on Oct. 1, 1888. He was detained on board the steamer.

OPINION BY MR. JUSTICE FIELD
(No evidence from the report that the decision was not unanimous.)

Question—Is the act of Congress in expelling Chinese laborers a violation of existing treaties of 1868 and 1880 between the United States and the Chinese government, and a violation of rights vested in them under the laws of Congress?

Decision—No.

Reason—Treaties of the United States and acts of Congress are both declared to be the supreme law of the land, with no authority of the one over the other. In either case, the last one enacted is in force. In this case the treaties and the rights were both superseded by the act of Congress of Oct. 1, 1888.

The right to determine admittance, or to reject is a privilege of sovereignty which belongs to the nation. Therefore the certificates, which are merely licenses, are revocable at will. Likewise, the power of Congress to exclude aliens and prevent their return is legitimate, even in peacetime.

"The treaties were of no greater legal obligation than the Act of Congress. By the Constitution, laws made in pursuance thereof and treaties made under the authority of the United States are both declared to be the supreme law of the land, and no paramount authority is given to one over the other.

A treaty, it is true, is in its nature a contract between nations, and is often merely promissory in its character, requiring legislation to carry its stipulations into effect. Such legislation will be open to future repeal or amendment. If the treaty operates by its own force, and relates to a subject within the power of Congress, it can be deemed in that particular only the equivalent of a legislative Act, to be repealed or modified at the pleasure of Congress. In either case the last expression of the sovereign will must control."

Corollary cases

Head Money Cases, 112 U. S. 580

Terrace v. Thompson, 263 U. S. 197

Jordan v. Tashiro, 278 U. S. 123

Oyama v. California, 332 U. S. 633

Whitney v. Robertson, 124 U. S. 190

Cook v. United States, 288 U. S. 102

Asakura v. Seattle, 265 U. S. 332

Nielsen v. Johnson, 279 U. S. 47

DUE PROCESS IN CRIMINAL PROCEDURE

Chambers v. Florida, 309 U. S. 227; 84 L. Ed. 716; 60 S. Ct. 472 (1940)

On May 13, 1933, Robert Darcy, white, was robbed and murdered in Pompano, Florida. The petitioners in this case were among the suspects rounded up for investigation. They were later removed to Dade County Jail at Miami as a measure of protection against mob violence. For a week's period the petitioners were continually questioned, and on the night of Saturday, May 20, the questioning routine became an all-night vigil. On Sunday, May 21, Woodward confessed. After one week of constant denial, all the petitioners "broke." These confessions were utilized by the state to obtain judgment. The petitioners were not, either in jail or in court, wholly removed from the constant observation, influence, custody and control of those whose persistent pressure brought about the sunrise confessions.

OPINION BY MR. JUSTICE BLACK
(Vote: 8-0)

Question—Was this an infringement of the due process of law guaranteed by the Fourteenth Amendment?

Decision—Yes.

Reason—The due process clause was intended to guarantee

adequate and appropriate procedural standards and to protect, at all times, people charged with or suspected of crime. This determination comes from the knowledge of past history that the rights and liberties of people suspected of crime cannot safely be left to secret processes. Those who have suffered most from these secret and dictatorial processes have always been the poor, the ignorant, the weak, and the powerless.

The requirement of conforming to the fundamental standards of procedure was made operative against the states by the Fourteenth Amendment. Such law enforcement methods as those described in this case are not necessary to uphold our laws. The Constitution prohibits such lawless means regardless of the end in view.

Corollary cases

Brown v. Mississippi, 297 U. S. 278
Powell v. Alabama, 287 U. S. 45
Norris v. Alabama, 294 U. S. 587
Gibbs v. Burke, 337 U. S. 773
Moore v. Dempsey, 261 U. S. 86

Ashcraft v. Tennessee, 322 U. S. 143
McNabb v. United States, 318, U. S. 332
Rochin v. California, 342 U. S. 165
Breithaupt v. Abram, 352 U. S. 432

CONGRESS AND INTERSTATE COMMERCE

Champion v. Ames (The Lottery Case), 188 U. S. 321; 23 S. Ct. 321; 47 L. Ed. 492 (1903)

Congress passed legislation in 1895 for the suppression of lottery traffic through national and interstate commerce and the postal service. The regulation was, in effect, a prohibition, since the law provided a prison term for each violation. Charles Champion was arrested for violating the act and he appealed that the act was unconstitutional since the commerce clause granted Congress only the power to regulate not to prohibit.

OPINION BY MR. JUSTICE HARLAN
(Vote: 5-4)

Question—Did Congress exceed its power in passing the legislation in question?

Decision—No.

Reason—Congress by the act did not assume to interfere with traffic or commerce in lottery tickets carried on exclusively within the limits of any state, but had in view only commerce of that kind among the several states. As a state may, for the purpose of guarding the morals of its own people, forbid all sales of lottery tickets within its limits, so Congress, for the purpose of guarding the people of the United States against the "widespread pestilence of lotteries" and to protect the commerce that concerns all the states, may prohibit the carrying of lottery tickets from one state to another. Congress alone has the power to occupy by legislation the whole field of interstate commerce. If the carrying of lottery tickets from one state to another be interstate commerce, and if Congress is of the opinion that an effective regulation for the suppression of lotteries, carried on through such commerce, is to make it a criminal offense to cause lottery tickets to be carried from one state to another, the Court knew of no authority to hold that the means was not appropriate. The Court held "that lottery tickets are subject to traffic among those who choose to sell or buy them; that the carriage of such tickets by independent carriers from one state to another is therefore interstate commerce; that under its power to regulate commerce among the several states Congress—subject to the limitations imposed by the Constitution upon the exercise of the powers granted—has plenary authority over such commerce, and may prohibit the carriage of such tickets from state to state; and that legislation to that end, and of that character, is not inconsistent with any limitation or restriction imposed upon the exercise of the powers granted to Congress."

Corollary cases

Phalen v. Virginia, 8 Howard 163

Stone v. Mississippi, 101 U. S. 814

Douglas v. Kentucky, 168 U. S. 488

Allgeyer v. Louisiana, 165 U. S. 578

Hoke v. United States, 227 U. S. 308

Brooks v. United States, 267 U. S. 432

Gooch v. United States, 297 U. S. 124

United States v. Darby, 312 U. S. 100

PUBLIC CONTRACTS

Charles River Bridge v. Warren Bridge, 11 Peter, 420; 9 L. Ed. 773 (1837)

This was an action by the Charles River Bridge Company to stop the construction of the Warren Bridge on the ground that the act authorizing its erection impaired the obligation of the contract between the Charles River Bridge Company and Massachusetts. The defendant received permission to erect another bridge of similar span within a few rods of the original bridge and was to give it to the state when paid for. The contention was that an original grant of ferry privileges to Harvard College in 1650 and a charter of 1785 incorporating the Proprietors of the Charles River Bridge (to which were transferred the rights of the College under the grant of 1650) constituted a contract whereby the plaintiffs were vested with an exclusive right to maintain a bridge "in that line of travel." Thus the Charles River Bridge Company implied that the privileges originally granted to Harvard College were transferred to them by means of the charter of 1785.

Opinion by Mr. Chief Justice Taney
(Vote: 5-2)

Question—Does the charter contain such a contract on the part of the state?

Decision—No.

Reason—"If a contract on that subject can be gathered from the charter, it must be by implication, and cannot be found in the words used. . . . In charters of this description, no rights are taken from the public, or given to the corporation, beyond those which the words of the charter, by their natural and proper construction, purport to convey." Implied privileges could prove to be unfavorable to the public and to the rights of the community; therefore it has always been the general operation of the Court to rule in favor of the public where an ambiguity exists in a contract between private enterprisers and the public.

Corollary cases

The Binghamton Bridge, 3 Wallace 51

Bridge Proprietors v. Hoboken Co., 1 Wallace 116

Larson v. South Dakota, 278 U. S. 429

Ogden v. Saunders, 12 Wheaton 213

West River Bridge v. Dix, 6 Howard 507

Long Island Water Supply Co. v. Brooklyn, 166 U. S. 685

CIVIL SUIT AGAINST A STATE

Chisholm v. Georgia, 2 Dallas 419; 1 L. Ed. 440 (1793)

Chisholm, a resident of the state of South Carolina, being an executor of an English creditor, brought suit against Georgia for money owed. It was brought in the Supreme Court because it was the only court that would accept jurisdiction. Georgia did not take part since she felt that she could not be sued.

OPINION BY MR. CHIEF JUSTICE JAY
(Vote: 5-1)

Question—Does the jurisdiction of the Supreme Court extend to suits by an individual citizen of a state against a state?

Decision—Yes.

Reason—The Constitution says that "The judicial power of the United States shall extend to controversies between a state and the citizens of another state." This was taken to mean that the power also extends to controversies between an individual and a state. The Constitution did not say that a state could not be sued, and hence the Court must judge all suits on the merits before it. There was no mention in the Constitution to exclude this type of suit; therefore the suit was properly brought before this court. (The rule of this case was abrogated by the Eleventh Amendment to the Constitution.)

Corollary cases

Cohens v. Virginia, 6 Wheaton 264
Osborn v. Bank of the United States, 9 Wheaton 738
Ex parte Young, 209 U. S. 123
New Hampshire v. Louisiana, 108 U. S. 76

South Dakota v. North Carolina, 192 U. S. 286
Hans v. Louisiana, 134 U. S. 1
Monaco v. Mississippi, 292 U. S. 313

PUBLIC PURPOSE IN TAXING AND SPENDING

Citizens Savings & Loan Ass'n. v. Topeka, 20 Wallace 655; 22 L. Ed. 455 (1874)

To encourage a bridge company to locate in Topeka the city made a gift to the company of a number of city bonds issued by virtue of authority granted to the city by an act of the legislature of Kansas. These bonds were transferred to the plaintiff and suit brought against the city to recover the interest due on them. The city contended the statute authorizing the issuance of the bonds was invalid because the purpose for which they were granted to the bridge company was not a public purpose.

OPINION BY MR. JUSTICE MILLER
(Vote: 8-1)

Question—Was the Kansas statute in this case valid.

Decision—No.

Reason—The Court said that there can be no lawful tax that is not laid for a public purpose. It may not be easy to draw the line in all cases so as to decide what is a public purpose; however, in this case if it be said that a benefit results to the local public of a town by establishing manufactures, the same may be said of any other business or pursuit that employs capital or labor. The merchant, the mechanic, the innkeeper, the banker, the builder, the steamboat owner are equally promoters of the public good, and equally deserving the aid of the citizens by forced contributions. The public treasury would be exhausted and no apparent good would result to the public. Therefore, the tax in this case was unlawful and the city was not bound to pay the interest on the bonds.

Corollary cases

Olcott v. Supervisors, 16 Wallace 689

McCulloch v. Maryland, 4 Wheaton 431

Jones v. Portland, 245 U. S. 217

CONGRESS AND THE FOURTEENTH AMENDMENT

The Civil Rights Cases, 109 U. S. 3; 3 S. Ct. 18; 27 L. Ed. 835 (1883)

Various colored persons had been denied by the proprietors of hotels, theaters, and railway companies, the full enjoyment of the accommodations thereof, contrary to the act of Congress requiring no discrimination. Those proprietors had been indicted or sued for the penalty prescribed by the act.

OPINION BY MR. JUSTICE BRADLEY
(Vote: 8-1)

Question—Does the Fourteenth Amendment compel a private citizen to refrain from the practice of discrimination?

Decision—No.

Reason—The law was founded on the Fourteenth Amendment, and this is concerned only with the state practicing discrimination. It makes no mention of individual persons infringing on individual rights. If the state does not assist the discrimination of an individual against another individual, it is purely a matter as between the two individuals. "In fine, the legislation which Congress is authorized to adopt in this behalf is not general legislation upon the rights of the citizen, but corrective legislation; that is, such as may be necessary and proper for counteracting such laws as the states may adopt or enforce, and which by the amendment they are prohibited from making or enforcing, or such acts and proceedings as the states may commit or take, and which by the amendment they are prohibited from committing or taking."

Corollary cases

United States v. Cruikshank, 92 U. S. 542

United States v. Harris, 106 U. S. 629

Virginia v. Rives, 100 U. S. 313

Shelley v. Kraemer, 334 U. S. 1

Hamilton v. Regents of University of California, 293 U. S. 245

Screws v. United States, 325 U. S. 91

Home Telegraph and Telephone Co. v. City of Los Angeles, 227 U. S. 278

Heart of Atlanta Motel, Inc. v. U. S., 379 U. S. 241

Katzenbach V. McClung, 379 U. S| 294

STATE AND INTERSTATE COMMERCE

Coe v. Errol, 116 U. S. 517; 6 S. Ct. 475; 29 L. Ed. 715 (1886)

Edward Coe cut certain logs in Maine and floated them down the Androscoggin River through New Hampshire bound for Lewiston, Maine. The logs were frozen in the river at Errol, New Hampshire. During that time they were taxed at Errol. Another group of logs had been cut in the state of New Hampshire, transported to Errol and there placed in the river and on the banks awaiting Spring floods. These also were taxed by the town of Errol.

OPINION BY MR. JUSTICE BRADLEY

(No evidence from the report that the decision was not unanimous.)

Question—Are the products of a state, though intended for exportation and partially prepared for that purpose by being deposited at a place or port of shipment within the state, liable to be taxed like other property within the state?

Decision—Yes.

Reason—The logs from Maine are already in the course of transportation and therefore not taxable, being protected by the Constitution. On the other hand, when products are brought to a town or station, such products are not yet exports. They are still part of the general mass of property of the state, and liable to state taxation, as long as they are not taxed with discrimination by reason of their being intended for export.

The point where state jurisdiction over commodities of commerce begins and ends is not easy to designate, but it is a matter of importance to the shipper and to the state. Products of a state intended for exportation to another state do not cease to be a part of the general mass of property within the state until they have been shipped, or started on their route on a common carrier, to another state. In this case, taking the logs to the depot where the journey was to commence was part of the preliminary work, and not interstate commerce. As long as they were taxed in the usual way as other similar property was taxed, there was no conflict. As long as the object is still part of the general mass of property and receives the same treatment, all is well. The river was the common carrier, and the law at this time stated that logs frozen in the river were not taxable, but logs on the bank were taxable for they were not in the hands of the common carrier.

Corollary cases

Joy Oil Co. v. State Tax Commission, 335 U. S. 812

Empresa Siderurgica, S. A. v. Merced County, 337 U. S. 154

Richfield Oil Corp. v. State Board, 329 U. S. 69

Bacon v. Illinois, 227 U. S. 504

Stafford v. Wallace, 258 U. S. 495

Minnesota v. Blasius, 290 U. S. 1

JURISDICTION OF FEDERAL COURTS

Cohens v. Virginia, 6 Wheaton 264; 5 L. Ed. 257 (1821)

To effect improvements in the City of Washington, Congress passed a law in 1802 authorizing the District of Columbia to conduct lotteries. Acting under this authority, the city passed an ordinance creating a lottery. The State of Virginia had a law forbidding lotteries except as established by that state. P. J. and M. J. Cohen were arrested in Norfolk, Va., charged with selling tickets for the Washington lottery. They were found guilty and fined $100. Then they appealed to the Supreme Court, to which Virginia did not object since the states were desirous of forcing the issue of the Supreme Court's authority over state actions.

Opinion by Mr. Chief Justice Marshall

(No evidence from the report that the decision was not unanimous.)

Question—Is the jurisdiction of the court excluded by the character of the parties, one of them a state and the other a citizen of that state?

Decision—No.

Reason—"Where, then, a state obtains a judgment against an individual, and the court, rendering such judgment, overrules a defense set up under the Constitution or laws of the United States, the transfer of this record into the Supreme Court, for the sole purpose of inquiring whether the judgment violates the Constitution or laws of the United States, can, with no propriety, we think, be denominated by a suit commenced or prosecuted against the state whose judgment is so far re-examined. Nothing is demanded from the state. No claim against it of any description is asserted or prosecuted. The party is not to be restored to the possession of anything. . . . Whether it be by writ of error or appeal, no claim is asserted, no demand is made by the original defendant; he only asserts the constitutional right to have his defense examined by that tribunal whose province it is to construe the Constitution and laws of the Union.

. . . .

It is, then, the opinion of the Court, that the defendant who removes a judgment rendered against him by a State court into this Court, for the purpose of re-examining the question, whether that judgment be in violation of the Constitution or laws of the United States, does not commence or prosecute a suit against the State, whatever may be its opinion where the effect of the writ may be to restore the party to the possession of a thing which he demands. . . ."

Corollary cases

Muskrat v. United States, 219 U. S. 346

Marbury v. Madison, 1 Cranch 137

Chisholm v. Georgia, 2 Dallas 431

Monaco v. Mississippi, 292 U. S. 313

Martin v. Hunter's Lessee, 1 Wheaton 304

THE COURTS AND LEGISLATIVE REDISTRICTING

Colegrove v. Green, 328 U. S. 549; 66 S. Ct. 1198; 90 L. Ed. 1432 (1946)

Three persons qualified to vote in a Congressional district with a larger population than other districts in

Illinois brought suit in federal court to restrain the officers of the state from arranging an election in which Representatives were to be elected. They alleged that the Congressional districts lacked compactness of territory and approximate equality of population.

OPINION BY MR. JUSTICE FRANKFURTER
(Vote: 4-3)

Question—Is this a matter for judicial determination?

Decision—No.

Reason—This issue is of a political nature. Article I, Section .4 of the Constitution states that the procedure for electing Representatives shall be prescribed by the legislature of each state, but that Congress may at any time by law make or alter such regulation. If Congress fails in exercising its powers, whereby standards of fairness are offended, the remedy ultimately lies with the people through the ballot. The courts cannot force a legislative body to take affirmative action.

Corollary cases

Wood v. Broom, 287 U. S. 1
Koenig v. Flynn, 285 U. S. 375
Smiley v. Holm, 285 U. S. 355
Luther v. Borden, 7 Howard 1
Pacific States Telephone and Tele-
graph Co. v. Oregon, 223 U. S. 118
Baker v. Carr, 369 U. S. 186 (1952)
Wesberry v. Sanders 376 U. S. 1 (1964)
Reynolds v. Sims, 377 U. S. 533 (1964)

THE AMENDING PROCESS AND JUDICIAL REVIEW

Coleman v. Miller, 307 U. S. 433; 59 S. Ct. 972; 83 L. Ed. 1385 (1939)

In June, 1924, Congress proposed an amendment to the Constitution known as the Child Labor Amendment. In January, 1925, the legislature of Kansas adopted a resolution rejecting the proposed amendment, and a certified copy was sent to the Secretary of State of the United States. In January, 1937, a resolution was introduced in the Senate of Kansas ratifying the proposed amendment. There were forty Senators, twenty in favor, and twenty rejecting it. The Lieutenant Governor, presiding officer of the Senate, cast his vote in favor of the resolution, which was later adopted by a majority of the members of the House of Representatives.

Petition was then brought challenging the right of the Lieutenant Governor to cast the deciding vote. The petition also challenged the vitality of the amendment, stating that a reasonable amount of time for ratification had elapsed.

Opinion by Mr. Chief Justice Hughes
(Vote: 7-2)

Questions—Two major issues were involved: (1) Can a state whose legislature has formally rejected a federal amendment later ratify it? (2) Do proposed amendments die of old age, if they remain before the states for too long a time?

Decisions—The Court decided that the case held enough interest for consideration. It upheld, without considering the merits, the decision of the state supreme court that the Lieutenant Governor had the authority to break the tie.

(1) The question of ratification in the light of previous rejection, or attempted withdrawal should be regarded as a political question, with ultimate authority for its decision residing in Congress.

(2) Congress, likewise, has the final say in the determination of whether or not an amendment has lost its vitality before the required ratifications.

Reasons—Article V of the Constitution says nothing of rejection, but only of ratification. The power to ratify is conferred upon a state by the Constitution, and persists, even if previously rejected.

The political departments of the government dealt with previous rejection and attempted withdrawal in the adoption of the Fourteenth Amendment. Both were considered ineffectual in the presence of an actual ratification. This is a political question pertaining to the political departments, with final authority for the matter in the hands of Congress.

Regarding the vitality of the amendment, an amendment is not open for ratification for all time, since amendments are prompted by necessity. However, if Congress does not set a limit, as it did in the Eighteenth Amendment (7 years), the Court may not take upon itself the responsibility of deciding what constitutes a reasonable time. No criteria for a judicial determination of any kind of time limit exist in the Constitution.

Congress has the power under Article V to fix a reasonable time limit. If the time is not fixed in advance, it is open for determination at the time of promulgating the adoption of the amendment. This decision of Congress would not be subject to review by the Court. These questions are essentially political and are not justiciable.

Corollary cases

Dillon v. Gloss, 256 U. S. 368
United States v. Sprague, 282 U. S. 716
Hawke v. Smith, 253 U. S. 221
Luther v. Borden, 7 Howard 1

Pacific States Telegraph and Telephone Co. v. State of Oregon, 223 U. S. 118
Leser v. Garnett, 258 U. S. 130

INTERGOVERNMENTAL TAXATION

Collector v. Day (Buffington v. Day), 11 Wallace 113; 20 L. Ed. 122 (1871)

Judge Day of the Probate Court for Barnstable County, Massachusetts, brought a suit against Buffington, Collector of Internal Revenue, to recover federal income tax assessments upon his salary during the years 1866 and 1867, as judge of the Court of Probate and Insolvency, Barnstable County, Mass. Judge Day, having paid the tax under protest, brought suit to recover the amount paid and obtained judgment. The Collector then sued for a writ of error.

OPINION BY MR. JUSTICE NELSON
(Vote: 8-1)

Question—Can Congress constitutionally impose a tax upon the salary of a judicial officer of a state?

Decision—No.

Reason—The work that a judge does is a vital function of the state. It is one of the reserved rights of the state coupled with the passing of laws and the administration of them. The federal government has only the delegated power that the states gave it, and since this is a part that the states reserved for themselves, these governmental actions are not properly subject to the taxing power of Congress.

The means and instrumentalities employed for carrying on the operations of state governments should not be liable to be crippled or defeated by the taxing power of another government. One of these means and instrumentalities is the judicial department of the state, and in its establishment the states are independent of the general government.

Although there is no express provision in the Constitution that prohibits the general government from taxing the means and instrumentalities of the states, the exemption rests upon necessary implication and is upheld by the law of self-preservation. (This case was overruled by Graves v. New York ex rel. O'Keefe.)

Corollary cases

McCulloch v. Maryland, 4 Wheaton 316

Lane County v. Oregon, 7 Wallace 76

Veazie Bank v. Fenno, 8 Wallace 533

Helvering v. Gerhardt, 304 U. S. 405

Graves v. New York ex rel. O'Keefe, 306 U. S. 466

New York ex rel. Rogers v. Graves, 299 U. S. 401

South Carolina v. United States, 199 U. S. 437

Dobbins v. Commissioners of Erie County, 16 Peters 435

Carson v. Roane-Anderson Co., 342 U. S. 232

JUDICIAL REVIEW

Commonwealth of Massachusetts v. Mellon (Frothingham v. Mellon), 262 U. S. 447, 43 S. Ct. 597, 67 L. Ed. 1078 (1923)

The Maternity Act of November 23, 1921 provided for annual federal appropriations to be apportioned among the states that might cooperate to reduce maternal and infant mortality and protect the health of mothers and infants. The State of Massachusetts, in an original suit against the Secretary of the Treasury, Andrew Mellon, stated that the Act of November 23, 1921, "The Maternity Act," was unconstitutional on the ground that the federal government usurped reserve powers of the states as guaranteed by the Constitution in the Tenth Amendment, since this Act invaded local powers and therefore should be enjoined by the Supreme Court.

Mrs. Frothingham appealed from a decision of the Circuit Court of Appeals of Washington, D. C., contesting the same act and endeavoring to have the Supreme Court enjoin the enforcement of the Act on the ground that the provisions of this Act would take her property under the guise of taxation.

OPINION BY MR. JUSTICE SUTHERLAND
(No evidence from the report that the decision was not unanimous.)

Questions—1. Can the Supreme Court issue an enjoining order on a federal appropriation act in a suit brought by the state?

2. Can a taxpayer invoke the power of the court to enjoin a federal appropriation act on the ground that it is invalid because it imposes hardship?

Decisions—1. No. Case dismissed.

2. No. Decision of lower court upheld.

Reason—The state cannot institute judicial proceedings to protect citizens of the United States who are also its citizens from the operation of statutes of the United States. Further, the Supreme Court has no jurisdiction to enjoin the enforcement of an Act of Congress, which is to become operative in any state only upon acceptance by it, on the grounds that Congress is legislating outside its power and into the reserved powers of the states, since this is a political question and not judicial in character. "His [the taxpayer's] interest in the moneys of the treasury—partly realized from taxation and partly from other sources—is shared with millions of others, is comparatively minute and indeterminable, and the effect upon future taxation, of any payment out of the funds, so remote, fluctuating, and uncertain, that no basis is afforded for an appeal to the preventive powers of a court of equity." A party invoking judicial action to hold a law of appropriation unconstitutional must show direct injury sustained or threatened, not merely that the individual is suffering in an indefinite way with the general public.

Corollary cases

Millard v. Roberts, 202 U. S. 429

Wilson v. Shaw, 204 U. S. 24

Bradfield v. Roberts, 175 U. S. 291

Gaines v. Thompson, 7 Wallace 347

Luther v. Borden, 7 Howard 1

United States v. Butler, 297 U. S. 1

Ex parte Levitt, 302 U. S. 633

Florida v. Mellon, 273 U. S. 12

Fairchild v. Hughes, 258 U. S. 126

New Jersey v. Sargent, 269 U. S. 328

Doremus v. Board of Education, 342 U. S. 420

Everson v. Board of Education, 330 U. S. 1

FEDERAL AND STATE REGULATION OF POWER

Cooley v. The Board of Wardens of the Port of Philadelphia, 12 Howard 299; 13 L. Ed. 996 (1851)

The Board of Wardens of the Port of Philadelphia, acting under a statute of the state of Pennsylvania which established an elaborate system of regulations regarding pilots in the port including monetary penalties for failure to comply with the regulations, attempted to enforce the regulations. Cooley violated the regulations and when tried alleged that they were unconstitutional.

OPINION BY MR. JUSTICE CURTIS
(Vote: 7-2)

Question—Is the power of Congress entirely exclusive in the regulation of commerce?

Decision—No.

Reason—The grant of this power to Congress does not contain any terms that expressly exclude the states from exercising any authority over this subject matter. Although Congress has the power to regulate pilots, its legislation manifests an intention not to regulate this subject but to let the states do it.

"Whatever subjects of this power are in their nature national, or admit only the one uniform system, or plan of regulation, may justly be said to be of such a nature as to require exclusive legislation by Congress. That this cannot be affirmed of laws for the regulation of pilots and pilotage, is plain."

Corollary cases

License Tax Cases, 5 Wallace 462
Louisiana Public Service Comm. v. Texas and N. O. R. Co., 284 U. S. 125
Gilman v. Philadelphia, 3 Wallace 713

Escanaba and L. M. Transportation Co. v. Chicago, 107 U. S. 678
Port Richmond and Bergen Point Ferry Co. v. Board of Chosen Freeholders of Hudson County, 234 U. S. 317
Hall v. De Cuir, 95 U. S. 485

EMPLOYER-EMPLOYEE RELATIONS
Coppage v. Kansas, 236 U. S. 1; 35 S. Ct. 240; 59 L. Ed. 441 (1915)

About July 1, 1911, one Hedges was employed as a switchman by the St. Louis and San Francisco Railroad Co., and was a member of a labor organization called the "Switchman's Union of North America." Coppage was employed by the railroad company as superintendent, and as such he requested Hedges to sign an argeement under which Hedges would be forced to withdraw from the union. Hedges refused to sign this, and refused to withdraw from the labor organization. Thereupon Coppage discharged him from service in the railroad company.

There had been enacted in Kansas a statute called "An Act to Provide a Penalty for Coercing or Influencing or Making Demands upon or Requirements of Employees, Servants, Laborers, and Persons Seeking Employment." This statute made it unlawful to sign an agreement not to join or remain a member of a labor organization. When the case came to the local county court in Kansas, Coppage was found guilty of violating the Act.

Opinion by Mr. Justice Pitney
(Vote: 6-3)

Question—Was the Kansas statute contrary to the due process clause of the Fourteenth Amendment?

Decision—Yes.

Reason—An individual has no inherent right to join a union and still hold his job if his employer does not consent to the union. The employer-employee relationship is a voluntary one, and if the former does not consent to his employees joining a labor union he does not have to keep the man on his payroll. If the man insists on joining a labor union he does not need to take the employment. The liberty of making contracts does not include the liberty to procure employment from an unwilling employer or without a fair understanding. Nor may the employer be denied by the legislature the same freedom of choice that is the right of the employee—the right to make employment contracts. To ask a man not to join a union in the future is not an infringement of his constitutional rights.

Corollary cases

Adair v. United States, 208 U. S. 161

Holden v. Hardy, 169 U. S. 366

N.L.R.B. v. Jones and Laughlin Steel Corp., 301 U. S. 1

Lincoln Federal Union, A.F.L. v. Northwestern Iron and Metal Co., 335 U. S. 525

C. B. and Q. R. R. Co. v. McGuire, 219 U. S. 549

Lochner v. State of New York, 198 U. S. 45

Allgeyer v. State of Louisiana, 165 U. S. 578

Olsen v. State of Nebraska, 313 U. S. 236

ANTITRUST LEGISLATION AND LABOR

Coronado Coal Co. v. United Mine Workers of America, 268 U. S. 295; 45 S. Ct. 551; 69 L. Ed. 963 (1925)

This was a suit for damages for the effect of an

alleged conspiracy of the defendants unlawfully to restrain and prevent plaintiffs' interstate trade in coal in violation of the first and second sections of the Federal Antitrust Act. The charge was that the defendants, in 1914, for the purpose of consummating the conspiracy, destroyed valuable mining properties of the plaintiffs. The case had appeared in the court earlier but failed on the part of the plaintiffs for lack of evidence. In this case the plaintiffs supplied the links lacking at the first trial.

OPINION BY MR. CHIEF JUSTICE TAFT

(No evidence from the report that the decision was not unanimous.)

Question—Was the Mine Workers Union guilty of a conspiracy in violation of the Antitrust Act?

Decision—Yes.

Reason—The court ruled that while the mere reduction in the supply of an article to be shipped in interstate commerce by the illegal or tortious prevention of its manufacture or production is ordinarily an indirect and remote obstruction to that commerce, nevertheless when the intent of those unlawfully preventing the manufacture or production is shown to be to restrain or control the supply entering and moving in interstate markets, their action is a direct violation of the Antitrust Act. The existence of that intent may be a necessary inference from proof of the direct and substantial effect produced by the employees' conduct. The Court listened to much testimony and evidence and deduced that the conspiracy existed in the local union of the United Mine Workers of America but the same could not be said for the International Union.

Corollary cases

United Mine Workers v. Coronado Coal Co., 259 U. S. 344

United Leather Workers International Union v. Herket & M. Trunk Co., 265 U. S. 457

Industrial Asso. v. United States, 268 U. S. 64

Loewe v. Lawlor, 208 U. S. 274

Bedford Cut Stone Co., v. Stone Cutters' Ass'n., 274 U. S. 37

N.L.R.B. v. Jones and Laughlin Steel Corp., 301 U. S. 1

STATE POLICE POWER AND CIVIL LIBERTIES

Cox v. New Hampshire, 312 U. S. 569; 61 S. Ct. 762; 85 L. Ed. 1049 (1941)

Cox, a member of the "Jehovah's Witnesses," was convicted of violating a city ordinance of the city of Manchester, New Hampshire. The ordinance forbade any parade or procession upon a public street unless a license had been obtained from the selectmen of the town. Cox said that he and the defendants did not have a parade but they also claimed that this ordinance was invalid under the Fourteenth Amendment of the Federal Constitution in that it deprived the appellants of their right of freedom of worship, freedom of speech and press, and freedom of assembly, vested unreasonable and unlimited arbitary and discriminatory powers in the licensing authority, and was vague and indefinite. Each of the defendants claimed to be a minister ordained to preach the gospel in accordance with his belief.

OPINION BY MR. CHIEF JUSTICE HUGHES
(No evidence from the report that the decision was not unanimous.)

Question—Is this ordinance a valid exercise of the police power of the state and not in conflict with the Constitution?

Decision—Yes.

Reason—The facts concerned here are not with the depriving of Cox of freedom of worship but of the ordinance governing the use of public streets. They were not prosecuted for anything other than that. Civil liberties, as guaranteed by the Constitution imply the existence of an organized society maintaining public order, without which liberty itself would be lost in the excess of unrestrained abuses. This use of the power of the local authorities is not inconsistent with civil liberties but a means of safeguarding them. The Court felt that the licensing was necessary to afford opportunity for proper policing.

"One would not be justified in ignoring the familiar red traffic light because he thought it his religious duty to disobey the municipal command or sought by that means to direct public attention to an announcement of his opinion." "We find it impossible to say that the limited authority conferred by the licensing provisions of the statute in question as thus construed by the state court contravened any constitutional right."

Corollary cases

Thornhill v. Alabama, 310 U. S. 88

Hague v. C.I.O., 307 U. S. 496

Cantwell v. Connecticut, 310 U. S. 296

Chaplinsky v. New Hampshire, 315 U. S. 568

Saia v. People of State of New York, 334 U. S. 558

Kovacs v. Cooper, 336 U. S. 77

POWER OF CONGRESS TO IMPOSE LIMITATIONS ON A TERRITORY BEFORE ADMISSION AS A STATE THAT WOULD BE BINDING AFTER ADMISSION

Coyle v. Smith, 221 U. S. 559; 31 S. Ct. 688; 55 L. Ed. 853 (1911)

When Oklahoma was admitted as a state in 1906, Congress provided that the capital should be located at Guthrie until the year 1913. In 1910 the Oklahoma legislature passed an act providing for the removal of the capital to Oklahoma City. Suit was brought to stop the move.

OPINION BY MR. JUSTICE LURTON
(Vote: 7-2)

Questions—1. May Congress, under penalty of denying admission, impose limitations on a new state at the time of admission?

2. Will those limitations be binding after admission as a state?

Decisions—1. Yes.

2. No.

Reasons—1. "The constitutional provisions concerning the admission of new states is not a mandate, but a power to be exercised with discretion." Therefore, Congress, in the exercise of this discretion, may impose conditions that a state-to-be must meet before Congress grants approval to its admission.

2. Any restraints imposed by Congress on a new state before its admission can be ignored with impunity by that state after admission except such as have some basis in the Constitution. Congress has no power to limit the rights of a state. The constitutional duty of guaranteeing to each state

a republican form of government does not allow Congress to place limits on them that would deprive them of equality with other states. The constitutional power of admission of states is based on the assumption that the new states will be on a par with other states. This is a union of equal states. If Congress could lay down binding conditions, as the one involved in this case on an incoming state, then the United States would include states unequal in power. When a state enters the Union, she at once becomes "entitled to and possessed of all the rights of dominion and sovereignty which belonged to the original states. She was admitted, and could be admitted, only on the same footing with them."

A clear distinction should be drawn between a matter involving political inequality of a new state (as here, and which is not binding after admission) and a matter involving a quid pro quo contractual relation (which is binding after admission).

Corollary cases

Stearns v. Minnesota, 179 U. S. 223

Van Brocklin v. Tennessee, 117 U. S. 151

Willmette Iron Bridge Co., v. Hatch, 125 U. S. 1

Pollard v. Hagan, 3 Howard 212

Escanaba and L. M. Transportation Co. v. Chicago, 107 U. S. 678

Permiol v. New Orleans, 3 Howard 589

Blue Jacket v. Johnson County, 5 Wallace 737

Texas v. White, 7 Wallace 700

Ervien v. United States, 251 U. S. 41

STATE BILLS OF CREDIT

Craig v. Missouri, 4 Peters 410; 7 L. Ed. 903 (1830)

This case had to do with the issuing by the state of certificates that were intended to circulate as money. When Missouri became a state in 1821, there was virtually no money in circulation within its borders. To provide a circulatory medium, the legislature established loan offices where citizens, in return for promissory notes, could purchase loan certificates issued by the state in denominations running from fifty cents to ten dollars. The certificates were receivable for taxes and other public debts, and for salt from the state salt mines. Redemption of the certificates was pledged by the state. Missouri defended the arrangement as a legitimate device for borrowing money, but it was challenged as the issuance of bills of credit in violation of the Constitution.

OPINION BY MR. CHIEF JUSTICE MARSHALL
(Vote: 4-3)

Question—Were these bills of credit issued in violation of the federal Constitution?

Decision—Yes.

Reason—The Court said that bills of credit in their larger sense are any instruments by which a state engaged to pay money at a future day, and thus included certificates given for money borrowed. Since the Missouri notes were intended to circulate as money, they were bills of credit, and the statute authorizing their issue was unconstitutional, even though it had not attempted to compel their acceptance by making them a legal tender in payment of debts. The Court at some length described the experiences of the states and of the United States in the Revolutionary period and thereafter which had resulted in the inclusion of the clause in the Constitution.

Corollary cases

Briscoe v. Bank of Kentucky, 11 Peters 257

Veazie Bank v. Fenno, 8 Wallace 533

Bank of United States v. Planters' Bank, 9 Wheaton 904

Darrington v. Bank of Alabama, 13 Howard 12

Poindexter v. Greenhow, 114 U. S. 270

Houston, E. and W. Texas Ry. Co. v. Texas 177 U. S. 66

COMMERCE, TAXATION, AND CITIZENSHIP

Crandall v. Nevada, 6 Wallace 35; 18 L. Ed. 744 (1868)

In 1865 the legislature of Nevada enacted that "there shall be levied and collected a capitation tax of one dollar upon every person leaving the state by any railroad, stage coach, or other vehicle, engaged or employed in the business of transporting passengers for hire," and that the proprietors, owners, and corporation so engaged (business of transporting passengers for hire) should pay the said tax of one dollar for each and every person so conveyed or transported from the state. For the purpose of collecting the tax, another section required from persons engaged in such business, or their agents, a report every month, under oath, of the number of passengers so transported. Crandall, who was the agent of a stage company engaged in carrying passengers through the State of Nevada, was arrested for refusing to report the number of passengers that had been transported.

OPINION BY MR. JUSTICE MILLER

(No evidence from the report that the decision was not unanimous.)

Question—Does a state have the right to levy such a tax?

Decision—No.

Reason—All citizens of the United States are members of the same community and must have the right to pass and repass through every part of it without interruption, as freely as in their own states. A tax imposed by a state for entering its territory or harbor is inconsistent with the right that belongs to citizens of other states as members of the Union and with the objects which this Union was intended to attain. Such a power in the states could produce nothing but discord and mutual irritation and they very clearly do not possess such a power.

"The views here advanced are neither novel nor unsupported by authority. The question of the taxing power of the States, as its exercise has affected the functions of the Federal government, has been repeatedly considered by this court, and the right of the States in this mode to impede or embarrass the constitutional operations of that government, or the right which the citizens hold under it, has been uniformly denied."

Corollary cases

Gibbons v. Ogden, 9 Wheaton 1
The Passenger Cases, 7 Howard 283

Slaughter-House Cases, 16 Wallace 36
Edwards v. California, 314 U. S. 160

NAVIGABLE WATERS

The Daniel Ball, 10 Wallace 557; 19 L. Ed. 999 (1871)

An Act of Congress provided that steam vessels engaged in transporting passengers upon navigable waters of the United States should be licensed and inspected. In 1868 the "Daniel Ball," a vessel that had not been licensed or inspected, was carrying goods between the cities of Grand Rapids and Grand Haven on the Grand River in the state of Michigan. The vessel was carrying goods coming from or going to points outside of Michigan, but was not operating in connection with any railway or steamship line, although both cities contained railways and steamship lines operating in interstate commerce.

OPINION BY MR. JUSTICE FIELD
(No evidence from the report that the decision was not unanimous.)

Question—Was the "Daniel Ball" operating on a navigable waterway of the United States and in interstate commerce?

Decision—Yes.

Reason—The common law interpretation of the navigability of waters has no application to this country. Any waterway is to be considered navigable if it can be used, or is capable of being used, in its ordinary condition, as a highway of commerce, over which trade and travel can be carried on in the usual methods. The Grand River is capable of bearing a steamer of 123 tons burden as far as Grand Rapids, 40 miles from its mouth in Lake Michigan. It is thus a highway for commerce with other states and also with foreign countries, and under direct control of the Congressional commerce power.

It was contended that the "Daniel Ball" was engaged only in internal commerce within the state of Michigan. This was not correct, since she was carrying goods from outside the state, and destined for places outside the state. The Daniel Ball, even though operating within the state entirely, was an instrument of interstate commerce, and subject to the legislation of Congress.

Corollary cases

Gilman v. Philadelphia, 3 Wallace 724

Gibbons v. Ogden, 9 Wheaton 194

The Thomas Jefferson, 10 Wheaton 428

United States v. Appalachian Electric Power Co., 311 U. S. 377

Oklahoma v. Guy F. Atkinson Co., 313 U. S. 508

Ashwander v. T.V.A., 297 U. S. 288

The Genesee Chief v. Fitzhugh, 12 Howard 443

STATE LAWS AND OBLIGATION OF CONTRACTS

Trustees of Dartmouth College v. Woodward, 4 Wheaton 518; 4 L. Ed. 629 (1819)

In 1769 Dartmouth College was chartered by the English Crown. Later, in 1816, the state legislature of New Hampshire passed a law completely reorganizing the government of the college and changing the name to Dartmouth University. The old trustees of the college brought an action of trover against Woodward, who was secretary and treasurer of the college, and who had joined in the new university movement. He held the seal, records, and account books. The state decided against the old college trustees.

OPINION BY MR. CHIEF JUSTICE MARSHALL
(Vote: 5-1)

Questions—1. Is this contract protected by the Constitution of the United States?
2. Does the act of 1816 impair the original charter, as contended by the old college trustees?

Decisions—1. Yes.
2. Yes.

Reason—"This is plainly a contract to which the donors, the trustees, and the crown (to whose rights and obligations New Hampshire succeeds) were the original parties. It is a contract made on a valuable consideration. It is a contract for the security and disposition of property. . . . It is then a contract within the letter of the Constitution, and within its spirit also."

The act of 1816 by the New Hampshire legislature gave the college a public and civil status, increased the number of trustees, and therefore in essence impaired the operations of the college as originally intended by the founders. The founders sought the charter in good faith, thus making a legally binding contract. Under the act of 1816, the charter as originally intended no longer existed. Thus the New Hampshire legislature violated the Constitution of the United States, and the act of 1816 was unconstitutional and void.

Corollary cases

Providence Bank v. Billings, 4 Peters 514
Stone v. Mississippi, 101 U. S. 814
Charles River Bridge v. Warren Bridge, 11 Peters 420
Ogden v. Saunders, 12 Wheaton 213
Home Building and Loan Ass'n. v. Blaisdell, 290 U. S. 398

Fletcher v. Peck, 6 Cranch 87
New Jersey v. Wilson, 7 Cranch 164
Pennsylvania Hospital v. Philadelphia, 245 U. S. 20
Long Island Water Supply Co. v. Brooklyn, 166 U. S. 685

DUE PROCESS AND PROPERTY

Davidson v. New Orleans, 96 U. S. 97, 24 L. Ed. 616, (1878)

The city of New Orleans sought to make an assessment on certain real estate within the parishes of Carroll and Orleans for the purpose of draining the swamp lands there. Included in the assessment was part of the estate of John Davidson, which was assessed for $50,000. The city brought suit to collect.

Opinion by Mr. Justice Miller
(No evidence from the report that the decision was not unanimous.)

Question—Is Mrs. Davidson being deprived of her property without due process of law?

Decision—No.

Reason—"Due process of the law" according to unanimous interpretation of the Court does not necessarily imply a regular proceeding in a court of justice, or after the manner of such courts. The "due process" clause is not to be looked upon as giving a blanket protection for anyone wishing to test the decision of a state court of justice against him. "That whenever by the laws of a State, or by state authority, a tax assessment, servitude, or other burden is imposed upon property for the public use, whether it be for the whole State or of some more limited portion of the community, and those laws provide for a mode of confirming or contesting the charge thus imposed, in the ordinary courts of justice, with such notice to the person, or such proceeding in regard to the property as is appropriate to the nature of the case, the judgment in such proceedings cannot be said to deprive the owner of his property without due process of law, however obnoxious it may be to other objections."

Whenever a state takes property for public use, and state laws provide a mode for contesting the charge in the ordinary courts, and if due notice is given to the person, and if there is a full and fair hearing, there is no cause for a suit charging lack of "due process" of the law.

Corollary cases

Murray's Lessee v. Hoboken Land & Improvement Company, 12 Howard 272

Citizens Savings and Loan Association v. Topeka, 20 Wallace 655

Kennard v. Morgan, 92 U. S. 480

INTERSTATE COMMERCE AND THE "RECAPTURE CLAUSE"

Dayton-Goose Creek Ry. Co. v. United States (Recapture Clause Case), 263 U. S. 456; 44 S. Ct. 169; 68 L. Ed. 388 (1924)

The Dayton-Goose Creek Railway Company is a corporation of Texas, engaged in intrastate, interstate, and foreign commerce. Its greatest volume of business is intrastate. In this case, the Dayton-Goose Creek Railway Company sought to obtain an injunction against the Interstate Commerce Commission from collecting a specified per cent of excess profits. The Commission determined what was to be a fair rate of return on the business and then collected a percentage in excess of that rate. The railroads that earned more were required to hold one-half of the excess primarily to preserve their sound economic condition and avoid wasteful expenditures and unwise dividends. As the Court pointed out, "Those who earn less are to be given help by credit secured through a fund made up of the other half of the excess. By the recapture clauses Congress is enabled to maintain uniform rates for all shippers and yet keep the net returns of railways, whether strong or weak, to the varying percentages which are fair respectively to them. The recapture provisions are thus the key provision of the whole plan."

OPINION BY MR. CHIEF JUSTICE TAFT
(No evidence from the report that the decision was not unanimous.)

Question—Was the "recapture" procedure within the power of Congress to regulate commerce?

Decision—Yes.

Reason—The constitutional power of Congress to regulate commerce means to foster, protect, and control the commerce with appropriate regard to the welfare of those who are immediately concerned, as well as of the public at large, and to promote its growth and insure its safety. A carrier owning and operating a railroad, however strong financially, is not entitled, as of constitutional right, to more than a fair net operating income upon the value of its properties that are being devoted to transportation. A carrier cannot raise the objection that the government cannot take over the excess profit earned by it above a reasonable return on the investment and that the amount be returned to the shippers, to whom it belongs. This cannot be done in equity. Therefore the government may properly appropriate for public use the excess of profit. It does not infringe on the constitutionally reserved power of the states although a portion of the income is derived from intrastate transportation. When the adequate maintenance of interstate commerce involves and makes necessary on this account the incidental and partial control of intrastate commerce, the power of Congress to exercise such control has been clearly established.

Corollary cases

Wisconsin R. R. Commission v. C. B. & Q. R.R. Co., 257 U. S. 563

California v. Central Pacific R.R. Co., 127 U. S. 1

Minnesota Rate Cases, 230 U. S. 352

Illinois Central R.R. Co., v. Behrens, 233 U. S. 473

Houston, East and West Texas Ry. Co., v. United States, 234 U. S. 342

New England Divisions Case, 261 U. S. 184

LABOR LEGISLATION

In re Debs, 158 U. S. 564; 15 S. Ct. 900; 39 L. Ed. 1092 (1895)

Eugene V. Debs and associates, officers of the American Railway Union, had instituted a strike against the Pullman Co. of Chicago. To enforce their demands they picketed the railway cars of that company and would not allow them either to enter or leave Chicago. In doing this they stopped interstate commerce and also the cars carrying United States mail. The company was granted an injunction by the federal court against the union picketing and when the order was not carried out Debs and the other officers of the union were convicted in contempt of it.

OPINION BY MR. JUSTICE BREWER

(No evidence from the report that the decision was not unanimous.)

Question—Is the federal government able to prevent a forcible obstruction of interstate commerce and of the mails?

Decision—Yes.

Reason—"The entire strength of the nation may be used to enforce in any part of the land the full and free exercise of all national powers and the security of all rights entrusted by the Constitution to its care. The strong arm of the national government may be put forth to brush away all obstructions to the freedom of interstate commerce or the transportation of the mails. If the emergency arises, the army of the Nation, and all its militia, are at the service of the Nation to compel obedience to its laws."

"It is obvious from these decisions that while it is not the province of the government to interfere in any mere matter of private controversy between individuals, or to use its great powers to enforce the rights of one against another, yet, whenever the wrongs complained of are such as affect the public at large, and are in respect of matters which by the Constitution are entrusted to the care of the Nation, and concerning which the Nation owes the duty to all the citizens of securing to them their common rights, then the mere fact that the government has no pecuniary interest in the controversy is not sufficient to exclude it from the courts, or prevent it from taking measures therein to fully discharge those constitutional duties."

Corollary cases

United States v. San Jacinto Tin Co., 125 U. S. 273

Coppage v. Kansas, 236 U. S. 1

Duplex Printing Press Co., v. Deering, 254 U. S. 443

Loewe v. Lawlor, 208 U. S. 274

Bedford Cut Stone Co., v. Journeymen Stone Cutter's Ass'n., 274 U. S. 37

United Leather Workers v. Herkert, 265 U. S. 457

DUE PROCESS AND ASSEMBLY

De Jonge v. Oregon, 299 U. S. 353; 57 S. Ct. 255; 81 L. Ed. 278 (1937)

De Jonge was indicted in Multnomah County, Oregon, for the violation of the Criminal Syndicalism Law of the state. This law made the doctrine which advocates crime, physical violence, sabotage, or any unlawful acts as methods of accomplishing industrial change or political revolution a crime. De Jonge was a member of the Communist Party, and spoke at an advertised meeting sponsored by the Communist Party.

OPINION BY MR. CHIEF JUSTICE HUGHES
(Vote: 8-0)

Question—Was this law a denial of due process?

Decision—Yes.

Reason—Apparently the only offense for which the accused was charged, convicted, and sentenced to imprisonment for seven years was taking part in a meeting held under the auspices of the Communist Party. While the states are entitled to protect themselves and the privileges of our institutions from abuse, none of the court decisions go to the length of such a curtailment of the right of free speech as the Oregon statute demanded.

Freedom of speech, press, and peaceful assembly are fundamental rights safeguarded by the due process clause of the Fourteenth Amendment. Holding a peaceful public meeting for lawful discussion cannot be made a crime. The Court was not here upholding the objectives of the Communist party. The defendant was still entitled to his personal right of free speech, although he was a member of the Communist Party, if the activity was carried on in a lawful manner, without incitement to violence or crime.

The Court held that the Oregon statute, as applied to the particular charge here, was repugnant to the due process clause of the Fourteenth Amendment.

Corollary cases

Gitlow v. New York, 268 U. S. 652
Whitney v. California, 274 U. S. 357
Near v. Minnesota, 283 U. S. 697
Grosjean v. American Press Co., 297 U. S. 233

Hague v. C.I.O., 307 U. S. 496
Herndon v. Lowry, 301 U. S. 242
Fiske v. Kansas, 274 U. S. 380
Stromberg v. California, 283 U. S. 359
Bates v. Little Rock, 361 U. S. 516
Terminiello v. Chicago, 337 U. S. 1

COMMUNISTS AND FREE SPEECH

Dennis v. United States, 341 U. S. 494; 71 S. Ct. 857; 95 L. Ed. 1137 (1951)

Eleven leaders of the Communist Party were convicted of violating the 1940 Smith Act. The defendants were convicted of conspiring to organize the Communist Party for the purpose of having it teach and advocate the overthrow and destruction of the United States government by force and violence. They claimed Articles Two and Three of the Act to be unconstitutional as violating the First Amendment and other provisions of the Bill of Rights and also as violative of the First and Fifth Amendments because of indefiniteness.

<u>OPINION BY MR. CHIEF JUSTICE VINSON</u>
(Vote: 6-2)

Questions—1. Did the Act violate the right of free speech?
2. Did it, because of indefiniteness, also violate the First and Fifth Amendments?

Decisions—1. No.
2. No.

Reasons—The Congress has the power to protect the United States government from armed rebellion, and the defendants were advocating the violent overthrow of the government. This law was not directed at discussion but against the advocacy of violence. These persons intended to overthrow the United States government as soon as conditions would permit. This represented a clear and present danger to the government. It was the existence of the highly organized conspiracy that created the danger. "Whatever· theoretical merit there may be to the argument that there is a 'right' to rebellion against dictatorial government is without force where the existing structure of the government provides for peaceful and orderly change. We reject any principle of governmental helplessness in the face of preparation for revolution, which principle, carried to its logical conclusion, must lead to anarchy."

Corollary cases

Frohwerk v. United States, 249 U. S. 204

Debs v. United States, 249 U. S. 211

Gitlow v. New York, 268 U. S. 652

Schaefer v. United States, 251 U. S. 466

American Communications Ass'n. v. Douds, 339 U. S. 382

Whitney v. California, 274 U. S. 357

Wieman v. Updegraff, 344 U. S. 183

Yates v. United States, 354 U. S. 298.

Communist Party of the United States v. Subversive Activities Control Board, 367 U. S. 1

Scales v. United States, 367 U. S. 203

Aptheker v. Secretary of State, 378 U. S. 500 (1964)

Zemel v. Rusk. 381 U. S. 1

United States v. Robel, 389 U. S. 258 (1967)

Schneider v. Smith, 389 U. S. 000 (1968)

THE AMENDING PROCESS

Dillon v. Gloss, 256 U. S. 368; 41 S. Ct. 513; 65 L. Ed. 994 (1921)

Dillon was taken into custody under Section 26 of Title 2 of the National Prohibition Act of October 28, 1919 on the charge of transporting intoxicating liquor in violation of Section 3 of Title 2. He petitioned the court and sought to be discharged on a writ of habeas corpus from the court on grounds, (1) that the Eighteenth Amendment was invalid because the Congressional resolution proposing the amendment declared that it should be inoperative unless ratified within seven years, and (2) that the act which he was charged with violating, and under which he was arrested, had not gone into effect at the time of the asserted violation nor at the time of the arrest. The Eighteenth Amendment was ratified January 16, 1919 but it was not proclaimed by the Secretary of State until January 29, 1919. Dillon committed the violation on January 17, 1920. By the terms of the Act it was to have gone into effect one year after being ratified. Dillon asserted it should have gone into effect one year after being proclaimed by the Secretary of State which would have been January 29, 1920.

<u>OPINION BY MR. JUSTICE VAN DEVANTER</u>
(No evidence from the report that the decision was not unanimous.)

Questions—1. Can Congress set a reasonable time limit on the ratification of an amendment?

2. On what date does the ratification take effect?

Decisions—1. Yes.

2. The day the last required state ratifies the amendment is the date the amendment becomes part of the Constitution.

Reasons—1. Article Five discloses that it is intended to invest Congress with a wide range of power in proposing amendments. That the Constitution contains no express provision on the time limit for ratification is not in itself controlling, for with the Constitution, as with a statute or other written instruments, what is reasonably implied is as much a part of it as what is expressed. Proposal and ratification are but necessary steps in a single endeavor. There is a fair implication that ratification must be sufficiently contemporaneous in the required number of states to reflect the will of the people in all sections at relatively the same period, and hence that ratification must be within some reasonable time after the proposal.

The court held that Article Five impliedly gives Congress a wide range of power in proposing amendments, and therefore a time limit of seven years for ratification is a reasonable use of this power.

2. The Court held that the amendment takes effect the day the last state ratifies it, that is, the state that gives the amendment the required majority. It is not necessarily the date when the Secretary of State proclaims the amendment.

Corollary cases

United States v. Babbit, 1 Black 55

Ex parte Yarbrough, 110 U. S. 651

McHenry v. Alford, 168 U. S. 651

South Carolina v. United States, 199 U. S. 437

Luria v. United States, 231 U. S. 9

The Pesaro, 225 U. S. 216

National Prohibition Cases, 253 U. S. 350

United States, v. Sprague, 282 U. S. 716

Hawke v. Smith, 253 U. S. 221

Coleman v. Miller, 307 U. S. 433

Hollingsworth v. Virginia, 3 Dallas 378

Leser v. Garnett, 258 U. S. 130

TERRITORIES AND THE CONSTITUTION

Dorr v. United States, 195 U. S. 138; 24 S. Ct. 808; 49 L. Ed. 128 (1904)

Dorr and O'Brien owned and edited a newspaper in Manila known as *Manila Freedom*. Don B. Legardes claimed that libelous headlines were false. Dorr was tried by a federal court in the Philippines without a jury.

OPINION BY MR. JUSTICE DAY
(Vote: 8-1)

Question—Does trial without jury deprive Dorr of his rights under the Constitution?

Decision—No.

Reason—The right to trial by jury and presentment by grand jury are not fundamental in their nature, but merely a method of procedure. The power to govern territory implied in the power to acquire it is given to Congress in the Constitution. It does not require Congress to enact for ceded territory, not made a part of the United States, a system of laws that shall include the right of trial by jury, and the Constitution does not without legislation carry such right to territory so situated. The Philippines were not a part of the United States in that the Constitution applied to them. If trial by jury were a fundamental right and went everywhere with United States jurisdiction then "no matter what the needs or capacities of the people, trial by jury, and in no other manner, must be forthwith established, although the result may be to work injustice and produce disturbance rather than to aid the orderly administration of justice." If the United States acquires territory where trial by jury is not known but where, due to customs and preference, the people have another method—are these considerations to be ignored and they "coerced to accept . . . a system of trial unknown to them and unsuited to their needs?"

Corollary cases

Hawaii v. Mankichi, 190 U. S. 197
DeLima v. Bidwell, 182 U. S. 1

Downes v. Bidwell, 182 U. S. 244
Balzac v. Porto Rico, 258 U. S. 298

THE CONSTITUTION AND THE TERRITORIES

Downes v. Bidwell, 182 U. S. 244; 21 S. Ct. 770; 45 L. Ed. 1088 (1901)

This was an action begun by Downes against Bidwell, Collector of the Port of New York, to recover back duties paid on oranges brought from Porto Rico. The duties were paid under protest beginning in 1900 as a result of the passage of the Foraker Act, which temporarily provided a civil government and revenues for the island.

OPINION BY MR. JUSTICE BROWN
(Vote: 5-4)

Question—Is Porto Rico a part of the United States for revenue purposes?

Decision—No.

Reason—Porto Rico did not become a part of the United States when it was ceded from Spain to the United States. Porto Rico came under the jurisdiction of the United States but it did not enjoy the advantage of being a part of the United States, that is, the Constitution did not extend to it. It would extend to Porto Rico only when Congress formally made provision for this. The United States government has the power to acquire and hold territory without immediately incorporating it into the United States.

"We are therefore of opinion that the Island of Porto Rico is a territory appurtenant and belonging to the United States, but not a part of the United States within the revenue clauses of the Constitution; that the Foraker act is constitutional so far as it imposes duties upon imports from such island, and that the plaintiff cannot recover back the duties exacted in this case." Thus, since it was not a part of the United States, the duties collected on the imports of that island were constitutional and the plaintiff could not recover the back duties.

Corollary cases

Yick Wo v. Hopkins, 118 U. S. 356

Wong Wing v. United States. 163 U. S. 228

Minor v. Happersett, 21 Wallace 162

De Lima v. Bidwell, 182 U. S. 1

Hawaii v. Mankichi, 190 U. S. 197

Dorr v. United States, 195 U. S. 138

Balzac v. Porto Rico, 258 U. S. 298

MARTIAL LAW IN THE TERRITORY OF HAWAII

Duncan v. Kahanamoku, 327 U. S. 304; 66 S. Ct. 606; 90 L. Ed. 688 (1946)

Immediately following the Pearl Harbor attack, Governor Poindexter of the Territory of Hawaii proclaimed martial law, suspended the writ of habeas corpus, closed the local courts, and turned over the powers of government to the commanding general of the United States Army in Hawaii. The President approved the measure, and the military ruled Hawaii until October 24, 1944, with minor relaxations.

The procedure aroused much opposition, and suits were brought to test the validity of the convictions of civilians by the military courts. In February 1944, Duncan, a civilian shipfitter employed by the Navy, was convicted of assault for engaging in a brawl with two Marine sentries. He was tried by a military tribunal rather than by a civil court.

OPINION BY MR. JUSTICE BLACK

(Vote: 6-2)

Question—Is the military government of Hawaii valid under the Hawaiian Organic Act?

Decision—No.

Reason—Civilians in Hawaii are entitled to their constitutional privilege of a fair trial. When, in 1900, Congress passed the

Hawaiian Organic Act it never intended to overstep the boundaries of military and civilian power. Martial law was never intended, in the meaning of the act, to supersede the civilian courts, but only to come to the assistance of the government, and maintain the defense of the island.

Corollary cases

Ex parte Milligan, 4 Wallace 2
Ex parte Quirin, 317 U. S. 1
In re Yamashita, 327 U. S. 1
Hirabayashi v. United States, 320 U. S. 81

Korematsu v. United States, 323 U. S. 214
Ex parte Endo, 323 U. S. 283

STATE POLICE POWER AND INTERSTATE COMMERCE

Edwards v. California, 314 U. S. 160; 62 S. Ct. 164; 86 L. Ed. 119 (1941)

Edwards was a citizen of the United States and a resident of California. He left Marysville, Calif., for Spur, Texas, with the intention of bringing his wife's brother, Frank Duncan, to Marysville. Duncan was a resident of Texas. Edwards knew that Duncan was employed by the W.P.A. and was aware that he was an indigent person throughout the case. They went to California in Edwards' car. Duncan had about $20 when he left Texas and nothing when he arrived in California. He lived unemployed with Edwards 10 days, then received assistance from the Farm Security Administration. The district court decided that Edwards violated the Welfare and Institutions Code of California by knowingly bringing into the state a nonresident indigent person.

OPINION BY MR. JUSTICE BYRNES
(No evidence from the report that the decision was not unanimous.)

Question—Is this law a valid exercise of the police power of the state of California?

Decision—No.

Reason—The California statute concerning the entry of indigent persons was a violation of the commerce clause of the federal Constitution. The passage of persons from state to state constitutes interstate commerce within the provisions of Article I, Section 8 of the Constitution delegating to Congress the authority to regulate interstate commerce, and the California law imposed an unconstitutional burden on such commerce. The concurring opinion noted that the right to move freely from state to state is an incident of national citizenship protected by the privileges and immunities clause of the Fourteenth Amendment against state interference.

Corollary cases

Hague v. C.I.O., 307 U. S. 496

Baldwin v. Seelig, 294 U. S. 511

City of New York v. Miln, 11 Peters 102

Milk Control Board v. Eisenberg Farm Products, 306 U. S. 346

Crandall v. Nevada, 6 Wallace 35

Southern Railway Co. v. King, 217 U. S. 524

South Carolina State Highway Dept. v. Barnwell Bros., 303 U. S. 177

Southern Pacific Co., v. Arizona, 325 U. S. 761

DUE PROCESS AND SEPARATION OF CHURCH AND STATE

Steven I. Engel et al. v. William J. Vitale, Jr. et al., 370 U.S. 421; 82 S. Ct.1261; 8 L. ed. 2d. 601 (1962)

The New York State Board of Regents had recommended, and the local school board had directed the school district's principal, that the following prayer be said aloud by each class in the presence of the teacher at the beginning of each school day:

"Almighty God, we acknowledge our dependence upon Thee, and we beg Thy blessings upon us, our parents, our teachers, and our country."

The parents of ten pupils brought action challenging the use of the prayer.

OPINION BY MR. JUSTICE BLACK
(Vote: 6-1)

Question — Does the use of the prayer violate the establishment clause of the First Amendment made applicable to the states by the Fourteenth Amendment?

Decision — Yes, this breaches the constitutional wall of separation between church and state.

Reason — Using the public school system to encourage recitation of the prayer is inconsistent with the establishment clause since this is a religious activity and the prayer was composed by governmental officials as a part of a governmental program to further religious beliefs. The fact that the prayer may be denominationally neutral and the fact that its observance on the part of the students is voluntary cannot change the application of the establishment clause. The establishment clause is violated by the enactment of laws which establish an official religion regardless of whether those laws coerce nonobserving individuals or not. It is an historical fact that governmentally-established religions and religious persecutions go hand in hand. "When the power, prestige, and financial support of government is placed behind a particular religious belief, the indirect coercive pressure upon religious minorities to conform to the prevailing officially-approved religion is plain."

"Under the First Amendment's prohibition against governmental establishment of religion, as reinforced by the provisions of the Fourteenth Amendment, government in this country, be it state or federal, is without power to prescribe by law any particular form of prayer which is to be used as an official prayer in carrying on any program of governmentally-sponsored religious activity."

Corollary cases

Everson v. Board of Education, 330 U. S. 1 (1947)

McCollum v. Board of Education, 333 U. S. 203 (1948)

Zorach v. Clauson, 343 U. S. 306 (1952)

West Virginia State Board of Education v. Barnette, 319 U. S. 624 (1943)

School District of Abington Twp. v. Schempp, 374 U. S. 203 (1963)

APPLICATION OF STATE LAW IN FEDERAL COURTS

Erie Railroad Co. v. Tompkins, 304 U. S. 64; 58 S. Ct. 817; 82 L. Ed. 1188 (1938)

Tompkins, a citizen of Pennsylvania, was injured on a dark night by a passing freight train of the Erie Railroad Co. while walking along its right of way at Hughestown in the state. He claimed that the accident occurred through negligence in the operation or maintenance of the train; that he was rightfully on the premises as licensee because on a commonly used footpath that ran for a short distance alongside the tracks; and that he was struck by something which looked like a door projecting from one of the moving cars. To enforce that claim he brought an action in the federal court for Southern New York, which had jurisdiction because the company is a corporation of that state. The Erie insisted that its duty to Tompkins was no greater than that owed to a trespasser. It contended among other things, that its duty to

Tompkins and hence its liability, should be determined in accordance with the Pennsylvania law; that under the law of Pennsylvania, as declared by the highest court, persons who use pathways along the railroad right of way are to be deemed trespassers; and that the railroad is not liable. Tompkins denied that any such rule had been established, and contended that since there was no statute of the state on the subject, the railroad's duty and liability was to be determined in federal courts as a matter of general law.

OPINION BY MR. JUSTICE BRANDEIS
(Vote: 6-2)

Question—Is the federal court bound by the alleged rule of Pennsylvania's common law as declared by the highest court of that state or free to exercise an independent judgment as to what the common law of the state is or should be?

Decision—Federal court bound by declaration of highest state court on the state law.

Reason—Except in matters governed by the federal Constitution or by Acts of Congress, the substantive law to be applied in any case is the law of the state. And whether the law of the state shall be declared by its legislature in a statute or by its highest court in a decision is not a matter of federal concern. There is no federal general common law. Congress has no power to declare substitute rules of common law applicable in a state whether they be local in their nature or "general," be they commercial law or part of the law of torts. And no clause of the Constitution purports to confer such a power upon the federal courts. The common law so far as it is enforced in the state is not common law generally but the law of that state existing by the authority of the state without regard to what it may have been in England or anywhere else. The authority and only authority is the state, and, if that be so, the voice adopted by the state as its own should utter the last word. (This case overruled Swift v. Tyson which said that there was a separate federal common law. This problem so plagued the federal courts for more than one hundred years that the Supreme Court finally grasped the Erie case to change the law.)

Corollary cases

Swift v. Tyson, 16 Peters 1

Black and White Taxicab & Transfer Co. v. Brown and Yellow Taxicab & Transfer Co., 276 U. S. 518

Sampson v. Channell, 110 F. 2nd 754

Baltimore and Ohio R.R. Co. v. Baugh, 149 U. S. 368

Rubbin v. New York Life Insurance Co., 304 U. S. 202

Guaranty Trust Co., of New York v. York, 326 U. S. 99

Meredith v. City of Winter Haven, 320 U. S. 228

DUE PROCESS AND COUNSEL

Escobedo v. Illinois, 378 U. S. 478; 84 S. Ct. 1758; 12 L. Ed. 2d 977 (1964)

Danny Escobedo was convicted of fatally shooting his brother-in-law in Chicago. During the police questioning following his arrest he was not permitted to consult with the attorney he had retained and who was at police headquarters. In the course of this questioning Escobedo was not advised of his constitutional right to remain silent and made some incriminating statements.

OPINION BY MR. JUSTICE GOLDBERG
(Vote: 5-4)

Question—Was the refusal by the police under the circumstances to honor the request of the accused to consult with his lawyer a violation of the Sixth Amendment?

Decision—Yes.

Reason—When an investigation is no longer a general inquiry into an unsolved crime but has begun to focus on a particular suspect who has been taken into custody, is being interrogated, and has requested and been denied counsel and has not been advised of his constitutional rights, as was the case here, the accused has been denied "the assistance of counsel" guaranteed by the Sixth Amendment. This guarantee was held to be obligatory on the states under the terms of the Fourteenth Amendment in *Gideon* v. *Wainwright*, 372 U. S. 335 (1963). When the investigatory process becomes accusatory then our adversary system begins to operate and the accused must be permitted to consult with his attorney.

Haynes v. Washington, 373 U. S. 503

Schmerber v. California, 384 U. S. 757

Massiah v. United States, 377 U. S. 201

Crooker v. California, 357 U. S. 433

Spano v. New York, 360 U. S. 315

Miranda v. Arizona, 384 U. S. 436

Johnson v. New Jersey, 384 U. S. 719

Gideon v. Wainwright, 372 U. S. 335

Jackson v. Denno, 378 U. S. 368

United States v. Wade, 388 U. S. 218

Gilbert v. California, 388 U. S. 263

Stovall v. Denno, 388 U. S. 293

DUE PROCESS AND ZONING

Village of Euclid, Ohio, v. Ambler Realty Co., 272 U. S. 365; 47 S. Ct. 114; 71 L. Ed. 303 (1926)

Appellee owned land within Euclid, Ohio. The village of Euclid passed a zoning law restricting the use of land to residential purposes. The Ambler Realty Company was holding it for industrial use because of its location and the resultant much higher value of the land than if used for residential lots.

OPINION BY MR. JUSTICE SUTHERLAND
(Vote: 6-3)

Question—Does the zoning ordinance take the company's property without due process of law contrary to the Fourteenth Amendment?

Decision—No.

Reason—The zoning ordinance is a valid exercise of the state's police power under which the state has the authority to abate a nuisance. Actually a nuisance may be merely a right thing in a wrong place. Noise, traffic, fire hazards, and the general desirability of an area for 'residential' purposes, including the rearing of children, certainly come under the power of the state and its agencies to care for the public safety, health, morals, and general welfare. Concern for the common good may properly override an individual's property rights.

Corollary cases

Terrace v. Thompson, 263 U. S. 197

Welch v. Swasey, 214 U. S. 91

Hebe Co. v. Shaw, 248 U. S. 297

Cusack Co. v. City of Chicago, 242 U. S. 526

Gorieb v. Fox, 274 U. S. 603

Nectow v. City of Cambridge, 277 U. S. 183

Queenside Hills Realty Co. v. Saxl, 328 U. S. 80

Berman v. Parker, 348 U. S. 26 (1954)

TAXATION OF JUDGES

Evans v. Gore, 253 U. S. 245; 40 S. Ct. 550; 64 L. Ed. 887 (1920)

This was a suit by Judge Walter Evans of the District Court of the Western District of Kentucky against J. R. Gore, Acting Collector of Internal Revenue, to recover the amount of a tax paid by him under protest on his salary as a judge. The tax was collected by the authority of the Revenue Act of 1919, whereas Judge Evans had been appointed in 1899. The Constitution in Article III, Section 1 provides that judges "shall, at stated times, receive for their services a compensation which shall not be diminished during their continuance in office."

OPINION BY MR. JUSTICE VAN DEVANTER
(Vote: 7-2)

Question—Is the tax imposed in this case an unconstitutional diminution of compensation?

Decision—Yes.

Reason—The Constitution provides that judges of both supreme and inferior courts shall hold office "during good behavior" and that their compensation "shall not be diminished during their continuance in office." The meaning of this phrase has to be determined. 1. Is it to benefit the judges and promote the public welfare by giving them the independence necessary for the impartial and courageous discharge of their office? 2. Does it not only forbid direct reduction but also indirect reduction in the form of a tax? 3. Does it mean that the judge shall have no fears for his support while he remains in office?

The Constitution provides for three separate departments of government with definite checks and balances to ensure their independence of each other. Of the three, the judiciary is the weakest, possessing only the power of judgment. However, it is the balance wheel of the entire system, preserving an adjustment between individual rights and governmental powers.

It is not without a set purpose that tenure during good behavior and an undiminishable compensation were coupled together. The prohibition was included, not to benefit the judges, but to attract good, competent men to the bench and to promote independence of action without respect to persons. The words of the prohibition in the Constitution are not qualified and therefore are taken by the Court to prohibit all diminution in salaries.

The Sixteenth Amendment does not justify the taxation of persons or things previously immune. It was intended only to remove all occasion for any apportionment of income taxes among the states. Therefore the tax in question was not supported by the Sixteenth Amendment. This tax was a diminution of salary, and therefore invalid.

Corollary cases

Miles v. Graham, 268 U. S. 501   O'Malley v. Woodrough, 307 U. S. 277

FREEDOM OF RELIGION AND SEPARATION OF CHURCH AND STATE

Everson v. Board of Education, 330 U. S. 1; 67 S. Ct. 504; 91 L. Ed. 711 (1947)

A New Jersey statute authorized local school districts to make rules and contracts for the transportation of children to schools. In this case, Ewing Township authorized a reimbursement to taxpayers using the public bus system in the township to transport their children. The reimbursement was also made to the parents of Catholic school children going to and from parochial schools. The appellant, a taxpayer, challenged the right of the board to reimburse parents of parochial school students.

OPINION BY MR. JUSTICE BLACK
(Vote: 5-4)

Question—Does the statute violate the Fourteenth Amendment and the First Amendment?

Decision—No.

Reason—The court reasoned that the transportation of children to their schools is considered in the same category as the provision of police protection near school crossings, the availability of fire protection, sanitary sewer facilities, public highways, and sidewalks. To cut off these facilities would make it far more difficult for the parochial schools to operate. The court held that such was not the intention of the First Amendment, and that under the First Amendment the state power is no more to be used so as to handicap religions than it is to favor them. Here the children attending Catholic schools were receiving no more than the benefits of public welfare legislation and therefore the New Jersey statute was not contrary to the constitution. It did not, as contended, run contrary to the concept of separation of church and state.

Corollary cases

Pierce v. Society of Sisters, 268 U. S. 510

Cochran v. Louisiana State Board of Education, 281 U. S. 370

Zorach v. Clauson, 343 U. S. 307

Doremus v. Board of Education, 342 U. S. 429

McCollum v. Board of Education, 333 U. S. 203

McGowan v. Maryland, 366 U. S. 420

Torcaso v. Watkins, 367 U. S. 488

Engel v. Vitale, 370 U. S. 421 (1962)

School District of Abington Twp. v. Schempp, 374 U. S. 203 (1963)

FREEDOM OF SPEECH

Feiner v. New York, 340 U. S. 315; 71 S. Ct. 303; 95 L. Ed. 295 (1951)

Irving Feiner, a student at Syracuse University, addressed a street meeting of about 75 people, urging them to attend a meeting that night on the subject of civil rights. He made derogatory remarks about President Truman, the American Legion, the mayor of Syracuse, and other local political officials. The police arrived and noted the restlessness of the crowd. Feiner was asked several times to stop talking, and was then arrested. He was convicted of creating a breach of the peace. Three lower courts in New York upheld his conviction.

OPINION BY CHIEF JUSTICE VINSON
(Vote: 6-3)

Question—If the police stop a lawful assembly when it passes the limits of persuasion and undertakes incitement to riot, is this contrary to the right of free speech as guaranteed by the First and Fourteenth Amendments?

Decision—No.

Reason—The officers making the arrest were concerned only with the preservation of law and order, and not with the suppression of Feiner's views and opinions. The deliberate defiance of Feiner and the imminent danger of reaction in the crowd constituted sufficient reason for state police action. The guarantee of free speech does not include the license of incitement to riot. Moreover, the state courts' approval of the action of the local police was entitled to the utmost consideration.

Corollary cases

Cantwell v. Connecticut, 310 U. S. 296

Sellers v. Johnson, 322 U. S. 851
Terminiello v. Chicago, 337 U. S. 1

Chaplinski v. New Hampshire, 315 U. S. 568

SEPARATION OF POWERS

Fergus v. Marks, 321 Ill. 510; 152 N. E. 557 (1926)

This involved a petition by John Fergus for a writ of mandamus to compel A. Marks and others, members of the General Assembly of Illinois, to meet and apportion the state into senatorial districts. Their duty was clear and unmistakable, Fergus claimed, because of Article IV, Section 6, of the Illinois Constitution of 1870. The duty had not been performed since 1901 and the Assembly was functioning under the Act of that year.

OPINION BY JUSTICE HEARD
(No evidence from the report that the decision was not unanimous.)

Question—Are the Illinois courts able to compel the legislature to reapportion the state?

Decision—No.

Reason—The judicial department has no jurisdiction to award mandamus against a coordinate department of the government. By the Constitution of Illinois, the departments are so separated that one cannot direct the other as to what acts it shall perform. Thus, even though the duty of the legislature was clear, the judiciary could not command it to perform the acts which constituted this duty. The legislative department is responsible to the people alone for failure to perform a legislative duty.

Corollary cases

Kelley v. Marron, 21 N. M. 239
South v. Peters, 339 U. S. 276

Colegrove v. Green, 328 U. S. 529
Baker v. Carr, 369 U. S. 186 (1962)

DELEGATION OF LEGISLATIVE POWER BY CONGRESS

Marshall Field & Co. v. Clark, 143 U. S. 649; 12 S. Ct. 495; 36 L. Ed. 294 (1892)

Marshall Field and Company sought to recover duties alleged to be illegally assessed by and at a Chicago port. The tariff was collected on certain imported goods (woolen dress goods, woolen wearing apparel, and silk embroideries imported by Marshall Field & Co.) under and according to the rates of the Tariff Act of Oct. 1, 1890. This act provided that certain goods should be admitted free but gave the President the power to place tariffs on these specified goods imported from countries where it appeared to him that the country producing these favored articles had imposed a tariff on American products that was "reciprocally unequal and unreasonable." Marshall Field contended that this part of the law gave the President legislative power and therefore was unconstitutional as a violation of the doctrine of separation of powers.

OPINION BY MR. JUSTICE HARLAN

(No evidence from the report that the decision was not unanimous.)

Question—Is such a statutory provision an improper delegation of power to the President?

Decision—No.

Reason—Congress did not delegate legislative powers to the President because nothing involving the subject or object of the law was left to the determination of the President. The legislative power was exercised when Congress declared that special tariffs on specific articles should take effect when deemed necessary by the President, and when, as in this case, the goods were being imported from countries where reciprocal tariff arrangements were unequal. The articles were specified by the law. What the President did was merely to execute the law. He was the agent of the lawmakers, ascertaining the necessity for the tariff and declaring the subject (limited by Congress) upon which the tariff would be assessed.

A subsidiary question in this case involved the validity of the Act of Congress. A section of the bill as passed was omitted in the copies signed by the presiding officers of the two Houses and by the President. The Court accepted these signatures and the deposit of the Act as law in the archives as incontrovertible evidence that the measure had properly become law. See also United States v. Ballin, 144 U. S. 1.

Corollary cases

Mulford v. Smith, 307 U. S. 38

J. W. Hampton, Jr. Co. v. United States, 276 U. S. 394

Panama Refining Co. v. Ryan, 293 U. S. 388

United States v. Curtiss-Wright Export Corp., 299 U. S. 304

Wayman v. Southard, 10 Wheaton 1

United States v. Grimaud, 220 U. S. 506

Schechter Poultry Corp., v. United States, 295 U. S. 495

Buttfield v. Stranahan, 192 U. S. 470

STATE LAWS AND IMPAIRMENT OF CONTRACTS

Fletcher v. Peck, 6 Cranch 87; 3 L. Ed. 162 (1810)

John Peck deeded to Robert Fletcher lands in the state of Georgia, which had been bought from the state of Georgia. The contract was executed in the form of a bill passed through the Georgia legislature in 1795. The next legislature rescinded the act and took possession of the land. Fletcher sued Peck to regain the purchase price.

OPINION BY MR. CHIEF JUSTICE MARSHALL
(No evidence from the report that the decision was not unanimous.)

Question—Can an executed contract in the form of a legislative grant of land by the state itself through its legislature be rescinded later by the state?

Decision—No.

Reason—A valid contract was executed. The state of Georgia was restrained either by general principles that are common to our free institutions or by particular provisions of the Constitution of the United States, from passing a law whereby the estate of the plaintiff in the premises so purchased could be constitutionally and legally impaired and rendered null and void. ". . . One legislature is competent to repeal any act which a former legislature was competent to pass; and that one legislature cannot abridge the powers of a succeeding legislature." However, "if an act be done under a law, a succeeding legislature cannot undo it. . . . When, then, a law is in its nature a contract, when absolute rights have vested under that contract, a repeal of the law cannot divest those rights; and the act of annulling them, if legitimate, is rendered so by a power applicable to the case of every individual in the community."

Corollary cases

Green v. Biddle, 8 Wheaton 1
Trustees of Dartmouth College v. Woodward, 4 Wheaton 518

Charles River Bridge v. Warren Bridge, 11 Peters 420
Ogden v. Saunders, 12 Wheaton 213

FEDERAL POWER OVER ALIENS

Fong Yue Ting v. United States, 149 U. S. 698; 13 S. Ct. 1016; 37 L. Ed. 905 (1893)

A federal statute of 1892 required all Chinese laborers, then lawfully in the United States and entitled to remain, to secure within one year from certain federal officers certificates of residence. Upon failure to do this they were to be deemed unlawfully within the country and deported to China or to the country to which they owed allegiance. The petitioners were arrested for deportation for failing to comply with this act.

<u>OPINION BY MR. JUSTICE GRAY</u>
(Vote: 6-3)

Question—Is the statute of 1892 constitutional?

Decision—Yes.

Reason—The right of a nation to expel or deport foreigners who have not been naturalized, or taken any steps toward becoming citizens of the country, is as absolute and unqualified as the right to prohibit and prevent their entrance into the country. The Court went on to say that the United States are a sovereign and independent nation, and are vested by the Constitution with the entire control of international relations, and with all the powers of government necessary to maintain that control, and to make it effective. The only government of this country that other nations recognize or treat with is the government of the Union, and the only American flag known throughout the world is the flag of the United States. "The power to exclude or to expel aliens, being a power affecting international relations, is vested in the political departments of the government, and is to be regulated by treaty or by act of Congress." Aliens residing in this country who fail to take steps toward citizenship remain under the power of Congress. Therefore, Congress has the power to expel them from the country when it is deemed necessary for the public interest.

Corollary cases

Nishimura Ekiu v. United States, 142 U. S. 651

Chae Chan Ping v. United States, 130 U. S. 581

Knox v. Lee, 12 Wallace 457

Lapina v. Williams, 232 U. S. 78

Wong Wing v. United States, 163 U. S. 228

Hines v. Davidowitz, 312 U. S. 52

Keller v. United States, 213 U. S. 138

Bridges v. Wixon, 326 U. S. 135

Harisiades v. Shaughnessy, 342 U. S. 580

Kessler v. Strecker, 307 U. S. 22

Shaughnessy v. United States ex rel. Mezei, 345 U. S. 206

STATE LEGISLATION AND INTERSTATE COMMERCE

Gibbons v. Ogden, 9 Wheaton 1; 6 L. Ed. 23 (1824)

The state of New York gave exclusive navigation rights to all water within the jurisdiction of the state of New York to R. R. Livingston and R. Fulton, who assigned Ogden the right to operate between New York City and New Jersey ports. Gibbons owned two steamships running between New York and Elizabethtown, which were licensed under Act of Congress. Ogden gained an injunction against Gibbons, who appealed.

OPINION BY MR. CHIEF JUSTICE MARSHALL
(No evidence from the report that the decision was not unanimous.)

Question—Can a state grant exclusive rights to navigate its waters?

Decision—No.

Reason—Congressional power to regulate commerce is unlimited except as prescribed by the Constitution. Commerce is more than traffic; it is intercourse and it is regulated by prescribing rules for carrying on that intercourse. Regulating power over commerce between states does not stop at jurisdictional lines of states, and may be exercised within a state, but it does not extend to commerce wholly within a state. When the state law and federal law conflict on this subject, federal law must be supreme. Thus the act of the state of New York was unconstitutional.

This case is noteworthy because it was the first one ever to go to the Court under the Commerce clause.

Corollary cases

Willson v. Blackbird Creek Marsh Co., 2 Peters 245

Cooley v. Board of Wardens of the Port of Philadelphia, 12 Howard 299

Baldwin v. Seelig, 294 U. S. 511

H. P. Hood and Sons v. Du Mond, 336 U. S. 525

United States v. South-Eastern Underwriters Ass'n., 322 U. S. 533

STATE LEGISLATION AND LABOR UNIONS

Giboney v. Empire Storage & Ice Co., 336 U. S. 490; 69 S. Ct. 684; 93 L. Ed. 834 (1949)

In this case the ice peddlers' union of Kansas City, Mo. sought to unionize all ice peddlers in Kansas City. The means used involved making an agreement with the ice wholesalers to refuse the sale of ice to nonunion peddlers. All agreed except the Empire Ice Company. The union proceeded to set up picket lines around the Empire Company's place of business and threatened the union members with the loss of their cards if they crossed the picket line. The avowed purpose of the picketing was to compel the Empire Company to stop selling ice to nonunion peddlers. There was a Missouri statute prohibiting competing dealers and their aiders and abettors from combining to restrain the freedom of trade.

OPINION BY MR. JUSTICE BLACK

(No evidence from the report that the decision was not unanimous.)

Question—Does Missouri have paramount constitutional power over a labor union to regulate and govern the manner in which certain trade practices shall be carried on within the state of Missouri?

Decision—Yes.

Reason—The court ruled that the Missouri statute regulated trade one way, and the union adopted a program to regulate trade another way. The state had provided for enforcement of its statutory rule by imposing civil and criminal sanctions. The union had provided for enforcement of its rule by sanctions against union members who crossed picket lines. The purpose of the statute was to prevent trust combinations such as the union sought to compel the Empire company to enter. The court ruled that the constitutional power to prevent such combinations by a state is beyond question. "The conditions developed in industry may be such that those engaged in it cannot continue their struggle without danger to the community. But it is not for judges to determine whether such conditions exist, nor is it their function to set the limits of permissible contest and to declare the duties which the new situation demands. This is the function of the legislature which, while limiting individual and group rights of aggression and defense, may substitute processes of justice for the more primitive method of trial by combat." Therefore the Court held that the state's power to govern in this field is paramount, and that nothing in the constitutional guaranties of speech or press compels a state to apply or not to apply its antitrade restraint law to groups of workers, businessmen or others.

Corollary cases

International Harvester Co. v. Missouri, 234 U. S. 199

Grenada Lumber Co., v. Mississippi, 217 U. S. 433

Allen Bradley Co., v. Union, 325 U. S. 797

Thornhill v. Alabama, 310 U. S. 88

Bridges v. California, 314 U. S. 252

Schneider v. State, 308 U. S. 147

Associated Press v. United States, 326 U. S. 1

Thomas v. Collins, 323 U. S. 516

Carlson v. California, 310 U. S. 106

COUNSEL AND DUE PROCESS

Gideon v. Wainwright, 372 U. S. 335; 83 S. Ct. 792; 9 L. Ed. 2d 799 (1963)

Clarence E. Gideon was charged in a Florida state court with having broken and entered a poolroom with intent to commit a misdemeanor. Under Florida law such an offense is a noncapital felony. Gideon appeared in court without funds and without a lawyer. He asked the court to appoint counsel for him. This the court refused to do because Florida law permitted the appointment of counsel for indigent defendants in capital cases only. Gideon appealed his conviction claiming violation of the constitutional guarantee of counsel.

OPINION BY MR. JUSTICE BLACK
(Vote: 9-0)

Question—Must an indigent defendant be provided counsel in a noncapital case?

Decision—Yes.

Reason—A provision of the Bill of Rights which is "fundamental and essential to a fair trial" is made obligatory upon the states by the Fourteenth Amendment. The Court noted that "reason and reflection require us to recognize that in our adversary system of criminal justice, any person haled into court, who is too poor to hire a lawyer, cannot be assured a fair trial unless counsel is provided for him. This seems to be an obvious truth. . . . The right of one charged with crime to counsel may not be deemed fundamental and essential to fair trials in some countries, but it is in ours." Thus was the guarantee of counsel in the Sixth Amendment applied to all cases in the state courts, capital and noncapital. In so holding, the Court overruled *Betts* v. *Brady* (316 U. S. 455, 1942).

Corollary cases

Powell v. Alabama, 287 U. S. 45

Hurtado v. California, 110 U. S. 516

Grosjean v. American Press Co., 297 U. S. 233

Bute v. Illinois, 333 U. S. 640

Johnson v. Zerbst, 304 U. S. 458

Adamson v. California, 332 U. S. 46

Palko v. Connecticut, 302 U. S. 319

Douglas v. California, 372 U. S. 353

FREEDOM OF PRESS AND OBSCENITY

Ginzburg v. United States, 383 U. S. 463; 86 S. Ct. 942; 16 L. Ed. 2d 31 (1966)

Ralph Ginzburg was convicted of violation of the federal obscenity statute by producing and selling obscene publications. The accusation was made that the advertising for the publications openly appealed to the erotic interest of potential customers. This case involved another application of what has come to be known as "the *Roth* test." This attempt to define obscenity was first set forth in *Roth* v. *United States* (354 U. S. 476, 1957) and has been elaborated in subsequent cases. Under this test three elements must coalesce to constitute obscenity. (1) The dominant theme of the material in question must appeal to a prurient interest in sex. (2) It must affront contemporary community standards. (3) The material must be utterly without redeeming social value.

OPINION BY MR. JUSTICE BRENNAN
(Vote: 5-4)

Question—Have the standards of "the *Roth* test" been correctly applied in this case?

Decision—Yes.

Reason—There was abundant evidence that pandering—the business of purveying textual or graphic matter openly advertised to appeal to the erotic interests of persons—was involved. The Court saw no threat to First Amendment guarantees in its holding but rather felt "the fact that each of these publications was created or exploited entirely on the basis of its appeal to prurient interests strengthens the conclusion that the transactions here were sales of illicit merchandise, not sales of constitutionally protected matter." The determination of the opinion is simply that questionable publications are obscene in a context—here the commercial exploitation of erotica solely for the sake of prurient appeal—which "brands them as obscene as that term is defined in *Roth*—a use inconsistent with any claim to the shelter of the First Amendment."

Corollary cases

Mishkin v. New York, 383 U. S. 502

A Book v. Attorney General of Massachusetts, 383 U. S. 413

Near v. Minnesota, 283 U. S. 697

Jacobellis v. Ohio, 378 U. S. 184

Kingsley Books v. Brown, 354 U. S. 436

Butler v. Michigan, 352 U. S. 380

Bantam Books v. Sullivan, 372 U. S. 58

A Quantity of Books v. Kansas, 378 U. S. 205

NATURALIZATION

Girouard v. United States, 328 U. S. 61; 66 S. Ct. 826; 90 L. Ed. 1084 (1946)

In 1943 Girouard filed a petition for naturalization in the District Court of Massachusetts. He stated in his application that he understood the principles of the United States government and that he was willing to take the oath of allegiance required of all citizens-to-be. However, he said that he would not bear arms in the defense of the country, but that he would serve as a noncombatant. He was a Seventh Day Adventist and his religious views did not permit him to bear arms. He was admitted to citizenship by the District Court, but this decision was reversed by the Court of Appeals.

OPINION BY MR. JUSTICE DOUGLAS
(Vote: 5-3)

Question—Does the fact that an alien refuses to bear arms deny him citizenship?

Decision—No.

Reason—The oath required of aliens does not in terms require that they promise to bear arms, nor has Congress expressly made any such finding a prerequisite to citizenship. To hold that it is required is to read it into the Act by unreasonable implication. The Court could not assume that Congress intended to make such an abrupt and radical departure from our traditions unless it spoke in unequivocal terms.

Religious scruples against bearing arms have been recognized by Congress in the various draft laws. This is evidence that one can support and defend our government even though his religious convictions prevent him from bearing arms. "We cannot believe that the oath was designed to exact something more from one person than from another."

Corollary cases

United States v. Schwimmer, 279 U. S. 644

United States v. Bland, 283 U. S. 636

United States v. Macintosh, 283 U.S. 605

DUE PROCESS AND THE STATES

Gitlow v. State of New York, 268 U. S. 652; 45 S. Ct. 625; 69 L. Ed. 1138 (1925)

Benjamin Gitlow was convicted in the Supreme Court of New York for having published and circulated, unlawfully, pamphlets and leaflets detrimental to the government. These advocated overthrowing organized government by violent and other unlawful means. Gitlow appealed the case through the Appellate Division and Court of Appeals of the New York system.

OPINION BY MR. JUSTICE SANFORD
(Vote: 7-2)

Question—Does the New York State Criminal Anarchy statute contravene the due process clause of the Fourteenth Amendment?

Decision—No.

Reason—There is no absolute right to speak or publish, without responsibility, whatever one may choose. A state in the exercise of its police power may punish those who abuse this freedom by utterances inimical to the public welfare. Utterances such as the statute prohibited, by their very nature, involve danger to the public peace and to the security of the state. The statute was not arbitrary or unreasonable.

This case has long been regarded as a "landmark" decision because here for the first time the Court held portions of the "Bill of Rights" applicable to the states by means of the Fourteenth Amendment. The Court said, "For present purposes we may and do assume that freedom of speech and the press—which are protected by the First Amendment from abridgment by Congress—are among the fundamental personal rights and 'liberties' protected by the due process clause of the Fourteenth Amendment from impairment by the states."

Corollary cases

See cases listed under Palko v. State of Connecticut.

Schenck v. United States, 249 U. S. 47

Abrams v. United States, 250 U. S. 616

Schaefer v. United States, 251 U. S. 466

Whitney v. People of State of California, 274 U. S. 357

Turner v. Williams, 194 U. S. 279

Toledo Newspaper Co. v. United States, 247 U. S. 402

Debs v. United States, 249 U. S. 211

Cantwell v. Connecticut, 310 U. S. 296

SEARCH AND SEIZURE

Goldman v. United States, 316 U. S. 114; 62 S. Ct. 993; 86 L. Ed. 1312 (1942)

Petitioner and another were indicted for conspiracy to violate the Bankruptcy Act by receiving, or attempting to obtain, money for acting, or forebearing to act, in a bankruptcy proceeding. They were convicted and sentenced, and the judgments were affirmed by the Circuit Court of Appeals. The petitioners were lawyers. One of them, Martin Goldman, approached Hoffman, the attorney representing an assignee for the benefit of creditors, with the proposition that the assignee sell the assets in bulk for an ostensible price which would net the creditors a certain dividend, but in fact at a secret greater price, and that Hoffman and the petitioners should divide the difference between them. Hoffman refused. Shulman, one of the petitioners, then filed an involuntary petition in bankruptcy. Again Hoffman was propositioned but refused. He consulted a federal investigator and was told to pretend to agree and negotiate with the petitioners. Meantime, two federal investigators set up a dictaphone in Shulman's office and reserved the next floor office for recording conversations. However, while the petitioners were conversing the dictaphone was found to be defective. Another device, a detectaphone, was used. This had a receiver so delicate that when placed against the partition wall it could pick up sound waves originating in Shulman's office, which were amplified, overheard, and recorded. This testimony was used to convict the petitioners.

OPINION BY MR. JUSTICE ROBERTS
(Vote: 5-3)

Question—Is the evidence gained in this way a violation of the Fourth Amendment of the federal Constitution?

Decision—No.

Reason—It was not a violation of the Fourth Amendment since there was no illegal search and seizure involved. To make use of the detectaphone, the agents did not have to trespass on the property of Goldman. The evidence obtained in this way was admissible in a federal court. This decision has been overruled by Katz v. United States, 389 U.S. 347 (1967).

Corollary cases

Olmstead v. United States, 277 U. S. 438

Agnello v. United States, 269 U. S. 20

Weeks v. United States, 232 U. S. 383

Gambino v. United States, 275 U. S. 310

Silverman v. United States, 365 U. S. 505

FEDERAL-STATE RELATIONS; INTER-GOVERNMENTAL TAXATION

Graves v. New York ex rel. O'Keefe, 306 U. S. 466; 59 Sup. Ct. 595; 83 L. Ed. 927 (1939)

O'Keefe, a resident of New York, was employed by the Home Owners' Loan Corporation, a federal government corporation. He contended that the New York Tax Commission had taxed him illegally because, as a federal employee, his salary was exempted from state income tax. The H.O.L.C., as designed by Congress, was completely a federal government project, but nowhere in the Act was there even intimated any congressional purpose to grant immunity from state taxation of employee salaries. In his income tax return, O'Keefe included his salary as subject to the New York state income tax and sought a tax refund on the basis of his federal employment.

OPINION BY MR. JUSTICE STONE
(Vote: 7-2)

Question—Does the tax laid by the state upon the salary of the respondent, employed by a corporate instrumentality of the federal government, impose an unconstitutional burden upon that government?

Decision—No.

Reason—The Court ruled that the state income tax is a nondiscriminatory tax on income applied to salaries at a specified rate. It is not in form or substance a tax upon the Home Owners' Loan Corporation or its property or income, nor is it paid by the corporation or the government from their funds. It was laid directly on the income of the respondent which he received as compensation for his services. These funds were his private funds and not the funds of the government. The only possible basis for implying a constitutional immunity from state income tax of the salary of an employee of the national government or of a governmental agency is that the economic burden of the tax is in some way passed on so as to impose a burden on the national government. Private funds received as compensation for services to the federal government constitute in no way a burden on the federal government when such funds are taxed by the state.

Tax immunity evolves from the premise that there is an implied immunity between the state and federal taxing powers as a limitation to prevent interference each by the other in the exercise of that power where the other government's activities are concerned. There is no implied restriction, therefore, no burden, on the federal government because the theory that a tax on income is legally a tax on its source is not tenable. The tax here is nondiscriminatory. Any burden that would exist here is one that the Constitution pre-supposes in a system of dual governments such as our federal system, and cannot be held to be within the implied taxing restrictions of the state. If such an immunity were implied it would impose too greatly on the taxing power confirmed to the state.

Corollary cases

McCulloch v. Maryland, 4 Whea-ton 435

Helvering v. Gerhardt, 304 U. S. 412

Collector v. Day, 11 Wallace 113

Metcalf & Eddy v. Mitchell, 269 U. S. 514

Dobbins v. Commissioners of Erie County, 16 Peters 435

New York v. United States, 326 U. S. 572

Ohio v. Helvering, 290 U. S. 360

Alabama v. King and Boozer, 314 U. S. 1

Federal Land Bank v. Bismark Lumber Co., 314 U. S. 95

Howard v. Commissioners of Sink-ing Fund, 344 U. S. 624

Esso Standard Oil v. Evans, 345 U. S. 495

DUE PROCESS AND PUBLIC FINANCE

Green v. Frazier, 253 U. S. 233; 40 S. Ct. 499; 64 L. Ed. 878 (1920)

A series of statutes enacted by the legislature of North Dakota in 1919 provided for the establishment of a state bank, deposits in which were to be guaranteed by the state, the building of mills and elevators to be owned and operated by the state, and the financing of private home-building projects. Bond issues were authorized to finance each of these projects and provision was made for their payment by taxation.

OPINION BY MR. JUSTICE DAY

(No evidence from the report that the decision was not unanimous.)

Question—Do the statutes in question amount to a taking of property without due process of law?

Decision—No.

Reason—Before the adoption of the Fourteenth Amendment there were no federal limitations upon the taxing power of the state. There are no specific limitations in the due process clause, but it has come to have the meaning that the state may not impose taxes for private purposes. Just what is "public" or "private" is judged upon the merits of the individual case.

The Supreme Court will not interfere unless it is clear beyond reasonable controversy that the rights secured by the Constitution have been violated. It would seem that, under the conditions existing in North Dakota, these statutes do not aid private enterprise, but promote the public welfare.

Corollary cases

Twining v. New Jersey, 211 U. S. 78

Fallbrook Irrigation District v. Bradley, 164 U. S. 112

Citizens Savings and Loan Association v. Topeka, 20 Wallace 655

Jones v. City of Portland, 245 U. S. 217

New State Ice Co. v. Liebmann, 285 U. S. 262

RIGHT OF PRIVACY

Griswold v. Connecticut, 381 U. S. 479; 85 S. Ct. 1678; 14 L. Ed. 2d 510 (1965)

Here the constitutionality of Connecticut's birth control law was involved. The statute provided that "any person who uses any drug, medical article or instrument for the purpose of preventing conception" was to be subject to fine or imprisonment or both. The statute further specified that a person who assisted another in committing any offense could be prosecuted and punished as if he were the principal offender. Estelle Griswold, Executive Director of the Planned Parenthood League of Connecticut, was convicted of being an accessory.

OPINION BY MR. JUSTICE DOUGLAS
(Vote: 7-2)

Question— Is the Connecticut statute valid under the Constitution?

Decision— No.

Reason— First, the appellants were held to have standing to raise the constitutional issue because they were accessories to violation of the criminal statute inasmuch as they were advising married persons as to the means of preventing conception. The decision established a new constitutional "right of privacy" really using the Ninth Amendment as a basis. The Court noted that "specific guarantees in the Bill of Rights have penumbras, formed by emanations from those guarantees that help give them life and substance . . . the right of privacy which presses for recognition here is a legitimate one. The present case, then, concerns a relationship lying within the zone of privacy created by several constitutional guarantees. . . . We deal with a right of privacy older than the Bill of Rights." In the course of the opinion the Court referred favorably to the Ninth Amendment's provision that "The enumeration in the Constitution, of certain rights, shall not be construed to deny or disparage others retained by the people." A concurring opinion emphasized the Ninth Amendment.

Corollary cases

Poe v. Ullman, 367 U. S. 497
Tileston v. Ullman, 318 U. S. 44
DeJonge v. Oregon, 299 U. S. 353

Pierce v. Society of Sisters, 268 U. S. 510
Meyer v. Nebraska, 262 U. S. 390
Mapp v. Ohio, 367 U. S. 643
Palko v. Connecticut, 302 U. S. 319

FREEDOM OF PRESS

Grosjean v. American Press Co., 297 U. S. 233; 56 S. Ct. 444; 80 L. Ed. 660 (1936)

This suit was brought by a group of newspapers in the State of Louisiana to prevent enforcement of a statute levying a 2 per cent gross receipts tax on them. The statute levied a tax only on newspapers having a circulation of 20,000 copies per week, making it applicable to only thirteen newspapers. Only one of these was not openly opposed to Senator Huey P. Long, under whose influence the law had been passed.

OPINION BY MR. JUSTICE SUTHERLAND

(No evidence from the report that the decision was not unanimous.)

Question—Does the Louisiana statute abridge the freedom of the press, being contrary to the due process clause of the Fourteenth Amendment?

Decision—Yes.

Reason—Justice Sutherland dealt at length with the various attempts in the history of the British government to tax newspapers. Inevitably such a tax produced two results, a hampering of the circulation, and more or less resistance on the part of citizens. The tax imposed by this statute was not one for the purpose of supporting the government, but a tax to limit the circulation of information to the public, which circulation is necessary for a free people and a free government. Even the form of this tax was suspicious, being based solely upon the amount of circulation.

Corollary cases

Twining v. New Jersey, 211 U. S. 78

Near v. Minnesota, 283 U. S. 697

Allgeyer v. Louisiana, 165 U. S. 578

Pennekamp v. Florida, 328 U. S. 331

Winters v. New York, 333 U. S. 507

Bridges v. California, 314 U. S. 252

Associated Press v. N.L.R.B., 301 U. S. 103

Associated Press v. United States, 326 U. S. 1

THE PARDON POWER AND CONTEMPTS

Ex parte Grossman, 267 U. S. 87; 45 S. Ct. 332; 69 L. Ed. 527 (1925)

Philip Grossman was sued for violation of the National Prohibition Act. An injunction against him had been granted by the District Court of Chicago. Two days later an information was filed against him, that he had violated the temporary order, and he was arrested, tried, found guilty of contempt, and sentenced to one year and $1,000 fine. The President granted a pardon, on the condition that the fine be paid. After he was released, he was sent by the court to the House of Correction to serve the sentence, in spite of the pardon.

OPINION BY MR. CHIEF JUSTICE TAFT

(No evidence from the report that the decision was not unanimous.)

Question—Does the President have power to pardon this type of offense?

Decision—Yes.

Reason—Contempts are crimes even though no trial by jury is allowed, as they are infractions of the laws and are intended as efforts to defeat the operation of a court order. That which violates the dignity and authority of federal courts, such as an intentional effort to defeat their decrees, violates a law of the United States and so is an offense against the United States. "For civil contempts, the punishment is remedial and for the benefit of the complainant, and a pardon cannot stop it. For criminal contempts, the sentence is punitive in the public interest to vindicate the authority of the court and to deter other like derelictions. The executive can reprieve or pardon all offenses after their commission, either before trial, during trial or after trial, by individuals, or by classes, conditionally or absolutely, and this without modification or regulation by Congress."

Corollary cases

United States v. Wilson, 7 Peters 150

Gompers v. Buck's Stove and Range Co., 221 U. S. 418

Ex parte Garland, 4 Wallace 333

United States v. Klein, 13 Wallace 128

Biddle v. Perovich, 274 U. S. 480

Brown v. Walker, 161 U. S. 591

In re Isserman, 345 U. S. 286

EQUAL PROTECTION AND SUFFRAGE

Grovey v. Townsend, 295 U. S. 45; 55 S. Ct. 351; 79 L. Ed. 1292 (1935)

This was a suit for damages for the refusal of officials in Texas to give Grovey, a Negro, an absentee ballot in the Texas Democratic primary. A resolution had been passed by the state Democratic Party at a state convention, in effect denying Negroes the right to vote in the Democratic Party primaries. The resolution read as follows: "Be it resolved that all white citizens of the State of Texas who are qualified to vote under the Constitution and laws of the state shall be eligible to membership in the Democratic Party and, as such, entitled to participate in its deliberations."

OPINION BY MR. JUSTICE ROBERTS

(No evidence from the report that the decision was not unanimous.)

Question—Can a political party deny membership because of race or color?

Decision—Yes.

Reason—The court held that the determination by the state convention of the membership of the Democratic Party was substantially different from a determination by the executive committee, as was the case in Nixon v. Condon. This was party action and voluntary in character. In the Nixon v.

Condon case it was by the authority of the state because of statutory warrant to the party committee. The managers of the primary election were therefore declared not to be state officials in such sense that their action was strictly state action. A state convention of a party was said not to be an official organ of the state. "This Court went on to announce that to deny a vote in a primary was a mere refusal of party membership with which 'the state need have no concern,' while for a state to deny a vote in a general election on the ground of race or color violated the Constitution. Consequently, there was found no ground for holding that the county clerk's refusal of a ballot because of racial ineligibility for party membership denied the petitioner any right under the Fourteenth or Fifteenth Amendments."

Corollary cases

Nixon v. Herndon, 273 U. S. 536

Nixon v. Condon, 286 U. S. 73

Newberry v. United States, 256 U. S. 232

United States v. Classic, 313 U. S. 299

Smith v. Allwright, 321 U. S. 649

SUFFRAGE AND THE "GRANDFATHER CLAUSE"

Guinn v. United States, 238 U. S. 347; 35 S. Ct. 926; 59 L. Ed. 1340 (1915).

In 1910 Oklahoma amended its constitution to read as follows: "No person shall be registered as an elector of this state or be allowed to vote in any election held herein, unless he be able to read and write any section of the constitution of the State of Oklahoma, but no person who was, on January 1, 1866, or at any time prior thereto, entitled to vote under any form of government, or who at that time resided in some foreign nation, and no lineal descendant of such person, shall be denied the right to register and vote because of his inability to so read and write sections of such constitution." In 1910, when certain Negro citizens of Oklahoma were denied the right to vote, the charge was made that the Oklahoma amendment was contrary to the Fifteenth Amendment.

OPINION BY MR. CHIEF JUSTICE WHITE.
(Vote: 8-0)

Question—Does the Oklahoma amendment violate the Fifteenth Amendment?

Decision—Yes.

Reason—The court reasoned that the Oklahoma amendment was designed to by-pass the provisions of the Fifteenth Amendment by setting the date of voting eligibility for those that could not read or write prior to the adoption of the Fifteenth Amendment. Since the negroes had no eligibility before that date, the court reasoned that this amendment was an attempt to deny voting because of color or race.

"We say this because we are unable to discover how, unless the prohibitions of the Fifteenth Amendment were considered, the slightest reason was afforded for basing the classification upon a period of time prior to the Fifteenth Amendment. Certainly it cannot be said that there was any peculiar necromancy in the time named which engendered attributes affecting the qualification to vote which would not exist at another and different period unless the Fifteenth Amendment was in view. . . ."

Corollary cases—

Ex parte Yarbrough, 110 U. S. 651

Neal v. Delaware, 103 U. S. 370

Lane v. Wilson, 307 U. S. 268

Grovey v. Townsend, 295 U. S. 45

United States v. Classic, 313 U. S. 299

Smith v. Allwright, 321 U. S. 649

South Carolina v. Katzenbach, 383 U. S. 301

Katzenbach v. Morgan, 384 U. S. 641

FREEDOM OF ASSEMBLY AND DUE PROCESS

Hague v. Committee for Industrial Organization, 307 U. S. 496; 59 S. Ct. 954; 83 L. Ed. 1423 (1939)

This case involved the validity of an ordinance of Jersey City that prohibited assemblies "in or upon public streets, highways, public parks, or public buildings" without a permit from the Director of Public Safety. In reliance on this ordinance, the officers of the city had enforced a policy against the distribution of circulars, leaflets, and handbills of the C.I.O., which was then organizing in the city.

OPINION BY MR. JUSTICE ROBERTS
(Vote: 5-2)

Question—Does this ordinance violate the due process clause of the Fourteenth Amendment?

Decision—Yes.

Reason—Although it has been held that the Fourteenth

Amendment created no rights in the citizen of the United States but merely secured existing rights against state abridgment, it is clear that the right peaceably to assemble and discuss topics and to communicate respecting them, whether orally or in writing, is a privilege inherent in the citizenship of the United States which the Amendment protects.

Citizenship of the United States would be little better than a name if it did not carry with it the right to discuss national legislation and the benefits, advantages, and opportunities that inure to citizens. However, the privileges and immunities section of the Fourteenth Amendment is applicable only to natural persons and not to artificial or legal persons.

Corollary cases

Slaughter-House Cases, 16 Wallace 36

United States v. Cruikshank, 92 U. S. 542

Colgate v. Harvey, 296 U. S. 404

Whitney v. California, 274 U. S. 357

Madden v. Kentucky, 309 U. S. 83

Crandall v. Nevada, 6 Wallace 35

COERCED CONFESSION

Haley v. State of Ohio, 332 U. S. 596; 68 S. Ct. 302; 92 L. Ed. 224 (1948)

A confectionery store was robbed near midnight on October 14, 1945, and its owner was shot. The petitioner, a Negro boy 15 years of age, was supposedly acting as a lookout while two others apparently committed the crime. The petitioner was arrested on October 19 and taken to police headquarters, where he was interrogated and questioned by police for five hours, the police working in relays throughout the time. No friend of the boy's was in attendance during this time and after these five hours of grilling the boy confessed. He was held incommunicado from October 20th to the 23rd without his mother or a lawyer being permitted to see him. He was tried and convicted of murder in the first degree.

OPINION BY MR. JUSTICE DOUGLAS
(Vote: 5-4)

Question—Was the due process clause of the Fourteenth Amendment violated in the securing of the confession and admitting it in evidence?

Decision—Yes.

Reason—"We do not think the methods used in obtaining this confession can be squared with the due process of law which the Fourteenth Amendment commands.

"The age of the petitioner, the hours when he was grilled, the fact that he had no friend or counsel to advise him, the callous attitude of the police toward his rights combine to convince us that this was a confession wrung from a child by means which the law should not sanction. Neither man nor child can be allowed to stand condemned by methods which flout constitutional requirements of due process of law.

"But we are told that this boy was advised of his constitutional rights before he signed the confession and that, knowing them, he nevertheless confessed. That assumes, however, that a boy of fifteen, without aid of counsel, would have a full appreciation of that advice and that on the facts of this record he had a freedom of choice. We cannot indulge those assumptions. Moreover, we cannot give any weight to recitals which merely formalize constitutional requirements. Formulas of respect for constitutional safeguards cannot prevail over the facts of life which contradict them. They may not become a cloak for inquisitorial practices and make an empty form of the due process of law for which free men fought and died. to obtain."

Corollary cases

Chambers v. Florida, 309 U. S. 227

Malinsky v. New York, 324 U. S. 401

Ashcraft v. Tennessee, 322 U. S. 143

Brown v. Mississippi, 297 U. S. 278

Watts v. State of Indiana, 338 U. S. 49

Gallegos v. Nebraska, 342 U. S. 55

Stroble v. California, 343 U. S. 181

Stein v. People of State of New York, 346 U. S. 156

WAR POWERS OF CONGRESS

Hamilton v. Kentucky Distilleries & Warehouse Co., 251 U. S. 146; 40 S. Ct. 106; 64 L. Ed. 194 (1919)

On November 11, 1918 the armistice with Germany was signed. On November 21, 1918, Congress passed and the President approved the War-Time Prohibition Act, which provided that alcoholic beverages held in bond should not be moved therefrom except for export. The purpose was to conserve the man power of the nation and to increase the efficiency of war production. The Kentucky Distilleries contended that the act was invalid since hostilities had ceased, thus, bringing an end to the wartime powers. Furthermore, they held that the government could not enforce such an act since the police power was reserved to the states.

OPINION BY MR. JUSTICE BRANDEIS
(No evidence from the report that the decision was not unanimous.)

Question—Was the War-Time Prohibition Act valid?

Decision—Yes.

Reason—The Court reasoned that the United States lacks general police power, and that this was reserved to the states by the Tenth Amendment. However, it is nonetheless true that when the United States exerts any of the powers conferred upon it by the Constitution, no valid objection can be based upon the fact that such exercise may be attended by the same incidents that attend the exercise by a state of its police power, or that it may tend to accomplish a similar purpose. As to the validity of the Act after cessation of hostilities, the Court held that the power of wartime emergencies is not limited to victories in the field and the dispersion of the insurgent forces. It carries with it inherently the power to guard against the immediate renewal of the conflict, and to remedy the evils that have arisen from its rise and progress. The Court was of the opinion that since the security of the nation was involved, the government had to be given a wide latitude of discretion as to the limitations of war powers.

Corollary cases

Woods v. Miller, 333 U. S. 138
Jacob Ruppert, Inc. v. Caffery, 251
   U. S. 264

Fleming v. Mohawk Wrecking and
   Lumber Co., 331 U. S. 111
Stewart v. Kahn, 11 Wallace 493
United States v. Central Eureka
   Mining Co., 357 U. S. 155

FEDERAL CONTROL OF CHILD LABOR

Hammer v. Dagenhart, 247 U. S. 251; 38 S. Ct. 529; 62 L. Ed. 1101 (1918)

In 1916 the Keating-Owen Act was passed. This provided that commodities produced under conditions in factories where children under fourteen years of age were employed or in mines where children under sixteen years of age were employed should be excluded from shipment in interstate or foreign commerce. Hours of employment were also specified for children between fourteen and sixteen years of age. Dagenhart, the father of two children, one under fourteen and the other between fourteen and sixteen, employed in a mill in North Carolina, brought suit to enjoin Hammer, United States District Attorney, from enforcing the law against the employment of his two children. He got this injunction and Hammer took an appeal to the Supreme Court. The penalties connected with the act made it financially impossible to employ children under the age of sixteen because any establishment producing goods with the aid of underaged children could not ship its products in interstate commerce until thirty days after cessation of the practice.

OPINION BY MR. JUSTICE DAY
(Vote: 5-4)

Question—Can Congress exclude from interstate commerce all goods manufactured by child labor?

Decision—No.

Reason—The making of goods and the mining of products is not commerce, nor does the fact that those things are to go afterwards into interstate commerce make them in their production interstate commerce *per se*. Congress has the power to regulate and deny to interstate commerce such products as impure foods, liquors, drugs, and others having possible harmful effects. However, there is nothing harmful, in themselves, in goods produced by child labor; therefore this power does not apply. Child labor may be regulated only under the police power of the states, and, therefore, Congress may not violate this state right. Thus the act "not only transcends the authority delegated to Congress over commerce, but also exerts a power as to a purely local matter to which the federal authority does not extend." (This latter notion—that Congress may not use its delegated powers to perform functions that are reserved to the states by the Tenth Amendment—came to be known as "dual federalism.")

Corollary cases

Gibbons v. Ogden, 9 Wheaton 1

United States v. Darby, 312 U. S. 100

In re Rahrer, 140 U. S. 545

Clark Distilling Co. v. Western Maryland R.R. Co., 242 U. S. 311

Whitfield v. Ohio, 297 U. S. 431

Kentucky Whip and Collar Co. v. Illinois Central R.R. Co., 299 U. S. 334

Mulford v. Smith, 307 U. S. 38

N.L.R.B. v. Jones and Laughlin Steel Corp., 301 U. S. 1

DELEGATION OF LEGISLATIVE POWER

J. W. Hampton, Jr., & Co. v. United States, 276 U. S. 394; 48 S. Ct. 348; 72 L. Ed. 624 (1928)

The J. W. Hampton, Jr., and Co. imported some goods at a New York port and was assessed a rate higher than fixed by statute. The collector of the port assessed the increase under authority of a proclamation by the President. The basis of the tariff was an Act of Congress setting up a Tariff Commission under the executive branch of the government. The act gave the President the power to fix and change duties on imports after investigation by the Commission and notice given to all parties interested to produce evidence. This was the so-called flexible tariff provision. The law provided that the increase or decrease of the tariff duties should not exceed 50 per cent of the rate set by Congress. The Hampton Co. contended that the act gave the President the power to legislate and therefore was unconstitutional.

OPINION BY MR. CHIEF JUSTICE TAFT
(No evidence from the report that the decision was not unanimous.)

Question—Does the act invoke improper delegation of legislative power?

Decision—No.

Reason—The Court held that the true distinction is between the delegation of power to make the law, which necessarily involves a discretion as to what it shall be, and conferring an authority or discretion as to its execution, to be exercised under and in pursuance of the law. The first cannot be done; the second, as was the case here, is valid.

The Court referred to the reasoning in Field v. Clark, 143 U. S. 649, to substantiate the point that Congress did not delegate legislative powers to the President, because nothing involving the contents of the law was left to the determination of the President. The legislative power was performed when Congress passed an act setting up the Tariff Commission as a part of the executive branch, placing the power to execute the law in the hands of the President, and setting down the general rules of action under which both the Commission and the President should proceed.

"What the President was required to do was merely in

execution of the act of Congress. It was not the making of law. He was the mere agent of the lawmaking department to ascertain and declare the event upon which its expressed will was to take effect."

The court also upheld the protection features of the tariff act as a proper exercise of its power over foreign commerce, as well as on the basis of action by the First Congress which was composed, in part, of framers of the Constitution.

Corollary cases

Buttfield v. Stranahan, 192 U. S. 470

Interstate Commerce Commission v. Goodrich Transit Co., 224 U. S. 194

Field v. Clark, 143 U. S. 649

Panama Refining Co. v. Ryan, 293 U. S. 388

Schechter Poultry Corp. v. United States, 295 U. S. 495

Yakus v. United States, 321 U. S. 414

Opp Cotton Mills v. Administrator, 312 U. S. 126

United States v. Curtiss-Wright Export Corp., 299 U. S. 304

SUABILITY OF A STATE

Hans v. Louisiana, 134 U. S. 1; 10 S. Ct. 504; 33 L. Ed. 842 (1890)

In 1874 Louisiana issued certain bonds, and by constitutional amendment pledged the proceeds of a certain special tax for their payment. In 1879 the new state constitution repudiated these obligations and forbade state officers to fulfill them. Hans, a citizen of Louisiana, sued the state in the federal court to recover the interest due upon some of said bonds held by him, alleging that the provisions of the new constitution violated the federal Constitution by impairing the obligation of these bond contracts. The state denied the court's jurisdiction and the suit was dismissed.

OPINION BY MR. JUSTICE BRADLEY
(No evidence from the report that the decision was not unanimous.)

Question—Can a state be sued in a Circuit Court of the United States by one of its own citizens upon a suggestion that the case is one that arises under the Constitution or laws of the United States?

Decision—No.

Reason—The Court was of the opinion that the Eleventh Amendment could be interpreted to imply that citizens of a state could not sue their own state. The amendment makes reference only to citizens of another state or foreign state. However, the court reasoned that the amendment undoubtedly would never have been ratified had it been interpreted to mean that citizens could bring suit against their own state. The suability of a state without its consent was a thing unknown to the law. "Neither a state nor the United States can be sued as defendant in any court in this country without their consent, except in the limited class of cases in which a state may be made a party in the Supreme Court of the United States by virtue of the original jurisdiction conferred on this court by the Constitution." The Court went on to say that while the state cannot be compelled by suit to perform its contracts, any attempt on its part to violate property or rights acquired under its contracts may be judicially resisted, and any law impairing the obligation of contracts under which such property or rights are held is void and powerless to affect their enjoyment.

Corollary cases

Louisiana v. Jumel, 107 U. S. 711

Chisholm v. Georgia, 2 Dallas 419

Hollingsworth v. Virginia, 3, Dallas 378

Wisconsin v. Insurance Co., 127 U. S. 265

Curran v. Arkansas, 15 Howard 304

Clark v. Barnard, 108 U. S. 436

Beers v. Arkansas, 20 Howard 527

Monaco v. Mississippi, 292 U. S. 313

South Dakota v. North Carolina, 192 U. S. 286

New Hampshire v. Louisiana, 108 U. S. 76

Cohens v. Virginia, 6 Wheaton 264

Virginia v. West Virginia, 246 U. S. 565

SEARCH AND SEIZURE

Harris v. United States, 331 U. S. 145; 67 S. Ct. 1098; 91 L. Ed. 1399 (1947)

The petitioner, George Harris, was arrested for using the mails for cashing a forged check for $25,000, in a scheme to defraud. A second warrant for his arrest was issued on the charge that he had caused the forged check to be transported in interstate commerce, a violation of the National Stolen Property Act. Five agents of the F.B.I., acting under the authority of the two warrants, went to Harris' apartment and there arrested him. Following the arrest in the living room, the entire apartment was searched. Near the end of the search a sealed envelope marked "George Harris, personal papers" was found in a bedroom. In the envelope were eight Selective Service Notice of Classification cards and eleven Registration Certificates. It was this evidence upon which was based his conviction of unlawful possession, concealment, and alteration of those cards. Harris charged that the evidence had been obtained by means of unreasonable search and seizure contrary to the provisions of the Fourth Amendment, and that to permit the introduction of that evidence would be to violate the self-incrimination clause of the Fifth Amendment.

OPINION BY MR. CHIEF JUSTICE VINSON
(Vote: 5-4)

Question—Was this an improper seizure since he was indicted for and convicted of a crime different from the one for which the search warrants were issued?

Decision—No.

Reason—This Court has consistently upheld the rights of privacy as protected by the Fourth Amendment. It has also pointed out that only unreasonable searches are violations of this Amendment, and that the test of reasonableness has to be decided for each case individually.

The Fourth Amendment does not require the authority of a search warrant for every valid search and seizure. Search and seizure may be conducted with every lawful arrest; also under appropriate circumstances, the premises under the immediate control of the one arrested may be searched, whether it be a dwelling place or a business establishment. In this case, the control extended to the other three rooms of the apartment, as well as the living room, where the arrest was made.

In this case, agents entered the apartment under lawful authority. The search was not a general exploratory search, but was directed toward the means by which the crimes charged had been committed, namely, two canceled checks of the Mudge Oil Company. Likewise, the objects sought and those actually discovered were proper objects of seizure. Nor was it important that the draft cards were not related to the crimes for which the petitioner was arrested. They were illegally possessed property of the United States. "If entry upon the premises be authorized and the search which follows valid, there is nothing in the Fourth Amendment which inhibits the seizure by law enforcement agents of government property the possession of which is a crime, even though the officers are not aware that such property is on the premises when the search is initiated." The evidence so obtained does not violate the petitioner's rights under the Constitution.

Corollary cases

Boyd v. United States, 116 U. S. 616

Weeks v. United States, 232 U. S. 383

Agnello v. United States, 269 U. S. 20

Segurola v. United States, 275 U. S. 106

Go-Bart Importing Co. v. United States, 282 U. S. 344

United States v. Rabinowitz, 339 U. S. 56

United States v. Lefkowitz, 285 U. S. 452

Abel v. United States, 362 U. S. 217

Trupiano v. United States, 334 U. S. 699

TERRITORIES AND THE CONSTITUTION

Hawaii v. Mankichi, 190 U. S. 197; 23 S. Ct. 787; 47 L. Ed. 1017 (1903)

Mankichi appealed in this case for a writ of habeas corpus from a conviction for manslaughter in a federal District Court in Hawaii. He had not been indicted in Hawaii by a grand jury and was convicted by the verdict of 9 out of 12 jurors. He was brought to trial on information by the attorney general, which was the common law practice in Hawaii prior to its acquisition by the United States as a territory. The United States District Court granted the writ of habeas corpus, ordering the prisoner discharged, and the attorney general appealed. Congress had passed the Newland resolution stating that municipal legislation, not contrary to the Constitution, should remain in effect until Congress should otherwise determine.

OPINION BY MR. JUSTICE BROWN
(Vote: 5-4)

Question—Did the rights to grand jury indictment and jury trial under the Constitution apply in Hawaii?

Decision—No.

Reason—The Court held that the Newland resolution was not intended to interfere with the existing practice of criminal procedure, since such interference would result in imperiling the peace and good order of Hawaii. To hold the people of Hawaii immediately subject to unfamiliar legislation would be an injustice to the people. Further, the Court held that guarantees in the Constitution differ as to force and authority. Some are fundamental, basic rights that apply automatically in all American territory. They "follow the flag." Others concern merely a method of procedure. They are formal in nature and may or may not be applied in the unincorporated territories as Congress sees fit. Since Congress had not indicated intention to incorporate Hawaii, the formal provisions of the Constitution—including those regarding grand and petit juries —did not apply there.

Corollary cases

Webster v. Reid, 11 Howard 437   United States v. Kirby, 7 Wallace
Thompson v. Utah, 170 U. S. 343   482

AMENDMENT OF THE CONSTITUTION

Hawke v. Smith, 253 U. S. 221; 40 S. Ct. 495; 64 L. Ed. 871 (1920)

Hawke, a citizen of Ohio, filed a petition for an injunction, seeking to enjoin the Secretary of State of Ohio from spending public money in preparing and printing forms of ballots for submission of a referendum to the electors of the state on the question of the ratification which the General Assembly had made of the proposed Eighteenth Amendment to the federal Constitution. The petition was sustained, this judgment was affirmed by the Court of Appeals and Supreme Court of Ohio, and then the Supreme Court of the United States was asked to decide the correctness of the judgment.

OPINION BY MR. JUSTICE DAY

(No evidence from the report that the decision was not unanimous.)

Question—Is the provision of the Ohio Constitution, extending the referendum to the ratification by the General Assembly of proposed amendments to the federal Constitution, in conflict with Article V of the Constitution of the United States?

Decision—Yes.

Reason—Article V of the federal Constitution says that, "The Congress, whenever two-thirds of both Houses shall deem it necessary, shall propose Amendments to this Constitution, or, on the application of the legislatures of two-thirds of the several states, shall call a convention for proposing amendments, which, in either case, shall be valid. . . . when ratified by the legislatures of three-fourths of the several states, or by conventions in three-fourths thereof. . . ." Article V is for the purpose of establishing an orderly manner in which changes in the Constitution can be accomplished. Ratification by a state of a constitutional amendment is not an act of legislation in the proper sense of the word. It is but an expression of the assent of the state to a proposed amendment. The power to legislate in the enactment of the laws of a state is derived from the people of the state, but the power to ratify a proposed amendment to the Constitution has its source in the federal Constitution. The act of ratification by the state derives its authority from the federal Constitution, to which the states and its people alike assent. The method of ratification is left to the choice of Congress. The determination of ratification is the exercise of a national power specifically granted by the Constitution. The language of Article V is plain. It is not the function of courts or legislative bodies, national or state, to alter methods which the Constitution has fixed.

Corollary cases

Coleman v. Miller, 307 U. S. 433
Chandler v. Wise, 307 U. S. 474
United States v. Sprague, 282 U. S. 716

Leser v. Garnett, 258 U. S. 130
National Prohibition Cases, 253 U. S. 350

TREATIES AND LAWS

Head Money Cases (Edye v. Robertson) 112 U. S. 580; 5 S. Ct. 247; 28 L. Ed. 798 (1884)

In 1882 Congress passed an act providing that a duty of fifty cents should be collected for each and every passenger who was not a citizen of the United States, coming from a foreign port to any port within the United States. Individuals and steamship companies brought suit against the Collector of Customs at New York, Mr. W. H. Robertson, for the recovery of the sums of money collected. The act was challenged on the grounds that it violated numerous treaties of our government with friendly nations.

OPINION BY MR. JUSTICE MILLER

(No evidence from the report that the decision was not unanimous.)

Question—Is this act void because of conflict with a treaty?

Decision—No.

Reason—A treaty is a compact between independent nations, which depends for its enforcement upon the interest and honor of the governments which are parties to the treaty. Treaties which regulate the mutual rights of citizens and subjects of the contracting nations are in the same category as Acts of Congress. When these rights are of such a nature as to be enforced by a court of justice, the court resorts to the treaty as it would to a statute. However, the Constitution gives a treaty no superiority over an Act of Congress. "In short, we are of the opinion, that, so far as a treaty made by the United States with a foreign nation can become the subject of judicial cognizance in the courts of this country, it is subject to such Acts as Congress may pass for its enforcement, modification or repeal."

Corollary cases

The Cherokee Tobacco Case, 11 Wallace 616

United States v. McBratney, 104 U. S. 621

State Railroad Tax Cases, 92 U. S. 612

Chae Chan Ping v. United States, 130 U. S. 581

Whitney v. Robertson, 124 U. S. 190

Asakura v. Seattle, 265 U. S. 332

Tucker v. Alexandroff, 183 U. S. 424

Nielsen v. Johnson, 279 U. S. 47

INTERSTATE COMMERCE AND CIVIL RIGHTS

Heart of Atlanta Motel, Inc. v. United States, 379 U. S. 241; 85 S. Ct. 348; 13 L. Ed. 2d 258 (1964)

The owner of a large motel in Atlanta, Georgia, which restricted its clientele to white persons, brought suit for a declaratory judgment and for an injunction to restrain enforcement of Title II of the Civil Rights Act of 1964, which outlawed distinguishing on the basis of race, color, religion, or national origin in making available public accommodations.

OPINION BY MR. JUSTICE CLARK
(Vote: 9-0)

Question—Does Congress have the power to enact this type of legislation under the power to regulate interstate commerce?

Decision—Yes.

Reason—The power of Congress over interstate commerce includes the power to regulate local incidents and activities in both the states of origin and destination of the commerce which might have a substantial and harmful effect on that commerce. The Court concluded that "the action of the Congress in the adoption of the Act as applied here to a motel which concededly serves interstate travelers is within the power granted it by the Commerce Clause of the Constitution as interpreted by this Court for 140 years." The Court made brief mention of the power to enforce the Fourteenth Amendment but its decision was basically that the commerce power was here being exercised. (This same statute was applied to a restaurant which purchased much of its food through interstate commerce in *Katzenbach* v. *McClung*, 379 U. S. 294, 1964.)

Corollary cases

The Civil Rights Cases, 109 U. S. 3

Hall v. De Cuir, 95 U. S. 485

Boynton v. Virginia, 364 U. S. 454

Bob-Lo Excursion Co. v. Michigan, 333 U. S. 28

Wickard v. Filburn, 317 U. S. 111

N.L.R.B. v. Jones and Laughlin Steel Corp., 301 U. S. 1

Burton v. Wilmington Parking Authority, 365 U. S. 715

Schechter v. United States, 295 U. S. 495

TAXATION AND SOCIAL SECURITY

Helvering v. Davis, 301 U. S. 619; 57 S. Ct. 904; 81 L. Ed. 1307 (1937)

Suits brought by a shareholder, George P. Davis, of the Edison Illuminating Company of Boston to restrain the corporation from making the payments and deductions called for by the Social Security Act under Titles VIII and II. The District Court held that the tax on employees was not the issue, and that the tax on employers was constitutional.

The Court of Appeals reversed the decision, holding that Title II was an invasion of powers reserved by the Tenth Amendment to the states, or to the people. The tax on employers was considered invalid for the additional reason that it was not the type of excise understood when the Constitution was adopted.

OPINION BY MR. JUSTICE CARDOZO
(Vote: 7-2)

Question—Two questions were included in a petition for a writ of certiorari: is the tax imposed upon employers contrary to the Tenth Amendment because of an invasion of powers reserved to the states, and are the purposes of expenditure legal?

Decision—The tax was not contrary to the Tenth Amendment, and the purposes were legal.

Reason—It is known that by the Constitution Congress can spend money for the general welfare. Yet difficulties are left when the power is conceded. The line must be drawn between one welfare and another: general and particular. There is a middle ground. The discretion is not confided to the courts. The discretion belongs to the Congress, unless the choice is clearly wrong. The spreading from state to state of unemployment is an ill not particular but general, which may be checked, if Congress so determines, by the resources of the nation. The ill is all one, or at least not greatly different, whether men are thrown out of work because there is no longer work to do or because the disabilities of age make them incapable of doing it. Consequently, when money is spent to promote the general welfare, the concept of welfare is shaped by Congress and not by the states.

Corollary cases

Steward Machine Company v. Davis, 301 U. S. 548

United States v. Butler, 297 U. S. 1

Alabama Power Co. v. Ickes, 302 U. S. 464

LABOR LEGISLATION

Holden v. Hardy, 169 U. S. 366, 18 S. Ct. 383, 42 L. Ed. 780 (1898)

The legislature of the State of Utah enacted an eight-hour day for workmen in underground mines, smelters, and similar places for the reduction of ore and metals, except in the event of an emergency. Violation of the statute was made a misdemeanor. Plaintiff in error was convicted of employing men contrary to the terms of the statute. He challenged the validity of the statute upon the ground of an alleged violation of the Fourteenth

Amendment, in that it abridged the privileges or immunities of citizens of the United States; deprived both the employer and the laborer of his property without due process of law, and denied to them the equal protection of the laws.

OPINION BY MR. JUSTICE BROWN
(Vote: 7-2)

Question—Is the Utah law unconstitutional?

Decision—No.

Reason—The Court reasoned that the act was a valid exercise of the police power of the state. The enactment did not profess to limit the hours of all workmen, but merely those who are employed in underground mines, or in the smelting, reduction, or refining of ores and metals. These employments, when too long pursued, the legislature has judged to be detrimental to the health of the employees, and so long as there are reasonable grounds for believing that this is so, its decision upon this subject cannot be set aside by the federal courts.

Corollary cases

Allgeyer v. Louisiana, 165 U. S. 578

Lochner v. New York, 198 U. S. 45

Muller v. Oregon, 208 U. S. 412

West Coast Hotel Co. v. Parrish, 300 U. S. 379

Bunting v. Oregon, 243 U. S. 426

Morehead v. New York ex rel. Tipaldo, 298 U. S. 587

Adkins v. Children's Hospital, 261 U. S. 525

THE PRESIDENT AND THE AMENDING PROCESS

Hollingsworth v. Virginia, 3 Dallas 378; 1 L. Ed. 644 (1798)

The decision of the court in the case of Chisholm vs. Georgia produced a proposition in Congress for amending the Constitution so that no state could be sued by citizens of another state, or by citizens or subjects of a foreign state. Upon its adoption this became the Eleventh Amendment.

OPINION BY MR. JUSTICE CHASE
(No evidence from the report that the decision was not unanimous.)

Question—Is the amendment valid since the original was never submitted to the President for his approbation?

Decision—Yes.

Reason—There is no necessity for an amendment to be shown to the President. The Constitutional requirement of Presidential signature applies only to ordinary legislation. The action of Congress in proposing an amendment is a constituent rather than a legislative act.

Corollary cases

Chisholm v. Georgia, 2 Dallas 419

National Prohibition Cases, 253 U. S. 350

Dillon v. Gloss, 256 U. S. 368

Hawke v. Smith, 253 U. S. 221

United States v. Sprague, 282 U. S. 716

Leser v. Garnett, 258 U. S. 130

United States v. Chambers, 291 U. S. 217

Coleman v. Miller, 307 U. S. 433

Edwards v. United States, 286 U. S. 482

The Pocket Veto Case, 279 U. S. 655

STATE POLICE POWER AND IMPAIRMENT OF CONTRACTS

Home Building and Loan Association v. Blaisdell, 290 U. S. 398; 54 S. Ct. 231; 78 L. Ed. 413 (1934)

The Home Building and Loan Association held a mortgage on the land of Blaisdell, the said mortgage containing a valid power of sale by advertisement, and, by reason of default, the mortgage was foreclosed. Blaisdell appealed to the Supreme Court of Minnesota, which affirmed his claim on the grounds that an act passed by the state legislature entitled "The Minnesota Mortgage Moratorium Law" provided that one who is unable to pay or retire a mortgage at the date of redemption can, by petitioning the court, be granted a moratorium from foreclosure sales. The Home Building and Loan Association appealed to the Supreme Court of the United States.

OPINION BY MR. CHIEF JUSTICE HUGHES
(Vote: 5-4)

Questions—1. Is the act contrary to the due process and equal protection clauses of the Fourteenth Amendment?

2. Does it violate the contract clause of the Constitution?

Decisions—1. No.

2. No.

Reasons—The obligations of a contract are impaired by a law that renders them invalid or releases or extinguishes them.

Here the integrity of the mortgage indebtedness was not impaired; interest continued to run, the mortgagor was to pay the rental value of the premises as ascertained in judicial proceedings. The obligation remained.

Too, not only are existing laws read into contracts in order to fix obligations as between the parties, but the reservation of essential attributes of sovereign power is also read into contracts as a postulate of the legal order. This power—called the police power—is paramount to any right under contracts between individuals. "An emergency existed in Minnesota which furnished a proper occasion for the exercise of the reserved power of the state to protect the vital interests of the community."

Corollary cases

Wilson v. New, 243 U. S. 332

East New York Savings Bank v. Hahn, 326 U. S. 230

Sturges v. Crowninshield, 4 Wheaton 122

Von Hoffman v. City of Quincy, 4 Wallace 535

Bronson v. Kinzie, 1 Howard 311

Boston Beer Co. v. Massachusetts, 97 U. S. 25

Manigault v. Springs, 199 U. S. 473

Honeyman v. Jacobs, 306 U. S. 539

Gelfert v. National City Bank, 313 U. S. 221

Providence Bank v. Billings, 4 Peters 514

Stone v. Mississippi, 101 U. S. 814

Charles River Bridge v. Warren Bridge, 11 Peters 420

Ogden v. Saunders, 12 Wheaton 213

Fletcher v. Peck, 6 Cranch 87.

New Jersey v. Wilson, 7 Cranch 164

Pennsylvania Hospital v. Philadelphia, 245 U. S. 20

Long Island Water Supply Co., v. Brooklyn, 166 U. S. 685

Trustees of Dartmouth College v. Woodward, 4 Wheaton 518

STATES AND INTERSTATE COMMERCE

H. P. Hood and Sons v. DuMond, 336 U. S. 525; 69 S. Ct. 657; 93 L. Ed. 865 (1949)

The Hood company was a Massachusetts milk distributor that obtained milk from farmers in New York. The milk was brought to Hood's three receiving plants, and from there it went to Boston. Hood applied to the New York Commissioner of Agriculture and Markets for permission to open a fourth receiving station, which was denied on the ground that the proposed plant would divert milk from the Troy, New York market.

OPINION BY MR. JUSTICE JACKSON
(Vote: 5-4)

Question—Does the New York Commissioner's order, and the statute on which it was based, put an unconstitutional burden on interstate commerce?

Decision—Yes.

Reason—New York, in its attempt to promote its own economic advantages in the milk industry, could not curtail or burden interstate commerce. This action neutralized the economic consequences of free trade among the states, and set up a barrier as effective as customs duties. A state may not use the power to tax nor its police power to establish an economic barrier to competition with the products of another state, even if it is to its own economic advantage. This discriminated against interstate commerce. "Our system, fostered by the Commerce Clause, is that every farmer and every crafts-man shall be encouraged to produce by the certainty that he will have free access to every market in the Nation, that no home embargoes will withhold his export, and no foreign state will by customs duties or regulations exclude them. Likewise, every consumer may look to the free competition from every producing area in the Nation to protect him from exploitation by any. Such was the vision of the Founders; such has been the doctrine of this Court which has given it reality."

Corollary cases

Baldwin v. Seelig, 294 U. S. 511
Milk Board v. Eisenberg, 306 U. S. 346

Dean Milk Co. v. City of Madison, 340 U. S. 349
Cities Service Co. v. Peerless Co., 340 U. S. 179

INTERSTATE COMMERCE CONTROL

Houston, E. & W. Texas Ry. Co. v. United States (The Shreveport Case), 234 U. S. 342; 34 S. Ct. 833; 58 L. Ed. 1341 (1914)

This case involved the power of Congress and its agent, the Interstate Commerce Commission, to control railroad rates between points within the same state. The Commission had fixed rates between the city of Shreveport, Louisiana, and certain points in eastern Texas for which Shreveport is the natural trade center. Motivated by a natural desire to keep Texas trade safe for the Texans, the government of that state had endeavored to fix the rates between the eastern Texas points and such cities as Dallas and Houston so low that these eastern points would trade with the Texas cities even though they were farther away than was Shreveport. At this point the I.C.C. ordered the intra-Texas rates raised to the same level as the interstate Texas-Louisiana rates.

OPINION BY MR. JUSTICE HUGHES
(Vote: 7-2)

Question—Under any conditions can Congress regulate local and intrastate commerce?

Decision—Yes.

Reason—The Supreme Court upheld the right of the federal government to regulate the local or intrastate commerce in this case on the theory that it had such a close and substantial relation to interstate commerce that the satisfactory control of one required the simultaneous and identical control of the other. "Congress, in the exercise of its paramount power, may prevent the common instrumentalities of interstate and intrastate commercial intercourse from being used in their intrastate operations to the injury of interstate commerce. This is not to say that Congress possesses the authority to regulate the internal commerce of a State, as such, but that it does possess the power to foster and protect interstate commerce, and to take all measures necessary or appropriate to that end, although intrastate transactions of interstate carriers may thereby be controlled."

Corollary cases

The Daniel Ball, 10 Wallace 557
Mobile County v. Kimball, 102 U. S. 691
Second Employers' Liability Cases, 223 U. S. 1

Minnesota Rate Cases, 230 U. S. 352
Wisconsin R.R. Commission v. C.B. & Q. R.R. Co., 257 U. S. 563
New York v. United States, 257 U. S. 591

CRIMINAL PROSECUTION AND DUE PROCESS

Hurtado v. California, 110 U. S. 516; 4 S. Ct. 111; 28 L. Ed. 232 (1884)

The plaintiff was charged by the district attorney with murder, by means of an information, in a California County Court. Upon this alone and in the same court, the plaintiff was tried, the jury rendered a verdict of murder in the first degree, and the court sentenced him to death. The Supreme Court of California upheld the judgment. The plaintiff contended that under the due process clause of the Fourteenth Amendment, he was entitled to a proper indictment by a grand jury before trial.

OPINION BY MR. JUSTICE MATTHEWS
(Vote: 7-1)

Question—In felony cases is an indictment by a grand jury a necessary part of "due process of law" guaranteed by the Fourteenth Amendment?

Decision—No.

Reason—The Court was of the opinion that the use of indictment by a grand jury was merely one process of the common law handed down to us from the courts of England. It is not a necessary part of the law but merely the way the law has been used. To hold that such a characteristic is essential to due process of law would be to render it incapable of progress or improvement. The information "is merely a preliminary proceeding, and can result in no final judgment, except as a consequence of a regular judicial trial, conducted precisely as in cases of indictments." Therefore the court reasoned that mere usage of the law at the time the due process clause was added to the Constitution does not imply that that usage is the only means of due process of law.

New procedure does not deny due process. Due process of law must mean more than the actual existing law of the land. "It follows that any legal proceedings enforced by public authority, whether sanctioned by age and custom, or newly devised in the discretion of the legislative power, in furtherance of the general public good, which regards and preserves these principles of liberty and justice, must be held to be due process of law."

Corollary cases

Munn v. Illinois, 94 U. S. 113

Kennard v. Louisiana ex rel. Morgan, 92 U. S. 480

Walker v. Savinet, 92 U. S. 90

Davidson v. New Orleans, 96 U. S. 97

Maxwell v. Dow, 176 U. S. 581

Twining v. New Jersey, 211 U. S. 78

Patton v. United States, 281 U. S. 276

STATE LEGISLATURE AND INTERSTATE COMMERCE

Interstate Transit, Inc. v. Lindsey, 283 U. S. 183; 51 S. Ct. 380; 75 L. Ed. 953 (1931)

Tennessee imposed a tax on concerns operating buses on highways graduated according to carrying capacity. Interstate Transit, an Ohio corporation, engaged exclusively in interstate commerce, challenged the tax.

OPINION BY MR. JUSTICE BRANDEIS
(Vote: 8-1)

Question—Is this tax a violation of the commerce clause?

Decision—Yes.

Reason—Because a state may not tax the privilege of engaging in interstate commerce, the tax cannot be sustained unless it appears affirmatively that it is only compensation for the use of the highways of the state. If it is a tax for the privilege of engaging in interstate commerce, it is a direct burden upon that commerce. Here, apparently, the tax was imposed for the privilege of doing business and not as compensation for the use of highways. The amount of tax was dependent not on the use made of the roads, nor even on the number of passengers actually carried. It was proportioned solely on the earning capacity of the vehicle.

Corollary cases

Kane v. New Jersey, 242 U. S. 168

Sprout v. South Bend, 277 U. S. 163

Hendrick v. Maryland, 235 U. S. 610

McCarroll v. Dixie Greyhound Lines, 309 U. S. 176

Aero Mayflower Transit Co. v Board of R.R. Comm. of Montana, 332 U. S. 495

DEFENSE USE OF PROSECUTION TESTIMONY

Jencks v. United States, 353 U. S. 657; 77 S. Ct. 1007; 1 L. Ed. 2d 1103 (1957)

The president of a labor union, Clinton E. Jencks, had been convicted of falsely swearing that he was not a member of the Communist Party. The Government's principal witnesses, Harvey F. Matusow and John W. Ford, were Communist Party members paid by the Federal Bureau of Investigation. These men had made regular oral and written reports to the F.B.I. on the matters about which they had testified. The accused had demanded that these reports be produced in court for inspection with a view to their possible use by the defense in impeaching the testimony. This motion was denied.

OPINION BY MR. JUSTICE BRENNAN
(Vote: 7-1)

Question—Is an accused person entitled to inspect relevant statements and reports of Government witnesses in the possession of the Government?

Decision—Yes.

Reason—Only the defense is adequately equipped to determine the effective use of such statements and reports for the purpose of discrediting the Government's witnesses. "Justice requires no less." "The burden is the Government's, not to be shifted to the trial judge, to decide whether the public prejudice of allowing the crime to go unpunished is greater than that attendant upon the possible disclosure of state secrets and other confidential information in the Government's possession." The Court noted also that a trial judge can determine the admissibility of Government documents and reports as evidence only after inspection by the accused.

Corollary Cases

Gordon v. United States, 344 U. S. 414

Goldman v. United States, 316 U. S. 129

Berger v. United States, 295 U. S. 78

United States v. Reynolds, 345 U. S. 1

Roviaro v. United States, 353 U. S. 53

Hannah v. Larche, 363 U. S. 420

Gonzales v. United States, 364 U. S. 59

FEDERAL-STATE RELATIONS

Johnson v. Maryland, 254 U. S. 51; 41 S. Ct. 16; 65 L. Ed. 126 (1920)

The plaintiff in error was an employee of the Post Office Department of the United States. While driving a government motor truck in the transportation of mail over a Maryland road to Washington, the plaintiff was arrested, tried, convicted, and fined for driving without a license from the State of Maryland.

OPINION BY MR. JUSTICE HOLMES
(Vote: 7-2)

Question—Has a state the power to require federal employees to obtain a license by submitting to an examination?

Decision—No.

Reason—It is the duty of the government to employ persons competent for their work, and that duty must be presumed to have been performed. However, an employee of the United States does not secure a general immunity from state law while acting in the course of his employment. Unless the United States rules otherwise, the state law would extend to a government employee as to the mode of carrying out the employment, as for example, a statute or ordinance regulating the turning at street corners. A state cannot hinder a government employee in the performance of his duties. In this case the driver was fined for not possessing a state driver's license. Such a ruling hinders the government employee in the performance of his duties, placing an additional qualification over and above what the government has determined sufficient.

Corollary cases

McCulloch v. Maryland, 4 Wheaton 316

Farmers & Mechanics Savings Bank v. Minnesota, 232 U. S. 516

Osborn v. Bank of the United States, 9 Wheaton 738

Ohio v. Thomas, 173 U. S. 276

In re Neagle, 135 U. S. 1

Keim v. United States, 177 U. S. 290

First National Bank of Louisville v. Commonwealth of Kentucky, 9 Wallace 353

LEGAL TENDER POWER

Juilliard v. Greenman, 110 U. S. 421; 4 S. Ct. 122; 28 L. Ed. 204 (1884)

Juilliard, the plaintiff, sued for the balance of $5,100 due on a cotton shipment to defendant. The balance had been paid in the form of two United States notes for $5,000 and $100 each, which plaintiff refused to accept as "legal tender."

OPINION BY MR. JUSTICE GRAY
(Vote: 8-1)

Question—Are notes of the United States legal tender in the payment of private debts in time of peace?

Decision—Yes.

Reason—The power, as incident to the power of borrowing money and issuing bills or notes of the government for money borrowed, and of impressing upon these bills or notes the quality of being legal tender for the payment of private debts, was a power universally understood to belong to sovereignty, in Europe and America, at the time of the framing and adoption of the Constitution of the United States. This power is not defeated or restricted by the fact that its exercise may affect the value of private contracts. Under the power to coin money and to regulate its value, Congress may issue coins of the same denominations as those already current by law, but of less intrinsic value, and thereby enable debtors to discharge their debts. A contract to pay a certain sum in money, without any stipulation as to the kind of money in which it shall be paid, may always be satisfied by payment of that sum in any currency that is lawful money at the place and time at which payment is to be made.

Corollary cases

Craig v. Missouri, 4 Peters 435
Briscoe v. Bank of Kentucky, 11 Peters 257
Legal Tender Cases, 12 Wallace 557

Norman v. Baltimore and Ohio R.R. Co., 294 U. S. 240
Darrington v. Bank of Alabama, 13 Howard 12

THE FEDERAL GOVERNMENT AND INHERENT POWERS

Kansas v. Colorado, 206 U. S. 46; 27 S. Ct. 655; 51 L. Ed. 956 (1907)

The State of Kansas brought suit to restrain the State of Colorado and certain corporations organized under its laws from diverting the waters of the Arkansas River for purposes of irrigation, thereby preventing its natural flow into Kansas. The United States, claiming a right to control water in the aid of reclamation of arid lands, filed an intervening petition. It made no claim that the navigability of the river was affected by the action taken by Colorado.

Question—Is the reclamation of arid lands one of the powers granted to the federal government?

Decision—No.

Reason—The proposition that there are legislative powers affecting the nation as a whole which belong to, although not expressed in, the grant of powers that Congress has, is in direct conflict with the doctrine that this government is one of enumerated powers. That this is such a government clearly appears from the Constitution, for otherwise it would be an instrument granting certain specified things made to operate so as to grant other and distinct things. This natural construction of the original body of the Constitution is made certain by the Tenth Amendment, which was seemingly adopted with the premonition of just such a contention. "It may well be that no power is adequate for their reclamation other than that of the national government. But, if no such power has been granted, none can be exercised."

Corollary cases

Fairbank v. United States, 181 U. S. 283

Carter v. Carter Coal Co., 298 U. S. 238

Arizona v. California, 283 U. S. 423

United States v. Curtiss-Wright Export Corp., 299 U. S. 304

Ashwander v. T.V.A., 297 U. S. 288

United States v. Appalachian Electric Power Co., 311 U. S. 377

Oklahoma v. Guy F. Atkinson Co., 313 U. S. 508

Knox v. Lee, 12 Wallace 457

Katz v. United States (See page 347)

INTERSTATE RENDITION

Kentucky v. Dennison, 24 Howard 66; 16 L. Ed. 717 (1861)

Kentucky had indicted Willis Lago for aiding in the escape of a Negro slave. Dennison, the governor of Ohio, refused to give up Lago, who was a fugitive, for he considered the offense as not being one of "treason, felony or other crime," in accordance with Article IV, Section 2, Clause 2 of the Constitution.

(No evidence from the report that the decision was not unanimous.)

Question—Has a governor any discretion in the rendition of a prisoner in accordance with Article IV, Section 2, Clause 2 of the Constitution?

Decision—Yes.

Reason—The Constitution says that if a fugitive from justice is found in another state, upon the demand of the executive authority of the state from which the fugitive fled, he is to be delivered up and returned to the state from which he fled. In 1793 an act of Congress made it the duty of the executive authority of one state to deliver upon demand the fugitive to the state from which he fled.

The key words are "it shall be the duty" in that Act of Congress, and the Court felt that they were not used as mandatory and compulsory but as declaratory of the moral duty which the Constitution created. This Act did not provide any means to compel the executive to do his duty, nor inflict any punishment for neglect or refusal on the part of the executive of the state; nor is there any clause or provision in the Constitution that arms the government of the United States with this power. If the federal government possessed the power to burden a state officer with a task and then, if it were not carried out, punish him "it might overload the officer with duties which would fill up all his time, and disable him from performing his obligations to the state, and might impose on him duties of a character incompatible with the rank and dignity to which he was elevated by the state."

If the governor of Ohio refuses to discharge his moral duty, there is no power for the federal government to use any coercive means to compel him to do so. The words of the Constitution and of the Act of Congress are mandatory in form but discretionary in fact.

Corollary cases

Roberts v. Reilly, 116 U. S. 80
Mahon v. Justice, 127 U. S. 700
Pettibone v. Nichols, 203 U. S. 192
Hyatt v. Corkran, 188 U. S. 691

Lascelles v. Georgia, 148 U. S. 537
Ex parte Reggel, 114 U. S. 642
Marbles v. Creecy, 215 U. S. 63
Sweeney v. Woodall, 344 U. S. 86

INTERSTATE COMMERCE

Kentucky Whip and Collar Co. v. Illinois Central R.R. Co., 299 U. S. 334; 57 S. Ct. 277; 81 L. Ed. 270 (1937)

The Ashurst-Sumners Act of 1935 makes it unlawful to ship in interstate commerce goods made by convict labor into any state where the goods are intended to be received, possessed, sold, or used in violation of its laws. Packages containing convict-made goods must be plainly labeled so as to show the names and addresses of shipper and consignee, the nature of the contents, and the name and location of the penal or reformatory institution where the article was produced. The petitioner manufactures in Kentucky, with convict labor, horse collars, harness, and strap goods that are marketed in various states. The Illinois Central received twenty-five separate shipments, for transportation in interstate commerce, none of which was labeled as required. The respondent refused to accept the shipments, and the petitioner brought suit for a mandatory injunction to compel shipment.

OPINION BY MR. CHIEF JUSTICE HUGHES
(Vote: 8-0)

Question—Does Congress have the power to prohibit in interstate commerce useful and harmless articles made by convict labor?

Decision—Yes.

Reason—The congressional power to regulate commerce is complete in itself, acknowledging no other limitations than those prescribed by the Constitution. The question here is whether this statute goes beyond the authority to "regulate."

The power to prohibit interstate transportation has been upheld in many cases. In fact, in the exercise of its control over interstate commerce, Congress may have the quality of police regulations. In so regulating, Congress may shape its policy to aid valid state laws in the protection of persons and property. Therefore, Congress may prevent transportation in interstate commerce of articles in which the state has the constitutional authority to forbid traffic in its internal commerce.

The Ashurst-Sumners Act has substantially the same provisions as the Webb-Kenyon Act. The subject matter is different, the effects are different, but the principle is the same. Where the subject of commerce is one on which the power of a state may be constitutionally exerted, Congress may, if it so chooses, put forth its power to prevent interstate commerce from being used to frustrate the state policy.

As far as the labels are concerned, they are but a reasonable provision for carrying out the purposes of the act.

Corollary cases

Gibbons v. Ogden, 9 Wheaton 1
Brooks v. United States, 267 U. S. 432
In re Rahrer, 140 U. S. 545
United States v. Hill, 248 U. S. 420

Whitfield v. Ohio, 297 U. S. 431
Rhodes v. Iowa, 170 U. S. 412
Clark Distilling Co., v. Western Maryland Railway Co., 242 U. S. 311

INVESTIGATORY POWER OF CONGRESS

Kilbourn v. Thompson, 103 U. S. 168; 26 L. Ed. 377 (1881)

Hallett Kilbourn refused to answer questions put to him by an investigating committee of the House of Representatives. He was found to be in contempt of this body and sentenced to prison for forty-five days. He brought damages against John Thompson, the sergeant-at-arms of the House and of the committee in which he was held to be in contempt. This investigation of the House concerned a real estate pool in which the government was a creditor.

OPINION BY MR. JUSTICE MILLER

(No evidence from the report that the decision was not unanimous.)

Question—Has the House of Representatives exceeded its power in directing one of its committees to make an investigation of this type?

Decision—Yes.

Reason—Parliamentary procedure holds no precedent for the punishment of a private citizen for refusal to testify before a committee of the House, and the power of the House to punish in such cases extends only to its own members. Further, the inquiries being made by the committee of the House were purely judicial in nature, and, under the principle of separation of powers, a legislative body such as the House of Representatives is not empowered to assume a judicial function. The bankruptcy case was then before the courts. Furthermore, the House had no authority to investigate the matter in question, so could not hold the witness in contempt. The Supreme Court held that the House could punish for contempt only when necessary to prevent interference with its powers.

Corollary cases

Anderson v. Dunn, 6 Wheaton 204

McGrain v. Daugherty, 273 U. S. 135

In re Chapman, 166 U. S. 661

Marshall v. Gordon, 243 U. S. 521

Jurney v. MacCracken, 294 U. S. 125

Sinclair v. United States, 279 U. S. 263

LABOR STANDARDS AND INTERSTATE COMMERCE

Kirschbaum Co. v. Walling, 316 U. S. 517; 62 S. Ct. 1116; 86 L. Ed. 1638 (1942)

The employees concerned in this case were engaged in the operation and maintenance of a loft building in which large quantities of goods for interstate commerce were produced. The Kirschbaum Co. was charged with paying lower wages for operation and maintenance help than required by the Fair Labor Standards Act.

OPINION BY MR. JUSTICE FRANKFURTER
(Vote: 8-1)

Question—Does the Fair Labor Standards Act extend to such employees?

Decision—Yes.

Reason—The Court reasoned that the operation and maintenance of the building was a necessary and important part of the work that was carried on within the building; therefore the employees concerned here were to be regarded as engaged in occupations necessary to the production of goods for interstate commerce. The Court further reasoned that cases of this sort are matters of degree. No mathematical formula was provided by the concepts of the Constitution on interstate commerce, due process, and equal protection.

Corollary cases

United States v. Darby, 312 U. S. 100

Opp Cotton Mills v. Administrator, 312 U. S. 126

Virginian Ry. Co. v. Federation, 300 U. S. 515

United Leather Workers v. Herkert, 265 U. S. 457

Levering & Garrigues Co. v. Morrin, 289 U. S. 103

N.L.R.B. v. Fainblatt, 306 U. S. 601

Heisler v. Thomas Colliery Co., 260 U. S. 245

Oliver Iron Co. v. Lord, 262 U. S. 172

Sunshine Coal Co. v. Adkins, 310 U. S. 381

Federal Trade Commission v. Bunte Bros., 312 U. S. 349

Santa Cruz Fruit Packing Co., v. N.L.R.B., 303 U. S. 453

DELEGATION OF LEGISLATIVE POWER

Knickerbocker Ice Co. v. Stewart, 253 U. S. 149; 40 S. Ct. 438; 64 L. Ed. 834 (1920)

William Stewart was employed by the Knickerbocker Ice Co. as a bargeman. He fell into the Hudson River and was drowned, August 1918. His wife filed a claim under the Workman's Compensation Law of New York and was given an award later upheld by the New York Court of Appeals. That court sustained the award on the basis of an Act of Congress of August 1917 which provided that the provisions of the Workmen's Compensation acts of any state could be applied to persons engaged in maritime labor.

OPINION BY MR. JUSTICE McREYNOLDS
(Vote: 5-4)

Question—Can Congress delegate to a state the power to pass compensation laws for maritime workers?

Decision—No.

Reason—The court invalidated the federal statute on the ground that the grant of power to Congress to legislate with respect to maritime matters was exclusive and could not be delegated to the states. The subject was entrusted to it by the terms of the Constitution to be dealt with according to its discretion, not for delegation to others. To say that because Congress could have enacted a compensation act applicable to maritime injuries, it could authorize the states to do so, as they might desire, is false reasoning. Congress cannot transfer its legislative power to the states.

Congress in the interest of uniform rules and adequate harmony was given power in maritime matters. Congress was given control in order to "relieve maritime commerce from unnecessary burdens and disadvantages incident to discordant legislation." Authorizing Congress to apply state compensations to matters within the special field of Congress would destroy the harmony and uniformity the Constitution sought, and substitute confusion and uncertainty.

Corollary cases

Southern Pacific Co. v. Jensen, 244 U. S. 205

Chelentis v. Luckenbach S. S. Co.,

Kentucky Whip and Collar Co., v. Illinois Central R.R. Co., 299 U. S. 334

247 U. S. 372

Union Fish Co. v. Erickson, 248 U. S. 308

In re Rahrer, 140 U. S. 545

Delamater v. South Dakota, 205 U. S. 93

Washington v. W. C. Dawson and Co., 264 U. S. 219

Clark Distilling Co., v. Western Maryland Railway Co., 242 U. S. 311

EVACUATION OF CIVILIANS UNDER THE WAR POWER

Korematsu v. United States, 323 U. S. 214; 65 S. Ct. 193; 89 L. Ed. 194 (1944)

Korematsu, an American citizen of Japanese ancestry, remained in California after it had been ordered cleared of all persons of Japanese descent under Executive Order 34, itself based on an Act of Congress. He refused to leave and was convicted under the law.

OPINION BY MR. JUSTICE BLACK
(Vote: 6-3)

Question—Was this a proper exercise of the war power?

Decision—Yes.

Reason—"Korematsu was not excluded from the Military Area because of hostility to him or his race. He was excluded because we are at war with the Japanese Empire, because the properly constituted military authorities feared an invasion of our West Coast and felt constrained to take proper security measures, because they decided that the military urgency of the situation demanded that all citizens of Japanese ancestry be segregated from the West Coast temporarily, and finally, because Congress, reposing its confidence in this time of war in our military leaders—as inevitably it must—determined that they should have the power to do just this. There was evidence of disloyalty on the part of some, the military authorities considered that the need for action was great, and time was short. We connot—by availing ourselves of the calm prespective of hindsight—now say that at that time these actions were unjustified."

Corollary cases

Hirabayashi v. United States, 320 U. S. 81

Chastleton Corporation v. Sinclair, 264 U. S. 543

Block v. Hirsh, 256 U. S. 136

Ex parte Mitsuye Endo, 323 U. S. 283

Duncan v. Kahanamoku, 327 U. S. 304

EQUAL PROTECTION

Kotch v. Board of River Port Pilot Commissioners for the Port of New Orleans, 330 U. S. 552; 67 S. Ct. 910; 91 L. Ed. 1093 (1947)

A Louisiana statute provides that all seagoing vessels moving between New Orleans and foreign ports must be navigated through the Mississippi River approaches to the port of New Orleans exclusively by pilots who are state officers. New state officers are appointed by the governor upon the certification of the State Board of River Pilot Commissioners, who are also pilots. Only those who have served a six-months apprenticeship under the incumbent pilots and possess other specified qualifications may be certified. The appellants have had at least fifteen years experience in the river, the port, and elsewhere, as pilots, but cannot qualify as state pilots because they have not served the six-months apprenticeship. They challenge the statute as giving the pilots an unfettered discretion in the selection of apprentices. Membership is closed to almost all except relatives and friends of the pilots.

Opinion by Mr. Justice Black
(Vote: 5-4)

Question—Does the pilotage law violate the equal protection clause of the Fourteenth Amendment?

Decision—No.

Reason—The history of pilotage proves that it is a highly personalized calling, requiring a detailed, and almost intuitive knowledge of the weather, waterways, and conformation of the harbor or river the pilot serves. This seems to be particularly true of the treacherous and shifting channel of the Mississippi. Likewise, "pilot towns" have grown up close to the places where the pilots board the ships, which give the young men an unusual opportunity to acquire special knowledge of the weather and water hazards of the locality.

The very first Congress left to the states the full power to regulate pilotage of certain kinds of vessels. Louisiana's legislation dates back to 1805, to territorial days, and seems to have accepted the idea that competition for appointments affects the public interest adversely in the matter of pilotage. Thus, the New Orleans practice has been existent for many years, and has the advantage of providing friendly supervision in early training, as well as the benefits to morale that the family and neighborly traditions contribute.

The equal protection clause cannot set a precise formula for every occasion. It is almost a necessary consequence of setting apart a classified group that there will be certain restrictions and advantages, but no constitutional safeguards are violated unless the grounds are wholly irrelevant to the objectives of the regulation.

There are no decisions of this Court which require a state governor to select state public officers by competitive tests or any other method. The object of the entire pilotage law is to ensure the safest and most efficacious system possible, and the Louisiana system is certainly related to this objective.

Corollary cases

Yick Wo v. Hopkins, 118 U. S. 356

Takahashi v. Fish and Game Commission, 334 U. S. 410

Goesaert v. Cleary, 335 U. S. 464

MacDougall v. Green, 335 U. S. 281

Borden's Farm Products Co. v. Ten Eyck, 297 U. S. 251

The Great A. & P. Tea Co. v. Grosjean, 301 U. S. 412

Railway Express Co. v. New York, 336 U. S. 106

FREE SPEECH AND THE "CAPTIVE AUDIENCE"

Kovacs v. Cooper, 336 U. S. 77; 69 S. Ct. 448; 93 L. Ed. 513 (1949)

An ordinance of Trenton, New Jersey makes it unlawful to play, use, or operate for advertising or any other purpose on public streets, alleys, or thoroughfares, sound trucks, loud speakers, sound amplifiers, calliopes, or any instrument which emits "loud and raucous noises."

OPINION BY MR. JUSTICE REED
(Vote: 5-4)

Question—Does this ordinance violate the right of freedom of speech and assembly, and the freedom to communicate information and opinions to others?

Decision—No.

Reason—Freedom of speech is not beyond control. The Court held that the legislation against "loud and raucous noises" is a permissible exercise of municipal authority. The citizen in his home or on the street is not in the position of the passerby who can refuse a pamphlet. He is helpless to escape this interference with his privacy except through the protection of the municipality.

"The preferred position of freedom of speech in a society that cherishes liberty for all does not require legislators to be insensible to claims by citizens to comfort and convenience. To enforce freedom of speech in disregard of the rights of others would be harsh and arbitrary in itself." This is not a restriction upon communication of ideas, but a reasonable protection from distraction.

Corollary cases

Winters v. New York, 333 U. S. 507

Saia v. New York, 334 U. S. 558

Martin v. Struthers, 319 U. S. 141

Palko v. Connecticut, 302 U. S. 319

Public Utilities Commission of the District of Columbia v. Pollak, 343 U. S. 451

PROCEDURAL DUE PROCESS AND PROPERTY

Lawton v. Steele, 152 U. S. 133; 14 S. Ct. 499; 38 L. Ed. 385 (1894)

> Steele, an officer of New York, acting under the authority of a New York statute for the protection of fisheries, destroyed fifteen fish nets used by Lawton for illegal fishing. The nets were worth $216, and Lawton sued for the value of the destroyed nets.

OPINION BY MR. JUSTICE BROWN
(Vote: 6-3)

Question—Does the statute in question deprive Lawton of his property without due process of law?

Decision—No.

Reason—The only question really involved here was the part of the act that declares that such articles used illegally may be destroyed. The legislature certainly may prohibit fishing in certain waters, make it a criminal offense, and take measures to prevent such occurrences in the future.

The value of the object illegally used may warrant judicial proceedings, if it is of great value. However, if the value of the article be trifling, it is within the power of the legislature to destroy it.

The person whose property is thus seized or destroyed is not without a remedy. If it has been used illegally, he has no reason for complaint; if there was no illegal use, he may replevy his nets from the officer, or if they have been destroyed, may recover their value.

Corollary cases

Callan v. Wilson, 127 U. S. 540 North American Cold Storage Co.
           v. Chicago, 211 U. S. 306

FEDERAL MONETARY POWERS

Legal Tender Cases (Knox v. Lee; Parker v. Davis), 12 Wallace 457; 20 L. Ed. 287 (1871)

Congress provided for the issuance of paper money by the United States and made such money legal tender for the payment of private debts. Knox had purchased a number of sheep that had been confiscated under the Confederacy in Texas during the Civil War. Lee, after the war, brought suit to recover the value of the sheep and won. The payment was to be made in United States Treasury certificates called "greenbacks," which were of less value than gold or silver. When Knox was about to pay the debt in greenbacks, Lee appealed the case to secure payment in gold or silver. In the second case, Davis asked for a writ of specific performance to compel Parker to transfer real estate upon payment of a set sum of money which Davis had previously offered to pay in legal tender notes.

OPINION BY MR. JUSTICE STRONG
(Vote: 5-4)

Question—Does Congress have the power to make the Treasury notes legal tender applicable to both previous and subsequent contracts.

Decision—Yes.

Reason—"And here it is to be observed it is not indispensable to the existence of any power claimed for the federal government that it can be found specified in the words of the Constitution, or clearly and directly traceable to some one of the specified powers. Its existence may be deduced fairly from more than one of the substantive powers expressly defined, or from them all combined. And it is of importance to observe that Congress has often exercised, without question, powers that are not expressly given nor ancillary to any single enumerated power. Powers thus exercised are what are called by Judge Story, in his *Commentaries on the Constitution,* resulting powers, arising from the aggregate powers of the government." The statute here was passed as a war measure to obtain credit for the equipment of armies, and the employment of money to an extent beyond the capacity of all ordinary sources of supply. If nothing else would have supplied the necessaries of the Treasury these acts would be valid. To say that some other means might have been chosen, is mere conjecture and if it be conceded, it proves nothing more than that Congress had the choice of means for a legitimate end, each appropriate and adapted to that end. The Court could not say that Congress ought to have adopted one rather than the other.

Corollary cases

Hepburn v. Griswold, 8 Wallace 603

Juilliard v. Greenman, 110 U. S. 421

Perry v. United States, 294 U. S. 330

McCulloch v. Maryland, 4 Wheaton 316

Lane County v. Oregon, 7 Wallace 71

Bronson v. Rodes, 7 Wallace 229

Roosevelt v. Meyer, 1 Wallace 512

Norman v. B. and O. R.R. Co., 294 U. S. 240

STATE LEGISLATION AND INTERSTATE COMMERCE

Leisy v. Hardin, 135 U. S. 100; 10 S. Ct. 681; 34 L. Ed. 128 (1890)

Leisy, a brewer of Peoria, Illinois, brought an action to recover a quantity of barrels and cases of beer that had been seized in a proceeding on behalf of the state, for violating the Iowa statute prohibiting the sale of intoxicating liquors in the state. The beer in question was shipped from Illinois and sold in the original packages.

OPINION BY MR. CHIEF JUSTICE FULLER
(Vote: 6-3)

Question—Can a state prohibit articles of commerce from being imported into the state, in the absence of legislation on the part of Congress?

Decision—No.

Reason—The power of Congress to regulate commerce is unlimited, except for those restrictions specified in the Constitution. If Congress does not regulate concerning certain phases of interstate commerce, that commerce shall be free and unhampered. Beer, therefore, may be brought into the state and sold, after which time it becomes mingled in the common mass of property of the state, and subject to its control. The right to sell any article brought into a state is an inseparable incident to the right to import the article.

Corollary cases

Brown v. Maryland, 12 Wheaton 419

License Cases, 5 Howard 504

Bowman v. Chicago & N. Ry. Co., 125 U. S. 465

South Carolina State Highway Department v. Barnwell Brothers, 303 U. S. 177

In re Rahrer, 140 U. S. 545

Clark Distilling Co. v. Western Maryland Ry. Co., 242 U. S. 311

United States v. Hill, 248 U. S. 420

Rhodes v. Iowa, 170 U. S. 412

Whitfield v. Ohio, 297 U. S. 431

Kentucky Whip and Collar Co. v. Illinois Central R.R. Co., 299 U. S. 334

SUPREME COURT JURISDICTION

Ex parte Albert Levitt, 302 U. S. 633, 58 S. Ct. 1, 82 L. Ed. 493 (1937)

Levitt, a lawyer, asked leave of the Supreme Court to file a petition for an order requiring Associate Justice Hugo Black of the U. S. Supreme Court to show cause why he should be permitted to serve as an associate justice of the Court. Two grounds were stated. Levitt contended that under Article I, Section 6, no senator should be appointed to any civil office under the authority of the United States, the salary whereof had been increased during the time for which he was elected. While Black was a senator, Congress had enacted a measure whereby a Justice could retire without discontinuance of the salary that he received as an active member of the Court. The second ground for the suit was that, since Justice Van Devanter had not resigned, but had merely retired, there was no vacancy on the Court to which Black might be appointed.

OPINION—PER CURIAM

(No evidence from the report that the decision was not unanimous.)

Question—Were there grounds sufficient for action by the Supreme Court?

Decision—No.

Reason—The court stated that the petitioning lawyer had shown no interest in the matter other than that of a citizen and a member of the bar of the court. Such an interest was insufficient to enable him to secure action from the Court. It was an established principle that, to entitle a private individual to invoke judicial power to determine the validity of executive or legislative action, he must show that he had sustained, or was in immediate danger of sustaining a direct injury as the result of that action. It was not sufficient that he had merely a general interest common to all members of the public.

Corollary cases

Tyler v. Judges of Ct. of Registration, 179 U. S. 405

Southern R.R. Co. v. King, 217 U. S. 524

Newman v. United States, 238 U. S. 537

Fairchild v. Hughes, 258 U. S. 126

Massachusetts v. Mellon, 262 U. S. 447

STATE LABOR LEGISLATION

Lincoln Federal Labor Union No. 19129, American Federation of Labor, et al., v. Northwestern Iron and Metal Co., et al., 335 U. S. 525; 69 S. Ct. 251; 93 L. Ed. 212 (1949)

A North Carolina statute made it unlawful for an employer to refuse employment to or to discharge anyone because of membership or nonmembership in a labor union, or for a labor organization and an employer to enter into a contract for a closed or union shop. In North Carolina an employer and officers of a labor union were convicted of a misdemeanor for entering into such a contract.

OPINION BY MR. JUSTICE BLACK

(No evidence from the report that the decision was not unanimous.)

Question—Do these state laws violate rights guaranteed employers, unions, and their members by the United States Constitution?

Decision—No.

Reason—Neither the due process clause nor the equal protection clause prohibits the states from outlawing closed or union shop agreements. The constitutional right of workers to assemble to discuss and formulate plans for the furthering of their own interest in jobs cannot be construed as a constitutional guarantee that none shall get and hold jobs except those who join in such plans. Where conduct affects the interest of others and the general public, the legality of that conduct must be measured by whether the conduct conforms to valid laws.

The liberty of contracts protected by the Fourteenth Amendment is not unqualified. Due process does not forbid a state to pass laws designed to safeguard the opportunity of nonunion members to get and hold jobs, free from discrimination because they are not members of a union. The Court rejected the earlier due process philosophy of the cases and returned to the even earlier philosophy that the states have the power to legislate against what are found to be injurious practices in their internal commercial and business affairs, so long as their laws do not run afoul of some specific federal Constitutional prohibition or some valid federal law. "Under this constitutional doctrine the due process clause is no longer to be so broadly construed that the Congress and state legislatures are put in a strait jacket when they attempt to suppress business and industrial conditions which they regard as offensive to the public welfare. Just as we have held that the due process clause erects no obstacle to block legislative protection of union members, we now hold that legislative protection can be afforded non-union workers."

Corollary cases

A. F. of L. v. American Sash Co., 335 U. S. 538

International Union v. Wisconsin, 336 U. S. 245

Daniel v. Family Security Life Insurance Co., 336 U. S. 220

West Coast Hotel Co. v. Parrish, 300 U. S. 379

Coppage v. Kansas, 236 U. S. 1

Adair v. United States, 208 U. S. 161

Phelps Dodge Corp. v. N.L.R.B., 313 U. S. 177

DUE PROCESS

Lochner v. New York, 198 U. S. 45; 25 S. Ct. 539; 49 L. Ed. 937 (1905)

A New York statute forbade any employee in a bakery or confectionery establishment to be permitted to work over 60 hours in any one week, or an average of over 10 hours a day. Lochner was convicted in Utica of requiring and permitting an employee to work more than sixty hours in one week.

OPINION BY MR. JUSTICE PECKHAM
(Vote: 5-4)

Question—Does this statute violate the Fourteenth Amendment?

Decision—Yes.

Reason—The right of an individual to make a contract with regard to his labor is part of the liberty of the individual protected by the Fourteenth Amendment. The right to purchase or sell labor is also part of this liberty, unless there are circumstances that exclude the right. Against these rights we have the police powers of the states, which under certain conditions may impose restrictions on the exercise of those rights. At times it is of great importance to determine which shall prevail—the right of the individual to labor for such a time as he may choose, or the right of the state to prevent an individual from laboring beyond a certain time prescribed by the state.

If this is a valid exercise of state police power, it involves the question of health. The Court held that there was no reasonable foundation for holding that this statute was necessary to safeguard the public health, or the health of bakers in general. The trade of a baker, while not the healthiest of occupations, does not affect health to such a degree that the legislature is warranted in interfering. At that rate, no trade or occupation would be able to escape acts of the legislature restricting the hours of labor.

The statute in question, the Court held, was an illegal interference in the rights of individuals, both employers and employees, for reasons entirely arbitrary. The Court was of the opinion that the only purpose of the act was to regulate the hours of labor in an occupation that is not dangerous in any degree to morals, nor in any substantial way injurious to health. This freedom to contract in relation to employment could not be interfered with, without violating the Constitution. (The doctrine of this case is no longer controlling.)

Corollary cases

Allgeyer v. Louisiana, 165 U. S. 578

Mugler v. Kansas, 123 U. S. 623

Holden v. Hardy, 169 U. S. 366

Nebbia v. New York, 291 U. S. 502

West Coast Hotel Co. v. Parrish, 300 U. S. 379

Atkin v. Kansas, 191 U. S. 207   Olsen v. Nebraska, 313 U. S. 236
Jacobson v. Massachusetts, 197   Phelps Dodge Corp. v. N.L.R.B.,
  U. S. 11   313 U. S. 177

LABOR AND ANTITRUST LEGISLATION

Loewe v. Lawlor, (The Danbury Hatters' Case), 208 U. S. 274; 28 S. Ct. 301; 52 L. Ed. 488 (1908)

Loewe and associates, known as the Danbury Hatters, were engaged in the manufacturing of hats. They refused to have a union in their shop. The union then boycotted the products of the concern. Loewe brought suit against Lawlor, agent for the United Hatters of North America, for triple damages for injuries inflicted upon his business by the United Hatters. Loewe charged that the United Hatters was a combination conspiring to restrain interstate commerce in violation of the Sherman Anti-Trust Act of 1890.

OPINION BY MR. CHIEF JUSTICE FULLER
(No evidence from the report that the decision was not unanimous.)

Question—Did the United Hatters of North America constitute a combination in restraint of interstate commerce under the Sherman Anti-Trust Act?

Decision—Yes.

Reason—It was proved beyond a doubt that the United Hatters was an organization of such power as to exert a tremendous influence over the hatmaking industry. The use by this organization of such means as boycotts, labor controls, intimidation of dealers, and other oppressive and coercive measures to gain control of the hat industry was definitely a restraint and hindrance of interstate commerce, which was not permitted to a state and certainly not permitted to any arbitrary collection of individuals. For this reason, the United Hatters constituted an illegal combination under the terms of the Sherman Anti-Trust Act.

Corollary cases

United States v. Hutcheson, 312   Duplex Printing Press Co. v. Dec-
  U. S. 219   ring, 254 U. S. 443

Bedford Cut Stone Co. v. Journeyman Stone Cutters Ass'n., 274
U. S. 37

United Mine Workers of America
v. Coronado Coal Co., 259 U. S.
344

Apex Hosiery Co. v. Leader, 310
U. S. 469

Michaelson v. U. S. ex rel. C., St.
P., M. & O. R.R. Co., 266 U. S.
42

PUNISHMENT AND DUE PROCESS

State of Louisiana ex rel. Francis v. Resweber, 329 U. S. 459; 67 S. Ct. 374; 91 L. Ed. 422 (1947)

Willie Francis, a colored citizen of Louisiana, was duly
convicted of murder in September, 1945 and sentenced
to be electrocuted for the crime. Upon a proper death
warrant, Francis was prepared for execution on May 3,
1946, and was placed in the electric chair of the State of
Louisiana in the presence of the authorized witnesses.
The executioner pulled the switch, but, because of mechanical difficulty, death did not result. A new death
warrant was issued by the governor of Louisiana, fixing
the execution for May 9, 1946. Because of this, an appeal
was made and execution of the sentence was delayed.

OPINION BY MR. JUSTICE REED
(Vote: 5-4)

Question—Did the experience through which Francis passed
violate the principles of the Fifth and Eighth Amendments
as to double jeopardy and cruel and unusual punishment, as
applied by the due process clause of the Fourteenth Amendment, and of equal protection?

Decision—No.

Reason—First, there was no case of double jeopardy. To
quote the Court, "We see no difference from a constitutional
point of view between a new trial for error of law at the
instance of the state that results in a death sentence instead
of imprisonment for life and an execution that follows a
failure of equipment." Second, there was no unusual and
cruel punishment involved in this case. The petitioner claimed
that the psychological strain was cruel and unusual punishment. The cruelty against which the Constitution protects a
convicted man is cruelty inherent in the method of punish-

ment, not the necessary suffering involved in any method employed to extinguish life humanely. Just because of mechanical failure there was not unusual or cruel punishment. Third, there was no denial of equal protection of the laws. The state of Louisiana did not single out Francis for special treatment that would not be applied to others. Equal protection does not extend to accidents. The Supreme Court after reviewing the records of the trial, said there was no evidence in any of the papers to show any violation of petitioner's constitutional rights.

Corollary cases

Lisenba v. California, 314 U. S. 219

Carter v. Illinois, 329 U. S. 173

Ex parte Lange, 18 Wallace 163

Adamson v. California, 332 U. S. 46

Palko v. Connecticut, 302 U. S. 319

Robinson v. California, 370 U. S. 660 (1962)

EQUAL PROTECTION AND INTERRACIAL MARRIAGE

Loving v. Virginia, 388 U. S. 1; 87 S. Ct. 1817; 18 L. Ed. 2d 1010 (1967)

Two residents of Virginia, a Negro woman and a white man, Richard Loving, were married in the District of Columbia. They then returned to Caroline County, Virginia. There they were indicted for violation of Virginia's ban on interracial marriages. Their conviction was upheld by the Supreme Court of Appeals of Virginia. The central provision of the state's Racial Integrity Act was the absolute prohibition of a "white person" marrying other than another "white person." The term "white person" was defined in the statute.

OPINION BY MR. CHIEF JUSTICE WARREN
(Vote: 9-0)

Question—Does the statutory scheme of Virginia to prevent marriages between persons solely on the basis of racial classification violate the Fourteenth Amendment?

Decision—Yes.

Reason—The statutes violate both the Equal Protection and Due Process Clauses of the Fourteenth Amendment. "There can be no question but that Virginia's miscegenation statutes rest solely upon distinctions drawn according to race. . . . There can be no doubt that restricting the freedom to marry solely because of racial classifications violates the central meaning of the Equal Protection Clause. . . . The freedom to marry has long been recognized as one of the vital personal rights essential to the orderly pursuit of happiness by free men. Marriage is one of the 'basic civil rights of man,' fundamental to our very existence and survival. . . . Under our Constitution, the freedom to marry or not marry, a person of another race resides with the individual and cannot be infringed by the State."

Corollary cases

Pace v. Alabama, 106 U. S. 583
McLaughlin v. Florida, 379 U. S. 184
Brown v. Board of Education, 347 U. S. 483

Strauder v. West Virginia, 100 U. S. 303
Skinner v. Oklahoma, 316 U. S. 535
Maynard v. Hill, 125 U. S. 190

DUE PROCESS AND PROPERTY

Louisville Joint Stock Land Bank v. Radford, 295 U. S. 555; 55 S. Ct. 854; 79 L. Ed. 1593 (1935)

This case involved the application of the Frazier-Lemke Act of 1934. Radford had mortgaged his farm to the Louisville Joint Stock Land Bank in 1924. In 1931 and subsequent years, Radford defaulted in the covenant to pay the taxes and in his promise to pay the installments of interest and principal. After Radford's refusal to refinance his indebtedness under the Emergency Farm Mortgage Act of 1933, the bank declared the entire indebtedness immediately payable and commenced a suit to foreclose the mortgage. Radford then sought relief under Section 75 of the Bankruptcy Act to effect a composition of his debts. Having failed in this, the bank offered to accept the deed to his property in full satisfaction of Radford's indebtedness to the bank and to assume the debt of the unpaid taxes. Meanwhile the Frazier-Lemke Act of 1934 was passed and Radford sought relief under this act. It provided Radford with the opportunity to purchase his property at its then-appraised value, acquiring title thereto by agreeing to make deferred payments over a period of six years. If the bank did not consent to this, then the court would stay all proceedings for five years and Radford would pay a rent to the court during that period. The money would be dispersed to the debtors. At the end of the five years, Radford would have the opportunity to purchase the property at its appraised value. The bank claimed that the Frazier-Lemke Act was, and the relief sought would be, unconstitutional.

Opinion by Mr. Justice Brandeis
(No evidence from the report that the decision was not unanimous.)

Question—Was application of the Frazier-Lemke Act of 1934 unconstitutional?

Decision—Yes.

Reason—The Court unanimously held the act unconstitutional as being in violation of the Fifth Amendment, because of taking from the bank rights in specific property which are of substantive value. For the Fifth Amendment, said the Court, commands that, however great the nation's need, private property shall not be thus taken without just compensation. If the public interest requires, and permits, the taking of property of individual mortgagees in order to relieve the necessities of individual mortgagors, resort must be had to proceedings by eminent domain; so that, through taxation, the burden of the relief afforded in the public interest may be borne by the public.

Corollary cases

Home Building & Loan Association v. Blaisdell, 290 U. S. 398

Long v. Bullard, 117 U. S. 617

Mitchell v. Clark, 110 U. S. 633

Local Loan Co. v. Hunt, 292 U. S. 234

W. B. Worthen Co. v. Kavanaugh, 295 U. S. 56

Wright v. Vinton Branch of Mountain Trust Bank of Roanoke, 300 U. S. 440

East New York Savings Bank v. Hahn, 326 U. S. 230

Manigault v. Springs, 199 U. S. 473

THE GUARANTEE OF A REPUBLICAN FORM OF GOVERNMENT

Luther v. Borden, 7 Howard 1; 12 L. Ed. 581 (1849)

In 1841 the people of the state of Rhode Island were still operating under the old colonial charter with a few minor revisions, using it as their state constitution. This constitution strictly limited the right to vote. Led by a man named Dorr, the people at various mass meetings throughout the state instituted a new constitution whereby suffrage was greatly increased. The state government claimed that this was an insurrection and appealed to the President to declare martial law. However, no federal forces were used. Members of the state militia led by Borden forced their way into the house of Luther, a Dorr adherent, who sued for trespass. Luther moved to Massachusetts in order to legalize a suit on the basis of diversity of citizenship.

OPINION BY MR. CHIEF JUSTICE TANEY
(Vote: 8-1)

Question—Can the Court decide as to the guaranty of a republican form of a state's government in accordance with Article IV, Section 4.

Decision—No.

Reason—This is a purely political question and must be left in the hands of the political branches of the government to decide. Their decision moreover may not be questioned in a judicial tribunal. It would constitute a usurpation of power for the Supreme Court to attempt to decide the question. The enforcement of the guarantee of a republican form of government rests with the President or Congress.

Corollary cases

Martin v. Mott, 12 Wheaton 19
Ex parte Dorr, 3 Howard 103
Pacific States Telephone and Telegraph Co. v. Oregon, 223 U. S. 118

Coleman v. Miller, 307 U. S. 433
Colegrove v. Green, 328 U. S. 549

SEARCH AND SEIZURE

Mapp v. Ohio, 367 U. S. 643; 81 S. Ct. 1684; 6 L. Ed. 2d 1081 (1961)

Cleveland police officers requested admission to a home to seek a fugitive who was reportedly hiding there. They had also received information that a large amount of policy paraphernalia was hidden in the house. Without a warrant, the police forced their way into the house. There they found obscene materials. This evidence was used to convict Miss Mapp in the state courts.

OPINION BY MR. JUSTICE CLARK
(Vote: 6-3)

Question — Is evidence obtained in violation of the search and seizure provisions of the Fourth Amendment admissible in a state court?

Decision — No.

Reason — Previous decisions have held that the security of one's privacy against arbitrary intrusion of the police is implicit in the concept of ordered liberty and as such enforceable against the states through the Due Process Clause. However, the Court has previously refused to exclude evidence thus secured from state courts as "an essential ingredient of the right." Since the Fourth Amendment's right of privacy has been declared enforceable against the states through the Due Process Clause of the Fourteenth Amendment, it is enforceable against them by the same sanction of exclusion as is used against the Federal Government. All evidence obtained by searches and seizures in violation of the Constitution is, by that same authority, inadmissible in a state court. The Court thus overruled Wolf v. Colorado, 338 U.S. 25, 1949.

Corollary cases

Weeks v. United States, 232 U. S. 383

Elkins v. United States, 364 U. S. 206

Benanti v. United States, 355 U. S. 596

Rea v. United States, 350 U. S. 214

United States v. Rabinowitz, 339 U. S. 56

McNabb v. United States, 318 U. S. 332

Rochin v. California, 342 U. S. 165

Irvine v. California, 347 U. S. 128

Breithaupt v. Abram, 352 U. S. 432

Stefanelli v. Minard, 342 U. S. 117

Ker v. California, 374 U. S. 23 (1963)

Linkletter v. Walker, 381 U. S. 618

COURT'S POWER TO PASS ON CONSTITUTIONALITY OF LAWS

Marbury v. Madison, 1 Cranch 137; 2 L. Ed. 60 (1803)

In compliance with the Act of Congress of February 1801, an act revising the judicial system, a commission for William Marbury, as a justice of the peace for the county of Washington, D. C., was signed by John Adams, then President of the United States, after which the seal of the

United States was affixed to it, but the commission never reached Marbury. It was held back by James Madison, Secretary of State under Jefferson. Marbury, desirous of the commission, filed an affidavit on which basis a rule was granted requiring the Secretary of State, Madison, to show cause why a mandamus should not be issued, directing him to deliver to Marbury his commission.

OPINION BY MR. CHIEF JUSTICE MARSHALL
(No evidence from the report that the decision was not unanimous.)

Questions—1. Has the applicant a right to the commission he demands?

2. If that right has been violated, do the laws of the United States afford him a remedy?

3. Is this remedy a mandamus issuing from this Supreme Court?

Decisions—1. Yes.

2. Yes.

3. No.

Reasons—1. By signing the commission of Mr. Marbury, John Adams, President, appointed him a justice of the peace, and the seal of the United States affixed thereto by the Secretary of State was conclusive testimony of the legitimacy of the signature, and of the completion of the appointment. That appointment, under its terms, conferred on Marbury a legal right to the office for the space of five years. Thus, Marbury had a right to the commission he demanded.

2. In all cases, it is a general and indisputable rule, that where there is a legal right, there is also a legal remedy by suit, or action at law, whenever that right is invaded. Marbury had a legal right, as shown above, and this right was obviously violated by the refusal of Madison to deliver to him the commission. Thus a remedy under United States laws was due Marbury.

3. The Supreme Court of the United States had no power to issue a mandamus to the Secretary of State since this would have been an exercise of original jurisdiction not warranted by the Constitution. Congress had no power to give to the Supreme Court original jurisdiction in other cases than those described in the Constitution. The Constitution says that the Supreme Court will have appellate jurisdiction except

in the cases in which it has original jurisdiction. The original jurisdiction of the Supreme Court is specifically stated by the Constitution, and Congress cannot enlarge or decrease this jurisdiction. "The particular phraseology of the Constitution of the United States confirms and strengthens the principle, supposed to be essential to all written constitutions, that a law repugnant to the constitution is void, and that courts, as well as other departments, are bound by that instrument." (This case derives its extreme importance from the fact that this was the first time the Supreme Court declared an act of Congress unconstitutional.)

Corollary cases

United States v. Ravara, 2 Dallas 297

Hylton v. United States, 3 Dallas 171

Fletcher v. Peck, 6 Cranch 87

United States v. Butler, 297 U. S. 1

Massachusetts v. Mellon, 262 U. S. 447

Norton v. Shelby County, 118 U. S. 425

Eakin v. Raub, 12 Sergeant and Rawle (Pa. Sup. Ct.), 330

Marchetti v. United States (See page 348)

FREEDOM OF SPEECH AND PRESS WITH HANDBILLS

Martin v. City of Struthers, Ohio, 319 U. S. 141; 63 S. Ct. 862; 87 L. Ed. 1313 (1943)

An ordinance of the city of Struthers made it unlawful for any person distributing circulars or handbills from door to door to ring the doorbell, sound the knocker, or in any way to summon the inmate of the residence to the door. The appellant, Thelma Martin, challenged this ordinance as violating the right of freedom of the press, and religion as guaranteed by the First and Fourteenth Amendments.

OPINION BY MR. JUSTICE BLACK
(Vote: 6-3)

Question—Does the city possess the power so to legislate in the light of the constitutional guarantee of freedom of speech and press?

Decision—No.

Reason—The freedom of the First Amendment embraces the right to distribute literature, and protects the right to receive it. Here is a case in which the civil rights of an individual and the rights of the individual householder to determine his willingness to accept a message conflict with the ordinance of this city protecting the interests of all its citizens, whether they want that protection or not.

Freedom to distribute literature is clearly vital to the preservation of a free society. The city may set reasonable police and health regulations, but must leave the individual householder free to decide for himself whether he will receive or reject the stranger at his door. Stringent prohibition can serve no purpose but that forbidden by the Constitution, the naked restriction of the dissemination of ideas. "We conclude that the ordinance is invalid because in conflict with the freedom of speech and press."

Corollary cases

Lovell v. Griffin, 303 U. S. 444
Schneider v. State, 308 U. S. 147
Cantwell v. Connecticut, 310 U. S. 296

Marsh v. Alabama, 326 U. S. 501
Tucker v. Texas, 326 U. S. 517
Prince v. Massachusetts, 321 U. S. 158

FEDERAL JUDICIARY

Martin v. Hunter's Lessee, 1 Wheaton 304; 4 L. Ed. 97 (1816)

In the case of Fairfax's Devisee v. Hunter's Lessee, 7 Cranch 603, the Court reversed the decision of the state court and sustained title to certain Virginia land previously held by Lord Fairfax, a citizen and inhabitant of Virginia until his death in 1781. He devised the land to Denny Fairfax (previously Denny Martin), a native-born British subject who resided in England until his death. The Court held that Denny Fairfax, although an alien enemy, whose property might have been confiscated, was in complete possession of the land at the time of the commencement of the suit in 1791 and up to the treaty of 1794. It was said to be clear "that the treaty of 1794 completely protects and confirms the title of Denny Fairfax, even admitting that the treaty of peace left him wholly unprovided for." Denny Fairfax died while the suit was still pending, and the Supreme Court vested title in his heirs. Hunter's lessee claimed title under the Commonwealth of Virginia.

OPINION BY MR. JUSTICE STORY
(No evidence from the report that the decision was not unanimous.)

Question—Does the appellate power of the United States extend to cases pending in the state courts?

Decision—Yes.

Reason—Appellate jurisdiction has been given by the Constitution to this Court in all cases under the Constitution where it has no original jurisdiction, subject, however, to such regulations and exceptions as Congress may prescribe. State judges in their official capacities are called on to decide cases, not according to the laws and constitution of their own state, but according to "the supreme law of the land"—the Constitution, laws, and treaties of the United States. Yet to all these cases, the judicial power of this Court is to extend, according to the Constitution. It cannot extend by original jurisdiction, so it must extend to them by appellate jurisdiction, or not at all.

A final motive, for the appellate power over the state tribunals, is the importance and necessity of uniformity of decisions throughout the United States. Different interpretations would result, and the laws, treaties, and the Constitution of the United States would never have the same construction or efficiency in any two states. For such an evil, the only remedy is the appellate jurisdiction of this Court.

Corollary cases

New Orleans Waterworks Co. v. Louisiana Sugar Refining Co., 125 U. S. 18

Cohens v. Virginia, 6 Wheaton 264

Kendall v. United States, 12 Peters 524

Palmer Oil Corp. v. Amerada Corp., 342 U. S. 35

PRESIDENTIAL POWER

Martin v. Mott, 12 Wheaton 19; 6 L. Ed. 537 (1827)

In August 1814, the governor of the state of New York, in compliance with a request from the President of the United States, ordered certain companies of militia to assemble in the city of New York for the purpose of entering the service of the United States. The President acted in accordance with a federal statute empowering him to call the militia wherever there shall be danger of invasion. Mott, a private in one of the companies called, refused to comply with the order of the governor. In 1818 a court martial imposed on him a fine of $96, and when he refused to pay he was sentenced to twelve months imprisonment. Martin, Deputy United States Marshal, seized certain goods of Mott, which Mott sought to recover by action of replevin.

OPINION BY MR. JUSTICE STORY
(No evidence from the report that the decision was not unanimous.)

Question—Can the President under the law, call forth the militia of the states when no invasion has taken place?

Decision—Yes.

Reason—One of the best means to repel invasion is to provid the necessary forces before the enemy has reached the soil. Who shall judge whether a state of emergency has arisen, if not the President? If any officer or inferior soldier were permitted to decide for himself, where would the case end? The power invested in the President for the faithful execution of his responsibility constitutes him the best judge of the facts. "Whenever a statute gives a discretionary power to any person, to be exercised by him, upon his own opinion of certain facts, it is a sound rule of construction, that the statute constitutes him the sole and exclusive judge of the existence of those facts. . . . It is no answer, that such a power may be abused, for there is no power which is not susceptible of abuse."

Corollary cases

Houston v. Moore, 5 Wheaton 1
Luther v. Borden, 7 Howard 1
Meyer v. Peabody, 212 U. S. 78

Sterling v. Constantin, 287 U. S. 378

FREEDOM OF RELIGION AND TRESPASS

Marsh v. State of Alabama, 326 U. S. 501; 66 S. Ct. 276; 90 L. Ed. 265 (1946)

Grace Marsh, a member of Jehovah's Witnesses, was distributing religious literature on the street of a privately owned town that adjoined the municipality of Mobile, Alabama, known as Chickasaw, and owned by the Gulf Shipbuilding Corporation. She was warned that she could not distribute literature without a permit and she would not be issued a permit. She refused to obey and was arrested for violation of the Alabama Code, which makes it a crime to enter upon or remain on the premises of another after being warned not to do so.

OPINION BY MR. JUSTICE BLACK
(Vote: 5-3)

Question—Is the Alabama statute constitutional?

Decision—No.

Reason—The Court took the view that a state statute seeking to punish the distribution of religious literature clearly violates the First and Fourteenth Amendments to the Constitution. The Court reasoned that one may remain on private property against the will of the owner and contrary to the law of the state so long as the only objection to his presence is that he is exercising an asserted right to spread his religious views.

"When we balance the Constitutional rights of owners of property against those of the people to enjoy freedom of press and religion, as we must here, we remain mindful of the fact that the latter occupy a preferred position. As we have stated before, the right to exercise the liberties safeguarded by the First Amendment 'lies at the foundation of free government by free men' and we must in all cases 'weigh the circumstances and . . . appraise . . . reasons in support of the regulation . . . of the rights,' Schneider v. State, 308 U. S. 147. In our view the circumstances that the property rights to the premises where the deprivation of liberty, here involved, took place, were held by others than the public, is not sufficient to justify the state's permitting a corporation to govern a community of citizens so as to restrict their fundamental liberties and the enforcement of such restraint by the application of a state statute. In so far as the state has attempted to impose criminal punishment on appellant for undertaking to distribute religious literature in a company town, its action cannot stand."

Corollary cases

Martin v. Struthers, 319 U. S. 141
Tucker v. Texas, 326 U. S. 517
Prince v. Massachusetts, 321 U. S. 158

Cantwell v. Connecticut, 310 U. S. 296

CONGRESS AND THE COURTS

Ex parte McCardle, 7 Wallace 506; 19 L. Ed. 264 (1869)

The Constitution assigns appellate jurisdiction to the Supreme Court with "such exceptions, and under such regulations, as the Congress shall make." In February, 1867 Congress passed an act providing for the exercise by the Supreme Court of appellate jurisdiction in the matter of writs of habeas corpus in cases where persons were restrained in violation of the Constitution, or of any treaty or law of the United States. McCardle was held in custody by military authority for trial before a military commission for the publication of incendiary and libelous articles in a newspaper that he edited. Before the judges acted upon his appeal, the act providing for the appellate jurisdiction was repealed.

OPINION BY MR. CHIEF JUSTICE CHASE

(No evidence from the report that the decision was not unanimous.)

Question—Does the Court have appellate jurisdiction in a case after the act pertaining to such jurisdiction has been repealed?

Decision—No.

Reason—Appellate jurisdiction is granted the Court by the Constitution, but with exceptions and regulations by Congress. This does not imply that Congress grants appellate jurisdiction, but that it can make exceptions to that power. Therefore, the act of 1868 repealing the act of 1867 deprived the Court of jurisdiction in this case. The general rule followed was that when an act is repealed, it must be considered, except as to transactions past and closed, as if it never existed.

The Court then had no choice but to decline jurisdiction of this case. This does not imply that the entire appellate jurisdiction of this Court over cases of habeas corpus was denied, but only appeals from the Circuit Courts under the act of 1867.

Corollary cases

Durousseau v. United States, 6 Cranch 312

Norris v. Crocker, 13 Howard 429

Maryland v. Baltimore Radio Show, 338 U. S. 912

Ex parte Yerger, 8 Wallace 85

Massachusetts v. Mellon, 262 U. S. 447

De La Rama S. S. Co., Inc. v. United States, 344 U. S. 386.

FEDERAL TAXATION AND REGULATION

McCray v. United States, 195 U. S. 27; 24 S. Ct. 769; 49 L. Ed. 78 (1904)

McCray was sued by the United States for a statutory penalty of $50. He purchased for resale a fifty-pound package of oleomargarine artificially colored to look like butter, to which were affixed internal revenue stamps of one-fourth of a cent per pound, upon which the law required stamps at the rate of ten cents per pound. The excise McGray paid was that imposed upon oleomargarine free from artificial coloration.

OPINION BY MR. JUSTICE WHITE
(Vote: 6-3)

Question—Was the tax upon the colored oleomargarine one which was in conflict with the Constitution as an attempt to use the federal taxing power so as to regulate a matter reserved to the states?

Decision—No.

Reason—"Undoubtedly, in determining whether a particular act is within a granted power, its scope and effect are to be considered. Applying this rule to the acts assailed, it is self-evident that on their face they levy an excise tax. That being their necessary scope and operation, it follows that the acts are within the grant of power." Therefore, the Supreme Court refused to go behind the appearance of a revenue act and inquire into the motives of indirect regulation that might have inspired Congress.

Corollary cases

McCulloch v. Maryland, 4 Wheaton, 431

Veazie Bank v. Fenno, 8 Wallace 533

License Tax Cases, 5 Wallace 462

Sonzinsky v. United States, 300 U. S. 506

Bailey v. Drexel Furniture Co., 259 U. S. 20

Hill v. Wallace, 259 U. S. 44

Carter v. Carter Coal Co., 298 U. S. 238

United States v. Butler, 297 U. S. 1

Helvering v. Davis, 301 U. S. 619

United States v. Constantine, 296 U. S. 287

United States v. Doremus, 249 U. S. 86

Steward Machine Co. v. Davis, 301 U. S. 548

IMPLIED POWER AND FEDERAL-STATE RELATIONS

McCulloch v. Maryland, 4 Wheaton 316; 4 L. Ed. 579 (1819)

Congress incorporated the Bank of the United States, a branch of which was established in Baltimore. The State of Maryland required all banks not chartered by the state to pay a tax on each issuance of bank notes. McCulloch, the cashier of the Baltimore branch of the Bank of the United States, issued notes without complying with the state law. Action was brought on the part of Maryland to recover the penalties.

OPINION BY MR. CHIEF JUSTICE MARSHALL
(No evidence from the report that the decision was not unanimous.)

Questions—1. Has Congress power to incorporate a bank?

2. May the state of Maryland tax a branch of the United States Bank located in Maryland?

Decisions—1. Yes.

2. No.

Reasons—1. The Constitution empowers the government with the right to lay and collect taxes; to borrow money; to regulate commerce; to declare and conduct war; and to raise and support armies and navies. Congress has also been granted the power "to make all laws which shall be necessary and proper for carrying into execution" the expressed powers in the Constitution. Therefore, by incorporating a bank, Congress is creating the means to attain the goals of the powers intrusted to them.

2. The Court contended that the Constitution and the laws made in pursuance thereof are supreme and cannot be controlled by the various states. If the State of Maryland could regulate the laws of the federal government to its own convenience, then the Constitution and federal laws would soon lose their significance. "Let the end be legitimate, let it be within the scope of the Constitution, and all means which are appropriate, which are plainly adapted to that end, which are not prohibited, but consist with the letter and spirit of the Constitution, are constitutional." The Court stated that when Maryland taxed the operations of the federal government, it acted upon institutions created not by their own constituents, but by people over whom they claimed no control.

The power to tax involves the power to destroy. Such a tax could be used to destroy an institution vitally necessary to carry out the operations of the federal government, and therefore is unconstitutional and void.

Corollary cases

United States v. Fisher, 2 Cranch 358

Osborn v. The Bank of the United States, 9 Wheaton 738

Dobbins v. Commissioners of Erie County, 16 Peters 435

Collector v. Day, 11 Wallace 113

Graves v. People of State of New York ex rel. O'Keefe, 306 U. S. 466

Smith v. Kansas City Title & Trust Co., 255 U. S. 180

LOCAL TAXATION AND INTERSTATE COMMERCE

McGoldrick v. Berwind-White Coal Mining Co., 309 U. S. 33; 60 S. Ct. 388; 84 L. Ed. 565 (1940)

New York City had imposed a city sales tax, the revenues being used for unemployment relief. The state authorized this tax for a limited period and ruled that it should be restricted to the territorial limits of New York City. The Comptroller of New York City assessed the coal company (a Pennsylvania corporation) on sales of coal transported interstate to New York. All sales contracts were entered into in New York City where the company had an office.

OPINION BY MR. JUSTICE STONE
(Vote: 6-3)

Question—Does the New York City tax laid upon sales of goods for consumption infringe the commerce clause of the federal Constitution?

Decision—No.

Reason—The Court reasoned that a nondiscriminatory taxation of the instrumentalities of interstate commerce is not prohibited. In imposing taxes for state purposes a state is not exercising any power that the Constitution has conferred upon Congress. It is only when the tax operates to regulate commerce between the states or with foreign nations to an extent that infringes the authority conferred upon Congress, that the tax can be said to exceed constitutional limitations. The court said that it was not the purpose of the commerce clause to relieve those engaged in interstate commerce of their just share of state tax burdens, merely because an incidental or consequential effect of the tax was an increase in the cost of doing the business. The Court held that the New York City sales tax did not aim at or discriminate against interstate commerce. It was laid upon every purchaser, within the state, of goods for consumption, regardless of whether they had been transported in interstate commerce.

Corollary cases

Gibbons v. Ogden, 9 Wheaton 1

Western Live Stock v. Bureau of Revenue, 303 U. S. 250

Henneford v. Silas Mason Co., 300 U. S. 577

Graybar Electric Co. v. Curry, 308 U. S. 513

Woodruff v. Parham, 8 Wallace 123

Robbins v. Shelby County Taxing District, 120 U. S. 489

McLeod v. Dilworth Co., 322 U. S. 327

Nippert v. Richmond, 327 U. S. 416

Norton Co., v. Department of Revenue, 340 U. S. 534

Emert v. Missouri, 156 U. S. 296

Memphis Steam Laundry Cleaner v. Stone, 342 U. S. 389

Scripto, Inc. v. Carson, 362 U. S. 207

CONGRESSIONAL INVESTIGATIONS

McGrain v. Daugherty, 273 U. S. 135; 47 S. Ct. 319; 71 L. Ed. 580 (1927)

The Senate decided to investigate the activities and inactivities of Harry M. Daugherty, former Attorney General of the United States. In the investigations they subpoened Mally S. Daugherty, a brother of the former Attorney General, to appear before the committee that was conducting the hearings. He refused, and the Senate issued a warrant to compel him to appear and testify. The Senate sent McGrain, its deputy sergeant-at-arms, to arrest him. Daugherty applied for and received a writ of habeas corpus to discharge him from custody on the ground that the Senate exceeded its powers under the Constitution.

OPINION BY MR. JUSTICE VAN DEVANTER
(Vote: 8-0)

Question—May either the Senate or House of Representatives compel a private individual to appear before it or one of its committees and give testimony?

Decision—Yes.

Reason—The power to legislate carries with it by necessary implication information needed in the rightful exercise of that power and to employ compulsory process for that purpose. Although it was investigating the former Attorney General, and the resolution that brought the committee into existence had not in turn avowed that it was intended to be in aid of legislation, plainly the subject was such that the information received could be of valuable help in enacting further laws.

Corollary cases

Anderson v. Dunn, 6 Wheaton 204
In re Chapman, 266 U. S. 661
Marshall v. Gordon, 243 U. S. 521
Barry v. United States ex rel. Cunningham, 279 U. S. 597
United States v. Rumely, 345 U. S.

Sinclair v. United States, 279 U. S. 263
Kilbourn v. Thompson, 103, U. S. 168
United States v. Rumley, 345 U. S. 41

SEGREGATION AND EQUAL PROTECTION

McLaurin v. Oklahoma State Regents, 339 U. S. 637; 70 S. Ct. 851; 96 L. Ed. 1149 (1950)

Mr. G. W. McLaurin, a Negro, applied to the University of Oklahoma to pursue studies leading to a doctorate in education. His application was denied solely because of his race. McLaurin filed complaint, alleging that the action of the school authorities and the statutes upon which their action was based were unconstitutional and deprived him of equal protection of the laws. A three-judge District Court held that the state had a constitutional duty to provide him with the education he sought as soon as it had provided that education for applicants of any other group. It held void the Oklahoma statutes that denied him admission.

The Oklahoma legislature amended its laws to permit admission of Negroes to institutions of higher learning, provided such courses were not available in Negro schools. Such instruction, however, was to be given on a segregated basis. McLaurin was required to sit at a desk in an anteroom adjoining the classroom, to sit at a designated desk on the mezzanine floor of the library, not to use the desks in the regular reading room, and to eat at a different time in the school cafeteria. McLaurin filed a motion to have these conditions removed, which the lower court rejected, holding that the Fourteenth Amendment was not violated. McLaurin then appealed to the United States Supreme Court.

OPINION BY MR. CHIEF JUSTICE VINSON

(No evidence from the report that the decision was not unanimous.)

Question—Can a state, in its state university, after admitting a student to graduate instruction, afford him different treatment from the other students solely because of his race?

Decision—No.

Reason—It was argued that the separations imposed were merely nominal, in order to comply with the statutory laws of Oklahoma, but it was significant that the state set McLaurin apart from the other students, thus hindering his pursuit of effective graduate study. "There is a vast difference—a Constitutional difference—between restrictions imposed by the state which prohibit the intellectual commingling of students and the refusal of individuals to commingle where the state presents no such bar." The conditions under which this appellant was forced to study deprived him of his personal and present right to equal protection of the laws.

Corollary cases

Missouri ex rel. Gaines v. Canada, 305 U. S. 337

Sipuel v. Board of Regents, 332 U. S. 631

Shelley v. Kraemer, 334 U. S. 1

Sweatt v. Painter, 339 U. S. 629

THE PRESIDENT AND HABEAS CORPUS
Ex parte Merryman, 17 Fed. Cas. No. 9487 (1861)

The petitioner, a citizen of Baltimore, was arrested by a military officer acting on the authority of his commanding officer. The petitioner was accused of treason against the United States. The Chief Justice of the Supreme Court, while on Circuit Court duty, issued a writ of habeas corpus directing the commanding officer to deliver the prisoner, and this was refused on the grounds that the officer was authorized by the President to suspend the writ.

OPINION BY MR. CHIEF JUSTICE TANEY WHILE ON CIRCUIT COURT DUTY

Question—Can the President suspend the writ of habeas corpus?

Decision—No.

Reason—The Court held that the petitioner was entitled to be set free on the grounds that (1) the President, under the Constitution cannot suspend the privilege of the writ of habeas corpus. This can be done under the Constitution only by Congress, since the provision appears in the Article of the Constitution dealing with Congress, and in a list of limitations on Congress. (2) A military officer cannot arrest a person not subject to the rules and articles of war, except in the aid of civil authority when the individual has committed an offense against the United States. In such a case the military officer must deliver the prisoner immediately to civil authority, to be dealt with according to law.

Corollary cases

Ex parte Bollman and Swartwout, 4 Cranch 75

Ex parte Milligan, 4 Wallace 2

Mississippi v. Johnson, 4 Wallace 475

Ex parte McCardle, 7 Wallace 506

Ex parte Vallandigham, 1 Wallace 243

THE FOURTEENTH AMENDMENT AND EDUCATION

Meyer v. Nebraska, 262 U. S. 390; 43 S. Ct. 625; 67 L. Ed. 1042 (1923)

In 1919 Nebraska passed a statute that prohibited the teaching of any subject in any other language except English. Languages could be taught only after the child has successfully passed the eighth grade. Meyer taught in a parochial school, and used a German bible history as a text for reading. The teaching served a double-purpose, teaching the German language and religious instruction.

OPINION BY MR. JUSTICE MCREYNOLDS
(Vote: 7-2)

Question—Is the statute in question a violation of the "liberty" protected by the Fourteenth Amendment?

Decision—Yes.

Reason—The Court has never attempted to define, with exactness, the liberty guaranteed by the Fourteenth Amendment. Certainly education and the pursuit of knowledge should be encouraged. Mere knowledge of the German language cannot be looked upon as harmful. Meyer's right to teach, and the right of parents to hire him so to teach were within the liberty of this Amendment.

The statute also forbade the teaching below the eighth grade, of any other language except English. The State Supreme Court had ruled that "ancient or dead languages" did not come within the meaning of this statute. This evidently interfered with the modern language teachers, with the opportunities of children to acquire knowledge, and with the power of parents to control the education of their children.

The state may go very far to improve the quality of its citizens, but certain fundamental rights of the individual must be respected, since the protection of the Constitution also extends to those who speak a language other than English. There are advantages to a ready knowledge of ordinary speech, but "a desirable end cannot be promoted by prohibited means."

No emergency has arisen that would render knowledge of another language so harmful as to justify its prohibition. Nor is this prohibition justified as a protection for mental health, since it is well known that a foreign language is more easily acquired at an early age. The Court cannot but conclude that this statute is arbitrary and without a reasonable relation to any end within the competency of the state.

Corollary cases

Bartels v. Iowa, Bohning v. Ohio, 262 U. S. 404

Pierce v. Society of Sisters, 268 U. S. 510

Minersville School District v. Gobitis, 310 U. S. 586

West Virginia State Board of Education v. Barnette, 319 U. S. 624

Cochran v. Louisiana State Board of Education, 281 U. S. 370

Everson v. Board of Education of Ewing Township, 330 U. S. 1

People of Illinois ex rel. McCollum v. Board of Education, 333 U. S. 203

Zorach v. Clauson, 343 U. S. 307

CONSTITUTIONAL RIGHTS AND WAR

Ex parte Milligan, 4 Wallace 2, 18 L. Ed. 281 (1866)

Milligan, who was not and never had been in the military service of the United States, was tried, convicted, and sentenced to be hanged by a military commission established under Presidential authority. The sentence was approved by the President. In a proceeding for a writ of habeas corpus Milligan contended the commission had no jurisdiction over him and that he was not accorded a jury trial. The Circuit Court asked the Supreme Court for an opinion.

OPINION BY MR. JUSTICE DAVIS
(No evidence from the report that the decision was not unanimous.)

Question—Did the military tribunal have any legal power and authority to try and to punish this man?

Decision—No.

Reason—The court stated that every trial involves the exercise of judicial power. No part of the judicial power of the country was conferred on the military commission because the Constitution expressly vests it "in one supreme court and in such inferior courts as the Congress may from time to time ordain and establish." The military cannot justify action on the mandate of the President because he is controlled by law, and has his appropriate sphere of duty, which is to execute, not make, the laws. The Court stated that in times of grave emergencies the Constitution allows the government to make arrests without a writ of habeas corpus but it goes no further; that is, that the citizen might be tried otherwise than by the course of the common law. The court further stated that martial law can be applied only when there is real necessity, such as during an invasion that would effectually close the courts and civil administration. However, as long as the civil courts are operating, as they were in this case, then the accused is entitled to a civil trial by jury.

"The Constitution of the United States is a law for rulers and people, equally in war and in peace, and covers with the shield of its protection all classes of men, at all times, and under all circumstances. No doctrine involving more pernicious consequences, was ever invented by the wit of men than that any of its provisions can be suspended during any of the great exigencies of government."

Corollary cases

Ex parte Quirin, 317 U. S. 1

In re Yamashita, 327 U. S. 1

Duncan v. Kahanamoku, 327 U. S. 304

Korematsu, v. United States, 323 U. S. 214

Hirabayashi v. United States, 320 U. S. 81

Ex parte Endo, 323 U. S. 283

Ex parte Merryman, 17 Fed. Cas. No. 9487

United States ex rel. Toth v. Quarles, 350 U. S. 11

Wilson v. Girard, 354 U. S. 524

Kinsella v. United States ex rel. Singleton, 361 U. S. 234

Reid v. Covert, 354 U. S. 1

STATE TAXATION AND INTERSTATE COMMERCE

State of Minnesota v. Blasius, 290 U. S. 1; 54 S. Ct. 34; 78 L. Ed. 131 (1933)

Blasius, a resident of Minnesota, was in the business of buying cattle mainly from outside the state, and then reselling the cattle chiefly outside the state. One of these shipments he had purchased on the day that the state was taxing personal property, and the state taxed this shipment. Blasius contended that the cattle were in the process of interstate travel, that he had purchased them that day and they would be sold out of the state the next day.

OPINION BY MR. CHIEF JUSTICE HUGHES

(No evidence from the report that the decision was not unanimous.)

Question—Was the tax by Minnesota in conflict with the power of Congress to regulate interstate commerce?

Decision—No.

Reason—The states may not tax property in transit in interstate commerce. But by reason of a break in the transit, the property may come to rest within a state and become subject to the power of the state to impose a nondiscriminatory property tax. Such an exertion of state power belongs to that class of cases in which, by virtue of the nature and importance of local concerns, the state may act until Congress, if it has paramount authority over the subject, substitutes its own regulation. If the interstate movement has not begun, the mere fact that such a movement is contemplated does not withdraw the property from the state's power to tax it. Where property has come to rest within a state, being held there at the pleasure of the owner, for disposal or use, so that he may dispose of it either within the state, or for shipment elsewhere, as his interest dictates, it is deemed to be a part of the general mass of property within the state and is thus subject to its taxing power. In this case the original shipment was not suspended; it was ended. The shipment was to Blasius, who became absolute owner and was free to deal with them as he liked. He could sell the cattle for use within the state or for shipment outside the state. They were not in transit, therefore there was no federal right to immunity from the tax.

Corollary cases

Swift & Co. v. United States, 196 U. S. 375

Stafford v. Wallace, 258 U. S. 495

Carson Petroleum Co. v. Vial, 279 U. S. 95

Coe v. Errol, 116 U. S. 517

Kelley v. Rhoads, 188 U. S. 1

Brown v. Houston, 114 U. S. 622

Bacon v. Illinois, 227 U. S. 504

Joy Oil Co. v. State Tax Commission of Michigan, 337 U. S. 286

Sonneborn Bros. v. Cureton, 262 U. S. 506

INTERSTATE COMMERCE CONTROL

Minnesota Rate Cases (Simpson v. Shepard) 230 U. S. 352; 33 S. Ct. 729; 57 L. Ed. 1511 (1913)

These suits were brought by the stockholders of the Northern Pacific Railway Company, and the Minneapolis & St. Louis Railroad, respectively, to restrain the enforcement of two orders of the Railroad and Warehouse Commission of the State of Minnesota, and two acts of the legislature of that state. The Minnesota legislature had established maximum rates for railroads in the state and sought to enforce them on both intrastate and interstate carriers while operating within the state. It was contended that the existence of federal interstate regulation was a bar to statewide intrastate regulation even though the state rates were reasonable.

OPINION BY MR. JUSTICE HUGHES
(No evidence from the report that the decision was not unanimous.)

Question—May the federal government exercise supreme control over interstate operations when they are intermingled with interstate operations?

Decision—Yes, but here state action held valid.

Reason—There is no room in our scheme of government for the assertion of state power in hostility to the authorized exercise of federal power. The authority of Congress extends to every part of interstate commerce and to every instrumentality or agency by which it is carried on; and the full control by Congress of the subjects committed to its regulation is not to be denied or thwarted by the commingling of interstate and intrastate operations. This is not to say that the nation may deal with the internal concerns of the state as such, but that the execution by Congress of its constitutional power to regulate interstate commerce is not limited by the fact that intrastate transactions may have become so interwoven therewith that the effective government of the former incidentally controls the latter. This conclusion necessarily results from the supremacy of the national power within its appointed sphere.

Of course, state rates cannot be confiscatory. "If this authority of the State be restricted, it must be by virtue of the paramount power of Congress over interstate commerce and its instruments, and, in view of the nature of the subject, a limitation may not be implied because of a dormant Federal power, that is, one which has not been exerted, but can only be found in the actual exercise of Federal control in such measure as to exclude this action by the State. . . . It is the function of this court to interpret and apply the law already enacted, but not under the guise of construction to provide a more comprehensive scheme of regulation than Congress has decided upon. Nor, in the absence of Federal action, may we deny effect to the laws of the State enacted within the field which it is entitled to occupy until its authority is limited through the exertion by Congress of its paramount constitutional power."

Corollary cases

McCulloch v. Maryland, 4 Wheaton 316
The Daniel Ball, 10 Wallace 557
Smith v. Alabama, 124 U. S. 465
Driscoll v. Edison Light and Power Co., 307 U. S. 104
Smyth v. Ames, 169 U. S. 466
Houston E. & W. Texas Ry. Co., v.

United States, 234 U. S. 342
Stone v. Farmers' Loan and Trust Co., 116 U. S. 307
Willcox v. Consolidated Gas Co., 212 U. S. 19
Cooley v. Board of Wardens, 12 Howard 299

SUFFRAGE FOR WOMEN

Minor v. Happersett, 21 Wallace 162; 22 L. Ed. 627 (1875)

This was an action in the Circuit Court of St. Louis County, Missouri, by Mrs. Virginia Minor against Happersett, a registering officer, for refusing to register her as a lawful voter. Mrs. Minor, held that the constitution of Missouri which stated that "every male citizen of the United States, . . . shall be entitled to vote" was in conflict with the Fourteenth Amendment.

OPINION BY MR. CHIEF JUSTICE WAITE

(No evidence from the report that the decision was not unanimous.)

Question—Is the right of suffrage one of the privileges and immunities which the states cannot abridge?

Decision—No.

Reason—The Constitution does not define privileges and immunities of citizens. In this case no definition is needed, but only the determination whether suffrage is necessarily among them. The Constitution nowhere adds the right of suffrage to the privileges and immunities of citizenship, so it is proper to inquire whether suffrage was coextensive with citizenship at the time of its adoption. An examination of the state constitutions of the time discloses that each state determined for itself who should have the right to vote, prescribing various qualifications. It is clearly evident that all the citizens were not invested with the right of suffrage, and in all the states, with the exception, perhaps, of New Jersey, this right was bestowed only on men and not even upon all of them. "Certainly, if the courts can consider any question settled, this is one. For nearly ninety years the people have acted upon the idea that the Constitution, when it conferred citizenship, did not necessarily confer the right of suffrage. If uniform practice long continued can settle the construction of so important an instrument as the Constitution of the United States confessedly is, most certainly it has been done here. Our province is to decide what the law is, not to declare what it should be."

Therefore the Constitution did not confer the right of suffrage upon anyone, and the statutes of the states bestowing suffrage on man only were not unconstitutional. (The 19th

Amendment, of course, has offset the practical effect of this case.)

Corollary cases

United States v. Wong Kim Ark, 169, U. S. 649

Ex parte Yarbrough, 110 U. S. 651

United States v. Classic, 313 U. S. 299

Smith v. Allwright, 321 U. S. 649

Slaughter-House Cases, 16 Wallace 36

Crandall v. Nevada, 6 Wallace 35

COERCED CONFESSION

Miranda v. Arizona, 384 U. S. 436; 86 S. Ct. 1602; 16 L. Ed. 2d 694 (1966)

Here four cases were decided by one opinion. They came from Arizona, New York, California, and the federal courts. In each of the cases the law enforcement officials had taken the defendant into custody and had interrogated him for the purpose of obtaining a confession. At no time did the police effectively advise a defendant of his right to remain silent or of his right to consult with his attorney. In the lead case, Ernesto Miranda had been arrested at his home and then taken to a Phoenix police station where he was questioned by two police officers. After two hours he made a written confession. He was subsequently convicted of kidnapping and rape. In the New York case the charge was first degree robbery, in the California case it was robbery and first degree murder, and in the federal case robbery of a savings and loan association and a bank in California.

OPINION BY MR. CHIEF JUSTICE WARREN
(Vote: 5-4)

Question—Are statements obtained from an individual subjected to custodial police interrogation under these circumstances admissible as evidence?

Decision—No.

Reason—An individual held for interrogation must be clearly informed that he has the right to consult counsel and to have his lawyer with him during interrogation. Financial inability of an accused person to furnish counsel is no excuse for the absence of counsel since in such an instance a lawyer must be appointed to represent the accused. If he answers some questions and gives some information on his own prior to invoking his right to remain silent this is not to warrant an assumption that the privilege has been waived. The Court noted that "the prosecution may not use statements, whether exculpatory or inculpatory, stemming from custodial interrogation of the defendant unless it demonstrates the use of procedural safeguards effective to secure the privilege against self-incrimination. By custodial interrogation, we mean questioning initiated by law enforcement officers after a person has been taken into custody or otherwise deprived of his freedom of action in any significant way."

Corollary cases

Escobedo v. Illinois, 378 U. S. 478

Johnson v. New Jersey, 384 U. S. 719

Davis v. North Carolina, 384 U. S. 737

Gideon v. Wainwright, 372 U. S. 335

Betts v. Brady, 316 U. S. 455

Mallory v. United States, 354 U. S. 449

Schmerber v. California, 384 U. S. 757

Chambers v. Florida, 309 U. S. 227

McNabb v. United States, 318 U. S. 332

Twining v. New Jersey, 211 U. S. 78

Jackson v. Denno, 378 U. S. 368

FEDERAL COURT JURISDICTION

Mississippi v. Johnson, 4 Wallace 475; 18 L. Ed. 437 (1867)

This case involved a bill in equity by which the State of Mississippi sought to enjoin President Johnson and the general in command of the military district of Mississippi and Arkansas from enforcing the Reconstruction Acts of 1867.

OPINION BY MR. CHIEF JUSTICE CHASE

(No evidence from the report that the decision was not unanimous.)

Question—Can the President be restrained by injunction from carrying into effect an Act of Congress?

Decision—No.

Reason—The Congress is the legislative department of the government. The President is the executive department. Neither can be restrained in its action by the judicial department, though the acts of both, when performed are, in proper cases, subject to its cognizance. The impropriety of such interference, the Court held, could be clearly seen upon consideration of its possible consequences. If the injunction were granted, the Court would have no power to enforce it. If the President did not enforce the bill according to the wishes of this Court, he would be subject to impeachment by the Congress and the Court could not stop the proceedings. "It is true that a state may file an original bill in this Court. And it may be true, in some cases, that such a bill may be filed against the United States. But we are fully satisfied that this Court has no jurisdiction of a bill to enjoin the President in the performance of his official duties, and that no such bill ought to be received by us."

Corollary cases

Georgia v. Stanton, 6 Wallace 50
Marbury v. Madison, 1 Cranch 137
Kendall v. United States, 12 Peters 524

Little v. Barreme, 2 Cranch 170
Kentucky v. Dennison, 24 Howard 66

EDUCATION AND EQUAL PROTECTION OF THE LAWS

Missouri ex rel. Gaines v. Canada, 305 U. S. 337; 59 S. Ct. 232; 83 L. Ed. 208 (1938)

Lloyd Gaines, a Negro, was refused admittance to the Law School of the University of Missouri on the ground that he was colored. He had completed his undergraduate training at Lincoln University, an all-Negro school. It had been the practice of the state of Missouri to separate the white students from the colored students all through the school system, but as yet the state had not added a law school to the course of study at Lincoln University. If a Negro student wanted to go to law school, the state would pay his tuition in an out-of-state school that accepted Negroes.

OPINION BY MR. JUSTICE ROBERTS
(Vote: 7-2)

Question—Was the equal protection guarantee of the Fourteenth Amendment violated by this practice?

Decision—Yes.

Reason—The actions of the curators of the University must be considered equivalent to the official actions of the state itself.

State policy is that Negroes attend Lincoln University while whites attend the University of Missouri. Meanwhile Negroes are granted the opportunity of studying, tuition paid, at any nearby state university pending the full development of Lincoln University to the level of the University of Missouri. While such an arrangement is praiseworthy, the fact that Lincoln University actually does not have a law school at present is a deprivation of equal privileges, since Gaines is denied this advantage extended to white students. The advantages of an alternate program allowing study in a nearby state and the relative excellence of that program with that offered by Missouri are beside the point since the whole consideration is whether or not Missouri had given equal privileges to both white and colored students within the state. This has not been done; therefore the state statute violates the Fourteenth Amendment by discrimination.

It was as an individual that he was entitled to the equal protection of the laws, and the state was bound to furnish him within its borders facilities for a legal education substantially equal to those that the state afforded for persons of the white race, even though he was the only Negro who wanted to study there.

Corollary cases

Yick Wo v. Hopkins, 118 U. S. 356

McCabe v. Atchison, Topeka, and Santa Fe R.R., 235 U. S. 151

Sipuel v. Regents of University of Oklahoma, 332 U. S. 631

Fisher v. Hurst, 333 U. S. 147

Berea College v. Kentucky, 211 U. S. 45

Cumming v. County Board of Education, 175 U. S. 528

Gong Lum v. Rice, 275 U. S. 78

McLaurin v. Oklahoma State Regents, 339 U. S. 637

Sweatt v. Painter, 339 U. S. 629

SCOPE OF THE TREATY-MAKING POWER

Missouri v. Holland, 252 U. S. 416; 40 S. Ct. 382; 64 L. Ed. 641 (1920)

The United States entered into a treaty with Great Britain for the protection of migratory birds. In the treaty was a provision that each of the contracting powers undertake to pass laws that would forbid the killing, capturing, or selling of the birds except in accordance with certain regulations. Congress enacted legislation and Missouri brought suit, saying its reserved powers under the Tenth Amendment were violated by the act and treaty.

OPINION BY MR. JUSTICE HOLMES
(Vote: 7-2)

Question—Do the treaty and statute interfere invalidly with the rights reserved to the states by the Tenth Amendment?

Decision—No.

Reason—Acts of Congress must be made in pursuance of the Constitution, but treaties are valid when made under the authority of the United States. "We do not mean to imply that there are no qualifications to the treaty-making power; but they must be ascertained in a different way. It is obvious that there may be matters of the sharpest exigency for the national well-being that an act of Congress could not deal with but that a treaty followed by such an act could, and it is not lightly to be assumed that, in matters requiring national action, 'a power which must belong to and somewhere reside in every civilized government' is not to be found. . . . Here a national interest of very nearly the first magnitude is involved. It can be protected only by national action in concert with that of another power. The subject matter is only transitorily within the state and has no permanent habitat therein.

"If the treaty is valid there can be no dispute about the validity of the statute under Article I, Section 8, as a necessary and proper means to execute the powers of the government."

Corollary cases

Nielson v. Johnson, 279 U. S. 47

Hauenstein v. Lynham, 100 U. S. 483

De Geofrey v. Riggs, 133 U. S. 258

United States v. Belmont, 301 U. S. 324

United States v. Pink, 315 U. S. 203

THE SUABILITY OF A STATE

Monaco v. Mississippi, 292 U. S. 313; 54 S. Ct. 745; 78 L. Ed. 1282 (1934)

The Principality of Monaco asked leave to bring suit in the Supreme Court against the State of Mississippi over the nonpayment of bonds issued by the state, and alleged to be absolute property of the Principality. The bonds were issued in 1833, were due in 1861 and 1866, issued in 1838 and due in 1850, issued in 1838 and due in 1858. They were handed down in a family of the state, but since private citizens cannot sue a state they were given to Monaco to use for the betterment of their country, on the theory that, since Monaco was a foreign country, it would be able to sue the state.

OPINION BY MR. CHIEF JUSTICE HUGHES
(No evidence from the report that the decision was not unanimous.)

Question—Can the State of Mississippi be sued by the Principality of Monaco without that state's consent?

Decision—No.

Reason—The Court ruled that the states of the Union retain the same immunity to suits by a foreign state that they enjoy with respect to suits by individuals whether citizens of the United States or subjects of a foreign power. The foreign state enjoys a similar immunity and without her consent cannot be sued by a state of the Union. The principle of the Eleventh Amendment applies to suits against a state by a foreign state.

Corollary cases

Williams v. United States, 289 U. S. 553

Hans v. Louisiana, 134 U. S. 1

South Carolina v. Georgia, 93 U. S. 4

South Dakota v. North Carolina, 192 U. S. 286

New Hampshire v. Louisiana, 108 U. S. 76

North Dakota v. Minnesota, 263 U. S. 365

Chisholm v. Georgia, 2 Dallas 419

MINIMUM WAGE LAWS AND DUE PROCESS

Morehead v. New York ex rel. Tipaldo, 298 U. S. 587; 56 S. Ct. 918; 80 L. Ed. 1347 (1936)

Tipaldo was sent to jail upon the charge that, as manager of a laundry, he failed to obey the mandatory order of the state industrial commissioner of New York, prescribing minimum wages for women employees. Some of the employees were receiving less than the minimum wages established by the state Industrial Commissioner operating under the state minimum wage law.

OPINION BY MR. JUSTICE BUTLER
(Vote: 5-4)

Question—Can a state fix minimum wages for women?

Decision—No.

Reason—It was claimed that this case differed from the Adkins case in which such legislation was declared unconstitutional, in that here the minimum wage was prescribed in cases where the given wage was less than the fair and reasonable value of the services rendered and insufficient to meet the minimum cost of living necessary for health. However, this did not change the principle of the case, namely, the exercise of legislative power to fix wages. The act left employers and men employees free to agree upon wages, but deprived employers and adult women of the same freedom. Likewise, women were restrained by the minimum wage in competition with men and were arbitrarily deprived of employment and a fair chance to find work. State legislation fixing wages for women is repugnant to the due process clause of the Fourteenth Amendment.

Corollary cases

Adkins v. Children's Hospital, 261 U. S. 525

West Coast Hotel Co., v. Parrish, 300 U. S. 379

Stettler v. O'Hara, 243 U. S. 629

Muller v. Oregon, 208 U. S. 412

Bunting v. Oregon, 243 U. S. 426

McLean v. Arkansas, 211 U. S. 539

INTERSTATE COMMERCE AND SEGREGATION

Morgan v. Commonwealth of Virginia, 328 U. S. 373; 66 S. Ct. 1050, 90 L. Ed. 1317 (1946)

This case involved a bus trip from Virginia, through the District of Columbia, to Baltimore. A state statute of Virginia required the assigning of separate seats or other space to white and colored persons, respectively. In this case the appellant, a Negro, was traveling on this bus. Upon her refusal to give up her seat to a white passenger and move to the rear of the bus, she was arrested, tried, and convicted under the Virginia statute.

OPINION BY MR. JUSTICE REED
(Vote: 7-1)

Question—Is the Virginia statute constitutional?

Decision—No.

Reason—As there was no federal act dealing with the separation of races in interstate transportation, the Court reasoned that they must decide the validity of this Virginia statute on the challenge that it interfered with commerce, as a matter of balance between the exercise of the local police power and the need for national uniformity in the regulations for interstate travel. It seemed clear to the Court that seating arrangements for the different races in interstate motor travel required a single, uniform rule to promote and protect national travel. Consequently, the Court held the Virginia statute in controversy invalid.

Corollary cases

Hatch v. Reardon, 204 U. S. 152
Federation of Labor v. McAdory, 325 U. S. 450
Hall v. DeCuir, 95 U. S. 485

Bob-Lo Excursion Co., v. Michigan, 333 U. S. 28
Plessy v. Ferguson, 163 U. S. 537
McCabe v. Atchison, Topeka and Sante Fe Ry. Co., 235 U. S. 151

INTERSTATE COMMERCE AND AGRICULTURE

Mulford v. Smith, 307 U. S. 38; 59 S. Ct. 648; 83 L. Ed. 1092 (1939)

The Agriculture Act of 1938, based upon the commerce power of the Constitution, regulated the marketing of various farm products. Congress set detailed limits in the Act and left it to the Secretary of Agriculture to put the Act into effect. The purpose of the Act was "to regulate interstate and foreign commerce in cotton, wheat, corn, tobacco, and rice to the extent necessary to provide an orderly, adequate, and balanced flow of such commodities in interstate and foreign commerce through storage of reserve supplies, loans, marketing, quotas, assisting farmers to obtain, in so far as practicable, parity prices for such commodities and parity of income, and assisting consumers to obtain an adequate and steady supply of such commodities at fair prices." The appellants brought suit under the portion of the Act dealing with marketing quotas for flue-cured tobacco.

OPINION BY MR. JUSTICE ROBERTS
(Vote: 7-2)

Questions—1. Is the act beyond the powers delegated to Congress?

2. Does it result in an unconstitutional delegation of legislative power to the Secretary of Agriculture?

3. Does it deprive farmers of their property without due process of law?

Decisions—1. No.

2. No.

3. No.

Reasons—1. The tobacco produced was for interstate commerce. The law did not limit the amount of the crop grown, but limited only what might be sold. It was a regulation of commerce granted to Congress in the Constitution. "The motive of Congress in exerting the power is irrelevant to the validity of the legislation."

2. There was no improper delegation of legislative power since definite standards were set down in the Act in both the fixing of quotas and in their allotment amongst states and farms.

3. The act dealt only with the marketing and not with the growing of crops. The farmers could hold over their tobacco until a later year if they saw fit.

Corollary cases

Wickard v. Filburn, 317 U. S. 111

United States v. Butler, 297 U. S. 1

United States v. Darby, 312 U. S. 100

United States v. Rock Royal Cooperative, 307 U. S. 533

Hood and Sons v. United States, 307 U. S. 588

Currin v. Wallace, 306 U. S. 1

Kentucky Whip and Collar Co., v. Illinois Central R.R. Co., 299 U.S. 334

WOMEN AND HOUR LEGISLATION

Muller v. Oregon, 208 U. S. 412; 28 S. Ct. 324; 52 L. Ed. 551 (1908)

An Oregon statute made illegal the employment of women in any mechanical establishment, factory, or laundry for more than ten hours during the day. Miller was convicted and fined for violating this statute in his laundry.

OPINION BY MR. JUSTICE BREWER

(No evidence from the report that the decision was not unanimous.)

Question—Is the Oregon statute constitutional?

Decision—Yes.

Reason—In Lochner v. New York the Court held that a law prohibiting a man from working more than ten hours a day was an unreasonable and arbitrary interference with his liberty to contract in relation to labor. A woman's physical well-being "becomes an object of public interest and care in order to preserve the strength and vigor of the race" and thus justifies the "special legislation restricting or qualifying the conditions under which she should be permitted to toil." The two sexes differ. This difference justifies a difference in legislation.

Corollary cases

Lochner v. New York, 198 U. S. 45

Bunting v. Oregon, 243 Wallace 426

West Coast Hotel Co. v. Parrish, 300 U. S. 379

Morehead v. New York ex rel. Tipaldo, 298 U. S. 587

Adkins v. Children's Hospital, 261 U. S. 525

Holden v. Hardy, 169 U. S. 366

PRICE FIXING BY STATES

Munn v. Illinois, 94 U. S. 113; 24 L. Ed. 77 (1877)

Ira Y. Munn, *et al.*, were grain warehousemen in Chicago, Illinois, and were sued by Illinois for transacting business without a state license in violation of a state statute that provided a maximum of charges for the storage of grain in a warehouse. The defendants admitted the facts charged, but alleged that the statute requiring said license was unconstitutional for attempting to fix that maximum rate of storage, on the ground that it was repugnant to the Constitution, which confers upon Congress the power to regulate commerce with foreign states and among the several states.

OPINION BY MR. CHIEF JUSTICE WAITE
(Vote: 7-2)

Question—Can the General Assembly of Illinois, under the limitations upon the legislative powers of the states imposed by the Constitution, fix by law regulations for the storage of grain in warehouses at Chicago and other places in the state?

Decision—Yes.

Reason—The Court reasoned that it has always been an established principle that where the public has a definite and positive interest in a business, they have a right to regulate the operations of that business. The Court held that such was the case here, and it did not matter that these plaintiffs had built their warehouses and established their business before the regulations complained of were adopted. What they did was from the beginning always subject to possible regulations promoting the common good. They entered upon their business and provided themselves with the means to carry it on, subject to this condition. If they did not wish to submit themselves to such interference, they should not have clothed the public with an interest in their concerns. "Property does become clothed with a public interest when used in a manner to make it of public consequence, and affect the community at large. When, therefore, one devotes his property to a use in which the public has an interest, he, in effect, grants to the public an interest in the use, and must submit to be controlled by the public for the common good, to the extent of the interest he has thus created. He may withdraw his grant by discontinuing the use; but so long as he maintains the use, he must submit to the control. We know that this is a power which may be abused; but that is no argument against its existence. For protection against abuses by legislatures the people must resort to the polls, not to the courts."

Corollary cases

Brown v. Maryland, 12 Wheaton 448

Gibbons v. Ogden, 9 Wheaton 232

Osborne v. Mobile, 16 Wallace 481

Nebbia v. People of State of New York, 291 U. S. 502

Olsen v. State of Nebraska, 313 U. S. 236

Cooley v. Board of Wardens of the Port of Philadelphia, 12 Howard 299

Brass v. North Dakota, 153 U. S. 391

FREEDOM OF RELIGION AND JEHOVAH'S WITNESSES

Murdock v. Commonwealth of Pennsylvania, 319 U. S. 105; 63 S. Ct. 870; 87 L. Ed. 1292 (1943)

The City of Jeannette, Pennsylvania, had an ordinance for forty years requiring that all persons soliciting get a license from the Treasurer of the Borough before doing so. The petitioners were Jehovah's Witnesses, who were arrested for asking people to purchase certain religious books, as they distributed literature.

OPINION BY MR. JUSTICE DOUGLAS
(Vote: 5-4)

Question—Is this an abridgement of the freedom of religion?

Decision—Yes.

Reason—It would hardly be denied that a tax laid specifically on the freedom of the First Amendment would be unconstitutional. Yet the license tax in this case was just that in substance. The custom of hand-distribution of religious literature is an old one and has the same claim to protection as other conventional exercises of religion. In this case payment of the license tax is a condition for pursuing their religious activities.

"The fact that the ordinance is 'nondiscriminatory' is immaterial. The protection afforded by the First Amendment is not so restricted. A license tax certainly does not acquire constitutional validity because it classifies the privileges protected by the First Amendment along with the wares and merchandise of hucksters and peddlers and treats them all alike. Such equality in treatment does not save the ordinance. Freedom of press, freedom of speech, freedom of religion are in a preferred position. . . .

"Jehovah's Witnesses are not 'above the law.' But the present ordinance is not directed to the problems with which the police power of the state is free to deal. It does not cover, and petitioners are not charged with, breaches of the peace. They are pursuing their solicitations peacefully and quietly. . . ."

Corollary cases

Jones v. Opelika, 316 U. S. 584

Jamison v. Texas, 318 U. S. 413

Douglas v. City of Jeannette, 319 U. S. 157

Cox v. New Hampshire, 312 U. S. 564

Chaplinsky v. New Hampshire, 315 U. S. 568

Martin v. Struthers, 319 U. S. 141

Follett v. Town of McCormick, 321 U. S. 573

Marsh v. Alabama, 326 U. S. 501

Tucker v. Texas, 326 U. S. 517

Prince v. Massachusetts, 321 U. S. 158

Cantwell v. Connecticut, 310 U. S. 296

Lovell v. Griffin, 303 U. S. 444

Minersville School District v. Gobitis, 310 U. S. 586

West Virginia State Board of Education v. Barnette, 319 U. S. 624

Largent v. Texas, 318 U. S. 418

Niemotko v. Maryland, 340 U. S. 268

Breard v. Alexandria, 341 U. S. 622

Bunger v. Green River, 300 U. S. 638

FEDERAL JUDICIAL POWER AND ADVISORY OPINIONS

Muskrat v. United States, 219 U. S. 346; 31 S. Ct. 250; 55 L. Ed. 246 (1911)

> An Act of Congress authorized Muskrat and others to bring suit in the federal Court of Claims, with an appeal to the federal Supreme Court to determine the validity of certain acts of Congress which altered terms of certain prior allotments of Cherokee Indian lands.

OPINION BY MR. JUSTICE DAY
(No evidence from the report that the decision was not unanimous.)

Question—Is the Supreme Court able to judge the validity of an Act of Congress as an abstract question rather than as an actual controversy or case?

Decision—No.

Reason—This is an attempt by Congress to have the Court pass upon the validity of laws before they are properly brought to the Court. Federal judicial power extends only to "cases" and "controversies," defined by Marshall as suits "instituted according to the regular course of judicial procedure." This matter is not presented in such a "case" or "controversy." "The whole purpose of the law is to determine the constitutional validity of this class of legislation, in a suit not arising between parties concerning a property right necessarily involved in the decision in question, but in a proceeding against the government in its sovereign capacity, and concerning which the only judgment required is to settle the doubtful character of the legislation in question. . . . If such actions as are here attempted, to determine the validity of legislation, are sustained, the result will be that this court, instead of keeping within limits of judicial power, and deciding cases or controversies arising between opposing parties, as the Constitution intended it should, will be required to give opinions in the nature of advice concerning legislative action,— a function never conferred upon it by the Constitution."

Corollary cases

Marbury v. Madison, 1 Cranch, 137

Alabama State Federation of Labor v. McAdory, 325 U. S. 450

United States v. Ferreira, 13 Howard 40

Altvater v. Freeman, 319 U. S. 359

United States v. Evans, 213 U. S.
297

Aetna Life Insurance Co., v. Haworth, 300 U. S. 227

Nashville, C. and St. L. Ry. v. Wallace, 288 U. S. 249

THE PRESIDENT'S REMOVAL POWER

Myers v. United States, 272 U. S. 52; 47 S. Ct. 21; 71 L. Ed. 160 (1926)

As a result of the President having exercised complete power of removal of officials from appointed offices, Congress passed the Tenure of Office Act which sought to prevent the removal of any official for whose appointment the concurrence of the Senate was required, without in turn obtaining Senatorial approval for his dismissal. This formula was subsequently re-enacted in a statute of 1876 pertaining to postmasters of the first three classes, concurrence of the Senate being stipulated as necessary for removal as well as appointment. In 1920, Myers, the postmaster of Portland, Oregon, was removed by President Wilson, without the consent of the Senate being obtained or even requested. Myers claimed that, under the terms of the 1876 statute, his removal was unlawful and sued for salary due him.

OPINION BY MR. CHIEF JUSTICE TAFT
(Vote: 6-3)

Question—May Congress limit the President's removal power?

Decision—No.

Reason—Section 6 of the Act of July 12, 1876, under which Myers was appointed provided that: "Postmasters of the first, second and third classes shall be appointed and may be removed by the President by and with the consent of the Senate, and shall hold their offices for four years unless sooner removed or suspended according to law." The Court referred to Madison's opinion given in the House of Representatives during the First Congress on Tuesday, May 18, 1789. The vesting of the executive power in the President was essentially a grant of the power to execute the laws. But the President alone and unaided can not execute the laws. He must execute them by the assistance of subordinates. This view has since been repeatedly affirmed by the Court. The further implication must be, in the absence of any express limitation respecting removals, that as the President's selection of administrative officers is essential to the execution of the laws by him, so is his power of removing those for whom he cannot continue to be responsible. The power to prevent the removal of an officer who has served under the President is different from the authority to consent to or reject his appointment. When a nomination is made, it may be presumed that the Senate is, or may become, as well advised as to the fitness of the nominee as the President, but in the nature of things defects in ability or intelligence or loyalty in the administration of the laws of one who has served under the President are facts as to which the President or his trusted subordinates must be better informed than the Senate, and the power to remove him may therefore be regarded as confined, for very sound practical reasons, to the governmental authority that has administrative control. The power of removal is incident to the power of appointment, not to the power of advising and consenting to appointment, and when the grant of the executive power is enforced, by the express mandate to take care that the laws be faithfully executed, it emphasizes the necessity for including within the executive power as conferred the exclusive power of removal. Such an opinion was held by all branches of the government for more than 74 years (1789-1863). The Court concluded that, for the reasons given, it must therefore hold that the provision of the law of 1876 by which the unrestricted power of removal of first-class postmasters was denied to the President was in violation of the Constitution and invalid.

Corollary cases

United States ex rel. Arant v. Lane, 249 U. S. 367

Nicholas v. United States, 257 U. S. 71

Kendall v. United States, 12 Peters 524

Kilbourn v. Thompson, 103 U. S. 168

Wilcox v. Jackson, 13 Peters 498

Rathbun v. United States, 295 U. S. 602

Morgan v. United States, 312 U. S. 701

Shurtleff v. United States, 189 U. S. 311

EMPLOYER-EMPLOYEE RELATIONS AND SIT-DOWN STRIKES

National Labor Relations Board v. Fansteel Metallurgical Corp., 306 U. S. 240; 59 S. Ct. 230; 83 L. Ed. 373 (1939)

The Fansteel Metallurgical Corp. of North Chicago, Illinois, was engaged in the manufacture and sale of products made of rare metal. On several occasions its employees attempted to organize labor unions within this plant. The company would not, however, recognize the "closed unions" and insisted on having a "company union" for its employees. This, however, proved abortive with the employees. When the employees did organize a union the company refused to deal with it because it was an "outside union." In a sit-down strike that resulted shortly thereafter many of the employees were fired. After the strike was broken and business was once more resumed, some but not all of the strikers were rehired. Next the employees organized again and the union was known this time as Local No. 1 of the Rare Metal Workers of America. This time, the National Labor Relations Board issued an order to the Fansteel Corp. to reinstate to their former positions with full back pay all fired employees who went on strike. The order also required Fansteel to desist from interfering with its employees in the exercise of their right to self-organization, and to bargain collectively through representatives of their own choosing. The corporation was also to desist from dominating or interfering with the formation or administration of the R.M.W.A., Local 1, because to do so was to violate the National Labor Relations Act. Then Fansteel took the case to the Circuit Court of Appeals to have the order of the Board set aside. When the Court did set aside the order, the Board, on certiorari, took the issue to the Supreme Court.

OPINION BY MR. CHIEF JUSTICE HUGHES
(Vote: 6-2)

Question—Can the National Labor Relations Board require a company to reinstate an employee who was discharged because of unlawful conduct in seizing a company's property in what was called a sit-down strike?

Decision—No.

Reason—Seizure and forcible retention of an employer's factory buildings in a sit-down strike was good cause for their discharge. They defied the law and the state courts when the employer called upon them to leave. The employees had been discharged by Fansteel for illegal seizure of the employer's property. On resuming operations, the company offered to re-employ and did re-employ many of the men engaged in the strike; the facts did not justify an order of the N.L.R.B. requiring the employer to reinstate other discharged employees. In ordering the reinstatement of such employees, the N.L.R.B. abused its discretion notwithstanding that the employer had been guilty of unfair labor practice. The National Labor Relations Act cannot be construed to encourage a defiance of the laws of the land. If a strike is lawful, the N.L.R.B. can order a reinstatement of the employee; if it is not lawful, they cannot.

Corollary cases

N.L.R.B. v. Jones and Laughlin Steel Corp., 301 U. S. 1

Associated Press v. N.L.R.B., 301 U. S. 103

N.L.R.B. v. Mackay Radio and Telegraph Co., 304 U. S. 333

N.L.R.B. v. Friedman-Harry Marks Clothing Co., 301 U. S. 58

N.L.R.B. v. Fruehauf Trailer Co., 301 U. S. 49

Washington, Virginia and M. Coach Co. v. N.L.R.B., 301 U. S. 142

INTERSTATE COMMERCE AND LABOR RELATIONS

National Labor Relations Board v. Jones & Laughlin Steel Corporation, 301 U. S. 1; 57 S. Ct. 615; 81 L. Ed. 893 (1937)

In a proceeding under the National Labor Relations Act of 1935, the National Labor Relations Board found that the Jones and Laughlin Steel Corporation had violated the Act by engaging in unfair labor practices. The unfair labor practices charged were that the corporation was discriminating against the members of the union with regard to hire and tenure of employment, and was coercing and intimidating its employees in order to interfere with their self-organization. The National Labor Relations Board tried to enforce the provisions of the Act, and the corporation failed to comply. The Circuit Court of Appeals refused to enforce the order of the board, holding that the order lay beyond the range of federal power. The Supreme Court granted certiorari.

Opinion by Mr. Chief Justice Hughes
(Vote: 5-4)

Question—Can Congress regulate labor relations under its interstate commerce power?

Decision—Yes.

Reason—"The fundamental principle is that the power to regulate commerce is the power to enact 'all appropriate legislation' for its protection or advancement . . . ; to adopt measures 'to promote its growth and insure its safety' . . . 'to foster, protect, control and restrain.' . . . That power is plenary and may be exerted to protect interstate commerce 'no matter what the source of the dangers which threaten it' . . . Although activities may be intrastate in character when separately considered, if they have such a close and substantial relation to interstate commerce that their control is essential or appropriate to protect that commerce from burdens and obstructions, Congress cannot be denied the power to exercise that control." "The fact remains that the stoppage of those operations by industrial strife would have a most serious effect upon interstate commerce. In view of respondent's far-flung activities, it is idle to say that the effect would be indirect or remote. It is obvious that it would be immediate and might be catastrophic. We are asked to shut our eyes to the plainest facts of our national life and to deal with the question of direct and indirect effects in an intellectual vacuum."

The Court stated that the cardinal principle of statutory construction is to save and not to destroy. The Court has repeatedly held that as between two possible interpretations of a statute, by one of which it would be unconstitutional and by the other valid, their plain duty is to adopt that which will save the Act. After reviewing the evidence in the case, it was determined that the main purpose of the Act was to obstruct interference with the flow of interstate commerce. The Court said that the steel industry is one of the great basic industries of the United States, affecting interstate commerce at every point. The Court referred to the steel strike of 1919-1920 with its far-reaching consequences. The fact that there appeared to have been no major disturbance in this case, did not dispose of the possibilities of the future. Therefore, the Court had no doubt that Congress had constitutional authority to safeguard the right of the employees to self-organization and freedom in the choice of representatives for collective bargaining.

Corollary cases

Schechter Corp. v. United States, 295 U. S. 495

Federal Trade Comm'n. v. American Tobacco Co., 264 U. S. 298

Panama R.R. Co., v. Johnson, 264 U. S. 375

Missouri Pacific R.R. Co., v. Boone, 270 U. S. 466

Blodgett v. Holden, 275 U. S. 142

Richmond Screw Anchor Co., v. United States, 275 U. S. 331

Texas & N. O. R.R. Co., v. Railway Clerks, 281 U. S. 548

American Steel Foundries v. Tri-City Central Trades Council, 257 U. S. 184

Baltimore & Ohio R.R. Co., v. Interstate Commerce Comm'n, 221 U. S. 612

Second Employers' Liability Cases, 223 U. S. 1

United States v. E. C. Knight Co., 156 U. S. 1

N.L.R.B. v. Fruehauf Trailer Co., 301 U. S. 49

N.L.R.B. v. Friedman-Harry Marks Clothing Co., 301 U. S. 58

Santa Cruz Fruit Packing Co. v. N.L.R.B., 303 U. S. 453

Consolidated Edison Co. v. N.L.R.B., 305 U. S. 197

Alstate Construction Co. v. Durkin, 345 U. S. 13

Thomas v. Hempt Bros., 345 U. S. 19

Kirschbaum v. Walling, 316 U. S. 517

AMENDMENT OF THE CONSTITUTION

National Prohibition Cases (Rhode Island v. Palmer), 253 U. S. 350; 40 S. Ct. 486, 64 L. Ed. 946 (1920)

The National Prohibition Cases consisted of seven cases of the same nature, and therefore were subject to the same interpretation. These cases questioned the constitutionality and legality of the Eighteenth Amendment and of the Volstead Act to enforce that amendment, and had asked the lower courts for a restraining order against the Volstead Act.

OPINION BY MR. JUSTICE VAN DEVANTER

(Vote: 7-2)

Question—Is the Eighteenth Amendment within the power to amend reserved by Article Five?

Decision—Yes.

Reason—The power to amend the Constitution was reserved by Article Five. The Court noted the following points:

"1. The adoption by both Houses of Congress, each by a two-thirds vote, of a joint resolution proposing an amendment to the Constitution, sufficiently shows that the proposal was deemed necessary by all who voted for it. An express declaration that they regarded it as necessary is not essential. None of the resolutions whereby prior amendments were proposed contained such a declaration.

"2. The two-thirds vote in each House, which is required in proposing an amendment is a vote of two-thirds of the members present—assuming the presence of a quorum—and not a vote of two-thirds of the entire membership, present and absent. . . .

"3. The referendum provisions of state constitutions and statutes cannot be applied, consistently with the Constitution of the United States, in the ratification or rejection of amendments to it. . . .

"4. The prohibition of the manufacture, sale, transportation, importation, and exportation of intoxicating liquors for beverage purposes, as embodied in the Eighteenth Amendment, is within the power to amend reserved by Article Five of the Constitution.

"5. That Amendment, by lawful proposal and ratification, has become a part of the Constitution, and must be respected and given effect the same as other provisions of that instrument."

According to the Constitution, this Amendment had been legally proposed by a two-thirds vote of the members present in each house, assuming the presence of a quorum, and ratified by a majority of the legislatures in three-fourths of the states. Incorporated into that Amendment was the provision "that Congress and the several states shall have concurrent power to enforce this article by appropriate legislation." This Section Two of the Amendment therefore authorized the Volstead Act. The words "concurrent power," giving concurrent power to Congress and the states to enforce that Amendment, do not mean a joint power or require that legislation thereunder by Congress, to be effective, shall be approved or sanctioned by the several states or any of them, and is in no wise dependent on or affected by action, or inaction, on the part of the states or any of them.

Corollary cases

FEDERAL OFFICERS AND STATE AUTHORITY

In re Neagle (Cunningham v. Neagle), 135 U. S. 1; 10 S. Ct. 658; 34 L. Ed. 55 (1890)

David Neagle was a deputy United States marshal traveling with Mr. Justice Field, who was holding Circuit Court, and whose life had been threatened by one Terry, who had been imprisoned on sentence imposed by Justice Field. Neagle was assigned by the Attorney General to accompany and protect Field. Mr. Justice Field was attacked by this man, whereupon Neagle shot and killed him. Neagle was arrested by local authorities for murder but was released on a writ of habeas corpus by the federal Circuit Court on the grounds that he was held for "an act done or omitted in pursuance of a law of the United States," within the meaning of the federal statute providing for the issuance of the writ in such cases. However, the law under which Neagle acted was an executive order of the President.

OPINION BY MR. JUSTICE MILLER
(Vote: 6-2)

Question—Was the federal Circuit Court interfering with the state in too great a degree?

Decision—No.

Reason—"It would be a great reproach to the system of government of the United States, declared to be within its sphere sovereign and supreme, if there is to be found within the domain of its powers no means of protecting the judges, in the conscientious and faithful discharge of their duties, from the malice and hatred of those upon whom their judgments may operate unfavorably. . . ."

Just as a sheriff must keep the peace of the state and local laws of California, thus Neagle, a United States deputy marshal was bound to keep the peace in regard to the federal laws. The attack on Mr. Justice Field was the breaking of the peace of the United States and it was the duty of Neagle to keep that peace.

"We cannot doubt the power of the President to take measures for the protection of a judge of one of the courts of the United States, who, while in the discharge of the duties of his office, is threatened with a personal attack which may probably result in his death. . . ."

Corollary cases

Tennessee v. Davis, 100 U. S. 257   Tarble's Case, 13 Wallace 397
Johnson v. Maryland, 254 U. S. 51   Martin v. Hunter, 1 Wheaton 363

FREEDOM OF PRESS

Near v. State of Minnesota ex rel. Olson, 283 U. S. 697; 51 S. Ct. 625; 75 L. Ed. 1357 (1931)

A Minnesota statute provided for the abatement, as a public nuisance, of a "malicious, scandalous and defamatory newspaper, magazine, or other periodical." The county attorney of Hennepin County brought action against a publication known as *The Saturday Press* published by the defendants in the city of Minneapolis. The periodical in various issues charged certain public officers with gross neglect of duty or grave misconduct in office.

OPINION BY MR. CHIEF JUSTICE HUGHES
(Vote: 5-4)

Question—Is this an infringement of the liberty of the press as guaranteed by the Fourteenth Amendment?

Decision—Yes.

Reason—It is no longer questioned that liberty of the press is one of the personal freedoms protected by the Fourteenth Amendment. However, the police powers of the state must be admitted and the limits determined.

The liberty of the press in the meaning of the Constitution is principally immunity from previous restraint. The statute cannot be justified by giving a publisher an opportunity to present his evidence. It would be only a step to a complete system of censorship. "The fact that the liberty of the press may be abused by miscreant purveyors of scandal does not make any the less necessary the immunity of the press from previous restraint in dealing with official misconduct. Subsequent punishment for such abuses as may exist is the appropriate remedy, consistent with constitutional privilege."

Scandal that tends to disturb the peace is a serious public evil, but the threat to liberty is an even more serious public evil. The Court held that the statute, by its operation and effect was unconstitutional, without any questioning of the truth of the charges contained in the particular periodical.

Corollary cases

Gompers v. Bucks Stove & Range Co., 221 U. S. 418

Schenck v. United States, 249 U. S. 47

Patterson v. Colorado, 205 U. S. 454

Grosjean v. American Press Co., 297 U. S. 233

Craig v. Harney, 331 U. S. 367

Associated Press v. United States, 326 U. S. 1

Associated Press v. N.L.R.B., 301 U. S. 103

Talley v. California, 362 U. S. 60

Smith v. California, 361 U. S. 147

Roth v. U. S., 354 U. S. 476

Ginzburg v. U. S., 383 U. S. 463

New York Times Co. v. Sullivan, 376 U. S. 254

Curtis Publishing Co. v. Butts, 388 U. S. 130

STATE PRICE CONTROL

Nebbia v. New York, 291 U. S. 502; 54 S. Ct. 505; 78 L. Ed. 940 (1934)

Nebbia, the proprietor of a grocery store in Rochester, New York, was convicted of violating an order of the New York Milk Control Board fixing the selling price of milk by selling two quarts of milk and a loaf of bread for 18¢, whereas the board had fixed the price of a quart of milk at 9¢. Nebbia, after losing the appeal to the New York Court of Appeals, appealed to the Supreme Court on grounds that the order and the statute authorizing the order contravene the equal protection clause and due process clause of the Fourteenth Amendment.

OPINION BY MR. JUSTICE ROBERTS
(Vote: 5-4)

Question—Does a state violate the Fourteenth Amendment when it fixes the minimum and maximum prices of articles such as milk?

Decision—No.

Reason—The milk industry in New York has been the subject of long standing and drastic regulation in the public interest.

Unrestricted competition in this industry aggravated existing evils, and the normal law of supply and demand was inadequate to correct maladjustments detrimental to the community. An inquiry disclosed trade practices that resulted in retail price cutting, and reduced the income of the farmer below the cost of production. In the light of this, the price fixing of the Control Board appeared not to be unreasonable, arbitrary, or without relation to the purpose of preventing ruthless competition from destroying the wholesale price structure on which the farmer depends for his livelihood and the community for an assured supply of milk.

The milk industry is of vital public interest since it is a basic food in our diet, and the legislature of New York, realizing this, passed this law to safeguard the public interest. The Constitution does not secure to anyone the liberty to conduct his business in such a fashion as to inflict injury upon the public at large or a substantial group of the public.

"The phrase 'affected with a public interest' can, in the nature of things, mean no more than that an industry, for adequate reason, is subject to control for the public good. . . . So far as the requirement of due process is concerned, and in the absence of other constitutional restriction, a state is free to adopt whatever economic policy may reasonably be deemed to promote public welfare, and to enforce that policy by legislation adapted to its purpose. If the laws passed are seen to have a reasonable relation to a proper legislative purpose, and are neither arbitrary nor discriminatory, the requirements of due process are satisfied. . . . Times without number we have said that the Legislature is primarily the judge of the necessity of such an enactment, that every possible presumption is in favor of its validity, and that though the court may hold views inconsistent with the wisdom of the law, it may not be annulled unless palpably in excess of legislative power."

Corollary cases

Wolff Packing Co. v. Court of Industrial Relations, 262 U. S. 522

Munn v. Illinois, 94 U. S. 113

Olsen v. Nebraska, 313 U. S. 236

Ribnik v. McBride, 277 U. S. 350

West Coast Hotel Co. v. Parrish, 300 U. S. 379

Tyson and Brothers v. Banton, 273 U. S. 418

FEDERAL CONTROL OF ELECTIONS

Newberry v. United States, 256 U. S. 232; 41 S. Ct. 469; 65 L. Ed. 913 (1920)

Newberry and others were found guilty of conspiring to violate the Federal Corrupt Practices Act. This Act made it illegal to spend more than $10,000 in procuring the nomination for United States Senator, whereas the indictment charged Newberry with the spending of more than $100,000 to secure his nomination.

OPINION BY MR. JUSTICE McREYNOLDS
(Vote: 5-4)

Question—Does the Congressional power to regulate the manner of holding elections include the regulation of primaries?

Decision—No.

Reason—The Constitution, while it gives Congress the power to regulate the times, places, and manner of holding elections, does not give Congress some indefinite, undefined power over the elections of Senators and Representatives. Elections, in the sense of the original Constitution, were not concerned about primaries, for they were unknown. A primary is not an election for office, but merely a choice by the party adherents of candidates. General provisions regarding elections do not necessarily apply to primaries. "We cannot conclude that authority to control party primaries or conventions for designating candidates was bestowed on Congress by the grant of power to regulate the manner of holding elections. The fair intendment of the words does not extend so far; the framers of the Constitution did not ascribe to them any such meaning. Nor is this control necessary in order to effectuate the power expressly granted. On the other hand, its exercise would interfere with purely domestic affairs of the State, and infringe upon liberties reserved to the people."

Corollary cases

Martin v. Hunter's Lessee, 1 Wheaton 304
Hawke v. Smith, 253 U. S. 221
Ex parte Siebold, 100 U. S. 371
Kidd v. Pearson, 128 U. S. 1
United States v. Classic, 313 U. S. 299

Nixon v. Herndon, 273 U. S. 536
Nixon v. Condon, 286 U. S. 73
Grovey v. Townsend, 295 U. S. 45
Smith v. Allwright, 321 U. S. 649
Rice v. Elmore, 333 U. S. 875

SUITS AGAINST STATES

New Hampshire v. Louisiana, 108 U. S. 76; 27 L. Ed. 656; 2 S. Ct. 176 (1883)

Louisiana issued bonds, which were held by citizens of the state of New Hampshire and New York. Since a citizen of one state cannot sue another state, the states of New York and New Hampshire in 1880 and 1879, respectively, passed bills similar in content called "an act to protect the rights of citizens of this state, holding claims against other states." A citizen of either of those states was thus admitted, through the state's attorney general, to bring suit against another state—the state thus representing its citizens. Suits were brought against the state of Louisiana by the said states because Louisiana had defaulted on bonds owned by the citizens of the plaintiffs.

OPINION BY MR. CHIEF JUSTICE WHITE
(No evidence from the report that the decision was not unanimous.)

Question—Can a citizen of a state sue in the name of his state after getting the consent of that state?

Decision—No.

Reason—The Eleventh Amendment was passed expressly for the purpose of not allowing this type of suit in the federal courts without the consent of the state being sued. "The evident purpose of the amendment, so promptly proposed and finally adopted, was to prohibit all suits against a state by or for citizens of other states, or aliens, without the consent of the state to be sued, and, in our opinion, the one state cannot create a controversy with another state, within the meaning of that term as used in the judicial clauses of the Constitution, by assuming the prosecution of debts owing by the other state to its citizens. Such being the case, we are satisfied that we are prohibited, both by the letter and the spirit of the Constitution, from entertaining these suits and the bill in each of them is dismissed."

Corollary cases

Chisholm v. Georgia, 2 Dallas 419
Hans v. Louisiana, 134 U. S. 1
Monaco v. Mississippi, 292 U. S. 313

North Dakota v. Minnesota, 263 U. S. 365
Virginia v. West Virginia, 246 U. S. 565

South Dakota v. North Carolina,   Wisconsin v. Illinois, 278 U. S. 367
    192 U. S. 286   Arizona v. California, 283 U. S.
                                     423

IMPAIRMENT OF OBLIGATION OF CONTRACT

New Jersey v. Wilson, 7 Cranch 164; 3 L. Ed. 303 (1812)

The remnant of the tribe of Delaware Indians had claims to a considerable portion of lands in New Jersey. A convention was held in February, 1785, at which the Indians agreed to specify particularly the lands that they claimed, release their claim to all others, and to appoint certain chiefs to treat with commissioners on the part of the government, for the final extinguishment of their whole claim.

In August, 1785, the Indian deputies met the commissioners and delivered to them a proposition that the government should purchase a tract of land on which they might reside, and that they would release their claim to all other lands in New Jersey.

This was assented to by the commissioners, and the state legislature passed an act authorizing the purchase of lands for the Indians. The act restrained them from granting leases or making sales and enacted that the lands should not be subject to any tax.

In 1801 the Indians became desirous of joining their brothers at Stockridge, in the state of New York. They applied and obtained an act from the legislature authorizing the sale of their land in the state. The act contained no expression in any manner respecting the privilege of taxation. In 1893 the lands were sold to the plaintiffs, George Painter and others.

In 1804, the legislature passed an act repealing that section of the act of August 1785, which exempted the lands from taxation. The lands were then assessed, and the taxes demanded.

OPINION BY MR. CHIEF JUSTICE MARSHALL

(No evidence from the report that the decision was not unanimous.)

Question—Does the repeal of the statute deprive the plaintiffs of a right secured to them by the Constitution?

Decision—Yes.

Reason—In Fletcher v. Peck, the Court held that impairment of contract extended to contracts to which a state was a party.

In this arrangement with the Delaware Indians there was every requisite for a contract, valid in all respects. The privilege, although for the benefit of the Indians, was attached to the land. New Jersey could have withdrawn the privilege at the time of sale. However, it was not withdrawn, and the purchaser succeeded to all the rights of the Indians, and these rights could not be withdrawn without an impairment of contract.

Corollary cases

Fletcher v. Peck, 6 Cranch 87
Dartmouth College v. Woodward, 4 Wheaton 518
Charles River Bridge v. Warren Bridge, 11 Peters 420

Piqua Branch of the Bank of Ohio v. Knoop, 16 Howard 369.
Mercantile Bank v. Tennessee, 161 U. S. 161

TAXATION OF STATE ACTIVITY BY CONGRESS

New York and Saratoga Springs Commission v. United States, 326 U. S. 572; 66 S. Ct. 310; 90 L. Ed. 326 (1946)

The issue was the validity of a federal tax on the sale of mineral waters, as applied to sales by the state of New York of water taken from Saratoga Springs. New York claimed the sales were immune from the tax on the ground that the state was engaged in the exercise of a usual, traditional, and essential governmental function.

OPINION BY MR. JUSTICE FRANKFURTER
(Vote: 6-2)

Question—Is the tax valid?

Decision—Yes.

Reason—The federal government is a government of all the states, and all the states share in the legislative process by which a tax of general application is levied. We have moved away from the notion of immunity of functionaries of one government from taxation by the other. "So long as Congress generally taps a source of revenue by whomsoever earned and not uniquely capable of being earned only by a State, the Constitution of the United States does not forbid it merely because its incidence falls also on a State . . ."

Corollary cases

South Carolina v. United States,
    199 U. S. 437
Helvering v. Gerhardt, 304 U. S.
    405
Graves   v.   New   York,   ex   rel.
    O'Keefe, 306 U. S. 240

Ohio v. Helvering, 292 U. S. 360
University of Illinois v. United
    States, 289 U. S. 48
Helvering v. Powers, 293 U. S. 214

EQUAL PROTECTION AND SUFFRAGE

Nixon v. Condon, 286 U. S. 73; 52 S. Ct. 484; 76 L. Ed. 984 (1932)

The petitioner, a Negro, brought this action against judges of a primary election in Texas for their refusal to allow him to vote by reason of his race or color. This was the second time Nixon had been denied the opportunity to vote. The first time the Supreme Court ruled a Texas statute denying the right of a Negro to vote in a party primary, was void. (See Nixon v. Herndon, 273 U. S. 536.) Then Texas passed a new statute stating that the state executive committee of each party should determine who can vote in primaries. Under this statute, the Democratic Party executive committee adopted a resolution allowing only white persons to vote in its party primary.

OPINION BY MR. JUSTICE CARDOZO
(Vote: 5-4)

Question—Was the new Texas statute in effect a violation of the Fourteenth Amendment, allowing for inequalities at the election polls for reasons of race and color?

Decision—Yes.

Reason—"The test is not whether the members of the Executive Committee are the representatives of the State in the strict sense in which an agent is the representative of his principal. The test is whether they are to be classified as representatives of the State to such an extent and in such a sense that the great restraints of the Constitution set limits to their action." The new statute placed the power in an executive committee, and thus the action was really state action and not private action, and was therefore subject to the limitations of the Fourteenth Amendment.

Corollary cases

Newberry v. United States, 256 U. S. 232

Grovey v. Townsend, 295 U. S. 45

United States v. Classic, 313 U. S. 299

Smith v. Allwright, 321 U. S. 649

Williams v. Mississippi, 170 U. S. 213

Guinn v. United States, 238 U. S. 347

Lane v. Wilson, 307 U. S. 268

Schnell v. Davis, 336 U. S. 933

Rice v. Elmore, 333 U. S. 875

Ex parte Siebold, 100 U. S. 371

Ex parte Yarbrough, 110 U. S. 651

United States v. Mosley, 238 U. S. 383

Minor v. Happersett, 21 Wallace 162

EQUAL PROTECTION AND SUFFRAGE

Nixon x. Herndon, 273 U. S. 536; 47 S. Ct. 446; 71 L. Ed. 759 (1927)

Nixon was refused permission to vote in a Texas Democratic primary solely because he was a Negro. A statute law of Texas forbade persons of colored descent the right to vote in a Democratic party primary.

OPINION BY MR. JUSTICE HOLMES

(No evidence from the report that the decision was not unanimous.)

Question—Is this law in violation of the Fourteenth Amendment?

Decision—Yes.

Reason—The Fourteenth Amendment gave citizenship and its privileges to persons of all colors, and it also denied to any state the power to withhold from them equal protection of the law. It said in effect that no state could discriminate against a person because of his color. The court said that "it seems to us hard to imagine a more direct and obvious infringement of the Fourteenth [Amendment]."

Corollary cases

Williams v. Mississippi, 170 U. S. 213

Guinn v. United States, 238 U. S. 347

Lane v. Wilson, 307 U. S. 268

Newberry v. United States, 256 U. S. 232

Smith v. Allwright, 321 U. S. 649

Schnell v. Davis, 336 U. S. 933

Rice v. Elmore, 333 U. S. 875

Ex parte Siebold, 100 U. S. 371

Ex parte Yarbrough, 110 U. S. 651

United States v. Mosley, 238 U. S. 383

Nixon v. Condon, 286 U. S. 73
Grovey v. Townsend, 295 U. S. 45
United States v. Classic, 313 U. S. 299

Minor v. Happersett, 21 Wallace 162

"GOLD CLAUSES" OF CONTRACTS

Norman v. Baltimore & Ohio Railroad Co., 294 U. S. 240; 55 S. Ct. 407; 79 L. Ed. 885 (1935)

The Baltimore & Ohio Railroad issued bonds that were to be paid in gold coin of the United States of or equal to the standard of weight and fineness existing on Feb. 1, 1930. In 1933, by a joint resolution, Congress nulified the gold clause in existing contractual obligations. The resolution provided that payment in gold was against public policy and that from then on all debts should be paid in the legal tender then in use in the United States.

OPINION BY MR. CHIEF JUSTICE HUGHES
(Vote: 5-4)

Question—Can Congress deny effect to "gold clauses" in existing contracts?

Decision—Yes.

Reason—The obligation is for payment of money and not for a specific number of grains of gold. Nor did the conditions specify gold value as claimed. Congress is empowered to coin money and to control its value. Even though the gold clauses in the bonds were a measure to avoid the payment of devalued money and were constitutional at the time they were made, the Congress has the power to devalue the dollar at its pleasure. Congress possesses this power as a delegated power, and even though it may invalidate certain contracts, it may exercise this power. The existence of such contracts cannot act as a bar to Congress in the exercise of its powers. Admission of the gold clauses in spite of the law would only tend to produce the opposite effect from that intended by Congress. Further it would place an unjust obligation on corporations, municipalities, and others whose sources of revenue, while being based on one standard, would have too many interests and debts on another standard.

Corollary cases

Perry v. United States, 294 U. S. 330

Nortz v. United States, 294 U. S. 317

Smyth v. United States, 302 U. S. 329

Guaranty Trust Co. v. Henwood, 307 U. S. 247

Craig v. Missouri, 4 Peters 410

Poindexter v. Greenhow, 114 U. S. 270

JURIES AND DUE PROCESS

Norris v. Alabama, 294 U. S. 587; 55 S. Ct. 579; 79 L. Ed. 1074 (1935)

Norris was one of nine Negro boys who were indicted in 1931 in Jackson, County, Alabama for the crime of rape. They were tried and convicted in Morgan County, Alabama, on change of venue. Norris claimed that his rights guaranteed to him by the Fourteenth Amendment had been violated because the juries that indicted and tried him were chosen to the exclusion of Negroes. The state contended that even if it were assumed that there was no name of a Negro on the jury roll, it was not established that race or color caused the omission. They said in this case the commission drawing up the jury did not take into consideration race or color, and that no one had been excluded because of race or color.

OPINION BY MR. CHIEF JUSTICE HUGHES
(Vote: 8-0)

Question—Was this a violation of the Fourteenth Amendment?

Decision—Yes.

Reason—The evidence produced disclosed that Negroes had never been called for jury duty in the two counties involved in this case. Furthermore, it was disclosed that there were some qualified Negroes in these counties. The court reasoned that this was prima facie evidence that Negroes were denied jury duty because of their race or color, and this was therefore contrary to the Constitution.

This is the second "Scottsboro case." The first was Powell v. Alabama.

Corollary cases

Powell v. Alabama, 287 U. S. 45

Carter v. Texas, 177 U. S. 442

Smith v. Texas, 311 U. S. 128

Hill v. Texas, 316 U. S. 400

Strauder v. West Virginia, 100
  U. S. 303
Neal v. Delaware, 103 U. S. 370
Thomas v. Texas, 212 U. S. 278

Akins v. Texas, 325 U. S. 398
Virginia v. Rives, 100 U. S. 313
Pierre v. Louisiana, 306 U. S. 354

ANTITRUST LEGISLATION

Northern Securities Co. v. United States, 193 U. S. 197, 24 S. Ct. 436, 48 L. Ed. 679 (1904)

The Northern Pacific and Great Northern Railroad Companies purchased most of the stock of the Burlington Railroad. The first two companies ran parallel lines and the Burlington was a connecting line. The Northern Pacific and Great Northern entered into a combination to form a New Jersey corporation, which came to be known as the Northern Securities Company. This company held three-fourths of the stock of the two companies. The United States charged them with violation of the anti-trust laws.

OPINION BY MR. JUSTICE HARLAN
(Vote: 5-4)

Question—Does this railroad combination restrain trade among the several states and therefore violate the anti-trust laws?

Decision—Yes.

Reason—The Court reasoned that this combination was, within the meaning of the act, a "trust," but, even if not, it was a combination in restraint of interstate and international commerce, and that was enough to bring it under the condemnation of the act. The mere existence of such a combination and the power acquired by the holding company as its trustee constituted a menace to, and a restraint upon, that freedom of commerce which Congress intended to recognize and protect, and which the public was entitled to have protected. Even if the state allowed consolidation, it would not follow that the stockholders of two or more state railroad corporations, having competing lines and engaged in insterstate commerce, could lawfully combine and form a distinct corporation to hold the stock of the constituent corporations, and by destroying competition between them in violation of the Act of Congress, restrain commerce among the states and with foreign nations.

Corollary cases

Gibbons v. Ogden, 9 Wheaton 197

United States v. South-Eastern Underwriters Ass'n., 322 U. S. 533

Swift and Co. v. United States, 196 U. S. 375

United States v. E. C. Knight Co., 156 U. S. 1

Times Picayune Pub. Co. v. United States, 345 U. S. 594

NAVIGABLE WATERS

Oklahoma ex rel. Phillips, Governor, v. Guy F. Atkinson Co., 313 U. S. 508; 61 S. Ct. 1050; 85 L. Ed. 1487 (1941)

In June, 1938 Congress authorized the Denison Dam and Reservoir Project on the Red River in Oklahoma and Texas. The project was part of a comprehensive scheme for controlling floods in the Mississippi River through reservoir control of its tributaries. It aimed also at protecting and improving navigation of the Red River (which lies below the state of Oklahoma), by averting damaging floods and regulating stream flow, and providing means for creating hydroelectric power, the disposition of which was to offset some of the costs.

Oklahoma alleged that the project would result in a net taxable loss from the tax rolls of about $40,000 annually. Besides being a direct invasion of the sovereign proprietary rights of Oklahoma, the boundary would be obliterated for about 40 miles, waters would be taken without just compensation, and a serious social and economic problem would arise, which would fall on Oklahoma with no compensation afforded.

OPINION BY MR. JUSTICE DOUGLAS

(No evidence from the report that the decision was not unanimous.)

Question—Is the project in conformity with the commerce power of the Congress?

Decision—Yes.

Reason—The Court did not find that the commerce power of Congress had been violated, since even nonnavigable parts of streams may be regulated in order to preserve and promote commerce on the navigable parts. One of the frequent benefits of flood control is the protection of navigation. Whether a particular project will benefit the arteries of interstate commerce is a question for Congress to decide, as well as the question of whether the benefits will outweigh the costs of the project.

In the Appalachian Electric Power Co. case the Court held that flood protection, watershed development, and recovery of the cost of improvements through the utilization of power are parts of commerce control. Nor can each reservoir project be viewed as an isolated unit. The tributaries of the Mississippi are generous contributors to its floods. "We now extend the power of flood control to the tributaries of navigable streams."

The fact that land included in a federal reservoir project is owned by a state, or that the state's revenues are impaired, or the state's boundary obliterated is beside the point. It constitutes no barrier, for the state must yield before the superior power of eminent domain of the United States.

Corollary cases

Economy Light and Power Co. v. United States, 256 U. S. 113

United States v. Appalachian Electric Power Co., 311 U. S. 377

United States v. Rio Grande Dam & Irrigation Co., 174 U. S. 690

United States v. Utah, 283 U. S. 64

Ashwander v. T.V.A., 297 U. S. 288

The Thomas Jefferson, 10 Wheaton 428

The Daniel Ball, 10 Wallace 557

The Genesee Chief v. Fitzhugh, 12 Howard 443

Gibbons v. Ogden, 9 Wheaton 1

Arizona v. California, 283 U. S. 423

SEARCH AND SEIZURE AND WIRE TAPPING

Olmstead v. United States, 277 U. S. 438; 48 S. Ct. 564; 72 L. Ed. 944 (1928)

This was a conspiracy to violate the National Prohibition Act by unlawfully possessing, transporting and importing intoxicating liquors and maintaining nuisances, and by selling intoxicating liquors. Olmstead was the leading conspirator and the general manager of the business. One of the chief men was always on duty at the main office to receive orders by telephone and to direct their filling by a corps of men stationed in another room. The information which led to the discovery of the conspiracy and its nature and intent was largely obtained by intercepting messages on the telephones of the conspirators by four federal prohibition officers. However, the wire tapping was done outside the residence, and not in the offices but in the basement of the building housing the offices. All conversations were recorded, and the evidence of the wiretapping was used in court against the conspirators.

OPINION BY MR. CHIEF JUSTICE TAFT
(Vote: 5-4)

Question—Does the use of evidence of private telephone conversations between the defendants and others, intercepted by means of wire tapping, amount to a violation of the Fourth Amendment and the Fifth Amendment?

Decision—No.

Reason—The court ruled that there is no room for applying the Fifth Amendment, unless the Fourth Amendment was first violated. Therefore, the court limited its consideration to the Fourth Amendment. The Amendment does not forbid what was done in this case. There was no searching. There was no seizure. The evidence was secured by the use of the sense of hearing and that only. There was no entry of the houses or offices of the defendants. By invention of the telephone, and its application for the purpose of extending communications, one can talk with another at a far distant place. The language of the Amendment cannot be extended and expanded to include telephone wires, reaching to the whole world from the defendant's house or office any more than to the highways along which they are stretched.

"A standard which would forbid the reception of evidence if obtained by other than nice ethical conduct by government officials would make society suffer and give criminals greater immunity than has been known heretofore. In the absence of controlling legislation by Congress, those who realize the difficulties in bringing offenders to justice may well deem it wise that the exclusion of evidence should be confined to cases where rights under the Constitution would be violated by admitting it . . ." This decision has been overruled by Katz v. United States, 389 U.S. 347 (1967).

Corollary cases

Adams v. New York, 192 U. S. 585

Gouled v. United States, 255 U. S. 298

United States v. Reid, 12 Howard 361

Goldstein v. United States, 316 U. S. 114

Goldman v. United States, 316 U. S. 129

Weiss v. United States, 308 U.S. 321

Weeks v. United States, 232 U. S. 383

Nardone v. United States, 302 U. S. 379

Schwartz v. State, 344 U. S. 199

Benanti v. United States, 355 U. S. 96

Lopez v. U. S., 373 U. S. 427

Berger v. New York, 388 U. S. 41

On Lee v. U. S., 343 U. S. 747

Silverman v. U. S., 365 U. S. 505

See also cases listed under Agnello v. United States.

STATE PRICE CONTROL

Olsen v. Nebraska ex. rel. Western Reference and Bond Association, Inc. et al., 313 U. S. 236; 61 S. Ct. 862; 85 L. Ed. 1305 (1941)

Olsen, the Secretary of Labor for the State of Nebraska, denied a license to operate a private employment agency for the year commencing May 1, 1940 to the Western Reference and Bond Association because of that Association's refusal to limit its maximum compensation as provided by state statute to 10 per cent of the first month's salary or wages of the person for whom employment was obtained. The Nebraska Supreme Court issued a writ of mandamus to license the said company on the grounds that the business of a private employment agency is not "vitally affected with a public interest" and not subject to the police power of the state.

OPINION BY MR. JUSTICE DOUGLAS

(No evidence from the report that the decision was not unanimous.)

Question—Does the statute violate the due process clause of the Fourteenth Amendment?

Decision—No.

Reason—The statute fixing the maximum compensation that an employment agency may collect as a $2.00 registration fee and 10 per cent of all monies paid or to be paid or earned by the applicant for the first month's service does not deny "due process of law" in violation of the Fourteenth Amendment. The need or wisdom of such a law is not determined by the United States Supreme Court, but by the states or by Congress. "We are not concerned, however, with the wisdom, need, or appropriateness of the legislation. Differences of opinion on that score suggest a choice which 'should be left where . . . it was left by the Constitution—to the states and to Congress.' There is no necessity for the state to demonstrate before us that evils persist despite the competition which attends the bargaining in this field. In final analysis, the only constitutional prohibitions or restraints which respondents have suggested for the invalidation of this legislation are those notions of public policy embedded in earlier decisions of this Court but which, as Mr. Justice Holmes long admonished, should not be read into the Constitution. . . . Since they do not find expression in the Constitution, we cannot give them continuing vitality as standards by which the constitutionality of the economic and social programs of the states is to be determined."

Corollary cases

Ribnik v. McBride, 277 U. S. 350

West Coast Hotel Co. v. Parrish, 300 U. S. 379

Nebbia v. New York, 291 U. S. 502

Tyson and Brothers v. Banton, 273 U. S. 418

New State Ice Co. v. Liebmann, 285 U. S. 262

Old Dearborn Distributing Co. v. Seagram-Distillers Corp., 299 U. S. 183

DELEGATION OF LEGISLATIVE POWER

Opp Cotton Mills v. Administrator of the Wage and Hour Division of the Department of Labor, 312 U. S. 126; 61 S. Ct. 524; 85 L. Ed. 624 (1941)

The Opp Cotton Mills, an Alabama Corporation, had received an order from the Administrator of the Wage and Hour Division of the Department of Labor to place a 32½ cents per hour minimum wage for the textile industry. The Opp Cotton Mills contended that the Fair Labor Standards Act was unconstitutional and infringed upon the Fifth and Tenth Amendments.

OPINION BY MR. JUSTICE STONE

(No evidence from the report that the decision was not unanimous.)

Question—Is the Act an unconstitutional delegation of the legislative power of Congress?

Decision—No.

Reason—The mandate of the Constitution that all legislative powers granted "shall be vested" in Congress has never been thought to preclude Congress from resorting to the aid of administrative officers or boards as fact-finding agencies whose findings, made in conformity to previously adopted legislative standards or definitions of Congressional policy, have been made prerequisite to the operation of its statutory command. The adoption of the declared policy by Congress, and its definition of the circumstances in which its command is to be effective, constitute the performance, in the constitutional sense, of the legislative function. The court held that the Fair Labor Standards Act satisfied these requirements. "In an increasingly complex society Congress obviously could not perform its functions if it were obliged to find all the facts subsidiary to the basic conclusions which support the defined legislative policy in fixing, for example, a tariff rate, a railroad rate, or the rate of wages to be applied in particular industries by a minimum wage law. The Constitution, viewed as a continuously operative charter of government, is not to be interpreted as demanding the impossible or the impracticable. The essentials of the legislative function are the determination of the legislative policy and its formulation as a rule of conduct. Those essentials are preserved when Congress specifies the basic conclusions of fact upon ascertainment of which, from relevant data by a designated administrative agency, it ordains that its statutory command is to be effective."

Corollary cases

United States v. Darby, 312 U. S. 100

United States v. Curtiss-Wright Export Corp., 299 U. S. 304

Schechter Poultry Corp. v. United States, 295 U. S. 495

Panama Refining Co. v. Ryan, 293 U. S. 388

J. W. Hampton, Jr., and Co. v. United States, 276 U. S. 394

Yakus v. United States, 321 U. S. 414

FEDERAL COURT JURISDICTION

Osborn v. Bank of the United States, 9 Wheaton 738; 6 L. Ed. 204 (1824)

The State of Ohio levied an annual tax on the Bank of the United States of $50,000. Officers of the Bank refused to pay the tax and the state officials collected by force. The Bank of the United States was chartered by Congress, and brought suit in the federal Circuit Court of Ohio, as authorized by its charter, to recover the funds collected and restrain Osborn, Auditor of Ohio, and other state officials from collecting the tax.

OPINION BY MR. CHIEF JUSTICE MARSHALL
(Vote: 6-1)

Question—Could Congress give the bank authorization to sue state officials in the Circuit Courts?

Decision—Yes.

Reason—In this case the Court reiterated the doctrine of McCulloch v. Maryland that Congress can establish a bank and that a state may not tax that bank. The Court then went on to answer the question noted above. It was held that the state was not a party on the record, so the case could not be construed as a violation of the Eleventh Amendment. "If the person who is the real principal, the person who is the true source of the mischief, by whose power and for whose advantage it is done, be himself above the law, be exempt from all judicial process, it would be subversive of the best established principles, to say, that the law could not afford the same remedies against the agent employed in doing the wrong, which they would afford against him, could his principal be joined in the suit."

A corporation chartered by Congress has the right to invoke the protection of the federal courts in any matter properly within the jurisdiction of the Court—a matter under Article III, Section 2 of the Constitution. "The constitution establishes the supreme court, and defines its jurisdiction. It enumerates cases in which its jurisdiction is original and exclusive; and then defines that which is appellate, but does not insinuate that, in any such case, the power cannot be exercised in its original form, by courts of original jurisdiction. It is not insinuated, that the judicial power, in cases depending on the character of the cause, cannot be exercised, in the first instance, in the courts of the Union, but must first be exercised in the tribunals of the state; tribunals over which the government of the Union has no adequate control, and which may be closed to any claim asserted under a law of the United States. We perceive, then, no ground on which the proposition can be maintained, that congress is incapable of giving the circuit court original jurisdiction, in any case to which the appellate jurisdiction extends."

Corollary cases

McCulloch v. Maryland, 4 Wheaton 316

Ableman v. Booth, 21 Howard 506

Ex parte McCardle, 7 Wallace 506

Muskrat v. United States, 219 U. S. 346

EQUAL PROTECTION

Oyama v. California, 332 U. S. 633; 68 S. Ct. 269; 92 L. Ed. 249 (1948)

The California Alien Land Law forbade aliens ineligible for citizenship to acquire, own, occupy, lease, or transfer agricultural land. The father, Kajiro Oyama, was a Japanese citizen not eligible for citizenship. He bought six acres of land in 1934, and the seller executed the deed to Fred Oyama, then six years old, and an American citizen. Some six months later, the father petitioned the court to be Fred's guardian, which was ordered, and the father posted the necessary bond. In 1937, two adjoining acres were acquired. In 1942, Fred and his family were evacuated from the Pacific Coast. In 1944 when he was sixteen, and still forbidden to return home, the state filed a petition to escheat the two parcels of land on the contention that there was an intent to violate and evade the Alien Land Law.

OPINION BY MR. CHIEF JUSTICE VINSON
(Vote: 6-3)

Question—Does this statute deprive Fred Oyama of equal protection of the laws and of his privileges as an American citizen?

Decision—Yes.

Reason—The State of California had discriminated against Fred Oyama, and this discrimination was based solely on his parents' country of origin. By the Fourteenth Amendment, and a federal statute, all states must accord to all citizens the right to take and hold real property. Under California law, infancy does not incapacitate a minor from holding real property. A minor citizen holding such property may have his father appointed his guardian, whether he be a citizen, an eligible alien, or an ineligible alien. At this point, the laws differ, pointing in one direction for minors whose parents cannot be naturalized, and in another direction for all other children.

Only the most exceptional circumstances can excuse such discrimination in the face of the equal protection clause and a federal statute giving all citizens the right to own land. In this case, the conflict was between a state's right to form a policy of landholding within its boundaries, and the right of American citizens to own land anywhere in the United States. When these two rights clash, the country of the father's origin may not be used as a pretense for subordinating the rights of the citizen.

Corollary cases

Hirabayashi v. United States, 320 U. S. 81

Truax v. Raich, 239 U. S. 33

Terrace v. Thompson, 263 U. S. 197

Cockvill v. California, 268 U. S. 258

Takahashi v. Fish and Game Commission, 334 U. S. 410

Frick v. Webb, 263 U. S. 326

REPUBLICAN FORM OF GOVERNMENT

Pacific States Telephone and Telegraph Co. v. State of Oregon, 223 U. S. 118; 32 St. Ct. 224, 56 L. Ed. 377 (1912)

In 1902 Oregon amended its constitution to give the people of the state the right of direct legislation through the initiative and the referendum. A tax law in 1906 was passed by the initiative under which corporations of certain types were assessed 2 per cent of their gross receipts, and the Pacific States Telephone and Telegraph Co. refused to pay it.

OPINION BY MR. CHIEF JUSTICE WHITE
(No evidence from the report that the decision was not unanimous.)

Question—Does this use of the initiative and referendum destroy the republican form of government in Oregon?

Decision—It is a political question and the Court has no jurisdiction in this case.

Reason—The case in question was not against the legality of the tax as such but was concerned with the framework and political character of the government by which the statute levying the tax was passed. It was the government, the political entity, that was called to the bar of the Court, not for the purpose of testing judicially some exercise of power assailed on the ground that its exertion has injuriously affected the rights of an individual because of some repugnancy to some constitutional limitation, but to demand of the state that it establish its right to exist as a state, republican in form.

These issues were political and governmental and out of the jurisdiction of this court.

Corollary cases

Luther v. Borden, 7 Howard 1

Colegrove v. Green, 328 U. S. 549

In re Cooper, 143 U. S. 472

Georgia v. Stanton, 6 Wallace 50

Cook v. Fortson, 329 U. S. 675

South v. Peters, 339 U. S. 276

McDougall v. Green, 335 U. S. 281

Coleman v. Miller, 307 U. S. 433

SECOND TRIAL IN A STATE COURT AS VIOLATIVE OF DUE PROCESS AS DOUBLE JEOPARDY

Palko v. State of Connecticut, 302 U. S. 319; 58 S. Ct. 149; 82 L. Ed. 288 (1937)

Palko was indicted in Connecticut for murder in the first degree. A jury found him guilty of murder in the second degree and sentenced him to life imprisonment. The state appealed this verdict and the Supreme Court of Errors for Connecticut ordered a new trial. The basis for this order was the discovery that there had been error of law to the prejudice of the state in the lower court. At the second trial additional evidence was admitted and additional instructions given to the jury. A verdict of first degree murder was returned and Palko was sentenced to death. He appealed the legality of this procedure under the due process clause of the Fourteenth Amendment, claiming double jeopardy.

OPINION BY MR. JUSTICE CARDOZO
(Vote: 8-1)

Question—Is the appellant, by the new trial and subsequent sentence to death, deprived of due process under the Fourteenth Amendment?

Decision—No.

Reason—The due process clause of the Fourteenth Amendment applies to the states only those provisions of the Bill of Rights (Amendments 1 to 8) which are of the very essence of a scheme of ordered liberty. These provisions are those that involve principles of justice "so rooted in the traditions and conscience of our people as to be ranked as fundamental." The Court noted that to date only the guarantees of the First Amendment and the right to benefit of counsel have been found to fit this test.

The Court noted further that there could be no valid charge of double jeopardy and no deprivation of due process unless the first trial had been without error. Since there was error in the conduct of the first trial and the second trial was requested by the state to rectify the errors of the first trial, and to further the purposes of justice, there was no deprivation of due process involved.

To bring the details of this case down to date, the guarantee of the Fourth Amendment against unreasonable searches and seizures (Mapp v. Ohio, 367 U.S. 643, 1961), the guarantee of the Fifth Amendment against self-incrimination (Malloy v. Hogan, 378 U.S. 1, 1964), the provisions of the Sixth Amendment guaranteeing a speedy trial (Klopfer v. North Carolina, 386 U. S. 216, 1967) an impartial jury (Parker v. Gladden, 385 U.S. 363, 1966), confrontation by witnesses (Pointer v. Texas, 380 U.S. 400, 1965), compulsory process for obtaining witnesses (Washington v. Texas, 388 U. S. 14, 1967), and the assistance of counsel in all criminal cases (Gideon v. Wainwright, 372 U. S. 335, 1963), and the provisions of the Eighth Amendment on cruel and unusual punishments (Robinson v. California, 370 U. S. 660, 1962) should be added as now applicable to the states by means of the Fourteenth Amendment. The right of privacy has also been deduced from the provisions of the Ninth Amendment (Griswold v. Connecticut, 381 U. S. 479, 1965).

Corollary cases

Hurtado v. California, 110 U. S. 516

Twining v. New Jersey, 211 U. S. 78

Near v. Minnesota, 283 U. S. 697

Adamson v. California, 332 U. S. 46

De Jonge v. Oregon, 299 U. S. 353

Herndon v. Lowry, 301 U. S. 242

Grosjean v. American Press Co., 297 U. S. 233

Cantwell v. Connecticut, 310 U. S. 296

Powell v. Alabama, 287 U. S. 45

Hamilton v. University of California, 293 U. S. 245

Pierce v. Society of Sisters, 268 U. S. 510

Walker v. Sauvinet, 92 U. S. 90

Maxwell v. Dow, 176 U. S. 581

Weeks v. United States, 232 U. S. 383

West v. Louisiana, 194 U. S. 258

Green v. United States, 355 U. S. 184

Wolf v. Colorado, 388 U. S. 25

DELEGATION OF LEGISLATIVE POWER

Panama Refining Co. v. Ryan, 293 U. S. 388; 55 S. Ct. 241; 79 L. Ed. 446 (1935)

Section 9 (c) of the National Industrial Recovery Act

had given the President the power to forbid the transportation in interstate commerce of oil produced or withdrawn from storage in violation of state law. The Panama Refining Company, as owner of an oil refining plant in Texas, sued to restrain the defendants, who were federal officials, from enforcing regulations from the Department of Interior based on the National Industrial Recovery Act, on the grounds that Section 9 (c) of the act was unconstitutional.

Opinion by Mr. Chief Justice Hughes
(Vote: 8-1)

Question—Does Section 9 (c) of the National Industrial Recovery Act delegate legislative power to the President?

Decision—Yes.

Reason—The statute did not contain any definition of the circumstances or conditions in which the transportation was to be permitted or prohibited. In other words, the power of the President was purely discretionary. He was not merely filling in the details of a legislative policy, since no legislative policy was outlined to guide or control him. Therefore the Court noted that, while very broad powers of administrative regulation may be delegated to the President, there must still be a legislative statement of policy sufficiently definite to prevent the exercise, upon his part, of pure discretion. Section 9 (c) of the N.I.R.A. in essence delegates the power to legislate to the President and is therefore unconstitutional and void.

Corollary cases

See Schechter Poultry Corp. v. United States, and cases there cited.

Wichita Railroad & Light Co., v. Public Utilities Commission, 260 U. S. 48

Mahler v. Eby, 264 U. S. 32

Opp Cotton Mills v. Administrator of Wage and Hour Division, 312 U. S. 126

United States v. Curtiss-Wright Export Corp., 299 U. S. 304

Yakus v. United States, 321 U. S. 414

Bowles v. Willingham, 321 U. S. 503

Norwegian Nitrogen Products Co. v. United States, 288 U. S. 294

Carter v. Carter Coal Co., 298 U. S. 238

Eubank v. Richmond, 226 U. S. 137

Washington ex rel. Seattle Trust Co. v. Roberge, 278 U. S. 116

STATE AGRICULTURAL LEGISLATION

Parker v. Brown, 317 U. S. 341; 63 S. Ct. 307; 87 L. Ed. 315 (1943)

> The California Agricultural Prorate Act instituted a program whereby raisin growers were to turn over two-thirds of their individual crops to a central committee that controlled the marketing of the crops to the packers. About 95 per cent of the raisin crop was destined for interstate or foreign commerce.

OPINION BY MR. CHIEF JUSTICE STONE

(No evidence from the report that the decision was not unanimous.)

Question—Is the California Agricultural Prorate Act rendered invalid by the Sherman Act, by the Agricultural Marketing Agreement as amended, or by the commerce clause of the Constitution?

Decision—No.

Reason—The Sherman Act makes unlawful any contract, combination, or conspiracy among persons to monopolize trade or commerce between the states. However, the prorate program was never intended to operate by the force of individual agreement or combination, but derived its authority and efficiency from the state legislature. There is nothing in the Sherman Act which proposes to restrain a state from activities directed by its legislature.

"The Agricultural Marketing Agreement Act is applicable to raisins only on the direction of the Secretary of Agriculture who, instead of establishing a federal program has, as the statute authorizes, cooperated in promoting the state program and aided it by substantial federal loans. Hence we cannot say that the effect of the state program on interstate commerce is one which conflicts with Congressional policy or is such as to preclude the state from this exercise of its reserved power to regulate domestic agricultural production."

The question on the commerce clause was whether in the absence of Congressional legislation prohibiting or regulating the product affected by the state program, the restrictions imposed on the sale of a commodity by its producer to a processor who worked upon the commodity before packing and shipping it in interstate commerce was a violation of the commerce clause. The Court held that in the absence of

Congressional legislation, the states may regulate matters of local concern, even though the measure somewhat restricts commerce. The regulation in question seemed to be within state power. Likewise, taxation or regulation, however drastic, is not in conflict with the commerce clause if it is imposed before any operation of interstate commerce occurs. The history of the raisin industry in California shows clearly a need for state regulation. The program did not discriminate against interstate commerce.

Corollary cases

Minnesota Rate Cases, 230 U. S. 352

Federal Compress Co., v. McLean, 291 U. S. 17

Kidd v. Pearson, 128 U. S. 1

Lemke v. Farmers Grain Co., 258 U. S. 50

DiSanto v. Pennsylvania, 273 U. S. 34

Oregon-Washington Co. v. Washington, 270 U. S. 87

Welch Co. v. New Hampshire, 306 U. S. 79

Hood and Sons v. Du Mond, 336 U. S. 525

STATE REGULATION OF COMMERCE

The Passenger Cases (Smith v. Turner) (Norris v. Boston), 7 Howard 283, 12 L. Ed. 702 (1849)

New York imposed on the masters of ships coming from foreign ports or the ports of other states a tax on the basis of each passenger aboard, the revenue to be used to defray the costs of examination of passengers for contagious diseases and to provide treatment for those found to be diseased. A similar tax was imposed by Massachusetts and made applicable to aliens, with the further requirement that the master should post a bond of $1,000 for each alien likely to become a public charge.

OPINION BY MR. JUSTICE MCLEAN
(Vote: 5-4)

Question—Were the New York and Massachusetts passenger laws an unconstitutional regulation of commerce?

Decision—Yes.

Reason—"It has been well remarked that the regulation of commerce consists as much in negative as in positive action. There is not a federal power which has been exerted in all its diversified means of operation. . . . Is a commercial regulation open to state action because the federal power has not been exhausted? The supposition of such a power in a State is utterly inconsistent with a commercial power, either paramount or exclusive, in Congress. . . ."

(Five majority justices wrote separate opinions.)

Corollary cases

Holmes v. Jennison, 14 Peters 570

Houston v. Moore, 5 Wheaton 23

Gibbons v. Ogden, 9 Wheaton 196

Brown v. Maryland, 12 Wheaton 446

Groves v. Slaughter, 15 Peters 511

New York v. Miln, 11 Peters 158

Sturges v. Crowninshield, 4 Wheaton 122

Willson v. Blackbird Creek Marsh Co., 2 Peters 250

Cooley v. Board of Wardens, 12 Howard 299

Henderson v. Mayor of New York, 92 U. S. 259

JURORS AND EQUAL PROTECTION

Patton v. State of Mississippi, 332 U. S. 463; 68 S. Ct. 184; 92 L. Ed. 76 (1948)

A Negro was indicted in the Circuit Court of Lauderdale County, Mississippi, by an all-white grand jury. He was charged with the murder of a white man. He was convicted by an all-white petit jury and sentenced to death by electrocution. The defendant Negro introduced evidence that in 30 years no Negro had served on a grand or petit jury in this county. He contended that this violated his rights under the Fourteenth Amendment.

OPINION BY MR. JUSTICE BLACK

(No evidence from the report that the decision was not unanimous.)

Question—Was there denial of equal protection in the selection of jurors?

Decision—Yes.

Reason—The Court recalled that, sixty-seven years before, this Court had held that the exclusion of Negroes from grand and petit juries solely because of their race denied Negro defendants in criminal cases equal protection of the laws required by the Fourteenth Amendment. The Court said there had been an unbroken line of decisions upholding the same principle, and held the facts to be the determining principle. The law provided that a juror must be a male citizen and a qualified elector in the state. The registration lists contained several hundred Negro electors. The circuit clerk of the county, charged with administrative duties, sent the names of eight Negroes to the jury commissioner. None was ever called, and the record showed that no Negro had served on a grand or petit jury for 30 years. This was evidence that administrative practice was responsible, and that the state should have corrected the situation. This evidence proved that there had been a systematic exclusion of Negroes from juries solely because of race, and such was a denial of the equal protection of the law for Negro defendants. Indictments and verdicts against Negroes under such circumstances cannot stand. The proper action of officials in such matters will have to be determined from the facts in cases as they arise.

Corollary cases

Strauder v. State of West Virginia, 100 U. S. 303

Hill v. State of Texas, 316 U. S. 400

Norris v. Alabama, 294 U. S. 587

Patton v. U. S., 281 U. S. 276

Akins v. Texas, 325 U. S. 398

Cassell v. Texas, 339 U. S. 282

Moore v. Dempsey, 261 U. S. 86

Shepherd v. Florida, 341 U. S. 50

Hernandez v. Texas, 347 U. S. 475

INSURANCE AS COMMERCE

Paul v. Virginia, 8 Wallace 168; 19 L. Ed. 357 (1869)

In May, 1866, S. Paul, a resident of the State of Virginia, was appointed agent of several insurance companies incorporated in New York. He complied with all requirements of a state statute respecting foreign insurance companies, except the provisions providing for a deposit of bond with the state treasurer. On this ground alone, a license to sell insurance was refused to Paul. However, he sold an insurance policy of the New York Company, and was arrested for violation of the statute.

OPINION BY MR. JUSTICE FIELD

(No evidence from the report that the decision was not unanimous.)

Question—Does the statute attempt to regulate interstate commerce and does it violate the privileges and immunities clause?

Decision—No.

Reason—The Court held that the sale of insurance did not involve interstate commerce, and that therefore it could be regulated by the state. "They are like other personal contracts between parties which are completed by their signature and the transfer of the consideration. Such contracts are not interstate transactions, though the parties may be domiciled in different States. The policies do not take effect—are not executed contracts—until delivered by the agent in Virginia. They are, then, local transactions, and are governed by the local law. They do not constitute a part of the commerce between the States any more than a contract for the purchase and sale of goods in Virginia by a citizen of New York whilst in Virginia would constitute a portion of such commerce." A corporation is not a citizen within the meaning of the privileges and immunities clause. The privileges secured are those that are common to the citizens of the state in question. Special privileges enjoyed by citizens in their own states are not secured in other states by this provision. It was not intended by the Constitution to give to the laws of one state any operation in any other state. They can have no such operation except by the permission of the other state. A grant of corporate existence is a grant of special privilege. A corporation is a mere creature of the law, and can have no legal existence beyond the limits of the sovereignty that created it. The recognition of its existence even by other states and the enforcement of contracts made therein depend entirely upon the comity of those states, a comity that is never extended where the existence of the corporation is prejudicial to the interests of the state or repugnant to its policies.

Corollary cases

United States v. South-Eastern Underwriters Ass'n., 322 U. S. 533

Hemphill v. Orloff, 277 U. S. 537

Asbury Hospital v. Cass County, N. D., 326 U. S. 207

Blake v. McClung, 172 U. S. 239

Welton v. Missouri, 91 U. S. 275

Prudential Insurance Co. v. Benjamin, 328 U. S. 408

STATE REGULATIONS AND FEDERAL AGENCIES

Penn Dairies, Inc., v. Milk Control Commission, 318 U. S. 261; 63 S. Ct. 617; 87 L. Ed. 748 (1943)

The Pennsylvania Milk Control Law established a Milk Control Commission with the authority to fix retail and wholesale milk prices within the Commonwealth of Pennsylvania. It gave the Commission authority to enforce its regulations. In 1940 a United States military camp was established in Pennsylvania on state-owned land under a permit from that Commonwealth, which stated that Pennsylvania should not lose its authority or jurisdiction over the area occupied by the camp. The Quartermaster Department at the camp asked bids to be submitted for supplying the camp with milk. The Milk Commission sent a notice to bidders that stated the minimum price to be allowed in the bids. Penn Dairies submitted a bid that was substantially lower than the minimum set by the Commission and received the contract. The Milk Commission denied a license to the Penn Dairies for refusing to comply with the Commission's price rule.

OPINION BY MR. CHIEF JUSTICE STONE
(Vote: 6-3)

Question—Did the law impose an unconstitutional burden on the United States or otherwise infringe the Constitution or the laws of the United States?

Decision—No.

Reason—Congressional legislation does not disclose a purpose to immunize government contractors from local price-fixing regulations, nor does the Constitution confer such immunity. Those who contract to furnish supplies or render service to the government are not federal agencies and do not perform governmental functions, and the mere fact that nondiscriminatory taxation or regulations of the contractors impose an economic burden on the government is no longer regarded as bringing the contract within the implied immunity of the government from state taxation or regulation. Thus this law does not violate any constitutional immunity possessed by the United States Government.

Corollary cases

Graves v. New York ex rel. O'Keefe, 306 U. S. 466

Ohio v. Thomas, 113 U. S. 276

Pittman v. Home Owners Loan Corp. 308 U. S. 21

State of Alabama v. King and Boozer, 314 U. S. 1

Baltimore and Ohio R.R. Co. v. Lichtenberg, 308 U. S. 525

James Stewart and Co., v. Sadrakula, 309 U. S. 94

Johnson v. Maryland, 254 U. S. 51

Mayo v. United States, 319 U. S. 441

FREE SPEECH, FREE PRESS AND CONTEMPT

Pennekamp v. Florida, 328 U. S. 331; 66 S. Ct. 1029; 90 L. Ed. 1295 (1946)

Petitioners, the publisher and associate editor of a

newspaper, were responsible for the publication of two editorials and a cartoon criticizing certain action previously taken by a Florida trial court of general jurisdiction in certain nonjury proceedings as being too favorable to criminals and gambling establishments. Two of the cases involved were dismissed. The third, a rape case, was at first dismissed and then a new indictment was granted and a trial was pending. Petitioners were convicted of contempt of court in that the publication reflected upon and impugned the integrity of the court, tended to create a distrust for the court, and also tended to obstruct the fair and impartial justice of pending cases.

OPINION BY MR. JUSTICE REED
(Vote: 8-0)

Question—Was the petitioners' right of free speech and freedom of the press violated by this conviction?

Decision—Yes.

Reason—On the record, the danger to fair judicial administration in this case had not the necessary clearness and immediacy to close the door of permissible public comment. Since the publication was concerned with the attitude of the judge toward those charged with crime, not comments on rulings during a jury trial or on evidence, their effect on the juries that might try the case was too remote to be a clear and present danger to justice.

This criticism of the judge's inclination or action in pending nonjury proceedings could not directly affect the administration of justice, although the cases were still pending on other points or might be revived by rehearings.

"It may influence some judges more than others. Some are of a more sensitive fiber than their colleagues. The law deals in generalities and external standards and cannot depend on the varying degrees of moral courage or stability in the face of criticism which individual judges may possess any more than it generally can depend on the personal equations or individual idiosyncrasies of the tort-feasor. We are not willing to say under the circumstances of this case that these editorials are a clear and present danger to the fair administration of justice in Florida."

Corollary cases

Bridges v. California, 314 U. S. 252   Schenck v. United States, 249 U. S.

Near v. Minnesota, 283 U. S. 697   47
Abrams v. United States, 250 U. S.   Toledo Newspaper Co. v. United
    616   States, 247 U. S. 402

FEDERAL-STATE RELATIONS

Pennsylvania v. Nelson, 350 U. S. 497; 76 S. Ct. 477; 100 L. Ed. 640 (1956)

An acknowledged member of the Communist Party, Steve Nelson, was convicted in Allegheny County, Pennsylvania, of violation of the Pennsylvania Sedition Act. He was sentenced to imprisonment and fine. While the Pennsylvania statute proscribes sedition against either the Government of the United States or the Government of Pennsylvania, this case was concerned only with alleged sedition against the United States.

OPINION BY MR. CHIEF JUSTICE WARREN
(Vote: 6-3)

Question—Does the Smith Act of 1940, which prohibits the knowing advocacy of the overthrow of the Government of the United States by force and violence, supercede the enforceability of the Pennsylvania Sedition Act.

Decision—Yes.

Reason—The Court examined the various federal acts on the subject, including the Internal Security Act of 1950 and the Communist Control Act of 1954, as well as the Smith Act, and concluded that Congress had intended to occupy the entire field of sedition. These acts, taken as a whole, "evince a Congressional plan which makes it reasonable to determine that no room has been left for the states to supplement it. . . . 'Sedition against the United States is not a *local* offense. It is a crime against the *Nation*'. . . . It is not only important but vital that such prosecutions should be exclusively within the control of the Federal Government." The Court went on to note that enforcement of state sedition statutes would present a serious danger of conflict with the administration of the federal program and would produce conflicting or incompatible court decisions.

"Since we find that Congress has occupied the field to the exclusion of parallel state legislation, that the dominant interest of the Federal Government precludes state intervention, and that administration of state acts would conflict with the operation of the federal plan, we are convinced that" the state statute cannot stand. "Without compelling indication to the contrary, we will not assume that Congress intended to permit the possibility of double punishment."

Corollary Cases

United States v. Lanza, 260 U. S. 377

Fox v. Ohio, 5 Howard 410

Gilbert v. Minnesota, 254 U. S. 325

Adler v. Board of Education of the City of New York, 342 U. S. 485

Campbell v. Hussey, 368 U. S. 297

American Communications Ass'n. v. Douds, 339 U. S. 382

Dennis v. United States, 341 U. S. 494

Hines v. Davidowitz, 312 U. S. 52

Rice v. Sante Fe Elevator Corp., 331 U. S. 218

Railway Employees' Dep't. AFL v. Hanson, 351 U. S. 225

THE FOURTEENTH AMENDMENT, EDUCATION AND THE SEPARATION OF CHURCH AND STATE

People of State of Illinois ex rel. McCollum v. Board of Education of School District No. 71, Champaign County, Illinois, 333 U. S. 203; 68 S. Ct. 461; 92 L. Ed. 648 (1948)

In the schools of Champaign County, Illinois, religious teachers were allowed to come into tax-supported public schools and give weekly religious instruction to the children who were attending school in these buildings. School authorities provided a thirty or forty-five minute religious period taken from the time of the regular school day. If the children did not attend the religious instruction, they were given something else to do in this time. The instructors were not paid by the school board and the children were required to have parental consent to attend these classes.

OPINION BY MR. JUSTICE BLACK
(Vote: 8-1)

Question—Is this use of the school building and school time a violation of the First and Fourteenth Amendments?

Decision—Yes.

Reason—The facts show there was a close cooperation between the secular and religious authorities in promoting religious education. Classes were conducted in the regular classrooms of the school building. The operation of the state's compulsory education system assisted in and was intregrated with the program of religious education carried on by the separate sects. Pupils compelled by law to attend school for a secular education were released in part from their duty if they went to these religious classes. This was beyond all question a utilization of the tax-supported public system to aid religious groups to spread their faith. And it fell squarely under the ban of the First Amendment (as made applicable to the states by the Fourteenth Amendment).

Corollary cases

Everson v. Board of Education of Ewing Township, 330 U. S. 1

Cochran v. Louisiana State Board of Education, 281 U. S. 370

Zorach v. Clauson, 343 U. S. 307

Doremus v. Board of Education, 342 U. S. 429

NECESSITY OF DECISION ON CONSTITUTIONAL QUESTIONS

Peters v. Hobby, 349 U. S. 331; 75 S. Ct. 790; 99 L. Ed. 1129 (1955)

The petitioner in this case, a Yale University professor of medicine, was employed by the United States Public Health Service, ultimately placed under the Department of Health, Education and Welfare, headed by Mrs. Oveta Culp Hobby, the respondent. The Loyalty Review Board in the Civil Service Commission determined that "there is reasonable doubt as to Dr. Peters' loyalty to the Government of the United States." This Board had been established by Executive Order 9835, issued by the President on March 21, 1947.

OPINION BY MR. CHIEF JUSTICE WARREN

(Vote: 7-2)

Question—Do Dr. Peters' removal and debarment deprive him of liberty and property without due process of law?

Decision—The difficulty here can be resolved without deciding this question.

Reason—"From a very early date, this Court has declined to anticipate a question of constitutional law in advance of the necessity of deciding it. . . . Applying this rule to the instant case, we must at the outset determine whether petitioner's removal and debarment were effected in accord with Executive

Order 9835. On consideration of this question, we conclude that the Loyalty Review Board's action was so patently in violation of the Executive Order—in fact, beyond the Board's delegated jurisdiction under the Order—that the constitutionality of the Order itself does not come into issue."

"There only remains for consideration the question of relief. Initially petitioner is entitled to a declaratory judgment that his removal and debarment were invalid. He is further entitled to an order directing the respondent members of the Civil Service Commission to expunge from its records the Loyalty Review Board's finding that there is a reasonable doubt as to petitioner's loyalty and to expunge from its records any ruling that petitioner is barred from federal employment by reason of that finding. His prayer for reinstatement, however, cannot be granted, since it appears that the term of petitioner's appointment would have expired on December 31, 1953, wholly apart from his removal on loyalty grounds."

Corollary cases

Bailey vs. Richardson, 341 U. S. 918

Wieman vs. Updegraff, 344 U. S. 182

U. S. vs. Lovett, 328 U. S. 303

Cole v. Young, 351 U. S. 536

Charles River Bridge vs. Warren Bridge, 11 Peters 420

Alma Motor Co. vs. Timken-Detroit Axle Co., 329 U. S. 129

Joint Anti-Fascist Refugee Committee vs. McGrath, 341 U. S. 123

Poe v. Ullman, 367 U. S. 497

Service v. Dulles, 354 U. S. 363

FEDERAL LABOR LEGISLATION

Phelps Dodge Corp. v. National Labor Relations Board, 313 U. S. 177; 61 S. Ct. 845; 85 L. Ed. 1271 (1941)

On June 10, 1935 a strike by the International Union of Mine and Smelter Workers at the Phelps Dodge's Copper Queen Mine at Bisbee, Arizona began. It ended August 24, 1935. During the time of the strike the National Labor Relations Act came into being. Following the strike a number of men had been refused employment because of their affiliations with the union. Most of these men were strikers, but two had ceased to be in the corporation's employ before the strike and sought employment after the close of the strike. The National Labor Relations Board concluded that the Phelps Dodge Corporation was guilty of unfair labor practices and ordered it to rehire the men that it had fired and to offer jobs to the men it had refused to hire solely because of their affiliation with the union and also to pay both the men that they fired because of the affiliation with the union (the cause of the strike) and the new employees the pay that they had lost.

OPINION BY MR. JUSTICE FRANKFURTER
(Vote: 8-0, Five justices dissented in part.)

Question—Can an employer subject to the National Labor Relations Act refuse to hire and to discharge an employee solely because of affiliation with a labor union?

Decision—No.

Reason—Congress explicitly disclosed its purpose in declaring the policy which underlies the Act. Its ultimate concern was to "eliminate the causes of certain substantial obstructions to the free flow of commerce." This vital national purpose was to be accomplished "by encouraging the practice and procedure of collective bargaining and by protecting the exercise of the workers full freedom of association." Protection of the rights of the worker to organize does not curtail the appropriate sphere of managerial freedom. The Act does not interfere with the rights of management to hire and fire employees but, under cover of this right, management may not intimidate or coerce its employees with respect to their self-organization and representation.

"We have already recognized the power of Congress to deny an employer the freedom to discriminate in discharging." . . . "Reinstatement is the conventional correction for discriminatory discharges. Experience having demonstrated that discrimination in hiring is twin to discriminaton in firing, it would indeed be surprising if Congress gave a remedy for the one which it denied for the other."

Corollary cases

N.L.R.B. v. Jones and Laughlin Steel Corp., 301 U. S. 1

N.L.R.B. v. Fansteel Metallurgical Corp., 306 U. S. 240

N.L.R.B. v. Friedman-Harry Marks Clothing Co., 301 U. S. 58

N.L.R.B. v. Fruehauf Trailer Co., 301 U. S. 49

THE FOURTEENTH AMENDMENT AND EDUCATION

Pierce v. Society of Sisters of the Holy Names of Jesus and Mary, 268 U. S. 510; 45 S. Ct. 571; 69 L. Ed. 1070 (1925)

In November, 1922, the state of Oregon passed a Compulsory Education Act requiring every child from the ages of eight to sixteen to attend public school. Parents or guardians who refused would be guilty of a misdemeanor. The plaintiff corporation conducted a group of private schools, according to the tenets of the Roman Catholic Church. They brought suit challenging that the statute conflicted with the right of parents to choose schools where their children would receive appropriate moral and religious training, and the right of schools and teachers to engage in a useful business or profession.

OPINION BY MR. JUSTICE McREYNOLDS

(No evidence from the report that the decision was not unanimous.)

Question—Can a state require children to attend public schools?

Decision—No.

Reason—Rights guaranteed by the Constitution may not be abridged by state legislation that has no reasonable relation to some purpose within the competency of the state. The liberty of the Constitution forbids the standardization of children by compelling them to attend public school instruction only. "The child is not the mere creature of the State; those who nurture him and direct his destiny have the right, coupled with the high duty, to recognize and prepare him for additional obligations.

"We think it entirely plain that the Act of 1922 unreasonably interferes with the liberty of parents and guardians to direct the upbringing and education of children under their control." Also, the corporations or schools involved had business and property for which they had a claim to protection under the Fourteenth Amendment. These rights, the Court held, were threatened with destruction through this unwarranted compulsion.

Corollary cases

Meyer v. Nebraska, 262 U. S. 390
Minersville School District v. Gobitis, 310 U. S. 586
West Virginia State Board of Education v. Barnette, 319 U. S. 624
Cochran v. Louisiana State Board of Education, 281 U. S. 370

Everson v. Board of Education of Ewing Township, 330 U. S. 1
People of Illinois ex rel. McCollum v. Board of Education, 333 U. S. 203
Zorach v. Clauson, 343 U. S. 307

FEDERAL TAX IMMUNITY

Pittman v. Home Owners' Loan Corporation, 308 U. S. 21, 60 S. Ct. 15, 84 L. Ed. 11 (1939)

The Home Owners Loan Corporation brought this proceeding in Baltimore for a writ of mandamus requiring the Clerk of the Superior Court of Baltimore to record a mortgage executed to the corporation upon the payment of the ordinary recording charge and without affixing stamps for the state recording tax. Since the Home Owners' Loan Corporation was expressly an instrumentality of the United States, it was contended that the tax as thus applied was invalid. The act of Congress setting up this corporation stated that it should be exempt from all state or municipal taxes.

OPINION BY MR. CHIEF JUSTICE HUGHES
(Vote: 8-0)

Question—Did Congress grant a tax immunity of a greater extent than was within its constitutional power?

Decision—No.

Reason—Congress has not only the power to create a corporation to facilitate the performance of governmental functions, but also has the power to protect the operations thus validly authorized. This power to preserve necessarily comes within the range of the express power conferred upon Congress to make all laws that shall be necessary and proper for carrying into execution all powers vested by the Constitution in the government of the United States. In this case, Congress had undertaken to safeguard the operations of the Home Owners' Loan Corporation by providing the described immunity. The Court construed this provision as embracing and prohibiting the tax in question. Since Congress had the constitutional authority to enact this provision, it was binding upon the Supreme Court as the supreme law of the land.

Corollary cases

Federal Land Bank v. Crosland, 261 U. S. 374

Graves v. New York ex rel. O'Keefe, 306 U. S. 466

McCulloch v. Maryland, 4 Wheaton 316

Smith v. Kansas City Title Co., 255

New York v. United States, 326 U. S. 572

Federal Land Bank of St. Paul v. Bismarck Lumber Co., 314 U. S. 95

Standard Oil Co. v. Johnson, 316 U. S. 481

U. S. 180

The Shreveport Case, 234 U. S. 342

Bank of New York v. Supervisors of New York County, 7 Wallace 26

Trotter v. Tennessee, 290 U. S. 354

Alabama v. King and Boozer, 314 U. S. 1

Oklahoma Tax Commission v. Texas Co., 336 U. S. 342

Carson v. Roane-Anderson Co., 342 U. S. 232

EQUAL PROTECTION AND SEGREGATION

Plessy v. Ferguson, 163 U. S. 537; 16 S. Ct. 1138; 41 L. Ed. 256 (1896)

In 1892, Plessy, a citizen of Louisiana, having seven-eighths Caucasian and one-eighth African blood, boarded a train from New Orleans to Covington in the same state. The conductor ordered him out of the car for white passengers and to sit in the Negro car. When Plessy refused to obey the order he was forcibly jailed by a policeman and convicted of violating a state statute of July 10, 1890, which required separate accommodations for white and colored passengers on railroads. An information was filed against him for the violation, and Plessy filed a demurrer against Ferguson, judge of the Criminal District Court. Plessy appealed on a writ of error when relief was denied him in the state court.

OPINION BY MR. JUSTICE BROWN
(Vote: 7-1)

Question—Does the Louisiana statute providing "equal but separate" railway carriages for the whites and colored violate the Thirteenth and Fourteenth Amendments?

Decision—No.

Reason—The object of the law is to ensure absolute equality of both races before the law. However, this is a political equality, not a social equality. The case hinges itself on the question of whether or not this is a reasonable regulation. Thus established usages, customs, and traditions, as well as the preservation of public peace and good order must be considered. Gauged by this standard, separate public conveyances are not unreasonable nor contrary to the Fourteenth Amendment.

If the colored race assumes that this separation makes them inferior, it is not by reason of the act. If the civil and political rights of both races be equal, that is sufficient. The Constitution cannot put them on the same plane socially.

Corollary cases

McCabe v. Atchison, Topeka and Santa Fe Ry. Co., 235 U. S. 151

Shelley v. Kraemer, 334 U. S. 1

Missouri ex rel. Gaines v. Canada, 305 U. S. 337

Sipuel v. Board of Regents of the University of Oklahoma, 332 U. S. 631

Sweatt v. Painter, 338 U. S. 865

Morgan v. Virginia, 328 U. S. 373

Hall v. De Cuir, 95 U. S. 485

FEDERAL INCOME TAX

Pollock v. Farmers' Loan and Trust Co., 158 U. S. 601; 15 S. Ct. 912; 39 L. Ed. 1108 (1895)

A bill was filed by Charles Pollock, a citizen of the State of Massachusetts, on behalf of himself and all other stockholders of the company against the Farmers' Loan and Trust Co., a corporation of the State of New York. The bill alleged that the defendant claimed authority under the provisions of the Act of August, 1894 (a statute providing for the imposition of a tax on incomes in excess of $4,000 received by individuals, associations, or corporations) to pay to the United States a tax of 2 per cent on the net profits of money in question including income derived from real estate and bonds of municipal corporations owned by it. Moreover, the bill alleged that such a tax was unconstitutional, in that the income from stocks and bonds of the states of the United States, counties, and municipalities therein is not subject to taxation.

OPINION BY MR. CHIEF JUSTICE FULLER
(Vote: 5-4)

Question—Is this a direct tax? Did any partial unconstitutionality of the 1894 income tax law render it void in its entirety?

Decision—Yes (to both questions).

Reason—"If the revenue derived from municipal bonds cannot be taxed because the source cannot be, the same rule applies to revenue from any other source not subject to the tax; and the lack of power to levy any but an apportioned tax on real estate and personal property equally exists as to the revenue therefrom."

The same statute may be in part constitutional and unconstitutional, and if the parts are wholly independent of each other, that which is constitutional may stand and that which is unconstitutional will be rejected. If they are dependent on each other for the outcome or purpose of the legislation then both parts or all of the statute is to be declared unconstitutional.

Here the income from realty formed a vital part of this scheme for taxation embodied therein. If that were to be stricken out and also all income from invested property, the largest part of the anticipated revenue would be eliminated and this would leave the burden of the tax to be borne by the professions, trades, and labor. In that way what was intended as a tax on capital would have remained in substance a tax on occupations and labor. This was not the intention of Congress and the whole law had to be declared unconstitutional.

Corollary cases

Springer v. United States, 102 U. S. 588

Frost v. Corporation Commission, 278 U. S. 515

Nicol v. Ames, 173 U. S. 509

Pollock v. Trust Co., 157 U. S. 429

Bromley v. McCaughn, 280 U. S. 124

Knowlton v. Moore, 178 U. S. 41

Flint v. Stone Tracy Co., 220 U. S. 107

Patton v. Brady, 184 U. S. 608

Hylton v. United States, 3 Dallas 171

Brushaber v. Union Pacific R.R. Co., 240 U. S. 1

COUNSEL AND DUE PROCESS

Powell v. Alabama, 287 U. S. 45; 53 S. Ct. 55; 77 L. Ed. 158 (1932)

Petitioners, nine Negro youths, were indicted for the rape of two white girls. They were tried by jury six days after the day upon which they were arrested, amidst an atmosphere of tense, hostile public sentiment. They were not represented by counsel, not asked if they desired counsel, the judge simply appointing "all members of the bar" to defend them. The jury returned the death penalty. This was affirmed on appeal although the chief justice of the state Supreme Court strongly dissented, claiming an unfair trial.

OPINION BY MR. JUSTICE SUTHERLAND
(Vote: 7-2)

Question—Were the petitioners denied the right of counsel, and, if so, did such denial infringe the due process clause of the Fourteenth Amendment?

Decision—Yes.

Reason—The basic elements comprising due process of law according to the Constitution are notice and hearing (preliminary steps) together with a legally competent tribunal having jurisdiction of the case. A hearing includes, in our country at least, the right and aid of counsel when so desired. The ordinary layman, even the intelligent and educated layman, is not skilled in the science of law, and needs the advice and direction of competent counsel. It is apparent from the settled facts that the Negroes were in effect denied the right to counsel. They were transients and all lived in other states, yet were given no chance to communicate with members of their families to obtain counsel. Further, the trial was carried out with such dispatch that they were accorded no time to prepare a defense employing a counsel of their own choice.

"In the light of the facts outlined in the forepart of this opinion—the ignorance and illiteracy of the defendants, their youth, the circumstances of public hostility, the imprisonment, and the close surveillance of the defendants by the military forces, the fact that their friends and families were all in other states and communications with them necessarily difficult, and above all that they stood in deadly peril of their lives—we think the failure of the trial courts to give them reasonable time and opportunity to secure counsel was a clear denial of due process."

This was the first of the famous "Scottsboro cases." The second was Norris v. Alabama.

Corollary cases

Betts v. Brady, 316 U. S. 455
Bute v. Illinois, 333 U. S. 640
Johnson v. Zerbst, 304 U. S. 458
Canizio v. People of State of New York, 327 U. S. 82
Gibbs v. Burke, 337 U. S. 773

De Meerleer v. Michigan, 329 U. S. 663
Carter v. Illinois, 329 U. S. 173
Norris v. Alabama, 294 U. S. 587
Smith v. O'Grady, 312 U. S. 329
Gideon v. Wainwright, 372 U. S. 335 (1963)
LaVallee v. Durocher, 377 U. S. 998 (1964)

THE PRESIDENT'S WAR POWERS

The Prize Cases, 2 Black 635; 17 L. Ed. 459 (1863)

By proclamations of April 15, April 19 and April 27, 1861, President Lincoln established a blockade of southern ports. These cases were brought to recover damages suffered by ships carrying cargoes to the Confederate states during the blockade. The blockade was declared before Congress had a chance to assemble and take action on the matter. These ships had been raided by public ships of the United States.

OPINION BY MR. JUSTICE GRIER
(Vote: 5-4)

Question—Did a state of war exist at the time this blockade was instituted that would justify a resort to these means of subduing the hostile force?

Decision—Yes.

Reason—Although a civil war is never publicly proclaimed, *eo nomine,* against insurgents, its actual existence is a fact in our domestic history which the court is bound to notice and to know. By the Constitution, Congress alone has the power to declare a national or foreign war. It cannot declare war against a state or any number of states, by virtue of any clause in the Constitution. The Constitution confers on the President the whole executive power. He is bound to take care that the laws be faithfully executed. He is commander-in-chief of the army and navy of the United States, and of the militia of the several states when called into the service of the United States. He has no power to initiate or declare war, either against a foreign nation or a domestic state. But he is authorized to call out the militia and use the military and naval forces of the United States in case of invasion by foreign nations, and to suppress insurrection against the government of a state or of the United States. If a war be made by invasion by a foreign nation, the President is not only authorized but bound to resist force by force. He does not initiate the war, but is bound to accept the challenge without waiting for any special legislative authority. And whether the hostile party be a foreign invader or domestic states organized in rebellion, it is none the less a war, although the declaration of it be unilateral. "The greatest of civil wars was not gradually developed by popular commotion, tumultuous assemblies, or local unorganized insurrections. However long may have been its previous conception, it nevertheless sprung forth suddenly from the parent brain, a

Minerva in the full panoply of war. The President was bound
to meet it in the shape it presented itself, without waiting
for Congress to baptize it with a name; and no name given to
it by him or them could change the fact. . . . Whether the
President in fulfilling his duties, as Commander-in-Chief, in
suppressing an insurrection, has met with such armed hostile
resistance, and a civil war of such alarming proportions as
will compel him to accord to them the character of bel-
ligerents, is a question to be decided by him, and this court
must be governed by the decision and acts of the Political
Department of the government to which this power was entrusted. 'He must determine what degree of force the crisis
demands.' The proclamation of blockade is, itself, official and
conclusive evidence to the court that a state of war existed
which demanded and authorized a recourse to such a measure,
under the circumstances peculiar to the case."

Corollary cases

Ex parte Milligan, 4 Wallace 2   Duncan v. Kahanamoku, 327 U. S.
Ex parte Quirin, 317 U. S. 1   304

TRIAL BY MILITARY COMMISSION
Ex Parte Quirin, 317 U. S. 1; 63 S. Ct. 1; 87 L. Ed. 3 (1942)

The petitioners were all born in Germany. All lived in
the United States and returned to Germany between 1933
and 1941. Petitioners attended sabotage school. After
completing this training, Quirin and two others boarded a
submarine and proceeded to Amagansett Beach, N. Y.
They landed on or about June 13, 1942, carrying a supply
of explosives and wearing German infantry uniforms. They
buried their uniforms and proceeded to New York City.
The four remaining petitioners proceeded by submarine to
Ponte Vedra Beach, Florida. These men were wearing caps
of German marine infantry and carrying explosives. They
buried uniform parts and proceeded to Jacksonville,
Florida, and thence to various points in the United States.
All were taken into custody by agents of the F.B.I. All
had received instructions to destroy war industries and
war facilities in the United States. The President of the
United States by order of July 2, 1942 appointed a Military Commission and directed it to try petitioners for
offenses against the law of war and Articles of War, and
prescribed regulations on trial and review of record of the
trial and any decision handed down by the Commission.

OPINION BY MR. CHIEF JUSTICE STONE
(Vote: 8-0)

Question—Was trial by a military commission without jury legal?

Decision—Yes.

Reason—It is necessary for the federal government to provide for the common defense. The President has the power to carry into effect all laws that Congress passes regarding the conduct of the war and all laws defining and punishing offenses against the law of nations, including those that pertain to the conduct of the war. These men were nothing more than spies. They fall under this category by their actions. "It has not hitherto been challenged, and, so far as we are advised, it has never been suggested in the very extensive literature of the subject that an alien spy, in time of war, could not be tried by military tribunal without a jury.

"We conclude that the Fifth and Sixth Amendments did not restrict whatever authority was conferred by the Constitution to try offenses against the law of war by military commission, and that petitioners, charged with such an offense not required to be tried by jury at common law, were lawfully placed on trial by the Commission without a jury."

Corollary cases

Ex parte Milligan, 4 Wallace 2

Ludecke v. Watkins, 335 U. S. 160

In re Yamashita, 327 U. S. 1

Hirabayashi v. United States, 320 U. S. 81

Korematsu v. United States, 323 U. S. 214

Ex parte Endo, 323 U. S. 283

Duncan v. Kahanamoku, 327 U. S. 304

United States ex rel. Toth v. Quarles, 350 U. S. 11

Reid v. Covert, 354 U. S. 1

McElroy v. United States ex. rel. Guagliardo, 361 U. S. 281

Grisham v. Hogan, 361 U. S. 278

STATE LEGISLATION AND INTERSTATE COMMERCE

In re Rahrer, 140 U. S. 545; 11 S. Ct. 865; 35 L. Ed. 572 (1891)

On August 8, 1890 Congress passed the Wilson Act, providing that all intoxicating liquors shipped into any state or territory and remaining there shall be subject to the laws of the state or territory as though the goods had been produced therein, and should not be exempt therefrom because introduced in original package or otherwise. Rahrer, an agent for liquor dealers in Missouri, sold in the original package in Kansas a four-gallon keg of beer and a pint of whiskey, part of a shipment received from the Missouri dealers. This was in violation of the Kansas general prohibition law passed before the Act of Congress.

OPINION BY MR. CHIEF JUSTICE FULLER

(No evidence from the report that the decision was not unanimous.)

Question—Does the Wilson Act convey to the state, power over interstate commerce delegated only to Congress?

Decision—No.

Reason—"No reason is perceived why, if Congress chooses to provide that certain designated subjects of interstate commerce shall be governed by a rule which divests them of that character at an earlier period of time than would otherwise be the case, it is not within its competency to do so." Congress did not use terms of permission to the state to act but simply removed an impediment to the enforcement of the state laws in respect to imported packages in their original condition, created by the absence of a specific utterance on its part. It imparted no power to the state not then possessed but allowed imported property to lose immunity at once upon arrival within the local jurisdiction. This is not the case of a law enacted in the unauthorized exercise of a power exclusively confided to Congress, but a law that was competent for the state to pass, that could not operate upon articles occupying a certain situation until the passage of an act of Congress.

Corollary cases

Cooley v. Board, of Wardens, 12 Howard 299

Robbins v. Shelby County Taxing District, 120 U. S. 489

Bowman v. Chicago and N. W. Railway Co., 125 U. S. 465

Rhodes v. Iowa, 170 U. S. 412

Brown v. Maryland, 12 Wheaton 419

Leisy v. Hardin, 135 U. S. 100

Clark Distilling Co. v. Western Maryland Ry. Co., 242 U. S. 311

United States v. Hill, 248 U. S. 420

Whitfield v. Ohio, 297 U. S. 431

Kentucky Whip and Collar Co. v. I. C. R.R. Co., 299 U. S. 334

STATES AND INTERSTATE COMMERCE

Railroad Commission of Wisconsin v. Chicago B. & Q. R.R. Co., 257 U. S. 563; 42 S. Ct. 232; 66 L. Ed. 371 (1922)

The Transportation Act of 1920, passed by Congress, empowered the Interstate Commerce Commission, after a prescribed investigation, to remove any undue advantage intrastate commerce might have over interstate commerce. Wisconsin set a minimum on intrastate fares below the rate prescribed by the Commission and this was considered by the Commission to be unjust discrimination.

OPINION BY MR. CHIEF JUSTICE TAFT

(No evidence from the report that the decision was not unanimous.)

Question—Under the Transportation Act had Congress employed a power reserved to the states, that is, the regulation of intrastate commerce?

Decision—No.

Reason—Commerce is a unit and does not always regard state lines, and while, under the Constitution, interstate and intrastate commerce are ordinarily subject to regulation by different sovereignties, yet when they are so mingled together that the supreme authority, the nation, cannot exercise complete effective control over interstate commerce without incidental regulation of intrastate commerce, such incidental regulation is not an invasion of state authority or a violation of the commerce clause. "Congress as the dominant controller of interstate commerce may, therefore, restrain undue limitation of the earning power of the interstate commerce system in doing state work. . . . In such development, it can impose any reasonable condition on a state's use of interstate carriers for intrastate commerce, it deems necessary or desirable. This is because of the supremacy of the national power in this field. . . .

"It does not involve general regulation of intrastate commerce. Action of the Interstate Commerce Commission in this regard should be directed to substantial disparity which operates as a real discrimination against, and obstruction to, interstate commerce, and must leave appropriate discretion to the state authorities to deal with intrastate rates as between themselves on the general level which the Interstate Commerce Commission has found to be fair to interstate commerce."

Corollary cases

Houston, East & West Texas Ry. Co. v. United States, 234 U. S. 342

North Carolina v. United States, 325 U. S. 507

Interstate Commerce Commission v. Goodrich Transit Co., 224 U. S. 194

New York v. United States, 257 U. S. 591

Dayton-Goose Creek Ry. Co. v. United States, 263 U. S. 456

THE PRESIDENT'S REMOVAL POWER

Rathbun, Humphrey's Executor v. United States, 295 U. S. 602; 55 S. Ct. 869; 79 L. Ed. 1611 (1935)

William E. Humphrey on December 10, 1931 was nominated by President Hoover to succeed himself as a member of the Federal Trade Commission, and was confirmed by the Senate. He was duly commissioned for a term of seven years, ending on September 25, 1938. On July 25, 1933 President Roosevelt asked the commissioner for his resignation, on the grounds that the aims of the administration would be carried out more effectively by his own personnel. Humphrey refused, and was removed by the President on October 7, 1933. Suit was brought by Samuel F. Rathbun, executor of the deceased Humphrey's estate.

OPINION BY MR. JUSTICE SUTHERLAND

(No evidence from the report that the decision was not unanimous.)

Question—Do the provisions of the Federal Trade Commission Act stating that "any commissioner may be removed by the President for inefficiency, neglect of duty, or malfeasance in office" restrict the power of the President to remove a commissioner except for one or more of the causes named, and, if so, is such a restriction valid under the Constitution?

Decision—Yes.

Reason—In the act setting up the Federal Trade Commission the term of office was set at seven years because the exacting and difficult character of the work made it desirable that the commissioners have an opportunity to acquire the expertness that comes from experience.

It was also the intention of Congress to create a commission not subject to the government, nor under any political domination or control, but separate from any existing department. It is clear that the length and certainty of tenure was considered a vital factor in setting up the commission, and that therefore executive removal power is limited to the causes mentioned.

As to the contention that the restriction is an unconstitutional interference with the executive power of the President, the government pointed to the Myers v. United States case. However, Myers was a postmaster, which is an executive function, subject to the control of the Chief Executive, which differs greatly from a commissioner having legislative and judicial power.

The power of Congress to create such quasi-legislative or quasi-judicial agencies cannot be doubted, nor the authority to fix the period of office, and to forbid their removal, except for specified causes. The Myers decision affirms the power of the President to remove purely executive officers, but for officers under consideration in this case, no removal may be made except for the causes mentioned. "We think it plain under the Constitution that illimitable power of removal is not possessed by the President in respect of officers of the character of those just named. The authority of Congress, in creating quasi-legislative or quasi-judicial agencies, to require them to act in discharge of their duties independently of executive control cannot well be doubted, and that authority includes, as an appropriate incident, power to fix the period during which they shall continue, and to forbid their removal except for cause in the meantime."

Corollary cases

Shurtleff v. United States, 189 U. S. 311

Standard Oil Co. v. United States, 283 U. S. 235

Federal Trade Commission v. Raladam Co., 283 U. S. 643

Myers v. United States, 272 U. S. 52

Morgan v. United States, 312 U. S. 701

Wiener v. United States, 357 U. S. 349

THE COURTS AND LEGISLATIVE REDISTRICTING

Reynolds v. Sims, 377 U. S. 533; 84 S. Ct. 1362; 11 L. Ed. 2d. 506 (1964)

A complaint was filed by a group of residents, taxpayers, and voters of Jefferson County, Alabama, challenging the apportionment of the Alabama legislature. The most recent apportionment of the Alabama legislature was based on the 1900 federal census despite the requirement of the state constitution that the legislature be apportioned decennially. As a result of population growth, Jefferson County and others were alleged to have suffered serious discrimination with respect to the allocation of legislative representation.

Also, there were two plans for apportionment pending. One was a proposed amendment to the state constitution. The other was a statute enacted as standby legislation to take effect if the proposed constitutional amendment should fail of adoption or be declared void by the courts. In neither of these plans was there provision for apportionment of either of the houses of the Alabama legislature on a population basis.

(In companion cases the Court held invalid the legislative apportionment of five other states, Colorado, Delaware, Maryland, New York, and Virginia.)

OPINION BY MR. CHIEF JUSTICE WARREN
(Vote: 8-1)

Question—Had there been violation of the Equal Protection Clause of the Fourteenth Amendment?

Decision — Yes.

Reason—A predominant consideration in determining whether a state legislative apportionment scheme constitutes an invidious discrimination violative of rights asserted under the Equal Protection Clause is that the rights allegedly impaired are individual and personal in nature. Legislators represent people, not trees or acres. The right to elect legislators in a free and unimpaired fashion is a bedrock of our political system. Overweighting and overvaluing the votes of persons living in one place has the certain effect of dilution and undervaluing the votes of those living elsewhere. Full and effective participation by all citizens in state government requires that each citizen have an equally effective voice in the election of members of his state legislature. As a basic constitutional standard the Equal Protection Clause requires that the seats in both houses of a bicameral state legislature must be apportioned on a population basis. An individual's right to vote for state legislators is unconstitutionally impaired when its weight is in a substantial fashion diluted when compared with the votes of citizens living in other parts of the state. This applies to both houses of the legislature. Attempted reliance on the federal analogy to state legislative apportionment arrangements "appears often to be little more than an after-the-fact rationalization offered in defense of maladjusted state apportionment arrangements." By apportionment on a population basis is meant an honest and good faith effort to set up districts on a practical basis. Mathematical exactness or precision is hardly a workable constitutional requirement.

Corollary cases

Colegrove v. Green, 328 U. S. 549 (1946)

Baker v. Carr, 369 U. S. 186 (1962)

Gray v. Sanders, 372 U. S. 368 (1963)

Wesberry v. Sanders, 376 U. S. 1 (1964)

WMCA, Inc. v. Lowenzo, 377 U. S. 633 (1964)

Lucas v. Forty-Fourth General As-sembly of Colorado, 377 U. S. 713 (1964)

Maryland Committee for Fair Representation v. Tawes, 377 U. S. 656 (1964)

Davis v. Mann, 377 U. S. 678 (1964)

Roman v. Sincock, 377 U. S. 695 (1964)

See also Swann v. Adams, 378 U. S. 533 (1964) and cases there noted.

STATE LEGISLATION AND INTERSTATE COMMERCE

Rhodes v. Iowa, 170 U. S. 412; 18 S. Ct. 664; 42 L. Ed. 1088 (1898)

A box labeled "groceries" and addressed to a party by the name of Horn in Iowa was received by the station agent at Brighton, Iowa. The package was sent from Illinois. The station agent placed the box in the station warehouse where, a few hours later, it was seized under a search warrant by a constable on what proved to be the the correct suspicion that it contained liquor. Iowa had a state law that only the state could control the sale of liquor in Iowa and made the transportation of liquor from one place to another an offense. The Wilson Act passed by Congress stated that goods were no longer regarded as being in interstate commerce upon arrival in a state. The purpose of this Act was the regulation of the transportation of intoxicating liquors between states.

OPINION BY MR. JUSTICE WHITE
(Vote: 6-3)

Question—Was the seizure under the Iowa law legal?

Decision—No.

Reason—The Court reasoned that, interpreting the statute in the light of all of its provisions, it was not intended to and did not cause the power of the state to attach to an interstate commerce shipment while the merchandise was in transit under such shipment, and until its arrival at the point of destination and delivery there to the consignee. Therefore arrival in such state, as stated in the Wilson Act, was interpreted by the Court to mean arrival in the hands of the consignee.

Corollary cases

Brown v. Maryland, 12 Wheaton 419

Bowman v. Chicago & N.W. Ry. Co., 125 U. S. 465

Leisy v. Hardin, 135 U. S. 100

In re Rahrer, 140 U. S. 545

Clark Distilling Co., v. Western Maryland Ry. Co., 242 U. S. 311

United States v. Hill, 248 U. S. 420

Whitfield v. Ohio, 297 U. S. 431

Kentucky Whip and Collar Co. v. I. C. R.R. Co., 299 U. S. 334

DELEGATION OF LEGISLATIVE POWER

A. L. A. Schechter Poultry Corp. v. United States, 295 U. S. 495; 55 S. Ct. 837; 79 L. Ed. 1570 (1935)

The A.L.A. Schechter Poultry Corp. was convicted in the District Court of the United States for the Eastern District of New York on an indictment charging violations of what was known as the "Live Poultry Code," established by executive order under the National Industrial Recovery Act. The Circuit Court of Appeals sustained the conviction in the District Court on sixteen counts for violation of the Code, but reversed the conviction on two counts that charged violation of requirements as to minimum wages and maximum hours of labor, as these were not deemed to be within the Congressional power of regulation.

The N.R.A. provided for the setting up of codes that would establish certain standards that were to be upheld under force of civil and criminal action. If an industry did not set up its own code, it would be up to the President to impose a code upon it. Schechter was a poultry dealer in New York City and disregarded the code. When tried, he was found guilty on eighteen counts. He then took the case to the Supreme Court.

OPINION BY MR. CHIEF JUSTICE HUGHES

(No evidence from the report that the decision was not unanimous.)

Questions—1. Was the act an illegal delegation of legislative powers?

2. Was the poultry in this case able to be considered within the interstate commerce power of Congress?

Decisions—1. Yes.

2. No.

Reason—1. The act set no standard, nor rules of conduct to be followed. It was too broad a declaration, leaving the

President too much room for descretion. The act left virtually untouched the field of policy. The President in approving a code could impose his own conditions. It was an unconstitutional delegation of legislative power.

The Constitution provides that "all legislative powers herein granted shall be vested in a Congress of the United States, which shall consist of a Senate and House of Representatives," and the Congress is authorized "to make all laws which shall be necessary and proper for carrying into execution" its general powers. The Congress is not permitted to abdicate or to transfer to others the essential legislative functions with which it is thus vested.

2. Although the poultry came from various states, when it arrived in New York it remained there and was processed. Congress could regulate it until it reached New York, after that it was intrastate commerce and as such it could not be controlled by Congress.

Corollary cases

See Panama Refining Co., v. Ryan and cases there cited.

Hampton, Jr. and Co. v. United States, 276 U. S. 394

McKinley v. United States, 249 U. S. 397

United States v. Grimaud, 220 U. S. 506

Hood and Sons v. United States, 307 U. S. 588

Sunshine Anthracite Coal Co. v. Adkins, 310 U. S. 381

New York Central Securities Corp. v. United States, 287 U. S. 12

United States v. Rock Royal Cooperative, 307 U. S. 533

FREEDOM OF PRESS AND SPEECH

Schenck v. United States, 249 U. S. 47; 39 S. Ct. 247; 63 L. Ed. 470 (1919)

Schenck was the general secretary of the Socialist Party. He sent out about 15,000 leaflets to men who had been called to military service, urging them to assert their opposition to the Conscription Act. He was indicted on three counts under the Espionage Act of 1917: (1) conspiracy to cause insubordination in the military service of the United States, (2) using the mails for the transmission of matter declared to be nonmailable by the Espionage Act, (3) the unlawful use of the mails for the transmission of the same matter as mentioned above.

OPINION BY MR. JUSTICE HOLMES

(No evidence from the report that the decision was not unanimous.)

Question—Does the statute in question violate the freedom of speech and the press guaranteed by the First Amendment?

Decision—No.

Reason—The defendants claimed that the tendency of the circular to obstruct the draft was protected by the First Amendment. That would be true in normal circumstances, but the character of every act must be judged according to the circumstances in which it was done. What must be ascertained is whether the words are used in such circumstances as "to create a clear and present danger" which would have brought about substantive evils which Congress had a right to prevent. It is a question of proximity and degree. Many things may not be said when a nation is at war, which may be of no consequence in time of peace. "The most stringent protection of free speech would not protect a man in falsely shouting fire in a theatre and causing a panic." The statute punishes conspiracies to obstruct as well as actual obstruction. There are no grounds for saying that success alone makes the action a crime.

Corollary cases

Gitlow v. New York, 268 U. S. 652

Bridges v. California, 314 U. S. 252

Gompers v. Bucks Stove and Range Co., 221 U. S. 418

Terminiello v. City of Chicago, 337 U. S. 1

Abrams v. United States, 250 U. S. 616

Herndon v. Lowry, 301 U. S. 242

Winters v. New York, 333 U. S. 507

Pennekamp v. Florida, 328 U. S. 331

Near v. Minnesota, 283 U. S. 697

Grosjean v. American Press Co., 297 U. S. 233

DUE PROCESS AND SELF-INCRIMINATION

Schmerber v. California, 384 U. S. 757; 86 S. Ct. 1826; 16 L. Ed. 2d 908 (1966)

Armando Schmerber had been convicted of driving an automobile while under the influence of intoxicating liquor. He had been arrested at a hospital while receiving treatment for injuries suffered in an accident involving the automobile he had apparently been driving. Under police direction a blood sample was taken from Schmerber by a physician at the hospital. This was done despite Schmerber's protests. Analysis of the sample of blood indicated intoxication, and the report of this analysis was admitted in evidence at the trial.

OPINION BY MR. JUSTICE BRENNAN
(Vote: 5-4)

Question—Does taking a blood sample under these circumstances (1) deny the accused due process of law, (2) abridge the privilege against self-incrimination, (3) deny the right to counsel, and (4) constitute unreasonable search and seizure?

Decision—The Court denied all four contentions.

Reason—(1) The case of *Breithaupt* v. *Abram* (352 U. S. 432, 1957) is controlling here. There a similar blood sample was taken while the individual was unconscious. This did not constitute offense against a "sense of justice" and thus there was no denial of due process. (2) *Breithaupt* also controls the self-incrimination aspect of the case. The privilege protects an accused person only from being compelled to testify against himself or otherwise provide the State with evidence of a testimonial or communicative nature. The taking and use of the blood sample did not involve compulsion to these ends. (3) Here there was no issue presented of counsel's ability to assist Schmerber in respect of any rights he did possess. (4) As to the search and seizure claim, there was plainly probable cause for the officer to arrest the accused. Further, the officer "might reasonably have believed that he was confronted with an emergency, in which the delay necessary to obtain a warrant, under the circumstances, threatened 'the destruction of the evidence'. . . . We are told that the percentage of alcohol in the blood begins to diminish shortly after drinking stops, as the body functions to eliminate it from the system." Finally the Court noted that the test was performed in a reasonable manner in a hospital environment according to accepted medical practices and emphasized that the judgment was only on the basis of the facts of the present case.

Corollary cases

Rochin v. California, 342 U. S. 165
Escobedo v. Illinois, 378 U. S. 478

Miranda v. Arizona, 384 U. S. 436
Twining v. New Jersey, 211 U. S. 78
Malloy v. Hogan, 378 U. S. 1
Mapp v. Ohio, 367 U. S. 643

DUE PROCESS AND SEPARATION OF CHURCH AND STATE

School District of Abington Township, Pa. v. Schempp, 374 U. S. 203; 83 S. Ct. 1560; 10 L. Ed. 2d. 844 (1963)

Pennsylvania by statute required that at least ten verses from the Bible should be read, without comment, at the opening of each public school on each school day. Any child could be excused from attending the Bible reading upon written request of his parent or guardian. The Schempp family, members of the Unitarian church, brought suit to enjoin enforcement of the statute. In a companion case (Murray v. Curlettt) Mrs. Murray and her son, professed atheists, brought similar action against a similar situation in Baltimore.

OPINION BY MR. JUSTICE CLARK
(Vote: 8-1)

Question — Does the requirement of Bible reading in public schools violate the Establishment Clause of the First Amendment made applicable to the states by the Fourteenth Amendment?

Decision — Yes.

Reason — The Court noted that the Establishment Clause withdrew all legislative power respecting religious belief or the expression thereof. "The test may be stated as follows: What are the purpose and the primary effect of the enactment? If either is the advancement or inhibition of religion then the enactment exceeds the scope of legislative power as circumscribed by the Constitution . . . The conclusion follows that in both cases the laws require religious exercises and such exercises are being conducted in direct violation of the rights of the appellees and petitioners. Nor are these required exercises mitigated by the fact that individual students may absent themselves upon parental request, for that fact furnishes no defense to a claim of unconstitutionality under the Establishment Clause.

Corollary cases

Engel v. Vitale, 370 U. S. 421 (1962)

Everson v. Board of Education, 330 U. S. 1 (1947)

McCollum v. Board of Education, 333 U. S. 203 (1948)

Zorach v. Clauson, 343 U. S. 306 (1952)

McGowan v. Maryland, 366 U. S. 420 (1961)

Torcaso v. Watkins, 367 U. S. 488 (1961)

CITIZENSHIP AND SLAVES

Scott v. Sandford, 19 Howard 393; 15 L. Ed. 691 (1857)

In 1834, Dred Scott, a Negro slave belonging to Dr. Emerson, a surgeon in the United States Army, was taken by his master to Rock Island, Illinois, where slavery was prohibited by statute. Later he was taken, in 1836, to Fort Snelling, in the Territory of Louisiana, which was north of the line of 36° 30′, and consequently an area in which slavery had been forbidden by the Missouri Compromise. In 1838, he was brought back to Missouri, and in 1847 brought suit in the Missouri Circuit Court to recover his freedom, basing his action on previous decisions that residence in free territory conferred freedom. Before the commencement of this suit, Scott was sold to Sandford, a citizen of New York.

OPINION BY MR. CHIEF JUSTICE TANEY
(Vote: 7-2)

Question—Can a Negro slave become a member of the political community formed and brought into existence by the Constitution of the United States and as such become entitled to all the rights and privileges guaranteed by the Constitution to the citizen?

Decision—No.

Reason—The Court held that the Negro was not included, and not intended to be included under the word "citizen" in the Constitution, and therefore could claim none of the rights and privileges secured to citizens of the United States.

This did not prevent a state from bestowing the right of state citizenship upon any person it thought proper. However, no state could by a law of its own, make a person a member of the United States by making him a member in its own territory. Nor could a state clothe an individual with the rights and privileges of the United States, or of any other state.

The history of our country and the language of the Declaration of Independence, as well as the legislation of the colonies, point to the fact that the Negro had no rights that the white man was bound to respect, and that he might justly and lawfully be reduced to slavery. The Constitution shows that public opinion had undergone no change, and pledged the states to maintain the property of the master, by returning any escaped slaves.

The next question involved was: was he, together with his family, free in Missouri by reason of the stay in the Territory of the United States? The plaintiff here relied on the act of Congress prohibiting involuntary servitude north of Missouri (36° 30′). The difficulty here was whether Congress was authorized to pass such a law, according to the Constitution.

The power of Congress over the person or property of an individual can never be a mere discretionary power, but must be regulated by the Constitution. Rights of property are identified with the rights of a person who may not be deprived of them without due process of law. Therefore, an act of Congress that deprives a man of his property because he came into a particular territory can hardly be called due process of law. It was therefore the opinion of the Court that the Act of Congress (The Missouri Compromise) which prohibited a citizen from holding property of this kind north of the line mentioned was not warranted in the Constitution, and was therefore void. Dred Scott and his family were not free by reason of being taken there.

The plaintiff also contended that he was free, by reason of being taken to Rock Island, in the State of Illinois, and that, being free, he was not again reduced to a state of slavery when brought back to Missouri. On the basis of the decision in Strader v. Graham, the Court held that the status of the slaves depended on the law of the state of residence. Therefore, Scott's status, free or slave, depended on the law of Missouri, not of Illinois.

In the light of these considerations, the plaintiff was not a citizen in the sense of the Constitution and the Courts had no jurisdiction in this case.

(All nine Justices wrote separate opinions on this case.)

Corollary cases

Strader *et al.* v. Graham, 10 Howard 82

United States v. Wong Kim Ark, 169 U. S. 649

American Insurance Co. v. Canter, 1 Peters 511

Bailey v. Alabama, 219 U. S. 219

Pollock v. Williams, 322 U. S. 4

STATE OFFICERS AND RIGHTS OF CITIZENS

Screws v. United States, 325 U. S. 91; 65 S. Ct. 1031; 89 L. Ed. 1495 (1945)

Screws was a county sheriff and enlisted the assistance of a policeman and a deputy to assist in an arrest. They arrested a Negro late at night on a warrant charging him with the theft of a tire. They placed handcuffs on the Negro. When they arrived at the Court House square, the petitioners immediately started to beat the Negro. They claimed he had reached for a gun. The Negro was beaten into unconsciousness and died at a hospital within an hour. An indictment returned against the petitioners charged violation of Section 20 of the Federal Criminal Code. This section makes it a criminal offense willfully to deprive one under color of law, of rights, privileges, or immunities secured to him by the Constitution and laws of the United States.

Opinion by Mr. Justice Douglas
(Vote: 5-4)

Question—Can Congress apply the Fourteenth Amendment to individual state officers when they act "under color of law?"

Decision—Yes.

Reason—Here the officers had deprived the accused of various rights guaranteed by the Fourteenth Amendment, "the right not to be deprived of life without due process of law; the right to be tried upon the charge on which he was arrested, by due process of law and if found guilty to be punished in accordance with the laws of Georgia." The Court stated that history shows that the word "willfully" was not added to the Act until 1909. The Court reasoned that the word "willfully" makes the act less severe by requiring proof of purposeful discriminatory action. The Court therefore required a specific intent to deprive a person of a federal right, leaving no possibility for charging the Act unconstitutional on grounds of vagueness.

The Court held that the petitioners acted "under color of law" in making the arrest since they were officers of the law. By their own admissions they assaulted the Negro in order to protect themselves. It was their duty under Georgia law to make the arrest effective. Therefore their conduct came within the statute.

The Court further reasoned that the problem is not whether state law has been violated, but whether an inhabitant of the state has been deprived of a federal right by one who acts under "color of any law." The fact that it is also a violation of state law does not make it any the less a federal offense punishable as such. Nor does its punishment by federal authority encroach on state authority or relieve the state from its responsibility for punishing state offenses.

The Screws case was remanded for a new trial.

Corollary cases

Shevlin-Carpenter Co. v. Minnesota, 218 U. S. 57

Snowden v. Hughes, 321 U. S. 1

Logan v. United States, 144 U. S. 263

United States v. Harris, 106 U. S. 629

Jerome v. United States, 318 U. S. 101

United States v. Cruikshank, 92 U. S. 542

United States v. Classic, 313 U. S. 299

Commonwealth of Virginia v. Rives, 100 U. S. 313

Mahnich v. Southern S. S. Co., 321 U. S. 96

Civil Rights Cases, 109 U. S. 3

Shelley v. Kraemer, 334 U. S. 1

Kentucky Finance Corp. v. Paramount Auto Exchange Corp., 262 U. S. 544

Monroe v. Pape, 365 U. S. 167

United States v. Williams, 341 U. S. 70, 97

INTERSTATE COMMERCE

Second Employers' Liability Cases, 223 U. S. 1, 32 S. Ct. 169; 56 L. Ed. 327 (1912)

The Employers' Liability Act of 1906 modified the fellow-servant doctrine of the common law, making common carriers engaged in commerce in the various states, territories, and districts liable for the death or injury of any of their employees that should result from the negligence of any of their officers, agents, or employees. This law was declared void by the Supreme Court on the ground that it applied to the carriers irrespective of the fact whether the person killed or injured was engaged at the time in interstate commerce. Congress then passed the Employers' Liability Act of 1908, similar to the law of 1906 except that its provisions were expressly limited to suits growing out of injuries or deaths to employees while actually engaged in interstate commerce. Several cases arose testing the validity of this law.

OPINION BY MR. JUSTICE VAN DEVANTER

(No evidence from the report that the decision was not unanimous.)

Question—May Congress, in the exertion of its power over interstate commerce, regulate the relations of common carriers and their employees while both are engaged in such commerce?

Decision—Yes.

Reason—"This power over commerce among the states, so conferred upon Congress, is complete in itself, extends incidentally to every instrument and agent by which such commerce is carried on, may be exerted to its utmost extent over every part of such commerce, and is subject to no limitations save such as are prescribed in the Constitution. But, of course, it does not extend to any matter or thing which does not have a real or substantial relation to some part of such commerce."

As to the change in the fellow-servant doctrine, a person has no property, no vested interest, in any rule of the common law. That is only one of the forms of municipal law, and is no more sacred than any other. Rights of property that have been created by the common law cannot be taken away without due process; but the law itself, as a rule of conduct, may be changed at the will of the legislature, unless prevented by constitutional limitations. The great office of statutes is to remedy defects in the common law as they are developed, and to adapt it to the changes of time and circumstances.

If any one proposition could command the universal assent of mankind, we might expect it would be that the government of the Union, though limited in its powers, is supreme within its sphere of action.

Rights arising under the act in question may be enforced, as of right, in the courts of the states when their jurisdiction, as prescribed by local laws, is adequate to the occasion.

Corollary cases

Howard v. Illinois Central R.R. Co. (Employers' Liability Cases), 207 U. S. 463

Mondou v. New York, N. H. & H. R.R. Co., 223 U. S. 1

Munn v. Illinois, 94 U. S. 113

McCulloch v. Maryland, 4 Wheaton 316

Southern Ry. Co. v. United States, 222 U. S. 20

Testa v. Katt, 330 U. S. 386

B. & O. R.R. Co. v. Interstate Commerce Commission, 221 U. S. 612

COMPULSORY MILITARY SERVICE

Selective Draft Law Cases (Arver v. United States) 245 U. S. 366; 38 S. Ct. 159; 62 L. Ed. 349 (1918)

By the Act of May 18, 1917, Congress provided that all male citizens between the ages of 21 and 30, with certain exceptions, should be subject to military service, and authorized the President to select from them a body of one million men. All persons made liable to service by the act were required to present themselves at a time appointed by the President for registration. The plaintiffs in error failed to present themselves as required and were prosecuted and convicted. They contended that Congress had no power to compel military service by selective draft.

OPINION BY MR. CHIEF JUSTICE WHITE

(No evidence from the report that the decision was not unanimous.)

Question—Does Congress have constitutional authority to draft men to raise military forces?

Decision—Yes.

Reason—The Court unanimously held that the power of conscription is included in the constitutional power to raise armies. The power is not limited by the fact that other powers of Congress over state militia are narrower in scope than powers over the regular army. The Court stated that when the Constitution came to be formed, one of the recognized necessities for its adoption was the want of power in Congress to raise an army and the dependence upon the states for their quotas. In supplying the power it was manifestly intended to give Congress all and leave none to the states, since, besides the delegation to Congress of authority to raise armies, the Constitution prohibited the states, without the consent of Congress, from keeping troops in time of peace or engaging in war.

"Finally, as we are unable to conceive upon what theory the exaction by government from the citizen of the performance of his supreme and noble duty of contributing to the defense of the rights and honor of the nation, as the result of a war declared by the great representative body of the people, can be said to be the imposition of involuntary servitude in violation of the prohibition of the Thirteenth Amendment, we are constrained to the conclusion that the contention to that effect is refuted by its mere statement."

Corollary cases

Cox v. Wood, 247 U. S. 3
Kneedler v. Lane, 45 Pa. 238
United States v. Williams, 302 U. S. 46

Billings v. Truesdale, 321 U. S. 542
Falbo v. United States, 320 U. S. 549

Northern Pacific Ry. v. North Dakota, 250 U. S. 135

Dakota Central Telephone Co. v. South Dakota, 250 U. S. 163

Reitman v. Mulkey, 387 U. S. 369

Estep v. United States, 327 U. S. 114

Orloff v. Willoughby, 345 U. S. 83

United States v. Nugent, 346 U. S. 1

EQUAL PROTECTION AND SEGREGATION

Shelley v. Kraemer, 334 U. S. 1; 68 S. Ct. 836; 92 L. Ed. 1161 (1948)

This case involves two instances of enforcement by state courts of private agreements, known as restrictive covenants, which barred Negroes from holding real property in certain sections of St. Louis and Detroit. Shelley, a Negro, purchased some property in a section of St. Louis covered by a restrictive covenant that barred such Negro ownership. Other owners of property in the same area requested relief, but a Missouri trial court refused it. However, the Supreme Court of Missouri reversed the ruling of the lower court and ordered the Negroes to vacate their newly occupied property. The Detroit case was similar. Negroes acquired property in a privately restricted zone and were ordered out by a state court. The Supreme Court of Michigan upheld the lower court.

OPINION BY MR. CHIEF JUSTICE VINSON
(Vote: 6-0)

Question—Are orders by state courts enforcing private restrictive covenants based on race and color a violation of the equal protection clause of the Fourteenth Amendment?

Decision—Yes.

Reason—Restrictive covenants drawn up by private individuals are not in themselves a violation of the Fourteenth Amendment. As long as they are completely private and voluntary they are within the law. Here, however, there was more. The state, through its courts, aided in the enforcement of the covenants. Indeed, if it were not for the courts, the purpose of the agreements would not be fulfilled. The fact that the state merely carries out something started by private individuals does not free the state from a part in the original intent; nor does the fact that it is the judicial branch of the government that carries out the discrimination. The Court has consistently held that the judicial branch of the government may violate the Constitution as well as the executive or legislative branches. Thus the states here involved were play-ing, through their judiciaries, an integral part in a policy of discrimination in clear violation of the Fourteenth Amend-ment, which prohibits the states from denying equal protection of the laws.

Corollary cases

Civil Rights Cases, 109 U. S. 3
Buchanan v. Warley, 245 U. S. 60
Corrigan v. Buckley, 271 U. S. 323
Hurd v. Hodge, 334 U. S. 24

Ex parte Yarbrough, 110 U. S. 65
Slaughter-House Cases, 16 Wallace 36
Barrows v. Jackson, 346 U. S. 249

FULL FAITH AND CREDIT AND DIVORCE

Sherrer v. Sherrer, 334 U. S. 343; 68 S. Ct. 1087; 92 L. Ed. 1429 (1948)

A wife went from her Massachusetts home to Florida and sued for a divorce in a court of that state after the expiration of the 90-day period of residence required by Florida law. Her husband appeared and denied all the allegations in the complaint, including that of the wife's Florida residence. The wife introduced evidence estab-lishing her residence, and the husband did not cross-examine. The court found that the wife was a bona fide resident of Florida and granted the divorce. The husband did not appeal. The wife married again and subsequently returned to Massachusetts. Her former husband then introduced proceedings in a Massachusetts court attacking the Florida decree. The Massachusetts court found that the wife under Massachusetts law was never domiciled in Florida and held the divorce void.

OPINION BY MR. CHIEF JUSTICE VINSON
(Vote: 7-2)

Question—Did the Massachusetts judgment deny full faith and credit to the Florida judgment, contrary to Article IV, Section 1, of the Constitution?

Decision—Yes.

Reason—The Court reasoned that the husband had his day in court in Florida with respect to every issue involved in the litigation, and there is nothing in the concept of due process that demands that he be given a second opportunity to litigate the existence of the jurisdictional facts. The court went on to say that if the application of the full faith and credit clause to cases of this nature requires that local policy be subordinated, that is a part of the price of our federal system. That vital interests are involved in divorce litigation makes it a matter of greater rather than lesser importance that, under the circumstances of this case, the litigation end in courts of the state in which the decree was rendered.

Corollary cases

Davis v. Davis, 305 U. S. 32
Williams v. North Carolina, 325
 U. S. 226

Andrews v. Andrews, 188 U. S. 14

EQUAL PROTECTION AND EDUCATION

Sipuel v. Board of Regents of the University of Oklahoma, 332 U. S. 631; 68 S. Ct. 299; 92 L. Ed. 247 (1948)

On January 14, 1946, the petitioner, a Negro, qualified to receive professional legal education as offered by the state, applied for admission to the School of Law of the University of Oklahoma, the only institution for legal education supported by the taxpayers of Oklahoma. Her petition was denied, solely because of her color.

OPINION PER CURIAM

(No evidence from the report that the decision was not unanimous.)

Question—Is this refusal a denial of equal protection of the laws?

Decision—Yes.

Reason—"The petitioner is entitled to secure legal education afforded by a state institution. To this time it has been denied her although during the same period many white applicants have been afforded legal education by the State. The State must provide it for her in conformity with the equal protection clause of the Fourteenth Amendment and provide it as soon as it does for applicants of any other group."

Corollary cases

Missouri ex rel. Gaines v. Canada,
 305 U. S. 337
Cumming v. County Board of Education, 175 U. S. 528

Berea College v. Kentucky, 211
 U. S. 45
Gong Lum v. Rice, 275 U. S. 78

PRIVILEGES AND IMMUNITIES OF U. S. CITIZENSHIP

Slaughter-House Cases, 16 Wallace 36; 21 L. Ed. 394 (1873)

These cases arose under a measure enacted in 1869 by the legislature of Louisiana. The act regulated the business of slaughtering livestock in New Orleans. It required that such activities for the city and for a vast area surrounding it should be restricted to a small section below the city of New Orleans, and provided that the slaughtering should be done in the houses of one corporation. The effect was virtually a monopoly grant of the business, even though the corporation was required to permit other butchers to have access to their facilities on payment of a reasonable fee.

OPINION BY MR. JUSTICE MILLER
(Vote: 5-4)

Question—Were the butchers of New Orleans denied rights under the Fourteenth Amendment?

Decision—No.

Reason—The Court declared that a glance at the Thirteenth, Fourteenth, and Fifteenth Amendments disclosed a unity of purpose. That purpose was the achievement of the freedom of the slave race, the security and firm establishment of that freedom, and the protection of the new freemen and citizens from oppression by their former owners. The Court held that the rights of others were not impaired because these Amendments did not speak of rights of citizens of the states. A sharp distinction was drawn between rights that were derived from state citizenship and those that were derived from citizenship of the United States. The Court held that the citizen derived his civil rights from state citizenship and therefore those rights were not protected by the Fourteenth Amendment against state action.

Corollary cases

Ward v. Maryland, 12 Wallace 430

Paul v. Virginia, 8 Wallace 180

Crandall v. Nevada, 6 Wallace 36

Colgate v. Harvey, 296 U. S. 404

Madden v. Commonwealth of Kentucky, 309 U. S. 83

Edwards v. California, 314 U. S. 160

Twining v. New Jersey, 211 U. S. 78

FEDERAL CONTROL OF CONGRESSIONAL PRIMARIES

Smith v. Allwright, 321 U. S. 649; 64 S. Ct. 757; 88 L. Ed. 987 (1944)

> Lonnie E. Smith, a Negro citizen of Texas, sued for damages for the refusal of election and associate election judges to give him a ballot to vote in the primary election of July 27, 1940 for the nomination of Democratic candidates for the United States Senate and House of Representatives, and other state officers. This refusal was based solely on race and color. He fulfilled all other requirements for voting. It was argued by those representing the election officials that those officials were acting under a State of Texas Democratic Party convention resolution that limited membership in the Democratic Party to white persons.

OPINION BY MR. JUSTICE REED
(Vote: 8-1)

Question—Is the action of the Democratic convention state action?

Decision—Yes.

Reason—The privilege of membership in a political party is of no concern to the state. However, when the privilege of membership in the party is an essential qualification for voting in the primary and selecting candidates for a general election, the action of the party is the action of the state. "When primaries become a part of the machinery for choosing officials, state and national, as they have here, the same tests to determine the character of discrimination or abridgment should be applied to the primary as are applied to the general election. If the state requires a certain electoral procedure, prescribes a general election ballot made up of party nominees so chosen and limits the choice of the electorate in general elections for state officers, practically speaking, to those whose names appear on such a ballot, it endorses, adopts and enforces the discrimination against Negroes practiced by a party entrusted by Texas law with the determination of the qualifications of participants in the primary. This is state action within the meaning of the Fifteenth Amendment . . ."

Corollary cases

Grovey v. Townsend, 295 U. S. 45
United States v. Classic, 313 U. S. 299
Nixon v. Herndon, 273 U. S. 536
Nixon v. Condon, 286 U. S. 73
Newberry v. United States, 256 U. S. 232

Guinn v. United States, 238 U. S. 347
Williams v. Mississippi, 170 U. S. 213
Lane v. Wilson, 307 U. S. 268
Rice v. Elmore, 333 U. S. 875
Terry v. Adams, 345 U. S. 461

TAXATION AND REGULATION

Sonzinsky v. United States, 300 U. S. 506; 57 S. Ct. 554; 81 L. Ed. 772 (1937)

The National Firearms Act of 1934 imposed a $200 annual license tax on dealers in firearms. The petitioner was convicted on two counts: (1) for failure to pay the firearms tax set down by Congress, and (2) for failure to register as a dealer in firearms as required by the National Firearms Act. The petitioner contended that the tax was for the purpose of suppressing the sale of certain types of firearms.

OPINION BY MR. JUSTICE STONE
(No evidence from the report that the decision was not unanimous.)

Question—Can Congress use a tax for the purpose of regulation?

Decision—Yes.

Reason—"Every tax is in some measure regulatory. To some extent it interposes an economic impediment to the activity taxed as compared with others not taxed. But a tax is not any the less a tax because it has a regulatory effect . . . and it has long been established that an Act of Congress which on its face purports to be an exercise of the taxing power is not any the less so because the tax is burdensome or tends to restrict or suppress the thing taxed." The court called attention to the fact that the tax "is productive of some revenue" and added "we are not free to speculate as to the motives which moved Congress to impose it or as to the extent to which it may operate to restrict the activities taxed. As it is not attended by an offensive regulation and since it operates as a tax, it is within the national taxing power. . . ."

Corollary cases

Weller v. New York, 268 U. S. 319

Field v. Clark, 143 U. S. 649

Hill v. Wallace, 259 U. S. 44

United States v. Doremus, 249 U. S. 86

McCray v. United States, 195 U. S. 27

Alaska Fish Co. v. Smith, 255 U. S. 44

Alston v. United States, 274 U. S. 289

Hampton & Co. v. United States, 276 U. S. 394

Carter v. Carter Coal Co., 298 U. S. 238

United States v. Butler, 297 U. S. 1

Bailey v. Drexel Furniture Co., 259 U. S. 20

Helvering v. Davis, 301 U. S. 619

United States v. Kahriger, 345 U.S. 22

Haynes v. United States, 389 U. S. 000 (1968)

Marchetti v. United States, 390 U. S. 39 (1968)

Grosso v. United States, 390 U. S. 62 (1968)

FEDERAL TAXATION OF STATE ACTIVITY

South Carolina v. United States, 199 U. S. 437; 26 S. Ct. 110; 50 L. Ed. 261 (1905)

> South Carolina was the sole dispenser of wholesale and retail liquor within the state. All profits went to the state treasury. Prior to 1901, the state paid the United States tax, but on April 14, 1901 the state authorities refused further payments.

OPINION BY MR. JUSTICE BREWER
(Vote: 6-3)

Question—Should this state agency be granted immunity from taxation by the federal government because they were exercising the sovereign power of a state?

Decision—No.

Reason—The necessity of regulation may induce the states to the possession of other fields such as tobacco and other objects of internal revenue tax. But "if one state finds it thus profitable, other states may follow, and the whole body of internal revenue tax be thus striken down." The national government would be crippled. If all the states exercised such power the efficiency of the national government could be destroyed. The exemption of state agencies and instrumentalities from national taxation is limited to those which are strictly governmental in character and does not extend to those which are used by the state in the carrying on of ordinary business. Thus "whenever a state engages in business which is of a private nature, that business is not withdrawn from the taxing power of the nation."

Corollary cases

Veazie Bank v. Fenno, 8 Wallace 533

United States v. Perkins, 163 U. S. 625

Ambrosini v. United States, 187 U. S. 1

Ohio v. Helvering, 292 U. S. 360

Helvering v. Powers, 293 U. S. 214

New York v. United States, 326 U. S. 572

STATE LEGISLATION AND INTERSTATE COMMERCE

South Carolina State Highway Department v. Barnwell Bros., Inc., 303 U. S. 177; 58 S. Ct. 510; 82 L. Ed. 734 (1938)

A South Carolina state law required that motor trucks and semitrailer trucks be limited to a gross weight of 20,000 pounds, with a width of 90 inches. Most trucks in interstate commerce are 96 inches wide, and carry a gross weight of more than 10 tons.

OPINION BY MR. JUSTICE STONE
(Vote: 7-0)

Question—Can a state, in the absence of regulations by Congress, so regulate that a burden is placed upon interstate commerce?

Decision—Yes.

Reason—While the commerce clause prohibits discrimination against interstate commerce, in the absence of congressional action, a state can maintain certain regulations, even though interstate commerce may be materially affected. "But so long as the state action does not discriminate, the burden is one which the Constitution permits because it is an inseparable incident of the exercise of a legislative authority, which, under the Constitution, has been left to the state.

"Congress, in the exercise of its plenary power to regulate interstate commerce, may determine whether the burdens imposed on it by state regulation, otherwise permissible, are too great, and may, by legislation designed to secure uniformity or in other respects to protect the national interest in the commerce, curtail to some extent the state's regulatory power."

In the absence of Congressional regulation, the only question to be considered is whether the state legislature has acted within its province, and whether the legislation is reasonably adapted to the desired end.

This was the case in South Carolina. Due to the construction and the materials used in its highways, South Carolina set its limits according to this statute. While these regulatory measures might seem a burden to interstate commerce, they were indispensable for the preservation and safety of the highways of the state. The measures of South Carolina therefore were reasonable and within its legislative power.

Corollary cases

Willson v. Black Bird Creek Marsh Co., 2 Peters 245

Cooley v. Board of Wardens, 12 Howard 299

Minnesota Rate Cases, 230 U. S. 352

Sproles v. Binford, 286 U. S. 374

Hood and Sons v. Du Mond, 336 U. S. 525

Southern Pacific Co. v. Arizona, 325 U. S. 761

Southern Railway Co. v. King, 217 U. S. 524

Bradley v. Public Utilities Commission, 289 U. S. 92

Edwards v. California, 314 U. S. 160

Bibb v. Navajo Freight Lines, Inc., 359 U. S. 520

SUABILITY OF A STATE

South Dakota v. North Carolina, 192 U. S. 286; 24 S. Ct. 269; 48 L. Ed. 448 (1904)

In 1866 the State of North Carolina authorized the issuance of bonds to complete the Western North Carolina Railway, with the provision that such bonds should be secured by mortgages of equivalent amount on the stock owned by the state in another railway. In 1901 the owners of a large part of the outstanding bonds presented ten of them to the State of South Dakota, which filed a bill asking that North Carolina be required to pay the amount due, and that, in default of payment, the railway shares on the security of which the bonds were issued might be sold.

Opinion by Mr. Justice Brewer
(Vote: 5-4)

Question—Does the Court have jurisdiction in such a controversy?

Decision—Yes.

Reason—In this case, South Dakota was not merely representing the owners of the bonds, for they were given outright to the state. The subject matter was evidently justiciable. The jurisdiction of "controversies between two or more States" was given to this Court with no constitutional limitations.

However, the contention was alleged that this Court had no power to enforce such a judgment, so that actions to recover money were an implied exception. This has been the policy of the Court, since the power to direct the levying of a tax was not extended to the judiciary.

Nevertheless, in this case there was a mortgage of property, and the sale of that property under foreclosure would not necessitate a personal judgment against a state. Equity would be satisfied by the foreclosure and the sale. If a deficiency should exist after the sale, that question would be taken up separately.

The Court decreed that the 100 shares of stock in the North Carolina Railway Company be sold at public auction, and that North Carolina pay the amount due ($27,400) and the costs of this suit. (The day before the public auction the Attorney General of the State of North Carolina went to Justice Brewer and paid the amount in full.)

Corollary cases

New Hampshire v. Louisiana, 108 U. S. 76

Missouri v. Illinois, 180 U. S. 208

Rees v. City of Watertown, 19 Wallace 107

Christian v. Atlantic & N. C. R.R. Co., 133 U. S. 233

Hans v. Louisiana, 134 U. S. 1

Monaco v. Mississippi, 292 U. S. 313

Cohens v. Virginia, 6 Wheaton 264

Arizona v. California, 283 U. S. 423

Chisholm v. Georgia, 2 Dallas 419

North Dakota v. Minnesota, 263 U. S. 365

Virginia v. West Virginia, 246 U. S. 565

STATE LEGISLATION AND INTERSTATE COMMERCE

Southern Pacific Co. v. Arizona, 325 U. S. 761; 65 S. Ct. 1515; 89 L. Ed. 1915 (1945)

> The Arizona Train Limit Law required that any person or corporation operating within the state a railroad train with more than 14 passenger cars or more than 70 freight cars would pay a penalty for each violation of the act.

OPINION BY MR. CHIEF JUSTICE STONE
(Vote: 7-2)

Question—Does the statute contravene the commerce clause of the federal Constitution?

Decision—Yes.

Reason—The court reasoned that the Arizona law, viewed as a safety measure, afforded at most slight and dubious advantage, if any, over unregulated train lengths, because it resulted in an increase in expense and in the number of trains and train operations and a consequent increase in train accidents of a character generally more severe than those due to slack action. Its effect on commerce was regulation without securing uniformity of the length of trains operated in interstate commerce. Thus it prevented the free flow of commerce by delaying it and by substantially increasing its cost and impairing its efficiency.

Corollary cases

Kelly v. Washington, 302 U. S. 1

Cooley v. Board of Wardens, 12 Howard 299

South Carolina Highway Dept. v. Barnwell Bros., 303 U. S. 177

Gibbons v. Ogden, 9 Wheaton 1

New York, N. H. & H. R.R. Co. v. New York, 165 U. S. 628

Atlantic Coast Line R.R. Co. v. Georgia, 234 U. S. 280

INTERSTATE COMMERCE

Stafford v. Wallace, 258 U. S. 495, 42 S. Ct. 397, 66 L. Ed. 735 (1922)

Stafford and Company, engaged in the buying and selling of livestock, brought suit against the Secretary of Agriculture, H. C. Wallace, in order to prohibit him from enforcing the Packers and Stockyards Act of 1921, which they contended was unconstitutional. The act provided for the supervision by federal authority of the business of the commission men and of the livestock dealers in the great stockyards of the country. Congress passed the act because, after extensive investigation, it found that the "Big Five" meat packers of the nation were engaged in a conspiracy in violation of the Anti-Trust Law, to control the business of the purchase of livestock, their preparation for use in meat products, and the distribution and sale thereof in this country and abroad.

OPINION BY MR. CHIEF JUSTICE TAFT
(Vote: 7-1)

Question—Did Congress have the authority under the commerce clause to supervise the activities of the meat-packers?

Decision—Yes.

Reason—The Court reasoned that Congress was exercising its established authority over interstate commerce. The stock-yards are not a place of rest or final destination. Thousands of head of livestock arrive daily by carload and must be promptly sold and disposed of and moved out to give place to the constantly flowing traffic that presses behind. The stockyards are but a throat through which the current flows, and the transactions that occur therein are only incident to this current from the west to the east, and from one state to another. Such transactions cannot be separated from the movement to which they contribute, and necessarily take on its character. The commission men are essential in making the sales without which the flow of the current would be obstructed, and this, whether they are made to packers or dealers. The dealers are essential to the sales to the stock farmers and feeders. The sales are not in this aspect merely local transactions. They create a local change of title, but they do not stop the flow; they merely change the private interests in the subject of the current, not interfering with, but on the contrary, being indispensable to its continuity. The origin of the livestock is in the west, its ultimate destination known to, and intended by all engaged in the business is in the middle west and east, either as meat products or stock for feeding and fattening. The stockyards and the sales are necessary factors in the middle of this current of commerce.

Corollary cases

Munn v. Illinois, 94 U. S. 113

United States v. Union Stock Yard Co., 226 U. S. 286

Swift & Co. v. United States, 196 U. S. 375

Chicago Board of Trade v. United States, 246 U. S. 231

Danciger v. Cooley, 248 U. S. 319

ANTITRUST LEGISLATION AND THE "RULE OF REASON"

Standard Oil Co. of New Jersey v. United States, 221 U. S. 1; 31 S. Ct. 502; 55 L. Ed. 619 (1910)

John D. Rockefeller and associates were convicted of violating the Sherman Anti-Trust Act. The specific charge of violation involved a combining of the stocks of a number of companies in the hands of Standard of New Jersey. The decree of the lower court enjoined the company from voting the stocks or exerting control over the various subsidiary companies, some thirty-seven in number. These companies, in turn, were ordered not to pay dividends to Standard Oil Co. of New Jersey or to cooperate in any way in making effective the combination. With this background the case went to the Supreme Court.

OPINION BY MR. CHIEF JUSTICE WHITE

(No evidence from the report that the decision was not unanimous.)

Question—Was this combination contrary to the Sherman Act?

Decision—Yes.

Reason—This was a combination that would result in the control of interstate and foreign commerce by this group rather than the only one authorized to do so, the Congress of the United States. Hence this was an illegal operation and it had to be abolished. The Court then proceeded to set forth what has come to be known as the "rule of reason." This, briefly, simply provides that the restraint of trade outlawed by the Sherman Act is not to apply to every contract or combination in restraint of trade, but only to those that do so unreasonably. "Undoubtedly, the words 'to monopolize' and 'monopolize,' as used in the section, reach every act bringing about the prohibited results. The ambiguity, if any, is involved in determining what is intended by monopolize. But this ambiguity is readily dispelled in the light of the previous history of the law of restraint of trade to which we have referred and the indication which it gives of the practical evolution by which monopoly and the acts which produce the same result as monopoly, that is, an undue restraint of the course of trade, all came to be spoken of as, and to be indeed synonymous with, restraint of trade. . . . It becomes obvious that the criteria to be resorted to in any given case for the purpose of ascertaining whether violations of the section have been committed is the rule of reason guided by the established law and by the plain duty to enforce the prohibitions of the Act, and thus the public policy which its restrictions were obviously enacted to observe. . . ."

Corollary cases

Swift and Co. v. United States, 196 U. S. 375

United States v. Northern Securities Co., 193 U. S. 197

Montague v. Lowery, 193 U. S. 38

United States v. American Tobacco Co., 221 U. S. 106

N.L.R.B. v. Jones and Laughlin Steel Corp., 301 U. S. 1

United States v. E. C. Knight Co., 156 U. S. 1

STATE CHAIN STORE TAX AND EQUAL PROTECTION

State Board of Tax Commissioners of Indiana v. Jackson, 283 U. S. 527; 51 S. Ct. 540; 75 L. Ed. 1248 (1931)

This was a suit by Jackson against the State Board of Tax Commissioners of Indiana to enjoin the enforcement against the plaintiff of a license tax prescribed by the Indiana Tax Law of 1929. The act made it a misdemeanor for any person, firm, association, or corporation to operate a store without first obtaining a license, and prescribed a graduated annual license fee based on the number of stores conducted under a single ownership or management. The fee for one store was $3.00; for two or more stores, but not exceeding five, $10.00 for each additional store beyond the first, etc. The plaintiff was engaged in the business of selling groceries, vegetables, and meats in Indianapolis, operating 225 stores in that city. The annual license tax charged against him was $5,443. He charged that the graduation of the tax per store according to the number of stores under a single ownership and management was based on no real difference between a store part of such a group and one separately owned and operated, or between the business transacted in them, and that the classification was unreasonable and arbitrary. He held that this resulted in depriving him of his property without due process of law, and denied him the equal protection of the laws.

OPINION BY MR. JUSTICE ROBERTS
(Vote: 5-4)

Question—Is this tax of Indiana discriminatory and a denial of equal protection under the law?

Decision—No.

Reason—The fact that a statute discriminates in favor of a certain class does not make it arbitrary, if the discrimination is founded upon a reasonable distinction. The Court stated that it was their duty to sustain the classification adopted by the legislature if there was substantial difference between the occupations separately classified. "In view of the numerous distinctions between the business of a chain store and other types of store, we cannot pronounce the classification made by the statute to be arbitrary and unreasonable. That there are differences and advantages in favor of the chain store is shown by the number of such chains established and by their astonishing growth. More and more persons, like the appellee, have found advantages in this method of merchandising. The Court below fell into the error of assuming that the distinction between the appellee's business and that of the other sorts of stores·mentioned was one of ownership. It disregarded the difference shown by the record. They consist not only in ownership, but in organization, management and type of business transacted. The statute treats upon a similar basis all owners of chain stores similarly situated." In the light of what was said the Court concluded that there was no contradiction with any clause of the Constitution, and the statute was not in opposition to the Fourteenth Amendment.

Corollary cases

Clark v. Titusville, 184 U. S. 329

American Sugar Refining Co. v. Louisiana, 179 U. S. 89

Armour Packing Co. v. Lacy, 200 U. S. 226

Louis K. Liggett Co. v. Lee, 288 U. S. 517

Great Atlantic and Pacific Tea Co. v. Grosjean, 301 U. S. 412

Fox v. Standard Oil Co. of New Jersey, 294 U. S. 87

Stewart Dry Goods Co. v. Lewis, 294 U. S. 550

Allied Stores of Ohio, Inc. v. Bowers, 358 U. S. 522

TAXATION FOR SOCIAL SECURITY

Charles C. Steward Machine Co. v. Davis, 301 U. S. 548; 57 S. Ct. 883; 81 L. Ed. 1279 (1937)

The petitioner, an Alabama corporation, paid a tax in compliance with the Social Security Act. It filed claim for refund with the Commissioner of Internal Revenue to recover the payment ($46.14) asserting a conflict between the statute and the Constitution. Funds realized are used to aid the states in the administration of their unemployment compensation laws.

OPINION BY MR. JUSTICE CARDOZO
(Vote: 5-4)

Question—Is the tax a valid exercise of federal power?

Decision—Yes.

Reason—It was contended that it is not lawful to tax a right, and that, as such, employment is not open to taxation. However, employment is a business relation, and business is a legitimate object of the taxing power.

There was also the contention that an ulterior motive was

contained in the structure of the Act, and that the motive was essentially contrary to the Tenth Amendment. However, neither the taxpayer nor the state was coerced in this matter. The taxpayer fulfilled the mandate of his local legislature. The state chose to administer unemployment relief under laws of her own making. Nor did the statute call for a surrender by the state of powers essential to their quasi-sovereign existence. The state did not bind itself to keep the law in force. The state might repeal the statute; the state was not forced.

Corollary cases

Knowlton v. Moore, 178 U. S. 41

Cincinnati Soap Co. v. United States, 301 U. S. 308

Sonzinsky v. United States, 300 U. S. 506

Florida v. Mellon, 273 U. S. 12

United States v. Butler, 297 U. S. 1

Helvering v. Davis, 301 U. S. 619

Carmichael v. Southern Coal and Coke Co., 301 U. S. 495

State of Oklahoma v. U. S. Civil Service Commission, 330 U. S. 127

Massachusetts v. Mellon, 262 U. S. 447

STATE LEGISLATION AND IMPAIRMENT OF CONTRACT

Stone v. Mississippi, 101 U. S. 814; 25 L. Ed. 1079 (1880)

The legislature of Mississippi passed an act, approved Feb. 16, 1867, entitled "An Act Incorporating the Mississippi Agricultural and Manufacturing Aid Society." Actually it was nothing but a lottery enterprise. The Constitution of the state, adopted in convention May 15, 1868, and ratified by the people Dec. 1, 1869, forbade the legislature to authorize any lottery. Criminal suit was brought against the lottery "society," which argued that it was operating under its charter.

OPINION BY MR. CHIEF JUSTICE WAITE

(No evidence from the report that the decision was not unanimous.)

Question—Was this impairment of the obligation of contract?

Decision—No.

Reason—Whether the contract existed depended on the authority of the legislature to bind the state and people of the state in this way in this case. A legislature cannot bargain away the police power of a state, which pertains to all matters affecting public health or morals. In their Constitution the people have expressed their wishes in this matter, so that no legislature can, by chartering a lottery company, defeat their wishes.

The contracts protected by the Constitution are property rights, not governmental rights. Lotteries are a species of gambling, which would disturb a well-ordered community. The right to suppress them is governmental, and may be invoked at will. Such an arrangement as this "is a permit, good as against existing laws, but subject to future legislative and constitutional control or withdrawal."

Corollary cases

Long Island Water Supply Co., v. Brooklyn, 166 U. S. 685

Boston Beer Co., v. Massachusetts, 97 U. S. 25

Grand Trunk Western R. Co. v. South Bend, 227 U. S. 544

Pennsylvania Hospital v. Philadelphia, 245 U. S. 20

Northwestern Fertilizing Co. v. Hyde Park, 97 U. S. 650

Texas and N. O. R.R. Co., v. Miller, 221 U. S. 408

EQUAL PROTECTION

Strauder v. West Virginia, 100 U. S. 303; 25 L. Ed. 664 (1880)

Strauder, a colored person of West Virginia, was indicted and convicted of murder by the state courts of West Virginia. The law of the state provided that "all white male persons who are twenty-one years of age and who are citizens of this State shall be liable to serve as jurors, except as herein provided." The persons excepted were state officials.

OPINION BY MR. JUSTICE STRONG
(Vote: 7-2)

Question—Were his constitutional rights violated by the law making all colored persons ineligible to sit on either a petit jury or grand jury?

Decision—Yes.

Reason—The West Virginia law that excluded colored persons from duty on the grand jury and petit jury involved discrimination, which the Fourteenth Amendment does not allow. The history of the Amendment indicates that its aim was against discrimination because of race or color. "The Fourteenth Amendment makes no attempt to enumerate the rights it designed to protect. It speaks in general terms, and those are as comprehensive as possible. Its language is prohibitory; but every prohibition implies the existence of rights and immunities, prominent among which is an immunity from inequality of legal protection, either for life, liberty or property. Any State action that denies this immunity to a colored man is in conflict with the Constitution."

Corollary cases

Norris v. Alabama, 294 U. S. 587
Hill v. Texas, 316 U. S. 400
Akins v. Texas, 325 U. S. 398
Patton v. Mississippi, 332 U. S. 463

Cassell v. Texas, 339 U. S. 282
Shepherd v. Florida, 341 U. S. 50
Moore v. Dempsey, 261 U. S. 86

IMPAIRMENT OF CONTRACTS

Sturges v. Crowninshield, 4 Wheaton 122; 4 L. Ed. 529 (1819)

Crowninshield was the maker of two promissory notes, both dated at New York, on March 22, 1811, for the sum of $771.86 each, and payable to the plaintiff, one on the 1st of August, and the other on the 15th of August, 1811. The defendant pleaded his discharge under "an act for the benefit of insolvent debtors and their creditors," passed by the legislature of the state of New York on April 3, 1811. Crowninshield was discharged, and a certificate given him on the 15th of February, 1812.

OPINION BY MR. CHIEF JUSTICE MARSHALL
(No evidence from the report that the decision was not unanimous.)

Question—Is the statute an act or law impairing contracts in the meaning of the Constitution since it discharges from liability for debts previously contracted.

Decision—Yes.

Reason—The obligation of contract binds a party to do something, as, in the case in question, to pay the plaintiff a sum of money on a certain day. Any law that releases this obligation impairs it.

The states have the power to pass bankruptcy laws, but are restrained from passing any law that impairs the obligation of contracts. The enumeration of all the various types of impairment could never have been attempted in the Constitution, without adding to the perplexity. The meaning of the phrase in the Constitution is not dubious—the full and obvious meaning is simply that contracts are inviolable. The making of paper money, emitting bills of credit, and others alleged, are not the reasons behind this part of the Constitution, for these powers are expressly forbidden to the states.

The Court held that a state might pass a bankruptcy law, provided it does not impair the obligation of contracts, and that there is no act of Congress in force, establishing a uniform bankruptcy law, with which it might conflict. The New York statute, in this case, constituted an impairment of contract, applying, as it did, to past debts.

Corollary cases

International Shoe Co. v. Pinkus, 278 U. S. 261

Home Building & Loan Ass'n. v. Blaisdell, 290 U. S. 398

Dartmouth College v. Woodward, 4 Wheaton 518

Ogden v. Saunders, 12 Wheaton 213

Bronson v. Kinzie, 1 Howard 311

Richmond Mortgage and Loan Corp. v. Wachoria Bank and Trust Co., 300 U. S. 124

Honeyman v. Jacobs, 306 U. S. 539

Gelfert v. National City Bank, 313 U. S. 221

W. B. Worthen v. Kavanaugh, 295 U. S. 56

EQUAL PROTECTION AND SEGREGATION

Sweatt v. Painter, 339 U. S. 629; 70 S. Ct. 848; 94 L. Ed. 1114 (1950)

Sweatt was denied admission to the University of Texas Law School solely because he was colored and Negroes by state law were prohibited from admission to the school. The state of Texas then established a Law School for Negroes that was not on an academic par with the Law School at the University of Texas.

OPINION BY MR. CHIEF JUSTICE VINSON

(No evidence from the report that the decision was not unanimous.)

Question—Was there denial of equal protection?

Decision—Yes.

Reason—As an individual Sweatt was entitled to the equal protection of the laws, and the state was bound to furnish facilities for legal education substantially equal to those the state afforded for persons of the white race. Such education was not available to him in a separate law school as offered by the state.

Corollary cases

Shelley v. Kraemer, 334 U. S. 1

Missouri ex rel. Gaines v. Canada, 305 U. S. 337

Sipuel v. Board of Regents, 332 U. S. 631

Fisher v. Hurst, 333 U. S. 147

McLaurin v. Oklahoma State Regents, 339 U. S. 637

ANTITRUST LEGISLATION

Swift and Co. v. United States, 196 U. S. 375; 25 S. Ct. 276; 49 L. Ed. 518 (1905)

This suit was brought against a number of corporations, firms, and individuals of different states, and charged, in summary, a combination of a dominant proportion of the dealers in fresh meat throughout the United States not to bid against each other in the livestock markets of the different states, to bid up prices to induce cattlemen to send their stocks to the yards, to fix selling prices, and to that end to restrict shipments of meat when necessary, to establish a uniform rule of credit to dealers, to keep a blacklist, and to make uniform and improper charges for cartage, and finally, to get less than lawful rates from the railroads to the exclusion of competitors.

OPINION BY MR. JUSTICE HOLMES

(No evidence from the report that the decision was not unanimous.)

Question—Is this an illegal monopoly in violation of the Sherman Anti-Trust Act.

Decision—Yes.

Reason—Although the combination alleged embraces restraint and monopoly of trade within a single state, its effect upon commerce among the states was not accidental, but rather the commerce was an object of attack. The commerce intended to be monopolized was undoubtedly interstate commerce protected from restraint by the Act of 1890, since the meat shipments and sales involved were between citizens of diverse states. Thus, any attempt to monopolize this commerce would be a violation of the Sherman Act. The actions in this case were directed to this purpose and thus violated the Act. "It is said that this charge was too vague and that it does not set forth a case of commerce among the States. Taking up the latter objection first, commerce among the States is not a technical legal conception, but a practical one, drawn from the course of business. When cattle are sent for sale from a place in one State, with the expectation that they will end their transit, after purchase, in another, and when in effect they do so, with only the interruption necessary to find a purchaser at the stock yards, and when this is a typical, constantly recurring course, the current thus existing is a current of commerce among the States, and the purchase of the cattle is a part and incident of such commerce. . . . It is immaterial if the section also embraces domestic transactions.

"It should be added that the cattle in the stock yard are not at rest. . . ."

Corollary cases

American Steel and Wire Co. v. Speed, 192 U. S. 500

Hopkins v. United States, 171 U. S. 578

Kidd v. Pearson, 128 U. S. 1

United States v. E. C. Knight Co., 156 U. S. 1

Addyston Pipe and Steel Co. v. United States, 175 U. S. 211

Minnesota v. Blasius, 290 U. S. 1

Stafford v. Wallace, 258 U. S. 495

EQUAL PROTECTION OF THE LAWS AND ALIENS

Takahashi v. Fish & Game Commission, 334 U. S. 410; 68 S. Ct. 1138; 92 L. Ed. 1478 (1948)

Takahashi, a Japanese alien ineligible to citizenship, brought suit for mandamus in the California Superior Court to compel issuance to him of a commercial fishing license. The commission denied him the license on the ground that a California law forbade giving a commercial fishing license to a person ineligible for citizenship. Holding this provision violative of the equal protection clause of the federal Constitution, the Superior Court granted the petition. The State Supreme Court reversed. In presenting the case to the United States Supreme Court, the Game Commission contended the California law was a conservation measure and that the fishing waters belonged to the state. Takahashi contended that the law was the outgrowth of racial antagonism.

OPINION BY MR. JUSTICE BLACK
(Vote: 7-2)

Question—Can California use the federally-created racial ineligibility to citizenship as a basis for barring Takahashi from a commercial fishing license?

Decision—No.

Reason—1. The power to regulate immigration and naturalization is a constitutional power given to the federal government. Furthermore the Fourteenth Amendment embodies the "general policy that all persons lawfully in this country shall abide 'in any state' on an equality of legal privilege with all citizens under non-discriminatory laws."

2. Whatever special public interests there may be, due to ownership of fish by California citizens, are inadequate to justify this legislation.

3. The barring of aliens from land ownership rests solely upon the power of the states to control the devolution and ownership of land within their borders, but cannot be extended to cover this case.

Corollary cases

Hines v. Davidowitz, 312 U. S. 52
Hurd v. Hodge, 334 U. S. 24
Truax v. Raich, 239 U. S. 33
Oyama v. California, 332 U. S. 633

Terrace v. Thompson, 233 U. S. 107
Heim v. McCall, 239 U. S. 175
Bayside Fish Co. v. Gentry, 297 U. S. 422

FEDERAL OFFICERS AND STATE AUTHORITY

Tennessee v. Davis, 100 U. S. 257; 25 L. Ed. 648 (1879)

> Davis, a federal revenue officer, was indicted for murder in Tennessee. Davis claimed he killed a man in self-defense while discharging his duties as deputy collector. He petitioned for the removal of the prosecution to the federal court.

OPINION BY MR. JUSTICE STRONG
(Vote: 7-2)

Question—Has Congress the power to pass an act making a criminal case involving a federal officer removable from a state court to a federal court?

Decision—Yes.

Reason—The Court ruled that the removal statute passed by Congress was a constitutional exercise of congressional power to prevent a state from obstructing the action of federal functionaries, as might come to pass if the federal courts could interfere only by reversing the judgment of the highest state court. Congress has "power to make all laws necessary and proper for carrying into execution not only all the powers previously specified but also all other powers vested by the Constitution in the government of the United States, or in any department or officer thereof." This jurisdiction over federal authority and rights is necessary not only for the preservation of the acknowledged powers of the government but also to provide a uniform and consistent administration of national laws and to preserve the supremacy that the Constitution gives to the federal government.

Corollary cases

Osborn v. The Bank of the United States, 9 Wheaton 738

Martin v. Hunter's Lessee, 1 Wheaton 304

Cohens v. Virginia, 6 Wheaton 264

The Mayor v. Cooper, 6 Wallace 247

In re Neagle, 135 U. S. 1

Tarble's Case, 13 Wallace 397

Ableman v. Booth, 21 Howard 506

EQUAL PROTECTION AND ALIENS

Terrace v. Thompson, 263 U. S. 197, 44 S. Ct. 15, 68 L. Ed. 255 (1923)

Terrace owned land in Washington which he desired to lease for 5 years to Nakatsuka, a Japanese alien who had not declared his intention of acquiring American citizenship. Under the Anti-Alien Land Law of Washington of 1921, it was made a criminal offense to sell or lease land to any alien who had not declared his intention of acquiring citizenship, and Thompson, the attorney general of the state, threatened to apply the full force of the Act against Terrace if the sale was made to Nakatsuka. Terrace challenged such action and filed to enjoin Thompson from enforcing the act.

OPINION BY MR. JUSTICE BUTLER
(Vote: 6-2)

Question—Were the appellants denied due process or the equal protection of the laws?

Decision—No.

Reason—The rights, privileges, and duties of aliens differ widely from those of citizens; and those of alien declarants differ substantially from those of nondeclarants. The inclusion of good faith declarants in the same class with citizens does not unjustly discriminate against aliens who are ineligible or against eligible aliens who have failed to declare their intention. The classification is based on eligibility and purpose to naturalize. Two classes of aliens inevitably result from the naturalization laws—those who may and those who may not become citizens. The rule established by Congress on this subject, in and of itself, furnishes a reasonable basis for classification in a state law withholding from aliens the privilege of land ownership as defined in the act.

"It is obvious that one who is not a citizen and cannot become one lacks an interest in, and the power to effectually work for the welfare of, the state, and, so lacking, the state may rightfully deny him the right to own and lease real estate within its boundaries. . . . The quality and allegiance of those who own, occupy and use the farm lands within its borders are matters of highest importance and affect the safety and power of the state itself."

Corollary cases

Truax v. Corrigan, 257 U. S. 312　Takahashi v. Fish and Game Com-
Oyama v. California, 332 U. S. 633　　mission, 334 U. S. 410
Truax v. Raich, 230 U. S. 33　　Yick Wo v. Hopkins, 118 U. S. 356

STATE COURTS AND FEDERAL LAW

Testa v. Katt, 330 U. S. 386; 67 S. Ct. 810; 91 L. Ed. 967 (1947)

The World War II Federal Emergency Price Control Act provided that persons charged over ceiling prices could sue for damages "in any court of competent jurisdiction." The defendant charged the plaintiff $210 in excess of the ceiling price on an automobile, and the plaintiff sued in a Rhode Island state court. Rhode Island held that its courts need not try the case, on the ground that the Act was a "penal statute in the international sense."

OPINION BY MR. JUSTICE BLACK
(No evidence from the report that the decision was not unanimous.)

Question—Does a state court have the power and the jurisdiction to enforce federal laws?

Decision—Yes.

Reason—The Court could not accept the mandate of the Rhode Island Supreme Court that it had no more obligation to enforce a valid penal law of the United States than it would have had to enforce a penal law of another state, or of a foreign country. Article VI of the Constitution provides that "this Constitution, and the laws of the United States which shall be made in pursuance thereof; and all treaties made, or which shall be made, under the authority of the United States, shall be the supreme law of the land; and the judges in every State shall be bound thereby, anything in the Constitution or laws of any State to the contrary notwithstanding."

Historically, there were no precedents for such an opinion as the state court handed down. The very first Congress conferred jurisdiction upon the state courts to enforce important federal laws. This was challenged, but in Claflin v. Houseman the Court reiterated, in a unanimous decision, that the Constitution and the laws pursuant are the supreme law of the land, binding alike upon states, courts, and people.

In the Mondou case, the Court held that Connecticut had no right to decline such action, since, when Congress speaks, it speaks and establishes a policy for all. Here Rhode Island likewise could hold no established policy by its courts against enforcing statutes of other states and of the United States. Her courts had adequate jurisdiction under established local law to judge this case.

Corollary cases

Claflin v. Houseman, 93 U. S. 130

Mondou v. New York, N. H. & H. R.R. Co., 223 U. S. 1

Minneapolis & St. L. R.R. Co. v. Bombolis, 241 U. S. 211

Prigg v. Pennsylvania, 16 Peters 539

United States v. Jones, 109 U. S. 513

Robertson v. Baldwin, 165 U. S. 275

Holmgren v. United States, 217 U. S. 509

McKnett v. St. Louis and S. F. Ry. Co., 292 U. S. 230

Young v. Ragen, 337 U. S. 235

Jennings v. Illinois, 342 U. S. 104

FREE SPEECH AND LABOR UNIONS

Thomas v. Collins, 323 U. S. 516; 65 S. Ct. 315; 89 L. Ed. 430 (1945)

A Texas statute required that all persons soliciting members for a labor organization obtain an organizer's card from the Secretary of State. Thomas, president of the International Union U.A.W. (United Automobile, Aircraft, and Agricultural Implements Workers) and a vice president of the C.I.O., was asked to address a mass meeting where the Oil Workers Industrial Union (O.W.I.U.) was campaigning to organize Local No. 1002.

Thomas arrived in Houston on the evening of September 21 for the meeting, which was to be held on September 23. His address had been announced in advance, and wide publicity was given to the meeting. On the afternoon of September 23 about 2:30 he was served with a restraining order.

Thomas consulted his attorneys, and went ahead with the meeting as planned, regarding the law and the citation as a restraint upon free speech and free assembly. The meeting was orderly and peaceful. Thomas closed his address with a general invitation to all who were not members of a union to join Local No. 1002, and solicited orally one Pat O'Sullivan. After the address, Thomas was arrested, and contempt proceedings filed for violation of the temporary restraining order.

Opinion by Mr. Justice Rutledge
(Vote: 5-4)

Question—Does the statute in question violate the First and Fourteenth Amendments by imposing a previous restraint upon freedom of speech and free assembly?

Decision—Yes.

Reason—Thomas based his case on the rule that requires that a clear and present danger must be evident to sustain a restriction upon freedom of speech or assembly. Texas contended that the statute was similar to statutes directed at business practices like selling insurance, dealing in securities, acting as a commission merchant, or pawnbroking, and that the appropriate standard was the commerce clause, which sustains state statutes regulating transportation. The Court was confronted with the delicate question of where the individual's freedom ends and the state's power begins, and, as in such cases, it is the character of the right, not of the limitation, that determines which standard to apply.

Restrictions upon these liberties must be justified by clear public interest; not by doubtful or remote threats, but by clear and present danger. Only the gravest abuses can give grounds for permissible limitations, especially when the right is exercised within a peaceable assembly. "If one who solicits support for the cause of labor may be required to register as a condition to the exercise of the rights to make a public speech, so may he who seeks to rally support for any social, business, religious or political cause. We think a requirement that one must register before he undertakes to make a public speech to enlist support for a lawful movement is quite incompatible with the requirements of the First Amendment.

"Once the speaker goes further, however, and engages in conduct which amounts to more than the right of free discussion comprehends, as when he undertakes the collection of funds or securing subscriptions, he enters a realm where a reasonable registration or identification requirement may be imposed. In that context such solicitation would be quite different from the solicitation involved here. . . ."

Corollary cases

Cantwell v. Connecticut, 310 U. S. 296

United States v. Carolene Products Co., 304 U. S. 144

De Jonge v. Oregon, 299 U. S. 353

Schneider v. State, 308 U. S. 147

Lovell v. Griffin, 303 U. S. 444

Hague v. C.I.O., 307 U. S. 496

Schenck v. United States, 249 U. S. 47

Gitlow v. New York, 268 U. S. 652

Herndon v. Lowry, 301 U. S. 242

Terminiello v. City of Chicago, 337 U. S. 1

Thornhill v. Alabama, 310 U. S. 88

Carlson v. California, 310 U. S. 106

PICKETING AND FREE SPEECH

Thornhill v. Alabama, 310 U. S. 88; 60 S. Ct. 736; 84 L. Ed. 1093 (1940)

Thornhill was convicted in Alabama of violating an Alabama statute that forbade loitering or picketing around a place of business for the purpose of inducing others not to trade with or work for the place of business. He was arrested for picketing the plant of the Brown Wood Preserving Co.

Opinion by Mr. Justice Murphy
(Vote: 8-1)

Question—Did the Alabama statute violate the First Amendment to the Constitution?

Decision—Yes.

Reason—The Court reasoned that the freedom of speech and of the press guaranteed by the Constitution embraces at the least the liberty to discuss publicly and truthfully all matters of public concern without previous restraint or fear of subsequent punishment. The Court stated that in the circumstances of our times the dissemination of information concerning the facts of a labor dispute must be regarded as within the area of free discussion that is guaranteed by the Constitution. The Court held that free discussion concerning the conditions in industry and the causes of labor disputes are indispensable to the effective and intelligent use of the processes of popular government to shape the destiny of modern industrial society. The court further stated that the streets are natural and proper places for the dissemination of information and opinion; and one is not to have the exercise of his liberty of expression in appropriate places abridged on the plea that it may be exercised in some other place.

Corollary cases

United States v. Carolene Products, 304 U. S. 144

De Jonge v. Oregon, 299 U. S. 353

Stromberg v. California, 283 U. S. 359

Lanzetta v. New Jersey, 306 U. S. 451

Duplex Printing Press Co., v. Deering, 254 U. S. 443

American Steel Foundries v. Tri-City Council, 257 U. S. 184

Schneider v. State, 308 U. S. 147

Hague v. C.I.O., 307 U. S. 496

Lovell v. Griffin, 303 U. S. 444

A.F.L. v. Swing, 312 U. S. 321

Carpenters and Joiners Union v. Ritter's Cafe, 315 U. S. 722

Carlson v. California, 310 U. S. 106

Local Union No. 10, United Ass'n of Journeymen Plumbers and Steamfitters of the United States and Canada of A.F.L. v. Graham, 345 U. S. 192

Youngdahl v. Rainfair, 355 U. S. 131

EQUAL PROTECTION OF THE LAWS

Tigner v. State of Texas, 310 U. S. 141, 60 S. Ct. 879, 84 L. Ed. 1124 (1940)

Tigner was charged with participation in a conspiracy to fix the retail price of beer. Such a conspiracy was made a criminal offense under the Texas penal code. Because the provisions of this law did not apply to agricultural products or livestock in the hands of the producer or raiser, Tigner challenged the validity of the entire statute and sought release in the local courts by habeas corpus. He contended that the law was offensive to the equal protection of the laws that the Fourteenth Amendment safeguards.

OPINION BY MR. JUSTICE FRANKFURTER
(Vote: 8-1)

Question—Could Texas promote its policy of freedom for

economic enterprise by utilizing the criminal law against various forms of combination and monopoly, but exclude from criminal punishment corresponding activities of agriculture?

Decision—Yes.

Reason—The Constitution does not require things that are different in fact or opinion to be treated in law as though they were the same. So the Court concluded that to write into law the differences between agriculture and other economic pursuits was within the power of the Texas legislature. At the core of the law was a conception of price and production policy for agriculture very different from that which underlies the demands made upon industry and commerce by antitrust laws. Agriculture expresses functions and forces different from the other elements in the total economic process. Therefore, equal protection of the laws was not denied.

Corollary cases

Connolly v. Union Sewer Pipe Co., 184 U. S. 540

Mulford v. Smith, 307 U. S. 38

United States v. Rock Royal Co-op., 307 U. S. 533

Nebbia v. New York, 291 U. S. 502

Liberty Warehouse Co. v. Burley, 276 U. S. 71

Frost v. Corporation Commission of Oklahoma, 278 U. S. 515

EQUAL PROTECTION AND DUE PROCESS IN LABOR DISPUTES

Truax v. Corrigan, 257 U. S. 312; 42 S. Ct. 124; 66 L. Ed. 254 (1921)

A restaurant owned by Truax in Bisbee, Arizona was picketed by Corrigan and others, cooks and waiters who were union members, who went on strike over the conditions of work in the restaurant. The defendants entered into a conspiracy and boycott to injure the plaintiff by picketing, carrying banners, advertising the strike, and other such measures. Truax filed for an injunction to stop this picketing and was refused under an Arizona statute forbidding the issuance of such type of injunction by the courts of that state. The picketing was coupled with threats of violence to the customers. An Arizona statute forbade the issuance of an injunction in labor disputes with some rather rare exceptions.

OPINION BY MR. CHIEF JUSTICE TAFT
(Vote: 5-4)

Question—Is Truax denied equal protection of the laws and deprived of his property by the law forbidding the issuance of this type of injunction?

Decision—Yes.

Reason—The type of picketing done in this case was illegal in the way in which it was done. It was not a mere appeal to the sympathetic aid of the would-be customers by presentation of the reason for the strike action. It was moral coercion by illegal annoyance and obstruction, and it was plainly a conspiracy. The action of the pickets was that of a tort and they were held liable in court. The laws of the country cannot favor one group over the other, for it would be denial of equal protection of the laws. "A law which operates to make lawful such a wrong as is described in plaintiffs' complaint deprives the owner of the business and the premises of his property without due process, and can not be held valid under the Fourteenth Amendment. . . ."

The law also offends against equal protection of the laws. The purpose of that provision of the Constitution was "to secure equality of protection not only for all but against all similarly situated. Indeed, protection is not protection unless it does so. Immunity granted to a class, however limited, of a personal or property right, is just as clearly a denial of equal protection of the laws to the latter class as if the immunity were in favor of, or the deprivation of right permitted worked against, a larger class. . . ."

Corollary cases

Duplex Printing Press Co., v. Deering, 254 U. S. 443

New York Central R.R. v. White, 243 U. S. 188

Hawkins v. Bleakly, 243 U. S. 210

Thornhill v. Alabama, 310 U. S. 88

Senn v. Tile Layers Protective Union, 301 U. S. 468

Borden's Farm Products Co., v. Ten Eyck, 297 U. S. 251

STATE LEGISLATION AND ALIENS

Truax v. Raich, 239 U. S. 33; 36 S. Ct. 7; 60 L. Ed. 131 (1915)

The State of Arizona passed a law to the effect that when any company, corporation, partnership, association, or individual employs more than five workers at any one

time, not less than 80 per cent must be qualified electors
or native born citizens of the United States or some sub-
division thereof. Raich, a native of Austria, but living
in Arizona, lost his job as a result of this legislation, since
his employer feared the penalty that might be incurred.
Raich filed his suit, asserting that the Act denied to him
equal protection of the laws.

OPINION BY MR. JUSTICE HUGHES
(Vote: 8-1)

Question—Is the Arizona Act repugnant to the Fourteenth
Amendment of the Constitution.

Decision—Yes.

Reason—The Court reasoned that Raich had been admitted
to the United States under federal law. He was thus admitted
with the privilege of entering and living anywhere in the
United States. Being lawfully an inhabitant of Arizona, the
complainant was entitled under the Fourteenth Amendment
to the equal protection of its laws. The Fourteenth Amendment states that all persons within the territorial jurisdiction
of the United States are entitled to the due process and equal
protection clauses of the Amendment. It has been frequently
held that this includes aliens. Although this law did not
totally exclude aliens from equal rights by setting down a
percentage, it did, however, if this law were to be declared
valid, give the state the power to exclude aliens totally from
equal protection within their borders. Thus the Arizona act
was against aliens as such in competition with citizens of a
defined category, and in the opinion of the Court it clearly
fell under the condemnation of the Constitution. The use of
the state's police power does not permit the state to deny to
lawful inhabitants the ordinary means of earning a livelihood.

Corollary cases

McCabe v. Atchison, Topeka &
Santa Fe Ry., 235 U. S. 151

Yick Wo v. Hopkins, 118 U. S. 356

Wong Wing v. United States, 163
U. S. 228

United States v. Wong Kim Ark,
169 U. S. 649

McCready v. Virginia, 94 U. S. 391

Patsone v. Pennsylvania, 232 U. S.
138

Fong Yue Ting v. United States,
149 U. S. 698

Takahashi v. Fish and Game Commission, 334 U. S. 410

Oyama v. State of California, 332
U. S. 633

Terrace v. Thompson, 263 U. S.
197

DUE PROCESS AND TRIAL

Tumey v. Ohio, 273 U. S. 510; 47 S. Ct. 437; 71 L. Ed. 749 (1927)

Tumey was arrested and brought before Mayor Pugh of the village of North College Hill in the State of Ohio on the charge of unlawfully possessing intoxicating liquor contrary to the prohibition act of that state. The mayor, under statutes of Ohio, had the authority to hear a case of one charged with violating this prohibition act. Tumey moved for a dismissal of the case because of the disqualification of the mayor to try him under the Fourteenth Amendment. The mayor denied the motion, proceeded to the trial, convicted Tumey of unlawfully possessing intoxicating liquor within Hamilton County, Ohio, fined him $100, and ordered that he be imprisoned until the fine and costs were paid. As a result of the conviction the mayor received a $12 fee from Tumey for his acting as judge in addition to his being mayor. The mayor would not have received this fee if the accused had not been convicted.

OPINION BY MR. CHIEF JUSTICE TAFT

(No evidence from the report that the decision was not unanimous.)

Question—Do certain statutes in Ohio, in providing for a trial by the mayor of a village of one accused of violating the prohibition act of the state deprive the accused of due process of law and violate the Fourteenth Amendment to the federal Constitution, because of the pecuniary and other interests that those statutes give the mayor in the result of the trial?

Decision—Yes.

Reason—"All questions of judicial qualification may not involve constitutional validity. Thus matters of kinship, personal bias, state policy, remoteness of interest would seem generally to be matters of legislative discretion. . . . But it certainly violates the Fourteenth Amendment and deprives a defendant in a criminal case of due process of law to subject his liberty or property to the judgment of a court, the judge of which has a direct, personal, substantial pecuniary interest in reaching a conclusion against him in his case."

No matter what the evidence against him, he has the right to have an impartial judge.

Corollary cases

Powell v. Alabama, 287 U. S. 45   Bute v. Illinois, 333 U. S. 640
Haley v. Ohio, 332 U. S. 596   Dugan v. Ohio, 277 U. S. 61

DUE PROCESS AND SELF-INCRIMINATION

Twining v. New Jersey, 211 U. S. 78; 29 S. Ct. 14; 53 L. Ed. 97 (1908)

Albert Twining and one, Cornell, directors of a bank in New Jersey, were indicted for having knowingly exhibited a false paper to a state bank examiner with intent to deceive him as to the condition of the bank. At the trial the defendants called no witnesses and did not testify in their own behalf. In his charge to the jury the judge said, "Because a man does not go upon the stand you are not necessarily justified in drawing an inference of guilt. But you have a right to consider the fact that he does not go upon the stand where a direct accusation is made against him." The defendants were convicted, and sentenced to imprisonment for six and four years, respectively.

OPINION BY MR. JUSTICE MOODY
(Vote: 8-1)

Question—Is the exemption from self-incrimination one of the privileges and immunities of citizens of the United States that states may not abridge?

Decision—No.

Reason—The defendants argued that the privilege of not incriminating oneself is one of the fundamental rights of national citizenship. If this be a right it is inherent in state citizenship only, for the privileges and immunities of citizens of the United States are only such as arise out of the nature and essential character of the national government, or are specifically granted by the Constitution.

The Court had previously enunciated that the personal rights enumerated in the first eight Amendments are not privileges and immunities of citizens, and that this clause of the Fourteenth Amendment does not apply to them. Exemption from compulsory self-incrimination, therefore, is not a privilege or immunity of national citizenship nor is it guaranteed by the due process clause of the Fourteenth Amendment from abridgement by the states.

Corollary cases

Barron v. Baltimore, 7 Peters, 243

Slaughter-House Cases, 16 Wallace 36

Maxwell v. Dow, 176 U. S. 581

Duncan v. Missouri, 152 U. S. 377

United States v. Cruikshank, 92 U. S. 542

O'Neil v. Vermont, 144 U. S. 323

Adamson v. California, 332 U. S. 46

Rochin v. California, 342 U. S. 165

Breithaupt v. Abram, 352 U.S. 432

Schmerber v. California, 384 U. S. 757

Palko v. Connecticut, 302 U. S. 319

Foster v. Illinois, 332 U. S. 134

Louisiana v. Resweber, 329 U. S. 459

Wolf v. Colorado, 338 U. S. 25

Hoffman v. United States, 341 U. S. 479

Malloy v. Hogan, 378 U. S. 1 (1964)

Murphy v. Waterfront Commission, 378 U. S. 52 (1964)

Griffin v. California, 380 U. S. 609

Tehan v. Shott, 382 U. S. 406

SELF-INCRIMINATION

Ullmann v. United States, 350 U. S. 422; 76 S. Ct. 497; 100 L. Ed. 511 (1956)

Congress in 1954 passed the Immunity Act providing that whenever, in the judgment of a United States Attorney, the testimony of any witness, or the production of books, papers, or other evidence by any witness, in any case or proceeding before any grand jury or court of the United States involving any interference with or endangering of national security (including certain specified federal statutes) is necessary to the public interest, the United States Attorney, upon the approval of the Attorney General, shall make application to the court for an order to the witness to testify. However, the witness cannot subsequently be prosecuted in any court on the basis of the testimony he then gives.

William L. Ullmann refused to answer questions regarding espionage activity before a grand jury of the Southern District of New York despite the statutory provision of immunity, and he was convicted of contempt.

OPINION BY MR. JUSTICE FRANKFURTER
(Vote: 7-2)

Question—Is the immunity provided by the Act sufficiently broad to displace the protection afforded by the Constitutional privilege against self-incrimination?

Decision—Yes.

Reason—The Immunity Act protects a witness who is compelled to answer to the extent of his Constitutional immunity, that is giving testimony that might possibly expose him to a criminal charge. The immunity thus granted by the statute is also effective as against state action. "We cannot say that Congress' paramount authority in safeguarding national security does not justify the restriction it has placed on the exercise of state power for the more effective exercise of conceded federal power." The Court noted that the sole concern of the privilege against self-incrimination "is, as its name indicates, with the danger to a witness forced to give testimony leading to the infliction of 'penalties affixed to the criminal acts . . . ' " "Immunity displaces the danger. Once the reason for the privilege ceases, the privilege ceases."

The Court also noted that the Act does not impose a non-judicial function on the District Court since this Court has no discretion to deny an application for an order requiring a witness to answer, assuming that the statutory requirements have been met.

Corollary Cases

Brown v. Walker, 161 U. S. 591

Hale v. Henkel, 201 U. S. 43

Adams v. Maryland, 347 U. S. 179

Boyd v. United States, 116 U. S. 616

Slochower v. Board of Higher Education of New York City, 350 U. S. 551

Adamson v. California, 332 U. S. 46

Reina v. United States, 364 U. S. 507

Beilan v. Board of Education, 357 U. S. 399

Marchetti v. United States, 390 U. S. 000 (1968)

Grosso v. United States, 389 U. S. 62 (1968)

THE CIVIL SERVICE AND POLITICAL ACTIVITY

United Public Workers of America v. Mitchell, 330 U. S. 75; 91 L. Ed. 754; 67 S. Ct. 556 (1947)

The Hatch Act, enacted in 1940, makes it unlawful for federal employees to engage in certain specified political activities. The appellants, with the exception of George Poole, asked for a declaration of the legally permissible limits of regulation. The Court held that this would be an advisory opinion, and refused to take jurisdiction. However, Poole was a ward executive committeeman of a political party and was politically active on election day as a worker at the polls and paymaster for other party workers. He had violated the Hatch Act.

OPINION BY MR. JUSTICE REED
(Vote: 4-3)

Question—Does the Hatch Act violate the political rights reserved to the people under the Ninth and Tenth Amendments?

Decision—No.

Reason—The practice of excluding classified employees from party offices and personal political activities at the polls is an old one. In Ex parte Curtis the decision was confirmed that prohibited employees from giving or receiving money for political purposes to or from other employees of the government because this was not a right protected by the Constitution, but one that was subject to regulation.

The prohibitions under discussion were not dissimilar, since they involved contributions of energy instead of money. Congress and the President are responsible for efficiency in the public service, and if they think prohibiting active political service will best obtain the objective, there is no constitutional objection. If Congress oversteps reasonable limits, the Courts will interfere, but only when congressional interference passes beyond the general existing conception of government power.

Corollary cases

Ex parte Curtis, 106 U. S. 371
United States v. Wurzbach, 280 U. S. 396

McAuliffe v. Mayor of New Bedford, 155 Mass. 216

ANTITRUST LEGISLATION AND THE "RULE OF REASON"

United States v. American Tobacco Co., 221 U. S. 106; 31 S. Ct. 632; 55 L. Ed. 663 (1911)

The American Tobacco Co., was charged with violating the first and second sections of the Anti-Trust Act of July 2, 1890. This company held controlling stock in five accessory corporations, thus exerting a control over them. They disguised this control by contracts and written agreements with the corporations. Furthermore, this control was extended to the subsidiary corporations belonging to the accessory corporations. These facts were undisputed before the court.

OPINION BY MR. CHIEF JUSTICE WHITE
(No evidence from the report that the decision was not unanimous.)

Question—Is every combination in restraint of trade illegal under the Sherman Act?

Decision—No.

Reason—Here the Court reiterated its "rule of reason" first set forth in United States v. Standard Oil Co. Reason must be used in deciding whether a particular contract in regard to interstate commerce should come within the prohibitions of the statute, else the statute would be too comprehensive to permit of application or else too uncertain to be enforced as a penal law. The Court was of the opinion that in view of the general language of the statute, there was no possibility of frustrating that policy by resorting to any disguise or subterfuge of form. Applying this reasoning to this case the Court held that the acts, contracts, agreements, and combinations of the American Tobacco Co. all resulted in the same thing, that is, the American Tobacco Co. as the principal organization had not restrained trade by exerting its power over accessory corporations and subsidiary corporations in the disguise of contracts and agreements, but actually by owning controlling stock in the accessory corporations. Therefore, the combination did violate the Sherman Act.

Corollary cases

United States v. Standard Oil Co., 221 U. S. 1

United States v. Trans-Missouri Freight Association, 166 U. S. 290

United States v. Joint Traffic Association, 171 U. S. 505

Swift and Co. v. United States, 196 U. S. 375

United States v. U. S. Steel Corp., 251 U. S. 417

NAVIGABLE WATERS

United States v. Appalachian Electric Power Co., 311 U. S. 377; 61 S. Ct. 291; 85 L. Ed. 243 (1940)

On June 25, 1925 the predecessor of the respondent Appalachian Electric Power Co. initiated the Radford Dam Project. There was some difficulty in determining whether the New River was navigable or not, so, in order to expedite matters, the respondent applied for a license, which could be withdrawn if it was found that no federal license was required. This application was later withdrawn. On October 12, 1932, without notice, the Commission pronounced the river navigable. The respondent began construction about June 1, 1934. On May 6, 1935 the United States filed this bill for an injunction against the construction or maintenance of the proposed dam otherwise than under a license from the Federal Power Commission and for a mandatory order of removal.

OPINION BY MR. JUSTICE REED
(Vote: 6-2)

Question—Was the New River navigable, and, if so, is the licensing power of the Federal Power Commission valid?

Decision—Yes.

Reason—"The plenary federal power over commerce must be able to develop with the needs of that commerce which is the reason for its existence. It cannot properly be said that the federal power over navigation is enlarged by the improvements to the waterways. It is merely that improvements make applicable to certain waterways the existing power over commerce. In determining the navigable character of the New River it is proper to consider the feasibility of interstate use after reasonable improvement which might be made."

"The state and respondent alike, however, hold the waters and the land under them subject to the power of Congress to control the waters, for the purpose of commerce. The power flows from the grant to regulate, i.e., to 'prescribe the rule by which commerce is to be governed'. . . . This includes the projection of navigable waters in capacity as well as use. This power of Congress to regulate commerce is so unfettered that its judgment as to whether a structure is or is not a hindrance is conclusive. Its determination is legislative in character. The Federal Government has domination over the water power inherent in the flowing stream. It is liable to no one for its use or non-use. The flow of a navigable stream is in no sense private property . . . Exclusion of riparian owners from its benefits without compensation is entirely within the Government's discretion. . . .

"The point is that navigable waters are subject to national planning and control in the broad regulation of commerce granted the Federal Government. The license conditions to which objection is made have an obvious relationship to the exercise of the commerce power. Even if there were no such relationship the plenary power of Congress over navigable waters would empower it to deny the privilege of constructing

an obstruction in those waters. It may likewise grant the
privilege on terms. . . ."

Corollary cases

Gibbons v. Ogden, 9 Wheaton 1

Oklahoma v. Guy F. Atkinson Co.,
  313 U. S. 508

Ashwander v. T.V.A., 297 U. S.
  288

The Daniel Ball, 10 Wallace 557

The Thomas Jefferson, 10 Wheaton
  428

The Genesee Chief v. Fitzhugh, 12
  Howard 443

Arizona v. California, 283 U. S.
  423

TAXATION AND REGULATION

**United States v. Butler, 297 U. S. 1; 56 S. Ct. 312; 80 L. Ed.
477 (1936)**

In accordance with the Agricultural Adjustment Act of
1933, the Secretary of Agriculture ordered the payment
of crop reduction benefits on cotton. To meet these,
processing taxes were levied on the processors. The act
provided also for the levying of floor taxes upon the
existent stocks of floor goods that would have been
subject to processing taxes had the law been effective
earlier. The receiver for a Massachusetts cotton mill,
the Hoosac Mills Corporation, attacked the constitutionality of the processing and floor taxes assessed against it.

OPINION BY MR. JUSTICE ROBERTS
(Vote: 6-3)

Question—Is this act a proper exercise of the federal taxing
  power?

Decision—No.

Reason—It was an act that invaded the rights reserved to the
states. It was a statutory plan to regulate and control agricultural production, a matter beyond the power delegated to the
federal government. "Resort to the taxing power to effectuate
an end which is not legitimate, not within the scope of the
constitution, is obviously inadmissible."

The tax was based on the general welfare clause of the
Constitution. This is a limitation on the power to tax, not an
enlargement of it. The law took money from one group for
the benefit of another group. This was not a tax.

It was claimed that the act was voluntary, but it was not.
It forced the farmer to comply with it under threat of financial
ruin. Congress cannot invade state jurisdiction to compel
individual action. "At best it is a scheme for purchasing with

federal funds submission to federal regulation of a subject reserved to the states."

Corollary cases

Mulford v. Smith, 307 U. S. 38

Bailey v. Drexel Furniture Co., 259 U. S. 20

Sonzinsky v. United States, 300 U. S. 506

McCray v. United States, 195 U. S. 27

Veazie Bank v. Fenno, 8 Wallace 533

Steward Machine Co., v. Davis, 301 U. S. 548

INTERSTATE COMMERCE AND DUE PROCESS

United States v. Carolene Products Co., 304 U. S. 144; 58 S. Ct. 778; 82 L. Ed. 123 (1938)

In March, 1923 Congress passed the "filled Milk Act" which prohibited the shipment in interstate commerce of skimmed milk compounded with any fat or oil other than milk fat, so as to resemble milk or cream. The appellee was indicted in southern Illinois for shipping in interstate commerce certain packages of a filled milk compound.

OPINION BY MR. JUSTICE STONE
(Vote: 6-1)

Question—Is this regulation beyond the power of Congress over interstate commerce, and is this a deprivation of property without due process of law?

Decision—No.

Reason—Filled milk is described by the statute as an adulterated article of food, injurious to health, and a fraud upon the public. "Even in the absence of such aids the existence of facts supporting the legislative judgment is to be presumed, for regulatory legislation affecting ordinary commercial transactions is not to be pronounced unconstitutional unless in the light of the facts made known or generally assumed it is of such a character as to preclude the assumption that it rests upon some rational basis within the knowledge and experience of the legislators."

In this case, it is at least debatable whether commerce in filled milk should be left unregulated, partially restricted, or entirely prohibited. That was a decision for Congress, and as such, the prohibition of shipment in interstate commerce of this product was a constitutional exercise of the power to regulate interstate commerce. Congressional power to regulate commerce is the power to prescribe the rules by which commerce is to be governed. This extends to the prohibition of shipments in such commerce. This power is complete and unlimited, except as limited by the Constitution. Congress is free to exclude from interstate commerce articles whose use in states may be injurious to public health, morals, or welfare, or that contravene the policy of the state of their destination.

The Court in this case indicated that it would give greater weight to the presumption of constitutionality in economic regulations than in matters covered by civil liberties.

Corollary cases

O'Gorman and Young v. Hartford Fire Ins. Co., 282 U. S. 251

Daniel v. Family Security Life Ins. Co., 336 U. S. 220

Polk Co. v. Glover, 305 U. S. 5

Champion v. Ames, 188 U. S. 321

Brooks v. United States, 227 U. S. 308

FEDERAL CONTROL OF CONGRESSIONAL PRIMARIES

United States v. Classic, 313 U. S. 299; 61 S. Ct. 1031; 85 L. Ed. 1368 (1941)

In Louisiana, a primary election to nominate a party candidate for Representative in Congress was conducted at public expense and regulated by state statute. Candidates to be voted on in the general election were restricted to primary nominees, to persons, not candidates in the primary, who filed nomination papers with the requisite number of signatures, and to persons whose names might lawfully be written on the ballot by the electors. Some of the votes of qualified voters were deliberately changed for the benefit of a different candidate. Classic, a Commissioner of Elections, was convicted under the federal Criminal Code which prohibits interference with constitutional rights.

OPINION BY MR. JUSTICE STONE
(Vote: 5-3)

Question—Has Congress the right to see that primary elections are carried on in accordance with the right of the people to vote?

Decision—Yes.

Reason—Although the state government has the power to regulate these primary elections, Congress still has the duty to see that the integrity of these elections is maintained. The state had made these primary elections an integral part of the act of choosing one's Representative. Thus it would fall under the meaning of elections of Article I, Sections 2 and 4 of the Constitution. "The right to participate in the choice of representatives for Congress includes, as we have said, the right to cast a ballot and to have it counted at the general election whether for the successful candidate or not. Where the state law has made the primary an integral part of the procedure of choice or where in fact the primary effectively controls the choice, the right of the elector to have his ballot counted at the primary, is likewise included in the right protected by Article I, Section 2."

Corollary cases

Newberry v. United States, 256 U. S. 232

Nixon v. Herndon, 273 U. S. 536

Ex parte Yarbrough, 110 U. S. 651

Ex parte Siebold, 100 U. S. 371

Screws v. United States, 325 U. S. 91

Grovey v. Townsend, 294 U. S. 699

United States v. Mosley, 238 U. S. 383

Minor v. Happersett, 21 Wallace 162

Nixon v. Condon, 286 U. S. 73

Smith v. Allwright, 321 U. S. 649

United States v. Raines, 362 U. S. 17

DELEGATION OF LEGISLATIVE POWERS

United States v. Curtiss-Wright Export Corp., 299 U. S. 304; 57 S. Ct. 216; 81 L. Ed. 255 (1936).

Curtiss-Wright Export Corp. sold to Bolivia, a country then engaged in armed conflict in the Chaco, certain arms of war. The sale was completed in the United States. The company was charged with violating the joint resolution of Congress empowering the President to forbid the sale of any articles of war to countries engaged in armed conflict if this prohibition of sale would act in the interest of peace between the combatants. This applied to sales within the United States. The President issued such a proclamation and made violation of it punishable as a crime.

OPINION BY MR. JUSTICE SUTHERLAND
(Vote: 7-1)

Question—Is this joint resolution of Congress an illegal delegation of legislative power to the President?

Decision—No.

Reason—"It is important to bear in mind that we are here dealing not alone with an authority vested in the President by an exertion of legislative power; but with such an authority plus the very delicate, plenary and exclusive power of the President as the sole organ of the federal government in the field of international relations—a power which does not require as a basis for its exercise an act of Congress, but which, of course, like every other governmental power, must be exercised in subordination to the applicable provisions of the Constitution. It is quite apparent that if, in the maintenance of our international relations, embarrassment—perhaps serious embarrassment—is to be avoided and success for our aims achieved, congressional legislation which is to be made effective through negotiation and inquiry within the international field must often accord to the President a degree of discretion and freedom from statutory restriction which would not be admissible were domestic affairs alone involved. . . .

"Practically every volume of the United States Statutes contains one or more acts or joint resolutions of Congress authorizing action by the President in respect of subjects affecting foreign relations which either leave the exercise of the power to his unrestricted judgment, or provide a standard far more general than that which has always been considered requisite with regard to domestic affairs. . . . A legislative practice such as we have here, evidenced not by only occasional instances, but marked by the movement of a steady stream for a century and a half of time, goes a long way in the direction of proving the presence of unassailable ground for the constitutionality of the practice, to be found in the origin and history of the power involved, or in its nature, or in both combined. . . ."

Corollary cases

Field v. Clark, 143 U. S. 649
Jones v. United States, 137 U. S. 202

Panama Refining Co. v. Ryan, 293 U. S. 388
Schechter Poultry Corp. v. United States, 295 U. S. 495

COMMERCE CONTROL AND LABOR STANDARDS

United States v. F. W. Darby Lumber Co., 312 U. S. 100; 61 S. Ct. 451; 85 L. Ed. 609 (1941)

The appellee was engaged, in the state of Georgia, in

the business of acquiring raw materials, which he manufactured into finished lumber with the intention of shipping it in interstate commerce to customers outside the state. Numerous counts charged the appellee with the shipment in interstate commerce from Georgia to points outside the state of lumber in which he employed workmen at less than the prescribed minimum wage or more than the prescribed maximum hours without payment of any wage for overtime. Another count charged the appellee with failure to keep records showing the hours worked each day a week by his employees, as required by the regulation of the administrator. The appellee sought to sustain the decision on the grounds that the prohibition of Congress was unauthorized by the commerce clause, and was prohibited by the Fifth Amendment.

Opinion by Mr. Justice Stone

(No evidence from the report that the decision was not unanimous.)

Question—Has Congress the constitutional power to prohibit the shipment in interstate commerce of lumber manufactured by employees whose wages are less than a prescribed minimum or whose weekly hours are greater than a prescribed maximum and to prohibit the employment of workmen in the production of goods for "interstate commerce" at other than prescribed wages and hours?

Decision—Yes.

Reason—The manufacture of goods in itself is not a matter of interstate commerce, but the shipment of such article is. It was contended that the regulations of Congress in the matter of wages and hours belong properly to the states. However, the power of Congress to regulate interstate commerce is complete in itself, with no other limitations except those prescribed in the Constitution.

The motive and purpose of the Act in question was to keep interstate commerce from being an instrument in the distribution of goods produced under substandard conditions, as such competition would be injurious to interstate commerce. This was a matter of legislative judgment perfectly within the bounds of congressional power, and over which the courts are given no control.

Congress has the power to regulate not only commerce between the states, but such intrastate activities that so affect interstate commerce as to make their regulation means to a legitimate end. As regards the congressional policy of excluding from interstate commerce all goods manufactured under substandards, the enforcement of wages and hours, even though intrastate, are a valid means of protection, and therefore, within the reach of the commerce power.

(This decision overruled Hammer v. Dagenhart, 247 U. S. 251.)

Corollary cases

Gibbons v. Ogden, 9 Wheaton 1

Kentucky Whip & Collar Co. v. Illinois Central R.R. Co., 229 U. S. 334

McCray v. United States, 195 U. S. 27

Sonzinsky v. United States, 300 U. S. 506

Veazie Bank v. Fenno, 8 Wallace 533

United States v. Carolene Products Co., 304 U. S. 144

Kidd v. Pearson, 128 U. S. 1

Martino v. Michigan Window Cleaning Co., 327 U. S. 173

United States v. Rock Royal Co-op., 307 U. S. 533

Sunshine Anthracite Coal Co. v. Adkins, 310 U. S. 381

Warren-Bradshaw Co. v. Hall, 317 U. S. 88

TAXATION AND REGULATION

United States v. Doremus, 249 U. S. 86; 39 S. Ct. 214; 63 L. Ed. 493 (1919)

Doremus, a physician, was indicted for violating Section 2 of the Harrison Narcotic Drug Act. It forbade any person to dispose of narcotic drugs except by a written order on a form issued by the Commissioner of Internal Revenue. It was not to apply to physicians who used drugs to treat patients. Section 1 of the act stated that all persons who would have contact with this type of drug in a commercial way must pay a special tax of one dollar per annum. Doremus was convicted of selling to one Ameris five hundred one-sixth grain heroin tablets without an order of the official type, and of selling not in professional practice but to relieve the appetite of a known drug addict. The lower court had held Section 2 of the Act unconstitutional as not a revenue measure but an invasion of state police power.

OPINION BY MR. JUSTICE DAY
(Vote: 5-4)

Question—Have the provisions in question any relation to the raising of revenue?

Decision—Yes.

Reason—That Congress might levy an excise tax upon such dealers and others named is not disputed. The provision in Section 2 aims to confine sales to registered dealers and to those dispensing the drugs as physicians. Congress, with full power over the subject, short of arbitrary and unreasonable treatment that is not to be assumed, inserted these provisions into the Act specifically to provide revenue. These provisions tend to keep traffic aboveboard and subject to inspection by those authorized to collect the revenue. They tend to restrain unauthorized persons from selling the drug and not paying the tax. Ameris might not have used all the drug himself but sold to others without paying the tax. At least Congress may have deemed it wise to prevent such possible dealings because of their effect on the collection of revenue. ". . . the fact that other motives may impel the exercise of Federal taxing power does not authorize the courts to inquire into the subject. If the legislation enacted has some reasonable relation to the exercise of the taxing authority conferred by the Constitution, it cannot be invalidated because of the supposed motives which induced it."

Corollary cases

License Tax Cases, 5 Wallace 462

Veazie Bank v. Fenno, 8 Wallace 533

McCray v. United States, 195 U. S. 27

Nigro v. United States, 276 U. S. 332

Bailey v. Drexel Furniture Co., 259 U. S. 20

Sonzinsky v. United States, 300 U. S. 506

Hill v. Wallace, 259 U. S. 44

Carter v. Carter Coal Co., 298 U. S. 238

ANTITRUST LEGISLATION

United States v. Hutcheson, 312 U. S. 219; 61 S. Ct. 463; 85 L. Ed. 788 (1941)

Anheuser-Busch, Inc., operating a large plant in St. Louis, contracted with Borsari Tank Corp. for the erection of an additional facility. Anheuser-Busch obtained the materials for its brewing and other operations through interstate commerce, as did the construction company for its building materials. Among the employees of Anheuser-Busch were members of the United Brotherhood of Carpenters & Joiners of America and the International

Association of Machinists. The conflicting claims of these two organizations, affiliated with the American Federation of Labor, in regard to erection and dismantling of machinery had long been a source of controversy between them. Anheuser-Busch had agreements with both, whereby the Machinists were given all disputed jobs and the Carpenters agreed to submit all disputes to arbitration. During the course of the construction of this new facility the Carpenters claimed certain jobs. Rejection by the employer of the Carpenters' demands and refusal of the Carpenters to arbitrate, was followed by a strike by the Carpenters, called by Hutcheson, against Anheuser-Busch, picketing of Anheuser-Busch, and a request that their union members and their friends cease buying Anheuser-Busch beer, this last-named activity carried on through circular letters and by official publication by the Carpenters. These activities on behalf of the Carpenters formed the basis of the charge of violation of Sherman Act.

OPINION BY MR. JUSTICE FRANKFURTER
(Vote: 6-2)

Question—Did the trade union conduct constitute a violation of the Sherman Law?

Decision—No.

Reason—The Court reasoned their decision in the light of the Clayton Act of 1914 and the Norris-LaGuardia Act of 1932. The opinion characterized the enactment of the Clayton Act of 1914 as an attempt to secure protection of labor against the application of the Sherman Act. The Court criticized early opinions of the Supreme Court devitalizing the Clayton Act as a protector of labor, and called attention to powerful judicial dissents and informed lay opinion that had disagreed with the majority of the Court. The Norris-LaGuardia Act of 1932, by narrowing the circumstances under which the federal courts could grant injunctions in labor disputes, had removed the fetters upon trade-union activities, which, according to judicial construction, the Clayton Act had left untouched. The Court stressed the statement of public policy as to labor included in the Norris-LaGuardia Act. Even though that act did not directly cover the kinds of situations involved in this case, the Court reached the conclusion that the statement of policy in it nullified an important part of the substance of the Sherman Act.

Corollary cases

Loewe v. Lawlor, 208 U. S. 274

Duplex Printing Press Co. v. Deering, 254 U. S. 443

Bedford Stone Co. v. Journeyman Stone Cutters Association, 274 U. S. 37

Allen Bradley Co. v. Local Union No. 3, I.B.E.W., 325 U. S. 797

Apex Hosiery Co. v. Leader, 310 U. S. 469

Hunt v. Crumboch, 325 U. S. 821

Coronado Coal Co. v. U.M.W.A., 268 U. S. 295

United States v. Employing Plasterer's Ass'n. et al., 347 U. S. 186 (1953)

MANUFACTURING AND COMMERCE

United States v. E. C. Knight Co., 156 U. S. 1; 15 S. Ct. 249; 39 L. Ed. 325 (1895)

The government charged that the E. C. Knight Company, with four others, had contracted with the American Sugar Refining Company for the purchase by the latter of the stocks and properties of these corporations, and for the issuance of stock in the American Sugar Refining Co. It charged that this transaction was intended to bring about control of the price of sugar in the United States, together with a monopoly of the manufacture and sale of refined sugar in this country, a violation of the Sherman Anti-Trust Act.

OPINION BY MR. CHIEF JUSTICE FULLER
(Vote: 8-1)

Question—Assuming the existence of a monopoly in manufacture, can the monopoly be directly suppressed under the act of Congress in the manner attempted by this action?

Decision—No.

Reason—The power to control manufacturing involves in a certain sense the control of its disposition, but only in a secondary sense. The exercise of that power brings the operation of commerce into play, but only indirectly. The regulation of commerce applies to subjects of commerce, not to those of internal police. The fact that an article is manufactured with an intent of export to another state does not of itself make such an article an item of interstate commerce. It becomes so when it begins its journey in interstate commerce.

The Act of 1890 did not attempt to deal with monopolies

as such, but with conspiracies to monopolize trade among the several states. In the case at hand, the object was private gain from manufacture of the commodity, not control of interstate or foreign commerce. There was nothing in the proofs to indicate any intention to put a restraint upon trade or commerce. (The rule of this case is no longer good law having been overruled by later cases, notably N.L.R.B. v. Jones and Laughlin Steel Corp.)

Corollary cases

Coe v. Errol, 116 U. S. 517

Kidd v. Pearson, 128 U. S. 1

Standard Oil Co. v. United States, 221 U. S. 1

United States v. American Tobacco Co., 221 U. S. 106

Swift and Co. v. United States, 196 U. S. 375

Miles Medical Co., v. Park and Sons, 220 U. S. 373

United States v. Northern Securities Co., 193 U. S. 197

Montague v. Lowry, 193 U. S. 38

Loewe v. Lawlor (Danbury Hatters' Case), 208 U. S. 274

Apex Hosiery Co. v. Leader, 310 U. S. 469

N.L.R.B. v. Jones and Laughlin Steel Corp., 301 U. S. 1

DOUBLE JEOPARDY

United States v. Lanza, 260 U. S. 377; 43 S. Ct. 141; 67 L. Ed. 314 (1922)

The State of Washington passed a prohibition law before the passage of the National Prohibition Act. Lanza was charged in the Federal Court of Washington and in the Supreme Court of Whatcom County, Washington for the violation of each of the respective acts. He was accused of making, selling, and transporting liquor and of having a still and material for the manufacture of liquor. He brought suit in the Federal Court to dismiss the suit of the United States on the grounds that he was placed in double jeopardy.

Opinion by Mr. Chief Justice Taft

(No evidence from the report that the decision was not unanimous.)

Question—Can the United States punish some one for an act for which the state has already punished him?

Decision—Yes.

Reason—We have two sovereignties, deriving power from different sources, capable of dealing with the same subject matter within the same territory. Each may, without interference from the other, enact laws determining what shall be an offense against its peace and dignity. In doing this, each is exercising its own sovereignty, not that of the other.

It follows that an act denounced as a crime by both national and state sovereignties is an offense against the peace and dignity of both and may be punished by each. The Fifth Amendment applies only to proceedings of the federal government, and the double jeopardy covered therein forbids a second prosecution under the authority of the federal government after a first trial for the same offense under the same authority. Here the same act was an offense against the State of Washington because of a violation of its laws and also an offense against the United States under the National Prohibition Act. The defendants thus committed two different offenses by the same act and a conviction by a court of Washington together with conviction in the Federal Court was not double jeopardy.

Corollary cases

Barron v. Baltimore, 7 Peters 243

National Prohibition Cases, 253 U. S. 350

Palko v. Connecticut, 302 U. S. 319

Wolf v. Colorado, 338 U. S. 25

Screws v. United States, 325 U. S. 91

Brock v. State of North Carolina, 344 U. S. 424

Baltimore and Ohio R.R. Co. v. United States, 345 U. S. 146

Abbate v. United States, 359 U. S. 187

Bartkus v. Illinois, 359 U. S. 121

BILL OF ATTAINDER

United States v. Lovett, 328 U. S. 303; 66 S. Ct. 1073; 90 L. Ed. 1252 (1946)

Lovett, Watson, and Dodd had been working for the government for several years, and the government agencies that had lawfully employed them were fully satisfied with their work, and wished to keep them employed. In 1943 Congress passed the Urgent Deficiency Appropriation Act, which provided that no salary should be paid respondents unless they were reappointed to their jobs by the President with the advice and consent of the Senate. Notwithstanding the failure of the President to reappoint them, they continued at their jobs, and sued for their salaries.

OPINION BY MR. JUSTICE BLACK
(Vote: 8-0)

Question—Is this a bill of attainder, which is forbidden by the Constitution?

Decision—Yes.

Reason—In Cummings v. Missouri the Court said, "A bill of attainder is a legislative act which inflicts punishment without a judicial trial." If the punishment be less than death, the act is termed a bill of pains and penalties, but both are included in the meaning of the Constitution.

Lovett, Watson, and Dodd were mentioned by Congressman Dies with thirty-six other named government employees as "irresponsible, unrepresentative, crackpot, radical bureaucrats" and affiliates of "communist front organizations." He urged that Congress refuse to appropriate money for their salaries. This in effect would force the governmental agencies to discharge them, and stigmatize their reputations, which would seriously impair their chances to earn a living. This clearly punished the individuals without a judicial trial, which is forbidden by the Constitution.

Corollary cases

United States v. Dickerson, 310 U. S. 554

Cummings v. Missouri, 4 Wallace 277

Ex parte Garland, 4 Wallace 333

Duncan v. Kahanamoku, 327 U. S. 304

U. S. v. Brown, 381 U. S. 437

SEARCH AND SEIZURE

United States v. Rabinowitz, 339 U. S. 56; 70 S. Ct. 430; 94 L. Ed. 653 (1950)

Rabinowitz was charged with the crime of altering postage stamps to defraud collectors. He was arrested under a proper arrest warrant, and the police, without a search warrant, then searched his one-room office, including desk, file cabinet, and safe and found the forged stamps. Rabinowitz was convicted on the evidence.

OPINION BY MR. JUSTICE MINTON
(Vote: 5-3)

Question—Was this unreasonable search and seizure under the Fourth Amendment?

Decision—No.

Reason—The Fourth Amendment says that the public is free from an unreasonable search. When there was an arrest with a proper arrest warrant, it was reasonable for the police officers to search the small business room, even if they had time to get a search warrant. "The relevant test is not whether it is reasonable to procure a search warrant, but whether the search was reasonable. That criterion in turn depends upon the facts and circumstances—the total atmosphere of the case."

Corollary cases

Go-Bart Importing Co. v. United States, 282 U. S. 344

Weeks v. United States, 232 U. S. 383

Trupiano v. United States, 334 U. S. 699

Harris v. United States, 331 U. S. 145

Wolf v. Colorado, 338 U. S. 25

Carroll v. United States, 267 U. S. 132

Lanzetta v. New Jersey, 306 U. S. 451

INSURANCE AS INTERSTATE COMMERCE

United States v. South-Eastern Underwriters Ass'n., 322 U. S. 533, 64 S. Ct. 1162, 88 L. Ed. 1440 (1944)

The South-Eastern Underwriters Association represented private stock companies in the business of selling fire insurance in six southeastern states. They were indicted in a federal district court for violations of the Sherman Anti-Trust Act by fixing and maintaining arbitrary and noncompetitive premium rates on fire insurance, and by monopolizing the trade and commerce in that line of insurance in and among the same states. They contended that selling insurance was not commerce and therefore did not come under the interstate commerce regulations.

OPINION BY MR. JUSTICE BLACK
(Vote: 4-3)

Question—Do fire insurance transactions which stretch across state lines constitute "commerce among the several States" so as to make them subject to regulation by Congress under the commerce clause?

Decision—Yes.

Reason—The Court reasoned that the basic responsibility in interpreting the commerce clause is to make certain that the power to govern intercourse among the states remains where the Constitution placed it. That power, as held by the Supreme Court from the beginning, is vested in Congress, available to be exercised for the national welfare as Congress shall deem necessary. No commercial enterprise of any kind that conducts its activities across state lines has been held to be wholly beyond the regulatory power of Congress under the commerce clause. The Court concluded that they could not make an exception of the business of insurance.

Corollary cases

Paul v. Virginia, 8 Wallace 168

Hooper v. California, 155 U. S. 648

New York Life Insurance Co. v. Deer Lodge County, 231 U. S. 495

Lottery Case, 188 U. S. 321

Hoke v. United States, 227 U. S. 308

United States v. Simpson, 252 U. S. 465

Brooks v. United States, 267 U. S. 432

Thornton v. United States, 271 U. S. 414

Gibbons v. Ogden, 9 Wheaton 1

Northern Securities Co. v. United States, 193 U. S. 197

Radovich v. National Football League, 352 U. S. 445

CITIZENSHIP BY BIRTH

United States v. Wong Kim Ark, 169 U. S. 649; 18 S. Ct. 456; 42 L. Ed. 890 (1898)

The Collector of the Port of San Francisco denied admission to the country of Wong Kim Ark, a Chinese person who was admitted to have been born in California, and was returning from a temporary visit to China. His parents were subjects of the emperor of China, but had a permanent domicile and residence here, and were carrying on business here. They were not employed in any official diplomatic capacity for the emperor of China.

Opinion by Mr. Justice Gray
(Vote: 7-2)

Question—Does a child in such circumstances become a citizen of the United States at birth?

Decision—Yes.

Reason—Wong Kim Ark became a citizen at birth by virtue of the first clause of the Fourteenth Amendment, "All persons born or naturalized in the United States, and subject to the jurisdiction thereof, are citizens of the United States and of the state wherein they reside." The Constitution nowhere defines the meaning of the word "citizen" or "natural-born citizen" either by way of inclusion or exclusion. The meaning of the phrase must therefore be interpreted in the light of common law.

The fundamental principle of the common law was birth within the allegiance of the king. Children of aliens born in England were natural-born subjects, as were children of ambassadors representing England, although born on foreign soil. Children of foreign ambassadors or diplomats or of alien enemies were not natural-born subjects since they were born outside the obedience of the king. This was the rule in all the English colonies up to the Declaration of Independence.

Roman law, which considered the citizenship of the child to be that of the parents, was not a principle of international law, since there was no settled and definite rule at the time the Fourteenth Amendment was adopted.

Corollary cases

Dred Scott v. Sandford, 19 Howard 393

Slaughter-House Cases, 16 Wallace 36

Elk v. Wilkins, 112 U. S. 94

Chirac v. Chirac, 2 Wheaton 259

Fong Yue Ting v. United States, 149 U. S. 698

United States v. Schwimmer, 279 U. S. 644

Girouard v. United States, 328 U. S. 61

Keller v. United States, 213 U. S. 138

Harisiades v. Shaughnessy, 342 U. S. 580

Mandoli v. Acheson, 344 U. S. 133

Kennedy v. Mendoza-Martinez, 372 U. S. 144

Afroyim v. Rusk, 387 U. S. 253

FOREIGN COMMERCE

University of Illinois v. United States, 289 U. S. 48; 53 S. Ct. 509; 77 L. Ed. 1025 (1933)

The University of Illinois imported scientific apparatus for use in one of its educational departments. Customs duties were exacted at the rates prescribed by the Tariff Act of 1922. The University paid under protest, insisting that as an instrumentality of the State of Illinois, and discharging a governmental function, it was entitled to import the articles duty free.

OPINION BY MR. CHIEF JUSTICE HUGHES
(No evidence from the report that the decision was not unanimous.)

Question—Is a university, as a state agent, immune from taxation by the federal government?

Decision—No.

Reason—It was the decision of the Court that the import duties in question were imposed by Congress in the exercise of its authority to regulate commerce with foreign nations. Congress had full power to regulate such commerce, even to the extent of prohibiting it altogether. No state has any right to engage in foreign commerce free from the restrictions which Congress might impose.

Corollary cases

Gibbons v. Ogden, 9 Wheaton 1
Groves v. Slaughter, 15 Peters 449
Fox Film Corp. v. Doyal, 286 U. S. 123
Graves v. New York, ex rel. O'Keefe, 306 U. S. 466

New York v. United States, 326 U. S. 572
Helvering v. Gerhardt, 304 U. S. 405

FEDERAL TAXATION AND REGULATION

Veazie Bank v. Fenno, 8 Wallace 533; 19 L. Ed. 482 (1869)

In 1866, Congress passed an act imposing a tax of 10 per cent on notes of private persons, state banks, and state banking associations. The Veazie Bank paid the tax under protest, alleging Congress had no power to pass such an act. This was a suit by the bank against the collector, Fenno, for reimbursement.

OPINION BY MR. CHIEF JUSTICE CHASE
(Vote: 5-2)

Question—Is this an unauthorized use of the taxing power of Congress?

Decision—No.

Reason—Congress had just undertaken to provide for a uniform currency for the country. To protect the newly established national bank from undue competition from the state banks, Congress was using its power indirectly when it could have used a direct method. Congress had to protect the newly established bank notes and restrain the notes of the state banks as money. Under its power to regulate the circulation of coin it was able to do this. "It cannot be doubted that under the Constitution the power to provide a circulation of coin is given to Congress. And it is settled by the uniform practice of the government and by repeated decisions, that Congress may constitutionally authorize the emission of bills of credit. . . . Having thus, in the exercise of undisputed constitutional powers, undertaken to provide a currency for the whole country, it cannot be questioned that Congress may, constitutionally, secure the benefits of it to the people by appropriate legislation. To this end, Congress has denied the quality of legal tender to foreign coins, and has provided by law against the imposition of counterfeit and base coin on the community. To the same end, Congress may restrain, by suitable enactments, the circulation as money of any notes not issued under its own authority. Without this power, indeed, its attempts to secure a sound and uniform currency for the country must be futile."

Corollary cases

McCray v. United States, 195 U. S. 27

Sonzinsky v. United States, 300 U. S. 506

Helvering v. Davis, 301 U. S. 619

Bailey v. Drexel Furniture Co., 259 U. S. 20

United States v. Butler, 297 U. S. 1

United States v. Constantine, 296 U. S. 287

United States v. Doremus, 249 U. S. 86

License Tax Cases, 5 Wallace 462

Nigro v. United States, 276 U. S. 332

Carter v. Carter Coal Co., 298 U. S. 238

INTERSTATE COMPACTS

Virginia v. Tennessee, 148 U. S. 503; 13 S. Ct. 728; 37 L. Ed. 537 (1893)

Virginia brought this suit to have the true boundary line between herself and Tennessee established. In 1801, some commissioners, appointed with the approval of both states, established a boundary, and subsequently in 1803 both legislatures approved the boundary. Since that date, the boundary established had been adhered to by both states and was recognized by Congress in districting for judicial, revenue, and federal election purposes. In this case, Virginia sought to have the agreement declared null and void as having been entered into without the consent of Congress. The Constitution provides that "no State shall, without the consent of Congress . . . enter into any agreement or compact with another state, or with a foreign power. . . ."

Opinion by Mr. Justice Field
(No evidence from the report that the decision was not unanimous.)

Question—Is the agreement, made without the consent of Congress between Virginia and Tennessee, to appoint commissioners to run and mark the boundary line between them, within the prohibition of the clause stated in the Constitution.

Decision—No.

Reason—It was the opinion of the Court that what the Constitution implied by "agreement or compact" was any compact or agreement that endangered the power of the federal government, such as a war alliance or increasing the political power in the states. The Court further noted that the clause in the Constitution did not state when Congress should approve of a compact or agreement. The approval by Congress of the compact entered into between the states upon their ratification of the action of their commissioners is fairly implied from its subsequent legislation and proceedings. The exercise of jurisdiction by Congress over the country as a part of Tennessee on one side, and as a part of Virginia on the other, for a long succession of years, without question or dispute from any quarter, is as conclusive proof of assent to it by that body as can usually be obtained from its most formal proceedings.

"Looking at the clause in which the terms 'compact' or 'agreement' appear, it is evident that the prohibition is directed to the formation of any combination tending to the increase of political power in the States, which may encroach upon or interfere with the just supremacy of the United States."

"The Constitution does not state when the consent of Congress shall be given, whether it shall precede or may follow the compact made, or whether it shall be express or may be implied."

Corollary cases

Rhode Island v. Massachusetts, 4 Howard 591

Holmes v. Jennison, 14 Peters 540

West Virginia v. Sims, 341 U. S. 22

New York v. New Jersey, 256 U. S. 296

Green v. Biddle, 8 Wheaton 1

Virginia v. West Virginia, 11 Wallace 39

South Carolina v. Georgia, 93 U. S. 4

Hinderlider v. La Plata Co., 304 U. S. 92

Kentucky v. Indiana, 281 U. S. 163

INTERSTATE SUITS

Virginia v. West Virginia, 264 U. S. 565; 62 L. Ed. 883; 38 S. Ct. 400 (1918)

When Virginia seceded from the Union at the outbreak of the Civil War, the western counties of the state remained loyal, and in 1863 were admitted to the Union as the State of West Virginia, on the condition that West Virginia take upon itself a just proportion of the public debt prior to January 1, 1861. Beginning in 1865, Virginia sought by negotiation to secure the sums due, but West Virginia showed no disposition to pay. In 1906 Virginia brought the first of nine successsive actions against West Virginia, trying again in 1907, 1908, twice in 1911, 1913, and 1914. In 1915 the Supreme Court held that it had jurisdiction to hear the case, and that West Virginia owed $12,393,929.50. In 1916 action was withheld until the West Virginia legislature had met. When they refused to do anything, Virginia asked for a mandamus to compel the levy of a tax.

OPINION BY MR. CHIEF JUSTICE WHITE

(No evidence from the report that the decision was not unanimous.)

Question—May a judgment rendered against a state as a state be enforced against it as such, including the right, to the extent necessary for so doing, of exerting authority over the governmental powers and agencies possessed by the state?

Decision—Yes.

Reason—The contention of Virginia was that the government had the power to make a judgment against a state, and the authority to enforce it. West Virginia held that power to be limited and inefficacious, saying, the reason on which such a general rule was based was the sovereignty of the state. But when the Constitution gave original jurisdiction to the Supreme Court in matters between the states, it must have intended to modify that sovereignty and bring the states within that judicial power. It is difficult to understand the position that one state may destroy the rights of any other state, with no right of redress on the part of the injured state. Therefore, the duty to enforce may be upheld, even if such exertion operates upon the governmental agencies of a state.

Corollary cases

New Hampshire v. Louisiana, 108 U. S. 76

South Dakota v. North Carolina, 192 U. S. 286

North Dakota v. Minnesota, 263 U. S. 365

INVESTIGATORY POWERS OF CONGRESS

Watkins v. United States, 354 U. S. 178; 77 S. Ct. 1173; 1 L. Ed. 2d 1273 (1957)

John T. Watkins, a labor union organizer, appeared as a witness in compliance with a subpoena issued by a Sub-Committee of the Committee on Un-American Activities of the House of Representatives. Although Watkins indicated he would answer questions about his relations with the Communist Party as well as questions concerning acquaintances currently members, he refused to answer those questions involving persons whom he believed had separated from the Party on the ground that these were not relevant to the work of this Committee and beyond the authority of the Committee to demand. He was indicted and convicted for contempt of Congress under a statute making criminal refusal to answer "any questions pertinent to the question under inquiry."

OPINION BY MR. CHIEF JUSTICE WARREN
(Vote: 6-1)

Question—May a witness at a Congressional committee hearing properly refuse to answer questions on the basis of their lack of pertinency?

Decision—Yes.

Reason—While the power of Congress to conduct investigations is inherent in the legislative process and is a broad power, the inquiry "must be related to and in furtherance of a legitimate task of the Congress." The Bill of Rights is applicable to investigations as to all forms of governmental actions, so the First Amendment freedoms of speech, press, religion, or political belief and association must not be abridged. Further, the First Amendment may be invoked against infringement of the protected freedoms by law or by lawmaking. There is a freedom *not* to speak. "Protected freedoms should not be placed in danger in the absence of a clear determination by the House or the Senate that a particular inquiry is justified by a specific legislative need." This requires that the instructions to an investigating committee spell out that group's jurisdiction and purpose with sufficient particularity. "There is no Congressional power to expose for the sake of exposure." In this instance, none of the several sources—the authorizing resolution, the remarks of the chairman, or the remarks of members of the Committee—was adequate to convey sufficient information as to the pertinency of the questions. Watkins was thus "not accorded a fair opportunity to determine whether he was within his rights in refusing to answer, and his conviction is necessarily invalid under the Due Process Clause of the Fifth Amendment."

Corollary cases

United States v. Rumely, 345 U. S. 41

Anderson v. Dunn, 6 Wheaton 204

In re Chapman, 166 U. S. 661

Kilbourn v. Thompson, 103 U. S. 168

McGrain v. Daugherty, 273 U. S. 135

Marshall v. Gordon, 243 U. S. 521

Jurney v. MacCracken, 294 U. S. 125

Sweezy v. New Hampshire, 354 U. S. 234

Barenblatt v. United States, 360 U. S. 109

Uphaus v. Wyman, 360 U. S. 72

THE COURTS AND LEGISLATIVE REDISTRICTING

Wesberry v. Sanders, 376 U. S. 1; 84 S. Ct. 526; 11 L. Ed. 2d. 481 (1964)

Action was brought by qualified voters of Georgia's Fifth Congressional District to have set aside a Georgia statute establishing Congressional districts. The population of the Fifth District was two to three times greater than that of some other Congressional districts in the state. Since there is only one Congressman for each district, it was claimed that there resulted a debasement of the people's right to vote because their Congressman represented two to three times as many people as did Congressmen from some other Georgia districts.

OPINION BY MR. JUSTICE BLACK
(Vote: 6-3)

Question — Does the districting statute abridge the requirement of Article I, Section 2 of the Constitution of the United States?

Decision — Yes.

Reason — The statute contracts the value of some votes and expands the value of others. In its historical context the command of Article I, Section 2 that Representatives be chosen "by the people of the several States" means that as nearly as practicable one man's vote in a Congressional election is to be worth as much as another's. "While it may not be possible to draw congressional districts with mathematical precision, that is no excuse for ignoring our Constitution's plain objective of making equal representation for equal numbers of people the fundamental goal for the House of Representatives. That is the high standard of justice and common sense which the Founders set for us."

Corollary cases

Colegrove v. Green, 328 U. S. 549 (1946)

Baker v. Carr, 369 U. S. 186 (1962)

Gray v. Sanders, 372 U. S. 368 (1963)

Wright v. Rockefeller, 376 U. S. 52 (1964)

Reynolds v. Sims, 377 U. S. 533 (1964)

STATE WAGE AND HOUR LEGISLATION

West Coast Hotel Co. v. Parrish, 300 U. S. 379; 57 S. Ct. 578; 81 L. Ed. 703 (1937)

Washington state laws prohibited wages below a living wage and conditions of labor detrimental to the health and morals of women and minors. Such wages were established by the state's Industrial Welfare Commission composed of members of management, labor, and the government. Elsie Parrish brought suit to recover the difference between her wages and those established by the Industrial Welfare Commission over a period of years during which she was employed by the West Coast Hotel Company.

OPINION BY MR. CHIEF JUSTICE HUGHES
(Vote: 5-4)

Question—Is the statute contrary to the due process clause of the Fourteenth Amendment?

Decision—No.

Reason—The principle controlling the decision—the Fourteenth Amendment—was not in doubt. Those attacking minimum wage regulation alleged that they were being deprived of freedom of contract. "What is this freedom? The Constitution does not speak of freedom of contract. It speaks of liberty and prohibits the deprivation of liberty without due process of law. In prohibiting that deprivation, the Constitution does not recognize an absolute, an uncontrollable liberty. Liberty in each of its phases has its history and connotation. But the liberty safeguarded is liberty in a social organization which requires the protection of law against the evils which menace the health, safety, morals and welfare of the people. Liberty under the Constitution is thus necessarily subject to the restraints of due process, and regulation which is reasonable in relation to its subject and is adopted in the interests of the community is due process."

The minimum wage requirement of the state of Washington did not seem to the Court to have gone beyond the boundary of its broad protective power. The wage was fixed after full consideration by representatives of employers, employees, and the public. No one was forced to pay anything, it simply forbade employment at rates fixed below the minimum requirement of health and right living. This the Court held was a valid exercise of state police power, and it was the conclusion of the Court that "the case of Adkins v. Children's Hospital should be, and it is overruled."

Corollary cases

Adkins v. Children's Hospital, 261 U. S. 525

Morehead v. New York ex rel. Tipaldo, 298 U. S. 587

Chicago, B. & Q. R.R. Co. v. McGuire, 219 U. S. 549

United States v. Darby, 312 U. S. 100

Atkin v. Kansas, 191 U. S. 207

Perkins v. Lukens Steel Co., 310 U. S. 113

Bunting v. State of Oregon, 243 U. S. 426

Muller v. Oregon, 208 U. S. 412

Lochner v. New York, 198 U. S. 45

RELIGIOUS LIBERTY AND EDUCATION

West Virginia State Board of Education v. Barnette, 319 U. S. 624; 63 S. Ct. 1178, 87 L. Ed. 1628 (1943)

Following the decision of the Supreme Court in Minersville School District v. Gobitis, 310 U. S. 586, the West Virginia legislature amended its statutes to require all schools to conduct courses in history, civics, and the Constitution. The Board of Education went further and required a salute and a pledge of allegiance to the flag. Failure to conform was insubordination, dealt with by expulsion. Readmission was denied by statute until compliance. Meanwhile the expelled child was unlawfully absent and the parents were subject to a fine. The appellees, who were Jehovah's Witnesses, sought to restrain the enforcement of this statute.

Opinion by Mr. Justice Jackson
(Vote: 6-3)

Question—Is the statute contrary to the First and Fourteenth Amendments?

Decision—Yes.

Reason—Denial of the freedoms guaranteed by the Constitution can only be due to present grave and immediate danger to interests that the state can lawfully protect. The limitations of the Constitution are applied with no fear that freedom to be intellectually and spiritually diverse or even contrary will disintegrate the social organization. Freedom of religion and expression cannot be hampered when the expressions and the religious practices dealt with are harmless to others and to the state, as is here the case. "If there is any fixed star in our constitutional constellation, it is that no official, high or petty, can prescribe what shall be orthodox in politics, nationalism, religion, or other matters of opinion or force citizens to confess by word or act their faith therein. If there are any circumstances which permit an exception, they do not now occur to us."

The Court felt that the action of the local authorities in compelling the flag salute and pledge transcended constitutional limitations on their power and invaded the sphere of intellect and spirit which it is the purpose of the First Amendment to our Constitution to reserve from all official control.

Therefore, the Court overruled the Minersville School District v. Gobitis decision and affirmed the order restraining the West Virginia regulations.

Corollary cases

Stromberg v. California, 283 U. S. 359

Minersville School District v. Gobitis, 310 U. S. 586

Meyer v. Nebraska, 262 U. S. 390

Cochran v. Louisiana State Board of Education, 281 U. S. 370

Everson v. Board of Education of Ewing Township, 330 U. S. 1

McCollum v. Board of Education, 333 U. S. 203

Zorach v. Clauson, 343 U. S. 307

Doremus v. Board of Education, 342 U. S. 429

FEDERAL CONTROL OF AGRICULTURE

Wickard v. Filburn, 317 U. S. 111; 63 S. Ct. 82; 87 L. Ed. 122 (1942)

The appellee for many years owned and operated a small farm in Montgomery County, Ohio, maintaining a herd of dairy cattle, selling milk, raising poultry, and selling poultry and eggs. He was accustomed to raise a small acreage of winter wheat, of which a portion was sold, part fed to poultry and livestock, part used for making flour for home consumption, and the rest kept for seeding the following year.

In 1940, according to the Agricultural Adjustment Act, he was given a wheat acreage of 11.1 acres and a normal yield of 20.1 bushels of wheat an acre. He sowed, however, 23 acres, and harvested from his excess acreage 239 bushels, which was subject to a penalty of 49 cents a bushel, or $117.11 in all. Filburn claimed that the excess wheat was not produced for the purpose of marketing but for his own consumption on his farm. He refused to pay the penalty, or to store the excess according to regulations.

OPINION BY MR. JUSTICE JACKSON

(No evidence from the report that the decision was not unanimous.)

Question—Does Congress possess the power under the commerce clause of the Constitution to regulate the production and consumption of wheat destined for personal use on the farm when the effect upon interstate commerce is at most indirect?

Decision—Yes.

Reason—Marketing, according to the Act, included, in addition to the conventional meaning, whatever might be consumed on the premises. Questions of federal power cannot be side-stepped by calling such activities indirect.

Whether the appellant's activity was local, or whether it was regarded as commerce or not, if it exerted a substantial economic effect on interstate commerce, such activity could be regulated by Congress. The consumption of homegrown wheat is the most variable factor in the disappearance of the wheat crop. Even though the appellant's contribution to the demand for wheat may have been trivial, it did not remove him from the field of federal regulation. His contribution, together with others in similar circumstances, had a substantial influence on price and market conditions. Therefore, home-grown wheat competes with wheat in commerce. The stimulation of commerce is a regulatory function clearly within the power of Congress.

Corollary cases

Mulford v. Smith, 307 U. S. 38

United States v. Butler, 297 U. S. 1

United States v. Darby, 312 U. S. 100

Gibbons v. Ogden, 9 Wheaton 1

United States v. E. C. Knight Co., 156 U. S. 1

Swift and Co. v. United States, 196 U. S. 375

Shreveport Rate Cases, 234 U. S. 342

N.L.R.B. v. Fainblatt, 306 U. S. 601

FULL FAITH AND CREDIT IN DIVORCE CASES

Williams et al. v. North Carolina, 325 U. S. 226; 65 S. Ct. 1092; 89 L. Ed. 1577 (1945)

The petitioners were accused of bigamous cohabitation and sentenced to prison. Williams married in 1916 Carrie Wyke and lived with her until 1940. Lillie Hendrix had married Thomas Hendrix in 1920 and lived with him until 1940. In 1940 Williams and Lillie Hendrix, petitioners, went to Las Vegas, Nevada, and established six-weeks residence there. They were awarded divorces on October 4, 1940, and married each other on that same day. Mrs. Williams (Carrie Wyke) remained in North Carolina and was notified by delivery to her by the sheriff of a copy of the complaint. Thomas Hendrix also remained in North Carolina and was notified by the mailing to him of a copy of a summons published in a Las Vegas newspaper. Petitioners appealed their arrest on grounds that the Nevada divorce was legal and binding in North Carolina through the full faith and credit clause. This the court did not pass upon in Williams v. North Carolina, 317 U. S. 287 (1942), since North Carolina had not questioned the domicile in Nevada. In this second case, the state of North Carolina did question Nevada's finding of domicile.

OPINION BY MR. JUSTICE FRANKFURTER
(Vote: 6-3)

Question—May full faith and credit be legally denied the Nevada decree by reason of the petitioners failing, in the opinion of North Carolina, to acquire domicile in Nevada.

Decision—Yes.

Reason—The avowed intention of petitioners in going to Nevada was to gain a divorce through the laxity of that state's laws. The opinion of North Carolina, in conformity with its laws, was that legal domicile was never acquired in Nevada and this was a valid conclusion. No one state by reason of its laxity in divorce laws can be allowed to exercise undue control over the established divorce requirements of other states. Therefore, North Carolina may refuse to recognize the Nevada decree on grounds of the nonacquisition of domicile on the part of the petitioners without violation of the full faith and credit clause. The issue of domicile was not contested in Nevada in any adversary proceeding.

Corollary cases

Andrews v. Andrews, 188 U. S. 14
Thompson v. Whitman, 18 Wallace 457
Haddock v. Haddock, 201 U. S. 562
Davis v. Davis, 305 U. S. 32

Popovici v. Agler, 280 U. S. 379
Bell v. Bell, 181 U. S. 175
Sherrer v. Sherrer, 334 U. S. 343
Estin v. Estin, 334 U. S. 541
May v. Anderson, 345 U. S. 528

DUE PROCESS AND CRIMINAL PROSECUTION

Wolf v. Colorado, 338 U. S. 25; 69 S. Ct. 1359; 93 L. Ed. 1782 (1949)

Julius A. Wolf was convicted in the courts of Colorado of conspiracy to commit abortions. Evidence was secured by a deputy sheriff going to a physician's office and, without a warrant, taking the office day book. From this appointment book were obtained the names of patients. These were subsequently questioned. On the basis of this, charges were brought by means of an information, and this evidence was also used at the trial.

OPINION BY MR. JUSTICE FRANKFURTER
(Vote: 6-3)

Question — Does a conviction by a state court for a state offense deny due process of law solely because evidence admitted at the trial was obtained under circumstances which would have rendered it inadmissible in a federal court?

Decision — No.

Reason — Due process of law is not confined to formal, fixed, narrow requirements. The security of one's privacy against arbitrary intrusion by the police is basic to a free society. It is therefore implicit in "the concept of ordered liberty" and as such enforceable against the states through the Due Process Clause. But the ways of enforcing such a basic right raise questions of a different order. Most of the English-speaking world does not regard as vital to such protection the exclusion of evidence thus obtained. There are other means to protect the right of privacy, such as the internal discipline of the police, an alert public opinion, and private action. Thus, in a prosecution in a state court for a state crime the Fourteenth Amendment does not forbid the admission of evidence obtained by an unreasonable search and seizure.

Corollary cases

Weeks v. United States, 232 U. S. 383

Benanti v. United States, 355 U. S. 96

Elkins v. United States, 364 U. S. 206

Mapp v. Ohio, 367 U. S. 643

Stefanelli v. Minard, 342 U. S. 117

Rea v. United States, 350 U. S. 214

Adamson v. California, 332 U. S. 46

PROCEDURAL DUE PROCESS

Wong Wing et al. v. United States, 163 U. S. 228; 16 S. Ct. 977; 41 L. Ed. 140 (1896)

On July 15, 1892, Wong Wing and three others were arrested on the charge of being Chinese persons unlawfully within the United States, and not entitled to remain within the United States. The Commissioner of the Circuit Court for the Eastern District of Michigan found that they were unlawfully within the United States, and sentenced them to be imprisoned at hard labor for a period of 60 days, and that at the expiration of that time, they were to be removed from the United States to China.

Opinion by Mr. Justice Shiras
(Vote: 8-0)

Question—Can Congress add to the exclusion and expulsion punishment of Chinese persons by imprisonment at hard labor to be inflicted by any justice, judge, or commissioner of the United States, without a trial by jury?

Decision—No.

Reason—The Court was of the opinion that detention or temporary confinement as a means to enforce the provisions for the exclusion or expulsion of aliens would be valid. Detention is a usual feature of arrest, even when an innocent person is wrongfully accused, but that is not imprisonment in a legal sense.

It would also be within the power of Congress to declare the act of an alien remaining unlawfully within the United States to be an offense punishable by fine or imprisonment, if it were established by a judicial trial. However, Congress may not subject aliens to infamous punishment at hard labor, or confiscate their property without a judicial trial to establish the guilt of the accused. Otherwise, there is lack of due process.

Corollary cases

Fong Yue Ting v. United States, 149 U. S. 698

United States v. Ju Toy, 198 U. S. 253

Quon Quon Poy v. Johnson, 273 U. S. 352

Nu Fung Ho v. White, 259 U. S. 276

Lawton v. Steele, 152 U. S. 133

Hepner v. United States, 213 U. S. 103

Ocean Steam Navigation Co. v. Stranahan, 214 U. S. 320

United States v. Regan, 232 U. S. 37

Trop v. Dulles, 356 U. S. 86

Tot v. United States, 319 U. S. 463

THE DURATION OF WAR LEGISLATION

Woods v. Cloyd W. Miller Co., 333 U. S. 138; 68 S. Ct. 421; 92 L. Ed. 596 (1948)

The District Court for the Northern District of Ohio declared unconstitutional Title II of the Housing and Rent Act of 1947, which continued in force rent control provisions of previous legislation. The Act became effective on July 1, 1947, and the following day the appellee demanded of its tenants 40 per cent and 60 per cent increases for rental accommodations in the Cleveland Defense-Rental Area. This was an admitted violation of the Act. The District Court declared the Act an unconstitutional violation of congressional war power.

OPINION BY MR. JUSTICE DOUGLAS

(No evidence from the report that the decision was not unanimous.)

Question—Does the right of Congress to establish rent controls by virtue of its war powers carry beyond the cessation of hostilities?

Decision—Yes.

Reason—The war power of Congress includes the power "to remedy the evils which have arisen from its rise and progress." This power continues for the duration of the emergency, and does not necessarily end with the cessation of hostilities. The deficit in housing caused by the heavy demobilization of veterans and the reduction in residential construction due to lack of materials during the period of hostilities still continued. Since the war effort contributed heavily to that deficit, Congress might retain controls, even after the cessation of hostilities.

War powers, used indiscriminately, may swallow up all the powers of Congress, as well as the Ninth and Tenth Amendments. Any power can be abused. However, such was not the case in this situation. Also, questions as to whether or not Congress has overstepped its war powers are open to judicial inquiry.

Corollary cases

Hamilton v. Kentucky Distilleries Co., 251 U. S. 146

Block v. Hirsh, 256 U. S. 135

Fleming v. Mohawk Wrecking and Lumber Co., 331 U. S. 111

Ruppert v. Caffey, 251 U. S. 264

Yakus v. United States, 321 U. S.   Arver v. United States, 245 U. S.
   414   366

Bowles v. Willingham, 321 U. S.
   503

DELEGATION OF POWER AND PRICE CONTROL

Yakus v. United States, 321 U. S. 414; 64 S. Ct. 660; 88 L. Ed. 834 (1944)

The petitioner was tried and convicted for the willful sale of wholesale cuts of beef prices above the maximum prices prescribed by the price regulations set down by the federal Price Administrator under the authority of the Emergency Price Control Act of January 30, 1942, and as amended by the Inflation Control Act of October 2, 1942.

OPINION BY MR. CHIEF JUSTICE STONE
(Vote: 6-3)

Question—Do the acts in question involve an unconstitutional delegation to the Price Administrator of the legislative power of Congress to control prices?

Decision—No.

Reason—"The essentials of the legislative function are the determination of the legislative policy and its formulation and promulgation as a defined and binding rule of conduct—here the rule, with penal sanctions, that prices shall not be greater than those fixed by maximum price regulations which conform to standards and will tend to further the policy which Congress has established. These essentials are preserved when Congress has specified the basic conditions of fact upon whose existence or occurrence, ascertained from relevant data by a designated administrative agency, it directs that its statutory command shall be effective. It is no objection that the determination of facts and the inferences to be drawn from them in the light of the statutory standards and declaration of policy call for the exercise of judgment, and for the formulation of subsidiary administrative policy within the prescribed statutory framework. . . . The standards prescribed by the present Act, with the aid of the 'statement of the considerations' required to be made by the administrator, are sufficiently definite and precise to enable Congress, the courts, and the public to ascertain whether the administrator, in fixing the designated prices, has conformed to those standards. Hence we are unable to find in them an unauthorized delegation of legislative power."

Corollary cases

Field v. Clark, 143 U. S. 649

Hampton, Jr. & Co. v. United States, 276 U. S. 394

Mulford v. Smith, 307 U. S. 38

United States v. Rock Royal Co-op., 307 U. S. 533

Sunshine Anthracite Coal Co. v. Adkins, 310 U. S. 381

Opp Cotton Mills v. Administrator, 312 U. S. 381

National Broadcasting Co. v. United States, 319 U. S. 190

Kiyoshi Hirabayashi v. United States, 320 U. S. 81

Union Bridge Co. v. United States, 204 U. S. 364

Bowles v. Willingham, 321 U. S. 503

Currin v. Wallace, 306 U. S. 15

Panama Refining Co. v. Ryan, 293 U. S. 388

Schechter Poultry Corp. v. United States, 295 U. S. 495

Woods v. Miller, 333 U. S. 138

MILITARY TRIBUNALS

In re Yamashita, 327 U. S. 1; 66 S. Ct. 340; 90 L. Ed. 499 (1946)

Yamashita, Commanding General of the Fourteenth Army Group of the Imperial Japanese Army in the Philippine Islands, was charged with violating the laws of war, in permitting members of his command to commit brutal atrocities and other high crimes against the people of the United States and its allies, particularly the Philippines.

OPINION BY MR. CHIEF JUSTICE STONE
(Vote: 6-2)

Question—Does the military commission have jurisdiction to try the prisoner? Is his detention lawful?

Decision—Yes.

Reason—In Ex parte Quirin the Court pointed out that Congress, in the exercise of the constitutional power to define and punish offenses against the law of nations recognized the "military tribunal" for the trial and punishment of offenses against the laws of war. Congress has conferred no power of judicial review over such tribunals except the power to grant a writ of habeas corpus for the purpose of an inquiry as to jurisdiction. Moreover, such commissions are not bound to observe due process.

An important consequence of the conduct of war is the seizure and subjection to disciplinary measures of those enemies who have violated the laws of war. Likewise such procedure may continue, even after hostilities have ceased, or at least until peace has been officially recognized by treaty or by proclamation. In fact, the practical administration of military justice would fail if such authority ended with the cessation of hostilities.

It cannot be denied that the acts in question directed against the civilian population of an occupied country and prisoners of war are recognized in international law as violations of the laws of war. It in no way lessened the guilt of the petitioner that he had not committed nor directed the commission of the acts. The laws of war presuppose that their violation is to be avoided through the control of commanders who are responsible for their subordinates.

Corollary cases

Ex parte Quirin, 317 U. S. 1

Ex parte Milligan, 4 Wallace 2

Madsen v. Kinsella, 343 U. S. 341

Eisentrager v. Johnson, 339 U. S. 763

United States ex rel. Toth v. Quarles, 350 U. S. 11

CONGRESS AND SUFFRAGE

Ex parte Yarbrough, 110 U. S. 651; 4 S. Ct. 152; 28 L. Ed. 274 (1884)

Yarbrough and others were convicted in a federal court for having conspired to intimidate a colored person from voting for a member of Congress, in violation of the federal statutes. Since, under the law in question in this case, Congress was aiming at activities of the Ku Klux Klan and similar organizations specializing in intimidation, this is sometimes called the "Ku Klux case."

OPINION BY MR. JUSTICE MILLER

(No evidence from the report that the decision was not unanimous.)

Question—Does Congress have the power to punish violations of election laws under the Constitution?

Decision—Yes.

Reason—The idea that Congress has no power to secure elections from violence, corruption, or fraud by making appropriate laws is startling. The proposition that every power of Congress must be expressly granted in the Constitution has never been adhered to by this Court. The Constitution itself recognizes this inherent inability to put into words all derived powers when it gives Congress the authority to pass all laws necessary and proper to carry out its functions.

Another objection was advanced, that the right to vote for a member of Congress is not dependent upon the Constitution, but upon the law of each state, respectively. Even if that were true, the election would still have to be free from bribery and corruption. However, the right to vote for a member of Congress does flow from the Constitution, for the Constitution adopts the qualifications of the state for electing the members of the "most numerous" branch of the state legislature. Therefore, the right does not depend exclusively on the law of the state.

It is essential that a government such as ours have within its constitutional framework the authority to provide against these evils, or it will soon be at the mercy of combinations of brute force.

Corollary cases

Minor v. Happersett, 21 Wallace 162

United States v. Reese, 92 U. S. 214

Ex parte Siebold, 100 U. S. 371

Guinn v. United States, 238 U. S. 347

Burroughs v. United States, 290 U. S. 534

Barry v. United States ex rel. Cunningham, 279 U. S. 597

United States v. Classic, 313 U. S. 299

Smith v. Allwright, 321 U. S. 649

EQUAL PROTECTION IN ADMINISTRATION OF LAWS

Yick Wo v. Hopkins, 118 U. S. 356; 6 S. Ct. 1064; 30 L. Ed. 220 (1886)

An ordinance of the City and County of San Francisco made it unlawful to operate a laundry without the consent of the board of supervisors unless it was located in a building constructed of brick or stone. Yick Wo and his associates were convicted of violating this ordinance.

OPINION BY MR. JUSTICE MATTHEWS
(No evidence from the report that the decision was not unanimous.)

Question—Is the enforcement of the ordinance in question a denial of equal protection of the laws?

Decision—Yes.

Reason—This ordinance of San Francisco permitted the supervisors, at their will and discretion, to reject or allow persons to follow this line of work. The idea that any man's livelihood depends on the mere will of another is the essence of slavery. Any ordinance, however fair and impartial it may appear on the surface, if it be administered "with an evil eye and an unequal hand," is a denial of equal justice. In the present case, the consent of the supervisors was withheld from some two hundred Chinese, while eighty others, not Chinese, were permitted to carry on the business under the same conditions. No reason was shown, except hostility to the race and nationality of the petitioners. This was illegal discrimination, and the public administration which enforced it was guilty of a denial of equal protection of the laws, and a violation of the Fourteenth Amendment. The provisions of the Fourteenth Amendment are not confined to the protection of citizens.

Corollary cases

Henderson v. Mayor of New York, 92 U. S. 259

Chy Lung v. Freeman, 92 U. S. 275

Ex parte Virginia, 100 U. S. 339

Neal v. Delaware, 103 U. S. 370

Soon Hing v. Crowley, 113 U. S. 703

Truax v. Raich, 239 U. S. 33

Murphy v. California, 225 U. S. 623

Takahashi v. Fish and Game Commission, 334 U. S. 410

Oyama v. California, 332 U. S. 633

Terrace v. Thompson, 263 U. S. 197

EXECUTIVE POWER AND PROPERTY RIGHTS

Youngstown Sheet & Tube Co. v. Sawyer, 343 U. S. 579; 72 S. Ct. 863; 96 L. Ed. 817 (1952)

In the latter part of 1951 a dispute arose between the steel companies and their employees over terms and conditions that should be included in new collective bargaining agreements. Long-continued conferences failed to settle the dispute. On Dec. 18, 1951, the employees' representative, United Steel Workers of America, C.I.O., gave notice of an intention to strike when the agreements expired on Dec. 31. The Federal Mediation and Conciliation Service intervened, but unsuccessfully, and the President then referred the dispute to the Federal Wage Stabilization Board to investigate and make recommendations for fair and equitable terms of settlement. This failing, the Union gave notice of a nationwide strike called to begin at 12.01 A.M., April 9. The indispensability of steel led President Truman to believe that the proposed strike would immediately jeopardize our national defense, and he issued an Executive Order directing Secretary of Commerce Sawyer to take possession of the steel mills and keep them running.

OPINION BY MR. JUSTICE BLACK
(Vote: 6-3)

Question—Is the seizure order within the constitutional power of the President?

Decision—No.

Reason—The power of the President to issue such an order must stem from an Act of Congress or from the Constitution itself. Only two statutes authorize seizure under certain conditions, but the government admitted these conditions were not met, since the procedure involved was too cumbersome and time-consuming. Moreover, in the consideration of the Taft-Hartley Act, the Congress rejected an amendment authorizing governmental seizures in an emergency.

Nor is there any provision in the Constitution that would warrant this seizure. As Commander in Chief of the Armed Forces the President still has no right to seize private property to keep labor disputes from stopping production. This was a matter for Congress only, not for military authorities. Neither does the Constitution permit the President to legislate—a function which belongs only to Congress, in good times or in bad times. "This seizure order cannot stand."

Corollary cases

Hooe v. United States, 218 U. S. 322

United States v. North American Co., 253 U. S. 330

Larson v. Domestic & Foreign Corp., 337 U. S. 682

United States v. Curtiss-Wright Corp., 299 U. S. 304

United States v. Russell, 13 Wallace 623

United States v. Causby, 328 U. S. 256

United States v. Caltex, 344 U. S. 149

LIQUOR AND THE STATES

Ziffrin v. Reeves, 308 U. S. 132; 60 S. Ct. 103; 84 L. Ed. 128 (1939)

Appellant, an Indiana corporation, had, since 1933, been receiving whisky from distillers in Kentucky for direct carriage to consignees in Chicago. It had permission under the Federal Motor Carriers Act of 1935 to operate as a contract carrier, and claimed the right to transport whisky in spite of the prohibitions of the Kentucky Alcoholic Beverages Control Law of 1938. It now sought to restrain the state from enforcing the contraband and penal provisions of the law. The Kentucky law forbade the carriage of intoxicating liquors by carriers other than licensed common carriers, and forbade distillers to deliver to an unauthorized carrier. Constant state control was exercised over the manufacture, sale, transportation, and possession of whisky. The Corporation was denied a common carrier's certificate and transportation license by Kentucky. The Corporation claimed that the law was unconstitutional because it was repugnant to the commerce, due process, and equal protection clauses.

Opinion by Mr. Justice McReynolds
(Vote: 8-0)

Question—Is the Kentucky law unconstitutional?

Decision—No.

Reason—The Twenty-First Amendment sanctions the right of the state to legislate concerning intoxicating liquor brought from without, unfettered by the commerce clause. Without doubt a state may absolutely prohibit the manufacture of intoxicants, their transportation, sale, or possession, irrespective of when or where produced or obtained or the use to which they are put. Further, she may adopt measures reasonably appropriate to effectuate these inhibitions and exercise full police authority in respect of them. Under its police power, the State of Kentucky can permit the manufacture and sale of liquors only under certain conditions and regulate the way in which they are sold. In this way they cannot properly be regarded as an article of commerce.

The record shows no violation of the equal protection clause. A licensed common carrier is under stricter control than an ordinary contract carrier and may be entrusted with privileges forbidden to the latter.

The Motor Carrier Act of 1935 is said to secure the appellant the right claimed, but the Court could find nothing there that undertakes to destroy state power to protect her people against the evils of intoxicants or to sanction the receipt of articles declared contraband. The Act has no such purpose or effect.

Corollary cases

South Carolina Highway Dept. v. Barnwell Bros., 303 U. S. 177

Kidd v. Pearson, 128 U. S. 1

Seaboard Air Line v. North Carolina, 245 U. S. 304

Finch Co., v. McKittrick, 305 U. S. 395

Duckworth v. Arkansas, 314 U. S. 390

Carter v. Virginia, 321 U. S. 131

United States v. Frankfort Distilleries, 324 U. S. 293

THE FOURTEENTH AMENDMENT AND EDUCATION

Zorach v. Clauson, 343 U. S. 306; 72 S. Ct. 679; 96 L. Ed. 954 (1952)

New York City arranged a program permitting its public schools to release students during the school day so that they might go to religious centers for religious instruction or devotional exercises. A student was released on the written request of his parents. The churches made a weekly list of the children released from the public school, but who had not reported for religious instruction. This "released time" program involved neither the use of the public school classrooms nor the expenditure of any public funds. All costs were paid by the religious organizations.

OPINION BY MR. JUSTICE DOUGLAS
(Vote: 6-3)

Question—Does the New York City statute violate the First Amendment, which, by reason of the Fourteenth Amendment, prohibits the states from establishing religion or prohibiting its free exercise?

Decision—No.

Reason—There was no issue concerned here with the prohibition of the "free exercise" of religion. No one was forced to attend the religious·instruction, nor was the religious training brought into the classrooms of the public schools.

The First Amendment does reflect the philosophy of "separation of Church and State," but does not say that in every and all respects there must be separation. It rather defines ways in which there shall be no dependency, one on the other. This is only common sense.

The concept of separation of church and state would have to be pressed to extreme views to condemn the present law on a constitutional basis. We are a religious people with a belief in a Supreme Being. Our government shows no partiality to any one group, but lets each flourish. The state follows the best of our traditions when it schedules its events so as to encourage religious instruction. The government may not finance religious groups, undertake religious instruction, blend secular and sectarian education, nor use secular institutions to force some religion on any person. However, there is no constitutional requirement for government to be hostile to religion. The McCollum case cannot be expanded to cover this case, unless separation of church and state means that public institutions cannot accommodate the religious needs of the people. "We cannot read into the Bill of Rights such a philosophy of hostility to religion."

Corollary cases

McCollum v. Board of Education, 333 U. S. 203

Everson v. Board of Education, 330 U. S. 1

Cochran v. Louisiana State Board of Education, 281 U. S. 370

Doremus v. Board of Education, 342 U. S. 429

SEARCH AND SEIZURE

**Katz v. United States, 389 U. S. 347; 88 S. Ct. 507; 19 L. Ed.
2d. 576 (1967)**

Charles Katz was convicted in federal District Court
in California of violation of federal communication statutes
by transmitting wagering information by telephone from
Los Angeles to Miami and Boston. At the trial evidence
was introduced of Katz's telephone conversations at his
end overheard by FBI agents who had attached an elec-
tronic listening and recording device to the outside of the
public telephone booth from which Katz had placed his
calls. The Court of Appeals had rejected the contention
that the recordings had been obtained in violation of the
Fourth Amendment because there was "no physical entrance into the area occupied" by the accused.

OPINION BY MR. JUSTICE STEWART
(Vote: 7-1)

Question—Was the search and seizure conducted in this case
in compliance with constitutional standards?

Decision—No.

Reason—The Fourth Amendment protects people and not
simply "areas" against unreasonable searches and seizures. The
reach of that amendment cannot turn upon the presence or
absence of a physical intrusion into any given enclosure. The
protection does not extend only to tangible property and to
incidents where there has been trespass. What a person seeks
to preserve as private, even in an area accessible to the public,
may be constitutionally protected.

In this case the surveillance was so narrowly circumscribed
that a judge could have authorized the search and seizure.
Omission of this authorization bypassed the safeguards provided by an objective predetermination of probable cause and
substituted instead the far less reliable procedure of an after-
the-event justification. This sort of bypassing leaves individuals
secure from Fourth Amendment violations only in the discretion of the police.

(The Court overruled Olmstead v. United States, 277 U. S.
438, 1928, and Goldman v. United States, 316 U. S. 129, 1942.)

Corollary cases

Berger v. New York, 388 U. S. 41 (1967)

Silverman v. United States, 365 U. S. 505 (1961)

Osborn v. United States, 385 U. S. 323 (1966)

Warden v. Hayden, 387 U. S. 294 (1967)

Rios v. United States, 364 U. S. 253 (1960)

On Lee v. United States, 343 U. S. 747 (1952)

Nardone v. United States, 302 U. S. 379 (1937); 308 U. S. 338 (1939)

Rathbun v. United States, 355 U. S. 107 (1957)

Benanti v. United States, 355 U. S. 96 (1957)

REGULATORY TAXES AND SELF-INCRIMINATION

Marchetti v. United States, 390 U. S. 39; 88 S. Ct. 697; 19 L. Ed. 2d 889 (1968)

James Marchetti was convicted in federal District Court in Connecticut (where there are numerous criminal penalties for gambling) for violation of federal statutes requiring the payment of an annual gambling occupational stamp tax and for failing to register before accepting wagers. These requirements were part of an intricate system of federal taxation applying to wagering, and the registration requirement was designed to aid the collection of the taxes. The arrangement was challenged as being unconstitutional.

OPINION BY MR. JUSTICE HARLAN
(Vote: 7-1)

Question—Are the methods employed by Congress in the federal wagering tax statutes consistent with the guarantee against self-incrimination contained in the Fifth Amendment?

Decision—The privilege against self-incrimination was properly asserted.

Reason—The federal Internal Revenue Service makes available to state law enforcement agencies the names and addresses of those who have paid the wagering tax. This creates a real and appreciable hazard of self-incrimination. The likelihood that any past or present gambling offenses will be discovered is increased. The tax provision obliges even a prospective gambler to accuse himself of conspiracy to violate laws. Further, the premise that the self-incrimination guarantee is entirely inapplicable to prospective acts is too narrow an application of the privilege. Not merely time or a chronological formula must be considered but also the substantiality of the risks of incrimination. Those persons who properly assert the constitutional privilege as to these wagering tax provisions may not be criminally punished for failure to comply with their requirements.

(The Court overruled United States v. Kahriger, 345 U. S. 22, 1953, and Lewis v. United States, 348 U. S. 419, 1955.)

Corollary cases

License Tax Cases, 5 Wallace 462 (1867)

United States v. Doremus, 249 U. S. 86 (1919)

United States v. Sullivan, 274 U. S. 259 (1927)

Shapiro v. United States, 335 U. S. 1 (1948)

Murphy v. Waterfront Commission, 378 U. S. 52 (1964)

Albertson v. Subversive Activities Control Board, 382 U. S. 70 (1965)

Sonzinsky v. United States, 300 U. S. 506 (1937)

Bailey v. Drexel Furniture Co., 259 U. S. 20 (1922)

Ullmann v. United States, 350 U. S. 422 (1956)

Grosso v. United States, 390 U.S. 62 (1968)

THE CONSTITUTION
OF THE UNITED STATES

> *We the people of the United States, in order to form a more perfect union, establish justice, insure domestic tranquillity, provide for the common defense, promote the general welfare, and secure the blessings of liberty to ourselves and our posterity, do ordain and establish this Constitution for the United States of America.*

ARTICLE I

Section 1. All legislative powers herein granted shall be vested in a Congress of the United States, which shall consist of a Senate and House of Representatives.

Section 2. 1. The House of Representatives shall be composed of members chosen every second year by the people of the several States, and the electors in each State shall have the qualifications requisite for electors of the most numerous branch of the State legislature.

2. No person shall be a representative who shall not have attained to the age of twenty-five years, and been seven years a citizen of the United States, and who shall not, when elected, be an inhabitant of that State in which he shall be chosen.

3. Representatives and direct taxes[1] shall be apportioned among the several States which may be included within this Union, according to their respective numbers, which shall be determined by adding to the whole number of free persons, including those bound to service for a term of years, and excluding Indians not taxed, *three-fifths of all other persons.*[2] The actual enumeration shall be made within three years after the first meeting of the Congress of the United States, and within every subsequent term of ten years, in such manner as they shall by law direct. The number of representatives shall not exceed one for every thirty thousand, but each State shall have at least one representative; and until such enumeration shall be made,

1 See the 16th Amendment.
2 See the 14th Amendment.

351

the State of New Hampshire shall be entitled to choose three, Massachusetts eight, Rhode Island and Providence Plantations one, Connecticut five, New York six, New Jersey four, Pennsylvania eight, Delaware one, Maryland six, Virginia ten, North Carolina five, South Carolina five, and Georgia three.

4. When vacancies happen in the representation from any State, the executive authority thereof shall issue writs of election to fill such vacancies.

5. The House of Representatives shall choose their speaker and other officers; and shall have the sole power of impeachment.

Section 3. 1. The Senate of the United States shall be composed of two senators from each State, *chosen by the legislature thereof*,[1] for six years; and each senator shall have one vote.

2. Immediately after they shall be assembled in consequence of the first election, they shall be divided as equally as may be into three classes. The seats of the senators of the first class shall be vacated at the expiration of the second year, of the second class at the expiration of the fourth year, and of the third class at the expiration of the sixth year, so that one third may be chosen every second year; and if vacancies happen by resignation, or otherwise, during the recess of the legislature of any State, the executive thereof may make temporary appointments until the next meeting of the legislature, which shall then fill such vacancies.[1]

3. No person shall be a senator who shall not have attained to the age of thirty years, and been nine years a citizen of the United States, and who shall not, when elected, be an inhabitant of that State for which he shall be chosen.

4. The Vice President of the United States shall be President of the Senate, but shall have no vote, unless they be equally divided.

5. The Senate shall choose their other officers, and also a president *pro tempore,* in the absence of the Vice President, or when he shall exercise the office of the President of the United States.

6. The Senate shall have the sole power to try all impeachments. When sitting for that purpose, they shall be on oath or affirmation. When the President of the United States is tried, the chief justice shall preside: and no person shall be convicted without the concurrence of two thirds of the members present.

7. Judgment in cases of impeachment shall not extend further than to removal from office, and disqualifications to hold and enjoy any office of honor, trust or profit under the United States: but the party convicted shall nevertheless be liable and subject to indictment, trial, judgment and punishment, according to law.

---

1 See the 17th Amendment.

Section 4. 1. The times, places, and manner of holding elections for senators and representatives, shall be prescribed in each State by the legislature thereof; but the Congress may at any time by law make or alter such regulations, except as to the places of choosing senators.

2. The Congress shall assemble at least once in every year, and such meeting shall be on the first Monday in December, unless they shall by law appoint a different day.

Section 5. 1. Each House shall be the judge of the elections, returns and qualifications of its own members, and a major ity of each shall constitute a quorum to do business; but a smaller number may adjourn from day to day, and may ·be authorized to compel the attendance of absent members, in such manner, and under such penalties as each House may provide.

2. Each House may determine the rules of its proceedings, punish its members for disorderly behavior, and, with the concurrence of two thirds, expel a member.

3. Each House shall keep a journal of its proceedings, and from time to time publish the same, excepting such parts as may in their judgment require secrecy; and the yeas and nays of the members of either House on any question shall, at the desire of one fifth of those present, be entered on the journal.

4. Neither House, during the session of Congress, shall, without the consent of the other, adjourn for more than three days, nor to any other place than that in which the two Houses shall be sitting.

Section 6. 1. The senators and representatives shall receive a compensation for their services, to be ascertained by law, and paid out of the Treasury of the United States. They shall in all cases, except treason, felony, and breach of the peace, be privileged from arrest during their attendance at the session of their respective Houses, and in going to and returning from the same; and for any speech or debate in either House, they shall not be questioned in any other place.

2. No senator or representative shall, during the time for which he was elected, be appointed to any civil office under the authority of the United States, which shall have been created, or the emoluments whereof shall have been increased during such time; and no person holding any office under the United States shall be a member of either House during his continuance in office.

Section 7. 1. All bills for raising revenue shall originate in the House of Representatives; but the Senate may propose or concur with amendments as on other bills.

2. Every bill which shall have passed the House of Representatives and the Senate, shall, before it becomes a law, be presented to the President of the United States; if he approves

he shall sign it, but if not he shall return it, with his objections to that House in which it shall have originated, who shall enter the objections at large on their journal, and proceed to reconsider it. If after such reconsideration two thirds of that House shall agree to pass the bill, it shall be sent, together with the objections, to the other House, by which it shall likewise be reconsidered, and if approved by two thirds of that House, it shall become a law. But in all such cases the votes of both Houses shall be determined by yeas and nays, and the names of the persons voting for and against the bill shall be entered on the journal of each House respectively. If any bill shall not be returned by the President within ten days (Sundays excepted) after it shall have been presented to him, the same shall be a law, in like manner as if he had signed it, unless the Congress by their adjournment prevent its return, in which case it shall not be a law.

3. Every order, resolution, or vote to which the concurrence of the Senate and the House of Representatives may be necessary (except on a question of adjournment) shall be presented to the President of the United States; and before the same shall take effect, shall be approved by him, or being disapproved by him, shall be repassed by two thirds of the Senate and House of Representatives, according to the rules and limitations prescribed in the case of a bill.

Section 8. The Congress shall have the power

1. To lay and collect taxes, duties, imposts, and excises, to pay the debts and provide for the common defense and general welfare of the United States; but all duties, imposts, and excises shall be uniform throughout the United States;

2. To borrow money on the credit of the United States;

3. To regulate commerce with foreign nations, and among the several States, and with the Indian tribes;

4. To establish a uniform rule of naturalization, and uniform laws on the subject of bankruptcies throughout the United States;

5. To coin money, regulate the value thereof, and of foreign coin, and fix the standard of weights and measures;

6. To provide for the punishment of counterfeiting the securities and current coin of the United States;

7. To establish post offices and post roads;

8. To promote the progress of science and useful arts, by securing for limited times to authors and inventors the exclusive right to their respective writings and discoveries;

9. To constitute tribunals inferior to the Supreme Court;

10. To define and punish piracies and felonies committed on the high seas, and offenses against the law of nations;

11.   To declare war, grant letters of marque and reprisal, and make rules concerning captures on land and water;

12.   To raise and support armies, but no appropriation of money to that use shall be for a longer term than two years;

13.   To provide and maintain a navy;

14.   To make rules for the government and regulation of the land and naval forces;

15.   To provide for calling forth the militia to execute the laws of the Union, suppress insurrections and repel invasions;

16.   To provide for organizing, arming, and disciplining the militia, and for governing such part of them as may be employed in the service of the United States, reserving to the States respectively, the appointment of the officers, and the authority of training the militia according to the discipline prescribed by Congress.

17.   To exercise exclusive legislation in all cases whatsoever, over such district (not exceeding ten miles square) as may, by cession of particular States, and the acceptance of Congress, become the seat of the government of the United States, and to exercise like authority over all places purchased by the consent of the legislature of the State in which the same shall be, for the erection of forts, magazines, arsenals, dockyards, and other needful buildings; and

18.   To make all laws which shall be necessary and proper for carrying into execution the foregoing powers, and all other powers vested by this Constitution in the government of the United States, or in any department or officer thereof.

Section 9.   1. The migration or importation of such persons as any of the States now existing shall think proper to admit, shall not be prohibited by the Congress prior to the year one thousand eight hundred and eight, but a tax or duty may be imposed on such importation, not exceeding ten dollars for each person.

2.   The privilege of the writ of *habeas corpus* shall not be suspended, unless when in cases of rebellion or invasion the public safety may require it.

3.   No bill of attainder or *ex post facto* law shall be passed.

4.   No capitation, or other direct, tax shall be laid, unless in proportion to the census or enumeration hereinbefore directed to be taken.[1]

5.   No tax or duty shall be laid on articles exported from any State.

6.   No preference shall be given by any regulation of commerce or revenue to the ports of one State over those of another: nor shall vessels bound to, or from, one State be obliged to enter, clear, or pay duties in another.

---

1 See the 16th Amendment.

7.   No money shall be drawn from the treasury, but in consequence of appropriations made by law; and a regular statement and account of the receipts and expenditures of all public money shall be published from time to time.

8.   No title of nobility shall be granted by the United States: and no person holding any office of profit or trust under them, shall, without the consent of the Congress, accept of any present, emolument, office, or title, of any kind whatever, from any king, prince, or foreign State.

Section 10.   1. No State shall enter into any treaty, alliance, or confederation; grant letters of marque and reprisal; coin money; emit bills of credit; make anything but gold and silver coin a tender in payment of debts; pass any bill of attainder, *ex post facto* law, or law impairing the obligation of contracts, or grant any title of nobility.

2.   No State shall, without the consent of the Congress, lay any imposts or duties on imports or exports, except what may be absolutely necessary for executing its inspection laws: and the net produce of all duties and imposts laid by any State on imports or exports, shall be for the use of the treasury of the United States; and all such laws shall be subject to the revision and control of the Congress.

3.   No State shall, without the consent of the Congress, lay any duty of tonnage, keep troops, or ships of war in time of peace, enter into any agreement or compact with another State, or with a foreign power, or engage in war, unless actually invaded, or in such imminent danger as will not admit of delay.

ARTICLE II

Section 1.   1. The executive power shall be vested in a President of the United States of America. He shall hold his office during the term of four years, and, together with the Vice President, chosen for the same term, be elected as follows:

2.   Each State shall appoint, in such manner as the legislature thereof may direct, a number of electors, equal to the whole number of senators and representatives to which the State may be entitled in the Congress: but no senator or representative, or person holding an office of trust or profit under the United States, shall be appointed an elector.

The electors shall meet in their respective States, and vote by ballot for two persons, of whom one at least shall not be an inhabitant of the same State with themselves. And they shall make a list of all the persons voted for, and of the number of votes for each; which list they shall sign and certify, and transmit sealed to the seat of the government of the United States, directed to the president of the Senate. The president of the Senate shall, in the presence of the Senate and House of Representatives, open all the certificates, and the votes shall then be counted. The person having the greatest number of votes shall be the President, if such number be a majority of the whole number of electors appointed; and if there be more than one who have such majority, and have an equal number of votes, then the House of Representatives shall immediately choose by ballot one of them for President; and if no person have a majority, then from the five highest on the list the said House shall in like manner choose the President. But in choosing the President, the votes shall be taken by States, the representation from each State having one vote; a quorum for this purpose shall consist of a member or members from two thirds of the States, and a majority of all the States shall be necessary to a choice. In every case, after the choice of the President, the person having the greatest number of votes of the electors shall be the Vice President. But if there should remain two or more who have equal votes, the Senate shall choose from them by ballot the Vice President.[1]

3.   The Congress may determine the time of choosing the electors, and the day on which they shall give their votes; which day shall be the same throughout the United States.

4.   No person except a natural born citizen, or a citizen of the United States, at the time of the adoption of this Constitution, shall be eligible to the office of President; neither shall any person be eligible to that office who shall not have attained to the age of thirty-five years, and been fourteen years a resident within the United States.

5.   In case of the removal of the President from office, or of his death, resignation, or inability to discharge the powers and duties of the said office, the same shall devolve on the Vice President, and the Congress may by law provide for the case of removal, death, resignation, or inability, both of the President and Vice President, declaring what officer shall then act as President, and such officer shall act accordingly, until the disability be removed, or a President shall be elected.

6.   The President shall, at stated times, receive for his services a compensation, which shall neither be increased nor diminished during the period for which he shall have been elected, and he shall not receive within that period any other emolument from the United States, or any of them.

7.   Before he enter on the execution of his office, he shall take the following oath or affirmation:—"I do solemnly swear (or affirm) that I will faithfully execute the office of President of the United States, and will to the best of my ability, preserve, protect and defend the Constitution of the United States."

1 Superseded by the 12th Amendment.

Section 2. 1. The President shall be commander in chief of the army and navy of the United States, and of the militia of the several States, when called into the actual service of the United States; he may require the opinion, in writing, of the principal officer in each of the executive departments, upon any subject relating to the duties of their respective offices, and he shall have power to grant reprieves and pardons for offenses against the United States, except in cases of impeachment.

2. He shall have power, by and with the advice and consent of the Senate, to make treaties, provided two thirds of the senators present concur; and he shall nominate, and by and with the advice and consent of the Senate, shall appoint ambassadors, other public ministers and consuls, judges of the Supreme Court, and all other officers of the United States, whose appointments are not herein otherwise provided for, and which shall be established by law: but the Congress may by law vest the appointment of such inferior officers, as they think proper, in the President alone, in the courts of law, or in the heads of departments.

3. The President shall have power to fill up all vacancies that may happen during the recess of the Senate, by granting commissions which shall expire at the end of their next session.

Section 3. He shall from time to time give to the Congress information of the state of the Union, and recommend to their consideration such measures as he shall judge necessary and expedient; he may, on extraordinary occasions, convene both Houses, or either of them, and in case of disagreement between them with respect to the time of adjournment, he may adjourn them to such time as he shall think proper; he shall receive ambassadors and other public ministers; he shall take care that the laws be faithfully executed, and shall commission all the officers of the United States.

Section 4. The President, Vice President, and all civil officers of the United States, shall be removed from office on impeachment for, and conviction of, treason, bribery, or other high crimes and misdemeanors.

ARTICLE III

Section 1. The judicial power of the United States shall be vested in one Supreme Court, and in such inferior courts as the Congress may from time to time ordain and establish. The judges, both of the Supreme and inferior courts, shall hold their offices during good behavior, and shall, at stated times, receive for their services, a compensation, which. shall not be diminished during their continuance in office.

Section 2. 1. The judicial power shall extend to all cases, in law and equity, arising under this Constitution, the laws of the United States, and treaties made, or which shall be made, under their authority;—to all cases affecting ambassadors, other public ministers and consuls;—to all cases of admiralty and maritime jurisdiction;—to controversies to which the United States shall be a party;—to controversies between two or more States; between a State and citizens of another State;[1]—between citizens of different States;—between citizens of the same State claiming lands under grants of different States, and between a State, or the citizens thereof, and foreign States citizens or subjects.

2. In all cases affecting ambassadors, other public ministers and consuls, and those in which a State shall be party, the Supreme Court shall have original jurisdiction. In all the other cases before mentioned, the Supreme Court shall have appellate jurisdiction, both as to law and to fact, with such exceptions, and under such regulations as the Congress shall make.

3. The trial of all crimes, except in cases of impeachment, shall be by jury; and such trial shall be held in the State where the said crimes shall have been committed; but when not committed within any State, the trial shall be at such place or places as the Congress may by law have directed.

Section 3. 1. Treason against the United States shall consist only in levying war against them, or in adhering to their enemies, giving them aid and comfort. No person shall be convicted of treason unless on the testimony of two witnesses to the same overt act, or on confession in open court.

2. The Congress shall have power to declare the punishment of treason, but no attainder of treason shall work corruption of blood, or forfeiture except during the life of the person attained.

ARTICLE IV

Section 1. Full faith and credit shall be given in each State to the public acts, records, and judicial proceedings of every other State. And the Congress may by general laws prescribe the manner in which such acts, records and proceedings shall be proved, and the effect thereof.

Section 2. 1. The citizens of each State shall be entitled to all privileges and immunities of citizens in the several States.[2]

2. A person charged in any State with treason, felony, or other crime, who shall flee from justice, and be found in another State, shall on demand of the executive authority of the State

---

1 See the 11th Amendment.
2 See the 14th Amendment, Sec. 1.

from which he fled, be delivered up to be removed to the State having jurisdiction of the crime.

3. No person held to service or labor in one State under the laws thereof, escaping into another, shall in consequence of any law or regulation therein, be discharged from such service or labor, but shall be delivered up on claim of the party to whom such service or labor may be due.[1]

Section 3. 1. New States may be admitted by the Congress into this Union; but no new State shall be formed or erected within the jurisdiction of any other State, nor any State be formed by the junction of two or more States, or parts of States, without the consent of the legislatures of the States concerned as well as of the Congress.

2. The Congress shall have power to dispose of and make all needful rules and regulations respecting the territory or other property belonging to the United States; and nothing in this Constitution shall be so construed as to prejudice any claims of the United States, or of any particular State.

Section 4. The United States shall guarantee to every State in this Union a republican form of government, and shall protect each of them against invasion; and on application of the legislature, or of the executive (when the legislature cannot be convened) against domestic violence.

ARTICLE V

The Congress, whenever two thirds of both Houses shall deem it necessary, shall propose amendments to this Constitution, or, on the application of the legislature of two thirds of the several States, shall call a convention for proposing amendments, which in either case, shall be valid to all intents and purposes, as part of this Constitution when ratified by the legislatures of three fourths of the several States, or by conventions in three fourths thereof, as the one or the other mode of ratification may be proposed by the Congress; Provided that no amendment which may be made prior to the year one thousand eight hundred and eight shall in any manner affect the first and fourth clauses in the ninth section of the first article; and that no State, without its consent, shall be deprived of its equal suffrage in the Senate.

ARTICLE VI

1. All debts contracted and engagements entered into, before the adoption of this Constitution, shall be as valid against the United States under this Constitution, as under the Confederation.[2]

1 See the 13th Amendment.
2 See the 14th Amendment, Sec. 4.

2. This Constitution, and the laws of the United States which shall be made in pursuance thereof; and all treaties made, or which shall be made, under the authority of the United States, shall be the supreme law of the land; and the Judges in every State shall be bound thereby, anything in the Constitution or laws of any State to the contrary notwithstanding.

3. The senators and representatives before mentioned, and the members of the several State legislatures, and all executive and judicial officers, both of the United States and of the several States, shall be bound by oath or affirmation to support this Constitution; but no religious test shall ever be required as a qualification to any office or public trust under the United States.

ARTICLE VII

The ratification of the conventions of nine States shall be sufficient for the establishment of this Constitution between the States so ratifying the same.

Done in Convention by the unanimous consent of the States present the seventeenth day of September in the year of our Lord one thousand seven hundred and eighty-seven, and of the independence of the United States of America the twelfth.. In witness whereof we have hereunto subscribed our names.　　　　　　　　[Names omitted]

Articles in addition to, and amendment of, the Constitution of the United States of America, proposed by Congress, and ratified by the legislatures of the several States pursuant to the fifth article of the original Constitution.

AMENDMENTS

First Ten Amendments passed by Congress Sept. 25, 1789.
Ratified by three-fourths of the States December 15, 1791.

ARTICLE I

Congress shall make no law respecting an establishment of religion, or prohibiting the free exercise thereof; or abridging the freedom of speech, or of the press; or the right of the people peaceably to assemble, and to petition the government for a redress of grievances.

ARTICLE II

A well regulated militia, being necessary to the security of a free State, the right of the people to keep and bear arms, shall not be infringed.

ARTICLE III

No soldier shall, in time of peace be quartered in any house, without the consent of the owner, nor in time of war, but in a manner to be prescribed by law.

ARTICLE IV

The right of the people to be secure in their persons, houses, papers, and effects, against unreasonable searches and seizures, shall not be violated, and no warrants shall issue, but upon probable cause, supported by oath or affirmation, and particularly describing the place to be searched, and the persons or things to be seized.

ARTICLE V

No person shall be held to answer for a capital, or otherwise infamous crime, unless on a presentment or indictment of a grand jury, except in cases arising in the land or naval forces, or in the militia, when in actual service in time of war or public danger; nor shall any person be subject for the same offense to be twice put in jeopardy of life or limb; nor shall be compelled in any criminal case to be a witness against himself, nor be deprived of life, liberty, or property, without due process of law; nor shall private property be taken for public use without just compensation.

ARTICLE VI

In all criminal prosecutions, the accused shall enjoy the right to a speedy and public trial, by an impartial jury of the State and district wherein the crime shall have been committed, which district shall have been previously ascertained by law, and to be informed of the nature and cause of the accusation; to be confronted with the witnesses against him; to have compulsory process for obtaining witnesses in his favor, and to have the assistance of counsel for his defense.

ARTICLE VII

In suits at common law, where the value in controversy shall exceed twenty dollars, the right of trial by jury shall be preserved, and no fact tried by a jury shall be otherwise reëxamined in any court of the United States, than according to the rules of the common law.

ARTICLE VIII

Excessive bail shall not be required, nor excessive fines imposed, nor cruel and unusual punishments inflicted.

ARTICLE IX

The enumeration in the Constitution of certain rights shall not be construed to deny or disparage others retained by the people.

ARTICLE X

The powers not delegated to the United States by the Constitution, nor prohibited by it to the States, are reserved to the States respectively, or to the people.

ARTICLE XI

Passed by Congress March 5, 1794. Ratified January 8, 1798.

The judicial power of the United States shall not be construed to extend to any suit in law or equity, commenced or prosecuted against one of the United States by citizens of another State, or by citizens or subjects of any foreign State.

ARTICLE XII

Passed by Congress December 12, 1803. Ratified September 25, 1804.

The electors shall meet in their respective States, and vote by ballot for President and Vice President, one of whom, at least, shall not be an inhabitant of the same State with themselves; they shall name in their ballots the person voted for as President, and in distinct ballots the person voted for as Vice President, and they shall make distinct lists of all persons voted for as President and of all persons voted for as Vice President, and of the number of votes for each, which lists they shall sign and certify, and transmit sealed to the seat of the government of the United States, directed to the President of the Senate;— The President of the Senate shall, in the presence of the Senate and House of Representatives, open all the certificates and the votes shall then be counted;—The person having the greatest number of votes for President, shall be the President, if such number be a majority of the whole number of electors appointed; and if no person have such majority, then from the persons having the highest numbers not exceeding three on the list of those voted for as President, the House of Representatives shall choose immediately, by ballot, the President. But in choosing the President, the votes shall be taken by States, the representation from each State having one vote; a quorum for this purpose shall consist of a member or members from two thirds of the States, and a majority of all the States shall be necessary to a choice. And if the House of Representatives shall not choose a President whenever the right of choice shall devolve upon them, before the fourth day of March next following, then the Vice President shall act as President, as in the case of the death or other constitutional disability of the President. The person having the greatest number of votes as Vice President shall be the Vice President, if such number be a majority of the whole number of electors appointed, and if no person have a majority, then from the two highest numbers on the list, the Senate shall choose the Vice President; a quorum for the purpose shall consist of two thirds of the whole number of Senators, and a majority of the whole number shall be necessary to a choice. But no person constitutionally ineligible to the office of President shall be eligible to that of Vice President of the United States.

ARTICLE XIII

Passed by Congress February 1, 1865. Ratified December 18, 1865.

Section 1. Neither slavery nor involuntary servitude, except as punishment for crime whereof the party shall have been duly convicted, shall exist within the United States, or any place subject to their jurisdiction.

Section 2. Congress shall have power to enforce this article by appropriate legislation.

ARTICLE XIV

Passed by Congress June 16, 1866. Ratified July 23, 1868.

Section 1. All persons born or naturalized in the United States, and subject to the jurisdiction thereof, are citizens of the United States and of the State wherein they reside. No State shall make or enforce any law which shall abridge the privileges or immunities of citizens of the United States; nor shall any State deprive any person of life, liberty, or property, without due process of law; nor deny to any person within its jurisdiction the equal protection of the laws.

Section 2. Representatives shall be apportioned among the several States according to their respective numbers, counting the whole number of persons in each State, excluding Indians not taxed. But when the right to vote at any election for the choice of electors for President and Vice President of the United States, representatives in Congress, the executive and judicial officers of a State, or the members of the legislature thereof, is denied to any of the male inhabitants of such State, being twenty-one years of age, and citizens of the United States, or in any way abridged, except for participation in rebellion, or other crime, the basis of representation therein shall be reduced in the proportion which the number of such male citizens shall bear to the whole number of male citizens twenty-one years of age in such State.

Section 3. No person shall be a senator or representative in Congress, or elector of President and Vice President, or hold any office, civil or military, under the United States, or under any State, who having previously taken an oath, as a member of Congress, or as an officer of the United States, or as a member of any State legislature, or as an executive or judicial officer of any State, to support the Constitution of the United States, shall have engaged in insurrection or rebellion against the same, or given aid or comfort to the enemies thereof. But Congress may by a vote of two thirds of each House, remove such disability.

Section 4. The validity of the public debt of the United States, authorized by law, including debts incurred for payment of pensions and bounties for services in suppressing insurrection or rebellion, shall not be questioned. But neither the United States nor any State shall assume or pay any debt or obligation incurred in aid of insurrection or rebellion against the United States, or any claim for the loss or emancipation of any slave; but all such debts, obligations, and claims shall be held illegal and void.

Section 5. The Congress shall have power to enforce, by appropriate legislation, the provisions of this article.

ARTICLE XV

Passed by Congress February 27, 1869. Ratified March 30, 1870.

Section 1. The right of citizens of the United States to vote shall not be denied or abridged by the United States or by any State on account of race, color, or previous condition of servitude.

Section 2. The Congress shall have power to enforce this article by appropriate legislation.

ARTICLE XVI

Passed by Congress July 12, 1909. Ratified February 25, 1913.

The Congress shall have power to lay and collect taxes on incomes, from whatever source derived, without apportionment among the several States, and without regard to any census or enumeration.

ARTICLE XVII

Passed by Congress May 16, 1912. Ratified May 31, 1913.

The Senate of the United States shall be composed of two senators from each state, elected by the people thereof, for six years; and each senator shall have one vote. The electors in each State shall have the qualifications requisite for electors of the most numerous branch of the State legislature.

When vacancies happen in the representation of any State in the Senate, the executive authority of such State shall issue writs of election to fill such vacancies: *Provided,* That the legislature of any State may empower the executive thereof to make temporary appointments until the people fill the vacancies by election as the legislature may direct.

This amendment shall not be so construed as to affect the election or term of any senator chosen before it becomes,valid as part of the Constitution.

ARTICLE XVIII

Passed by Congress December 17, 1917. Ratified January 29, 1919.

After one year from the ratification of this article, the manufacture, sale, or transportation of intoxicating liquors within, the importation thereof into, or the exportation thereof from the United States and all territory subject to the jurisdiction thereof for beverage purposes is hereby prohibited.

The Congress and the several States shall have concurrent power to enforce this article by appropriate legislation.

This article shall be inoperative unless it shall have been ratified as an amendment to the Constitution by the legislatures of the several States, as provided in the Consitution, within seven years from the date of the submission hereof to the states by Congress.

ARTICLE XIX

Passed by Congress June 5, 1919. Ratified August 26, 1920.

The right of citizens of the United States to vote shall not be denied or abridged by the United States or by any State on account of sex.

The Congress shall have power by appropriate legislation to enforce the provisions of this article.

ARTICLE XX

Passed by Congress March 3, 1932. Ratified January 23, 1933.

Section 1. The terms of the President and Vice President shall end at noon on the 20th day of January, and the terms of

Senators and Representatives at noon on the 3d day of January, of the years in which such terms would have ended if this article had not been ratified; and the terms of their successors shall then begin.

Section 2. The Congress shall assemble at least once in every year, and such meeting shall begin at noon on the 3d day of January, unless they shall by law appoint a different day.

Section 3. If, at the time fixed for the beginning of the term of the President, the President-elect shall have died, the Vice President-elect shall become President. If a President shall not have been chosen before the time fixed for the beginning of his term, or if the President-elect shall have failed to qualify, then the Vice President-elect shall act as President until a President shall have qualified; and the Congress may by law provide for the case wherein neither a President-elect nor a Vice President-elect shall have qualified, declaring who shall then act as President, or the manner in which one who is to act shall be selected, and such person shall act accordingly until a President or Vice President shall have qualified.

Section 4. The Congress may by law provide for the case of the death of any of the persons from whom the House of Representatives may choose a President whenever the right of choice shall have devolved upon them, and for the case of the death of any of the persons from whom the Senate may choose a Vice President whenever the right of choice shall have devolved upon them.

Section 5. Sections 1 and 2 shall take effect on the 15th day of October following the ratification of this article.

Section 6. This article shall be inoperative unless it shall have been ratified as an amendment to the Constitution by the legislatures of three-fourths of the several States within seven years from the date of its submission.

ARTICLE XXI

Passed by Congress February 20, 1933. Ratified December 5, 1933.

Section 1. The Eighteenth Article of amendment to the Constitution of the United States is hereby repealed.

Section 2. The transportation or importation into any State, Territory, or possession of the United States for delivery or use therein of intoxicating liquors in violation of the laws thereof, is hereby prohibited.

Section 3. This article shall be inoperative unless it shall have been ratified as an amendment to the Constitution by conventions in the several States, as provided in the Constitution, within seven years from the date of the submission thereof to the States by the Congress.

ARTICLE XXII
Passed by Congress March 24, 1947. Ratified February 26, 1951.

Section 1. No person shall be elected to the office of the President more than twice, and no person who has held the office of President, or acted as President, for more than two years of a term to which some other person was elected President shall be elected to the office of the President more than once. But this article shall not apply to any person holding the office of President when this article was proposed by the Congress, and shall not prevent any person who may be holding the office of President, or acting as President, during the term within which this article becomes operative from holding the office of President or acting as President during the remainder of such term.

Section 2. This article shall be inoperative unless it shall have been ratified as an amendment to the Constitution by the legislatures of three-fourths of the several States within seven years from the date of its submission to the States by the Congress.

ARTICLE XXIII
Passed by Congress June 16, 1960. Ratified Mar. 29, 1961.

Section 1. The district constituting the seat of Government of the United States shall appoint in such manner as the Congress may direct:

A number of electors of President and Vice President equal to the whole number of Senators and Representatives in Congress to which the District would be entitled if it were a State, but in no event more than the least populous State; they shall be in addition to those appointed by the States, but they shall be considered, for the purposes of election of President and Vice President, to be electors appointed by a State; and they shall meet in the District and perform such duties as provided by the twelfth article of amendment.

Section 2. The Congress shall have the power to enforce this article by appropriate legislation.

ARTICLE XXIV
Passed by Congress Aug. 27, 1962. Ratified Jan. 23, 1964

Section 1. The right of citizens of the United States to vote in any primary or other election for President or Vice President, for electors for President or Vice President, or for Senator or Representative in Congress, shall not be denied or abridged by the United States or any State by failure to pay any poll tax or other tax.

Section 2. The Congress shall have the power to enforce this article by appropriate legislation.

ARTICLE XXV
Passed by Congress July 6, 1965. Ratified February 10, 1967.

Section 1. In case of the removal of the President from office or of his death or resignation, the Vice President shall become President.

Section 2. Whenever there is a vacancy in the office of the Vice President, the President shall nominate a Vice President who shall take office upon confirmation by a majority vote of both Houses of Congress.

Section 3. Whenever the President transmits to the President pro tempore of the Senate and the Speaker of the House of Representatives his written declaration that he is unable to discharge the powers and duties of his office, and until he transmits to them a written declaration to the contrary, such powers and duties shall be discharged by the Vice President as Acting President.

Section 4. Whenever the Vice President and a majority of either the principal officers of the executive departments or of such other body as Congress may by law provide, transmit to the President pro tempore of the Senate and the Speaker of the House of Representatives their written declaration that the President is unable to discharge the powers and duties of his office, the Vice President shall immediately assume the powers and duties of the office as Acting President.

Thereafter, when the President transmits to the President pro tempore of the Senate and the Speaker of the House of Representatives his written declaration that no inability exists, he shall resume the powers and duties of his office unless the Vice President and a majority of either the principal officers of the executive department or of such other body as Congress may by law provide, transmit within four days to the President pro tempore of the Senate and the Speaker of the House of Representatives their written declaration that the President is unable to discharge the powers and duties of his office. Thereupon Congress shall decide the issue, assembling within forty-eight hours for that purpose if not in session. If the Congress, within twenty-one days after receipt of the latter written declaration, or, if Congress is not in session, within twenty-one days after Congress is required to assemble, determines by two-thirds vote of both Houses that the President is unable to discharge the powers and duties of his office, the Vice President shall continue to discharge the same as Acting President; otherwise, the President shall resume the powers and duties of his office.

INDEX

INDEX

INDEX OF CASES
By Subject Matter

See *Table of Contents* for alphabetical listing of cases.